South Africa's Environmental History
Cases & Comparisons

South Africa's Environmental History
Cases & Comparisons

EDITED BY

STEPHEN DOVERS, RUTH EDGECOMBE AND BILL GUEST

OHIO UNIVERSITY PRESS
Series in Ecology and History
Athens

DAVID PHILIP PUBLISHERS
Cape Town

First published in 2002 in Africa by David Philip Publishers,
an imprint of New Africa Books (Pty) Ltd, 99 Garfield Rd, Claremont 7780,
South Africa

Published in 2003 in North America in the Ohio University Press Series in Ecology
and History by Ohio University Press, Scott Quadrangle, Athens, Ohio 45701,
United States of America

ISBN 0-86486-492-2 (David Philip)
ISBN 0-8214-1498-4 (Ohio University Press)

US CIP data available upon request.

Printed in South Africa by Creda Communications (Pty) Ltd.

Contents

Contributors

Sean Archer, a member of the School of Economics, University of Cape Town, was born in the Karoo region to which he returns regularly. The environmental history of the Karoo is his long-term research interest, aimed in particular at understanding the decisions and actions of the users of the land that led to its degradation in the past.

William Beinart is author of *Twentieth-century South Africa* (Oxford, 2001), and *Environment and history: the taming of nature in the USA and South Africa* (Routledge, 1995). He is Rhodes Professor of Race Relations at the University of Oxford and is currently teaching and writing in the field of southern African environmental history.

Jane Carruthers is senior lecturer in the Department of History, University of South Africa, and a leading environmental historian of southern Africa. Her books include *The Kruger National Park: a social and political history* (University of Natal Press, 1995), *The life and work of Thomas Baines* (Fernwood Press, 1995), and *Wildlife and warfare: the life of James Stevenson-Hamilton* (University of Natal Press, 2001). She has contributed to a number of books and academic journals and been historical consultant to a number of environmental organisations. Recently she has become engaged in historical comparisons between South Africa and Australia.

Stephen Dovers is a senior fellow with the Centre for Resource and Environmental Studies, Australian National University. He researches and writes on policy and institutional dimensions of sustainability, decision making and uncertainty, natural resource management and Australian environmental history. His most recent edited volume is *Environmental history and policy: still settling Australia* (Oxford, 2000).

Ruth Edgecombe was a professor in Historical Studies in the School of Human and Social Studies at the University of Natal, Pietermaritzburg.

Beverley Ellis is a science and history graduate who teaches biology at Girls' High School in Pietermaritzburg.

Bill Guest is a professor of Historical Studies in the School of Human and Social Studies at the University of Natal, Pietermaritzburg.

Nancy Jacobs holds a Ph.D. from Indiana University and is assistant professor of History and African Studies at Brown University. Her book *Eyes on the thornveld: a socio-environmental history of the Kalahari's edge* is forthcoming with Cambridge University Press.

Elna Kotze is an Ashoka Fellow, and a committed environmentalist and social entrepreneur. While involved in her rural renewal and grassland conservation work in Wakkerstroom, she worked in close association with the University of Natal, Pietermaritzburg, and particularly with Professor Ruth Edgecombe, who was a valued mentor. She is currently Operations Director for the New Economics Foundation in London, with whom she shares a commitment to creating a just and sustainable economy.

John Lambert is an associate professor in the Department of History at the University of South Africa. He has published extensively in the field of Natal colonial history, concentrating in particular on rural African societies and the homestead economy.

Gregory H. Maddox is associate professor of History at Texas Southern University in Houston. He is a specialist on East African history, has taught at the University of Dar es Salaam, was co-editor with James Giblin and I.N. Kimambo of *Custodians of the land: ecology and culture in Tanzanian history* (Ohio University Press, 1996), and the author of several pieces on the environmental and social history of central Tanzania.

John McAllister worked in bird and grassland conservation in South Africa for nearly twenty years. He now runs a small tourism operation, based in the Wakkerstroom grasslands, specialising in birding tours in South and East Africa.

John (JR) McNeill has taught at Georgetown University's School of Foreign Service since 1985, where he has been professor of history since 1993. His research interests lie in the environmental history of the Mediterranean world, the tropical Atlantic world and Pacific Islands. His books are *The Atlantic empires of France and Spain* (University of North Carolina Press, 1985), *Atlantic American societies from Columbus to abolition* (Routledge, 1992), *The mountains of the Mediterranean world* (Cambridge, 1992), and *Something new under the sun: an environmental history of the twentieth-century world* (Norton, 2000), which was awarded the World History Association book prize. He is currently working on the history of yellow fever.

S. Ravi Rajan is assistant professor of Environmental Studies at the University of California, Santa Cruz. His most recent work is *Modernizing nature: tropical forestry and the contested legacy of colonial eco-development* (Oxford: forthcoming).

Jabulani Sithole is a lecturer in Historical Studies in the School of Human and Social Studies at the University of Natal, Pietermaritzburg.

Georgina Thompson is an environmentalist working and living in KwaZulu-Natal. She is currently the implementing agent for a Department of Environmental Affairs and Tourism (Coastal Management) sustainable livelihoods project which forms part of their programme to realise the goals of the White Paper for Sustainable Coastal Development in South Africa. Her interests lie in sustainable development, and she was recently co-compiler and author of the preliminary state of environment report for KwaZulu-Natal.

Lance van Sittert is a lecturer in the Department of History at the University of Cape Town. His interests are in marine economies and the environmental history of the nineteenth- and twentieth-century Cape Colony/Province.

Harald Witt is a lecturer in the Economic History and Development Studies Programme at the University of Natal, Durban, teaching environmental history among other topics, and is an active member of a number of environmental groups.

Preface

This book conveys some of the richness and potential of the growing field of South African environmental history, presenting a diverse sample of research and writing on South Africa along with perspectives from other parts of the world. There are many significant individual contributions that show at once the depth of existing scholarship and the scope for the future. We hope that the volume will spark further recognition and endeavours in this emerging, interdisciplinary field in a deeply fascinating country.

The book had its genesis at a meeting of environmental historians hosted by the University of Natal, Pietermaritzburg, in 1996. That meeting was a significant event, its organisation a significant task, and gratitude is expressed to all those who helped make it happen. The sad loss of Ruth Edgecombe in 2001 took from that university a scholar and warm human being, from this endeavour its central initiator, and from environmental history a tireless and valued pioneer.

Since that meeting, original papers have been further developed, additional chapters commissioned, and many people have helped in bringing the project to fruition against the complications of distance, time, technology and resources. The contributors to this volume are thanked for their effort, patience and dedication. In South Africa, Russell Martin of David Philip Publishers has been crucial in supporting and managing the project, and the book has benefited greatly from the editorial vigilance of Andrea Nattrass. In Canberra, Katrina Proust provided editorial assistance, and Clive Hilliker prepared most of the figures. The participation of Ohio University Press has provided further international reach in the increasingly global field of environmental history.

Steve Dovers and Bill Guest

Dedicated to the life and memory of Ruth Edgecombe, 1944–2001

Part I
Introduction

Environmental history in southern Africa: An overview

Jane Carruthers

This book had its genesis in July 1996 at an Environmental History Workshop convened by the late Ruth Edgecombe together with Bill Guest of the Department of Historical Studies of the University of Natal, Pietermaritzburg, and held on that campus. It was a memorable few days. Very atypically for a country of generally mild climate, there was snow in South Africa that week – the heaviest fall ever recorded. Together with exceptional storms, this harsh weather played havoc with carefully planned travel schedules. The province of KwaZulu-Natal was isolated, even the main highways were closed to traffic. The landscape around Pietermaritzburg was littered with fallen trees and broken branches, indigenous and exotic plants alike unable to bear the weight of the snow. A shallow-rooted, tree-sized succulent *Euphorbia*, vulnerable to high wind, collapsed, destroying one participant's motor vehicle. A few delegates were not able to reach Pieter-maritzburg; some arrived terrified after experiencing extreme aircraft turbulence; others came late, stranded for hours in snow-drifts or bogged down in mud. For a gathering dedicated to environmental history it was certainly clear that the elements intended to remind us very directly of the impact of natural phenomena on human behaviour. The intellectual consequences were extremely propitious. In a large draughty hall we all huddled around a single small radiator; the academic camaraderie was palpable and the papers were provocative and stimulating. Many of the chapters in this volume are based on the conference presentations, and they have been augmented with the inclusion of work from other scholars in the field.

Environmental history in southern Africa has only quite recently come into its own as a distinct field of historical inquiry. The wide variety of subject matter and high standard of contributions offered here attest both to its vigour and to its challenging potential. That environmental history took off slowly in southern

Africa can be explained on the one hand by the fact that the academic community is relatively small. On the other hand, and perhaps more importantly, the majority of historians and other social scientists have for many decades been engaged in investigating the overwhelming and critical importance of the antecedents and ramifications of apartheid. In short, the politics of race relations – whether written in the traditions of Afrikaner nationalism, liberalism or neo-Marxism – have dominated southern African historiography.

Environmental history grew out of the Marxist social history tradition and was launched in the context of the end of the apartheid state and a changing political dispensation from the late 1980s onwards. It has been asserted that social and environmental history are in many respects similar and that the outgrowth of one from the other is organic. Common elements include a preoccupation with the previously inconspicuous, the empirical examination of fresh sources, and a political sympathy with those (not necessarily human, in the case of environmental history) less powerful and most exploited. There is, in addition, a strong sense of engagement with issues which are morally important and politically relevant.[1] As the contributions in this volume show, environmental history in southern Africa encompasses all these elements.

Defining environmental history

Subdisciplines of history are traditionally defined in terms of their subject fields or their methodology. While some people are dubious about whether a definition is truly constructive, there may be merit in trying to outline the boundaries of the discipline by way of introduction. I think that some clarity could be helpful because environmental history is so wide-ranging, so disparate in subject matter, methodology and output, that there is a danger of relegating it to being merely a trendy catch-phrase, applied willy-nilly to any study which includes the word 'environment' and which does not fit neatly elsewhere. While one does not wish to be exclusive in any way, it would be a pity to dilute intellectual rigour to the extent that environmental history loses any value as a useful epistemological category.

Although methods, sources and focus vary, at the core of environmental history is a deliberation on how people use, manage or interrelate with natural resources and the natural environment, in specific circumstances at given times and places. The essential element is the nexus between humanity and the environment interacting as partners in a distinctive historical context. Stephen Dovers (an editor of this volume) dislikes the word 'subdiscipline' for environmental history, preferring to call it an 'interdisciplinary arena'.[2] Providing that all the issues in that arena relate to natural resources, he makes a good point.

Natural resources – whether contests over them, ideologies and cultures relating to them, their exploitation or conservation, their scientific or ecological particularities and vulnerabilities – certainly lie at the heart of environmental history. But within that broad parameter, concerns can vary enormously and individual interests and a wide range of sources can be accommodated: the evidence is in this book.

William Cronon, an eminent and popular environmental historian in the United States, takes the view that environmental history examines the place of human societies in particular but changing ecosystems.[3] He also believes that 'environmental history offers unusual opportunities for synthesis across historical sub-fields, [and] it is even stronger for the many disciplines that analyse environmental change'.[4] Donald Worster, another influential proponent of environmental history, would agree.[5] He thinks that the 'examination of changes in people's attitudes towards the natural world have been among the most dramatic stories our field has described'.[6] Another authoritative word comes from Australian Tom Griffiths: 'Environmental history's distinctiveness … resides in its closer affiliations with environmental politics, its explicit engagement with the scientific insights and metaphors of ecology, a determination to give the non-human world some agency in the historical narrative, and a stronger self-definition as a humanities discipline.'[7] British historians William Beinart and Peter Coates[8] call environmental history a series of 'dialogues over time between people and the rest of nature, focusing on reciprocal impacts'.[9] Thinking of nature as humanity's collaborator in historical interaction is underscored by Alfred Crosby, famous for introducing 'ecological imperialism' into the vocabulary, who argues that environmental history's achievement has been to include the natural world in historical explanation.[10] The crucial elements of examining change over time and its narrative power – the essence of history and its special strength – have brought different categories of knowledge together in the field of environmental history.

Environmental historiography in southern Africa

Despite the earlier observation that environmental history is a newcomer to southern African historiography, its antecedents go back well into the past, although they were not called environmental history at that time. There was the trilogy of P.J. van der Merwe on the trekboer economy, for example, which was published in the 1930s and 1940s.[11] Van der Merwe examined frontier subjects which are familiar to modern environmental historians. B.H. Dicke's study of the tsetse fly's effect on historical events is another in the same vein.[12] Also ahead of its time as an environmental history was N.C. Pollock and Swanzie Agnew's *An historical geography of*

South Africa, published in the early 1960s.[13] (Historical geography is not identical to environmental history of course, but it certainly speaks the same kind of language.[14]) Some years later, a number of social historians (particularly those working on agrarian and rural history) began to incorporate elements of environmental history into their work.[15] These included Robert Wagner's account of the hunting community in the Soutpansberg,[16] and Jeff Guy's powerful environmental arguments for the rise of the Zulu kingdom.[17] Ian Phimister analysed the link between conservationism and development in 1986,[18] and there were historical explorations of environmental issues in the work of William Beinart, Peter Delius, Timothy Keegan, Jeff Peires and Kevin Shillington.[19]

In moving away from social history and becoming independently recognisable, southern African environmental history was advanced by academic journals and essay collections. Leading the way in 1987 was *Conservation in Africa: people, policies and practice*, edited by David Anderson and Richard Grove, which brought the natural and social sciences together for the first time in a seminal collection of essays.[20] This was followed two years later by a special issue of the *Journal of Southern African Studies* devoted to 'The politics of conservation in Southern Africa'.[21] What these publications lacked in coherence was outweighed by the novelty and pioneering significance of bringing within the mainstream historical ambit issues such as conservation ideology in the nineteenth-century Cape (with special emphasis on soil erosion), hunting, pastoralism and overgrazing, the emergence and political and cultural implications of national parks, as well as agricultural planning and policy in the Eastern Cape, Lesotho and Zimbabwe.

Access to other publications grew, and specialist journals such as the American *Environmental History* (formerly *Environmental History Review*) began to include contributions from southern Africa – on Swaziland, the African National Soil Conservation Association and crayfish conservation in the Cape.[22] Also proactive in this regard was *Environment and History*, the journal started by Richard Grove. The *South African Historical Journal* and other journals now have regular environmental contributions as part of their established repertoire.[23] An analysis of the emerging environmental historiography of southern Africa came fairly early, and two review articles were published in 1990: William Beinart's 'Empire, hunting and ecological change in southern and central Africa',[24] and Jane Carruthers's 'Towards an environmental history of southern Africa: some perspectives'.[25] Phia Steyn has entered this field more recently with an article in *New Contree* in 1999.[26]

Environmental historians have been forced by their subject matter to become more adept at interdisciplinary work. Indeed, it is one of the very essences of the subject and one of its most innovative aspects. The natural and geographical sciences are obvious collaborative disciplines, but economics and hard sciences (as well as other fields of study) provide fresh source material and prisms through which to engage with the past. Obviously, ecology is extremely important in this regard. In his comparative chapter, 'South African environmental history in the African context', William Beinart points out a number of productive areas of interdisciplinary research. Together with JoAnn McGregor, Richard Grove and the *Journal of Southern African Studies* team, Beinart was instrumental in arranging a significant conference at St Antony's College, Oxford, in July 1999, entitled 'African environments: past and present'. This was an extremely productive interdisciplinary meeting which has resulted in a special issue of the *Journal of Southern African Studies*,[27] as well as a book which is in the process of publication. The special issue of the journal contains some innovative contributions which expand historical horizons literally and figuratively. For the first time there is a variety of contributions on matters relating to water impoundment, long-range synthetic accounts of soil conservation in South Africa over a 40-year period, and colonial constructs of the Kenyan environment from 1920 to 1945, among many others. There is also what used to be thought of as a strictly 'scientific' contribution from M. Timm Hoffman and Simon Todd, 'A national review of land degradation in South Africa: the influence of biophysical and socio-economic factors'. Collaborative ventures such as this are extremely encouraging.

Essays in South African environmental history

All the contributors to this book add appreciably to the historiographical literature. There are, however, no pretensions at being comprehensive. There is, for example, no chapter on the renowned Cape floral kingdom, nor on recent urban environmental tragedies such as sullied cholera-infested rivers lined with squatter camps, or industrial pollution. A number of chapters relate to social justice, but none addresses it directly as a historio-political issue, nor links it to current environmental activism. Pre-colonial societies are perhaps neglected, together with issues relating to indigenous knowledge, which are touched upon rather than explored in any detail. Gender is a field which is not dealt with here. Nonetheless, this publication aims to advance environmental history by expanding the framework of conceptualisation as well as the body of research material. History – change over time – is the focus of the contributions, and theoretical positions differ from author to author.

Because environmental history is locality- (or biome-) based it often feeds into notions of 'place'. As Griffiths has explained, environmental historians analyse what 'place' means, 'how it is constructed and understood, and what connects people to it'.[28] Such studies are not storms in teacups, but looking at the 'local' often illuminates the limits of state power and may even redirect or erode it by facilitating changes in national policy and legislation. Environmental activism is important for this reason. The chapters by Elna Kotze on Wakkerstroom and Georgina Thompson on St Lucia illuminate such activism well, covering two important limited – and threatened – biomes in South Africa: highveld grassland and vlei systems in the case of Wakkerstroom, and coastal fresh-water lake systems in the case of St Lucia. Both these contributions are significant not only in terms of their content, but also in how they meet Dovers' pragmatic assessment of the importance of environmental history as 'contribut[ing] directly to pressing societal concerns'.[29] Kotze is personally connected to environmental conservation initiatives in the Wakkerstroom district and her chapter outlines human occupation over many centuries. Thompson's St Lucia interest – under the guidance of the late Ruth Edgecombe – was sparked by the heated national debate over mining in the St Lucia area in the 1970s and 1980s. These chapters, like many others, use the perspective of 'green' politics to explore the theme that apartheid has been the cause of the environmental 'degradation' of South Africa. An early book in this vein was *Going green: people, politics and the environment in South Africa*, published in 1991, edited by sociologist Jacklyn Cock and award-winning environmental journalist Eddie Koch.[30] This work explored how a secretive, centrally planned industrial economy and pockets of affluence caused poverty, rural and urban squalor, and ignorance.

Every contribution in the first part of this book elucidates more than one important thread and speaks to the others at various levels, both thematically and geographically. Many are situated within a particular geographical space, and events in a specific place are analysed in a certain period of time. Nancy Jacobs uses her space – the Kuruman area in the late nineteenth century – to test a theoretical model proposed by Carolyn Merchant, which used colonialism in New England as the canvas. Using comparisons sparingly and judiciously, Jacobs finds that a number of crucial elements of the model simply do not fit the more flexible and fluid southern African situation. The notion of cultural and environmental hegemony, even in the colonial context, is slippery, because traditional societies, such as the Tswana whom Jacobs has studied and come to know well, have significantly underestimated capacities for adaptation and transformation. By way of contrast, John Lambert's chapter on rural Natal in the same period explores the limits of such adaptation among certain Zulu groups. With his detailed knowledge of land transactions in Natal, he shows how colonial demands for land can impact so greatly on pre-colonial structures that they preclude survival strategies from operating as they should. Creative responses to environmental impacts become constrained (even absent), particularly at times when crisis is exacerbated by an outbreak of disease or the occurrence of drought.

How settlers were able to maximise land-use in a way that indigenous societies were never able to do, also comes through in economist Sean Archer's chapter on the alterations to the environment resulting from western technological innovations of the nineteenth century. In particular he looks at paddock fencing and the use of windmills to increase water points for livestock in the Sneeuberg of the Cape's Karoo. An additional strength of Archer's chapter is its theoretical position which resonates with Jacobs's, and also his strong comparative suggestions with outback Australia, a region which shares similar climatic, environmental and economic elements with the Karoo. Just as in the rangelands of arid Australia, farmers in the Karoo appear to prefer to see their sheep die of starvation rather than of thirst. But, just as importantly, Archer brings an economist's reasoning to the problem. One of his crucial ideas concerns the question of passing on to each future generation a piece of land – an inheritable capital asset – in worse shape with each transfer.

Along with mechanical introductions such as windpumps and barbed wire, white settlers brought living biological material – plants and animals – in their colonial baggage. Some of these introductions went awry, becoming dangerous invaders. Prickly pear is a particularly cogent example of such a case, and *Opuntia* has certainly made its mark on the South African landscape and in its environmental mythology. While the windmills discussed by Archer represent a 'controlled invasion', the prickly pear in Lance van Sittert's contribution was not. Rather than an asset, it was – as the author explains – a menace to the pastoral economy in the late nineteenth and well into the twentieth century, additionally bringing panic to elements of society in its wake. Prickly pear was invested with a variety of 'meanings': it was destructive of livestock (yet provided feed), seductive as alcohol, helpful to vagrants as a refuge, useful for culinary purposes and many more. Van Sittert is a master at balancing prickly pear's advantages against its disadvantages and in explaining how difficult these made it for any legislative action to be taken against the weed or for substantial state funding to be allocated for its removal.[31]

Harald Witt's chapter also focuses on introduced plant species, particularly those from Australia. His eucalypts and wattles were initially more sympathetically welcomed than prickly pear because they made an important contribution to the South African economy – indeed, they still do. Plantations of alien woods provide timber and paper pulp and their export earns good international currency exchange for South Africa. They also provide tannin, firewood and a measure of employment. As anyone who travels around South Africa can see, these trees have altered the landscape and the ecology significantly. Moist grassland, often on mountain slopes, is now densely vegetated and many copses of indigenous hardwoods have been felled to make way for the aggressive invaders. Witt not only shows how tree cultivation fitted into an economic ideology, but he analyses other issues too, including how forestry was regarded as environmentally (and culturally) desirable, being more 'beautiful' than wild nature, more 'progressive' and 'modern' a landscape, and also how trees would assist in bringing about a more benign and wetter climate at the same time as promoting patriotism.[32] The luckless prickly pear was never invested with all these aesthetic and beneficent qualities.

William Beinart has contributed two chapters to this book and the first has strong resonances with Harald Witt's contribution on forestry. The obverse of planting exotic trees is the conservation of native ones, and Beinart – whose special field of research includes Pondoland in the Eastern Cape – dissects two competing worldviews of indigenous forests. He shows how the 1960 Pondoland revolt against the state had some of its origins in resource control and in different cultural perspectives on those resources. Beinart deals with violent contest relating to ecological imperialism between state and rural people over control of land and how best to care for it. He shows also how environmental concerns are closely allied to local politics and cannot ever merely be solved by scientific or rational argument alone. Resource optimisation feeds into traditional views of society and structures of control. A similar theme of protest and resistance is taken up by Jabulani Sithole. This contribution on violence in the Pinetown district between 1920 and 1936 links up with Lambert's chapter, taking it further into modern social dilemmas of overcrowding and urban politics. Another urban study comes from Beverly Ellis, who describes how the natural environment in the Durban area inexorably made way for a settler city. Ellis's point of view can also be interpreted as a contest, not between warring parties for a greater share of environmental bounty, but between a growing town and its natural surroundings in the period 1845 to 1870.[33]

Humans were directly active in changing the environment through introducing exotic trees and other plant or animal species, in utilising new technologies and in a variety of other ways. John McAllister's chapter takes a different approach: he debates the role of humans in creating a major biome in South Africa, 'grassland', which covers almost a third of the country. He picks up on what 'climax' vegetation might really be and what creates it. In the case of grassland, McAllister argues that, contrary to the view that grasslands are maintained by grazing and other human-induced pressures, grassland may well be the most ancient vegetation of the African continent, maintained by natural forces. He finds no fault with the opinion that fire is the mechanism which keeps bush from swallowing grassland, but he ranges the opposing views of agency for fire. Is fire principally climatic or is it engineered by humans? Carefully weighing the evidence, McAllister concludes that climate is the controlling factor.

Commentaries and comparisons

It is possible to regard the twelve chapters in the second part of this book as case studies. However, in tandem with the lens of the 'local', globalisation demands recognition that 'local' and 'global' often cannot be divorced. The third section, 'Commentaries and comparisons', has much to offer environmental history generally, but particularly in situating southern African studies within a broader comparative historiography. These chapters certainly substantiate Tom Griffiths's observation that 'environmental history often makes best sense on a regional and global scale, and rarely on a national one'.[34] Understanding environmental history from an international perspective has been assisted by Richard Grove's monumental and detailed *Green imperialism: colonial expansion, tropical island Edens and the origins of environmentalism*.[35] Emphasising the role of an expanding Europe, Grove investigated the imperialist origins of environmentalism in a story which drew together the environmental history of former colonies and, by extension, the 'third world'. Far from having their origins in the American national parks movement of the late nineteenth century or the technological advances of the twentieth, Richard Grove reminds us that environmental and conservation issues are old ones and that exploring unusual historical links between various places at the time of the expansion of Europe is extremely productive.

Comparing the South African environmental experience has indeed proven to be a profitable avenue of investigation and the five comparative chapters presented here add substantially to it. *Environment and history: the taming of nature in the USA and South Africa*, by William Beinart and Peter Coates, which was published in 1995, paved the way.[36] It was directly comparative and explored many fruitful points of comparison between South Africa and the United States. *Environment and history* is important because of its synthetic approach and because it is an overview of relevant environmental concepts and writings as they relate to the 'taming of nature' in the service of humanity in the United States and South Africa. Needless to say, there is far more to tell about the United States than about South Africa, yet the authors raise a wide array of environmental concerns which are common to the history of both countries – the frontier, race relations, hunting, agriculture, national parks and forestry among them. In his chapter, John McNeill turns the kaleidoscope to South America in order to explore whether comparisons between South Africa and South America are possible. Because he begins with great knowledge of South America, McNeill raises questions of early environmental disturbances, for example decimation of the population of pre-colonial societies and their domestic stock by introduced diseases, which are given scant attention in the South African literature. He also explores the introduction of plants and animals – making connections with earlier chapters on these themes – and also on mining, a topic not covered elsewhere.

When South African history is discussed in the context of other histories, it is frequently singled out as an 'exception' because of its apartheid past. Certainly, southern Africa's political history is aberrant but, as this book elucidates, there is value and insight to be gained by shifting focus more widely. Looking through a global prism, as authors Beinart, Dovers, McNeill, Maddox and Rajan do in their respective chapters, is exciting and challenging and adds suggestive insights to the study of southern Africa. During the conference at which many of the chapters in this volume were originally presented, Terence Ranger made the strong point that because South Africa was no longer politically isolated from its neighbours, a shared natural and human environment could play a pivotal historiographical role.[37] In consequence, a strong southern African environmental historiography could – and should – develop. William Beinart's chapter explores some of these issues, as well as pointing out those areas where research is lacking.

Elements of environmental comparison within southern Africa were already tentatively explored in the 1989 special issue of the *Journal of Southern African Studies*,[38] and a stimulating issue of *Environment and History* in 1995 was devoted to Zimbabwe.[39]

In this context there are also the well-known works of imperial historian John Mackenzie, *The empire of nature* and *Imperialism and the natural world*. These provide a cogent reminder of the complex tensions between the metropole and periphery which could be pursued with merit.[40] Nonetheless, as Gregory Maddox warns in his chapter on degradation narratives and population time bombs, Africa remains a continent of colonial mythology. Caution is therefore needed when comparisons are made so that shorthand phrases such as 'land shortage', 'deforestation' and the like are critically examined in a particular historical and geographical context and deconstructed from their political moorings. Evidence needs to be carefully evaluated and creatively handled. Not all myths are colonial constructs, of course, and the oft-repeated notion that pre-colonial societies were idyllically living as the first ecologists in complete harmony with nature, needs also to be questioned.

While the Americas and other parts of Africa provide obvious comparisons, there may be fruitful investigation to be done in exploring southern African environmental history in conjunction with other 'Commonwealth' countries, as fire historian Stephen Pyne of Arizona State University calls them.[41] Australia is an obvious choice. An important comparative publication appeared in 1996 along these lines after a conference hosted by the Sir Robert Menzies Centre for Australian Studies in London. Entitled *Ecology and Empire: environmental history of settler societies* and edited by Tom Griffiths and Libby Robin, this book includes themes such as science, nationhood and economy.[42] These contributions, while themselves marking a substantial advance in comparative environmental history, also serve to point out just how much more could be usefully achieved. As far as Australia is concerned, there is a particularly profitable number of valid comparisons, from indigenous or autochthonous communities, British colonial penetration, nationalism, common climatic conditions and even similar floral kingdoms. While omitting South Africa from his survey, Thomas Dunlap raises some of these concerns in a comparative way in *Nature and the English diaspora: environment and history in the United States, Canada, Australia, and New Zealand*.[43]

Stephen Dovers powerfully takes up the Australian–South African linkages in his chapter on 'Commonalities and contrasts'. In outlining those similarities and differences, he uses the analogy of societies which are still in the process of settlement. The process continues, he argues, and recognising settlement as ongoing is helpful to environmental management as well as to historical issues. Dovers looks at pre-colonial Australians as experimenting with their environment in the same way as later white settlers have done and evaluates current experiments within their historical and geographical contexts. Dovers also reminds historians that at a time when history is losing popularity and power, returning the discipline to political and social relevance – public history, applied history and people's history – through environmental history may be a survival strategy as well as an academic one.

India and south-east Asia is a part of the world which also may give some guidance to southern Africanists and there are a number of works which would reward comparative scrutiny.[44] Ravi Rajan rounds off 'Commentaries and comparisons' with just such a chapter and he gives an extensive list of useful literature for southern Africanists. Rajan sees the whole colonial process in terms of an exciting stage drama played out in five acts in different environments. Using this metaphor, he extracts a remarkable number of themes common to colonised areas in all regions of the globe.

Teaching and research

While congratulations are in order for a book such as this, the mere fact of putting these chapters together suggests only too clearly what is missing and how much more could be done. Many research lacunae have been mentioned above, and many of the contributions in this book deal with them too, some in considerable detail. But often it is students by way of postgraduate theses rather than established historians who contribute to the research profile of any discipline.[45] How history is taught is therefore fundamental to the future of the discipline. Beinart emphasises the need for university history programmes which combine an interdisciplinary approach in a post-apartheid country. Environmental history, he argues, could be a lifeline for a beleaguered discipline. Dovers also takes up this point with his emphasis on environmental history being able to inform and influence policy. Without keeping relevance in mind (as some of the case studies in this book do so well), neither interest nor funding will be forthcoming.

The most vital omissions remain a strong pre-colonial African perspective and in the area of indigenous knowledge. This perspective is fundamental. Animal rights issues are becoming more complex in southern Africa; intellectual history, aesthetics, even gender issues (so vibrant elsewhere) are lacking.[46] Public history – the scrutiny of museum collections and private non-governmental organisations – needs to be done, as well as an analysis of the rich travel and exploration literature of the nineteenth century. Industrial and urban-related environmental issues must find a place.[47] That most elementary historical production – biography – has yet to be written.[48] Frontier studies need to be imbued with a strong environmental dimension. And, as Beinart reminds us, fundamentally there has to be an active engagement with the world of science and its cultural adjuncts.[49]

Co-operation with scientists brings novel historical sources into play and the cross-fertilisation of ideas can only be beneficial. A few of the disciplines with which history can co-operate symbiotically include historical geography, which, in Australia, is a strong suit.[50] Medicine – both animal and human – is also productive. Environmental law could be usefully employed,[51] as could zoology, wildlife management and agronomy. New sources as well as new issues breathe fresh life into history.

When interdisciplinary environmental programmes are being compiled history often receives short shrift from geographers and others who feel that ecology and environmental management are 'theirs'. History is therefore relegated to an 'elective' rather than a 'core' of the programme. Historians need to work with other disciplines and a wider range of evidence in order to alter the impression that what they have to say is peripheral to the 'real' issues. It is not. It seeks to contextualise, critique and explain within a timespan. In doing so, history can elucidate substantially on important current issues – as Dovers so correctly points out. Many South African university history departments seek to reposition history within environmental parameters – to add ecological factors to historical explanation and to help senior students select appropriate themes for postgraduate work. In this they are assisted by the tourism and heritage initiatives which are popular with politicians and public alike. It is, however, fitting to pay tribute to one particular South African historian, the late Professor Ruth Edgecombe, whose enthusiasm and inspiration lie behind this book and many of its contributions. Ruth came to environmental history in the 1990s from an economic history background and she campaigned for it with characteristic passion. Based at the University of Natal, Pietermaritzburg, she not only motivated and guided her students, but was also instrumental in the establishment of the Centre for Environment and Development. The aim of this centre is to combine human and biophysical studies in order to create a context in which current and future environmental problems can be explored and to produce confident and skilled problem-solvers. This book is dedicated to her memory for this reason.

Part II
Essays in South African environmental history

The colonial ecological revolution in South Africa: The case of Kuruman

Nancy Jacobs

In 1989 Carolyn Merchant published *Ecological revolutions: nature, gender and science in New England*. In addition to being an environmental history of New England, the work was intended to contribute to the theory of a young field: environmental history. The book identified and described new historical phenomena, ecological revolutions, defined as 'major transformations in human relations with nonhuman nature'.[1] Merchant noted two such transformations in the history of New England – one colonial and one capitalist – and postulated that a global ecological revolution was currently under way. She was explicit in her belief that ecological revolutions had been repeated throughout North America, other temperate regions, and in the developing world. The concept has been cited in Africanist environmental historiography for the history of Ethiopia,[2] but the theory remains to be tested. Southern Africa, with its long history of colonisation, is especially well suited for a preliminary test. The present study is not a comparison of the environmental history of New England and southern Africa. Rather, it is a summary of Merchant's model for environmental history and her theory of the colonial ecological revolution, and an evaluation of their contributions to our understanding of one southern African case.

The model and the theory

The introduction to Merchant's book models the interplay between forces arising from four loci: ecology, production, reproduction and consciousness. The 'core' of this model is ecology, by which she means the community of plants and animals in a particular habitat. Three levels of human interaction with the habitat rest upon this core, the most immediate being production, 'the extraction, processing and exchange of natural resources'.[3] The next level is the reproduction of human society, divided into two categories: biological (the reproduction of life), and social (the reproduction of the community).[4] It is the interactions between the biological core and these two levels which generate ecological revolutions, whose impact is felt at the ecological core, and also on the last level, that of consciousness. Regarding consciousness, Merchant emphasises the human construction of nature.[5]

The theory of ecological revolutions explains how interactions between these forces lead to turning points in human relations with the environment. The two ecological revolutions correspond to major processes whose environmental repercussions are often overlooked: the establishment of colonialism and capitalism. In contrast, this theory elevates the environmental implications to the highest importance. Regarding the colonial ecological revolution, Merchant states:

> [It] was externally generated. It resulted in the collapse of indigenous Indian ecologies and the incorporation of a European ecological complex of animals, plants, pathogens and people. The colonial revolution extracted native species from their ecological contexts and shipped them overseas as commodities. It was legitimated by a set of symbols that placed cultured European humans above wild nature, other animals, and 'beastlike savages'.[6]

Obviously, the ecological revolution is an ambitious concept. Merchant indicates the breadth of her scope by identifying both Thomas Kuhn's theory of scientific revolutions as well as Marxist concepts of social revolutions as the two 'frameworks of analysis which offer springboards for discussing the structure of such ecological revolutions'.[7]

Ecology, production, reproduction and consciousness in Kuruman before the 1820s

Outlined above, in brief, is Merchant's model for understanding the interactions between humans and the environment and the theory of how these relationships build to points of revolutionary change. With reference to one South African case, this chapter will explore whether the interactions between the core and successive levels have built revolutionary tension. It will also consider to what extent the theory is able to transcend the North American experience to serve as a tool for world environmental history. An immediate issue arises from the definition of the colonial ecological revolution, which states that this is a phenomenon of the temperate world. Studies of environmental aspects of imperialism have given much attention to the temperate world, as 'lands of demographic takeover' where settlers established 'neo-Europes'.[8] However, imperialism and colonialism were not limited to the temperate world, and their environmental impact is not limited to areas of white settlement. Merchant explains no ecological characteristics of the temperate world that make it more susceptible than other zones to ecological revolutions. Nor does she explain why she restricts her concept of 'colonialism' to areas of mass European immigration. Since there are no environmental or historical explanations limiting the theory to temperate zones it is reasonable to test it in a subtropical case.

This model necessitates beginning with a description of the 'ecology', the non-human environment of the region under consideration. Kuruman lies on the border of the Northern Cape and North West provinces. As described here, it corresponds to a magisterial district defined after colonial annexation. In area it is roughly the size of Belgium, but the Tswana-speaking people of the Tlhaping and Tlharo chief-doms in Kuruman probably numbered below 20 000 until well into the twentieth century.[9] Despite its size, little environmental variation occurs: the entire savannah is now classified as Kalahari thornveld, with a profile of large camelthorns, smaller acacias, some bushes and grass.[10] Lying just barely within the subtropical summer rainfall system, and far inland from the humid coast, Kuruman qualifies as semi-arid.[11] The highest rainfall in the district, 420 millimetres per year, falls in the south-east.[12] The south-eastern plateau has scores of fountains, ranging in size from seasonal small springs to the Eye of Kuruman, yielding approximately twenty million litres of water a day. The district becomes progressively drier to the west, and the Langeberg – mountains 100 kilometres south-west of the Eye – receive as little as 250 millimetres of rainfall per year. The even drier Kalahari circles from west of the Langeberg to north of the plateau, into Botswana.

Similar to the case of New England before white settlement, the most basic interactions between humans and this ecological core before the 1820s occurred through subsistence production. In contrast to the Native Americans of New England, who cultivated, hunted and gathered, Kuruman people also herded stock. Divisions of labour by gender and class determined which activity individuals pursued. Men in towns herded goats and cattle and women grew sorghum, beans and melons. A few rich and powerful men controlled cattle keeping, the most valuable use of the natural environment. They minimised their labour and risk by dispersing their herds among poorer clients through *mafisa*. A contemporary observer described the arrangement:

The care of cattle is entrusted to poor people who have none of their own. Such people are hired by the wealthy cattle owners who give them food and a small part of the annual profit…A poor Beetjuana with one wife and half a dozen head of cattle seeks the protection of a richer one. He adds his few oxen to the large herd of the rich one and for a share in the 'profit' he serves as a herdsman.[13]

All households supplemented their food production with gathering wild plants and hunting wild animals. However, a lower class of the unfortunate and oppressed, the *balala*, did not subsist through their own food production. Underemployed as herding clients, they tended others' fields and crops, or subsisted as full-time foragers. It is essential that early observers did not think of the *balala* as Khoisan bushmen, but recognised them as genuine Tswana.[14] Divided from the food producers by class rather than ethnicity, they interacted with town dwellers in a dynamic in some ways similar to the ecological cycle identified by Richard Elphick among Khoikhoi and San in the western Cape.[15]

This dynamic of the ecological cycle involved only men. Women worked instead as cultivators, a less propitious form of production. Cultivation had developed only in the late eighteenth century in this region. A variety of factors connected with the establishment of the Tlhaping and Tlharo chiefdoms promoted this intensification. Nevertheless, grain remained a less durable, higher-risk commodity than stock. It could not flee from danger or drought. For fewer rewards, it required more work: sowing, weeding, scaring birds, harvesting and threshing. The disadvantages of cultivation explain why those with power dominated herding. Yet women's work provided households with a hedge against the vagaries of the ecological cycle. Growing grain gave women a way to supplement milk and wild foods in the diet. Most human labour was given over to subsistence production and directly oriented towards the reproduction of society. Women's reproductive capacity was particularly valued and transferred between families through bridewealth, or *bogadi* in Tswana. These were gifts of stock from the groom's to the bride's family.[16]

Consciousness is the final level of Merchant's model. As stated above, the treatment of consciousness in this theory puts heavy emphasis on human perceptions of their environment. The anthropologists Jean and John Comaroff have considered such issues among the southern Tswana. Significant in their descriptions of the worldview is a schematic of spatiality, concentric circles with the chief's court at the core, ringed by residences in the town, gardens, pastures and cattle posts, and the bush. They postulate that people understood a devolution from a social sphere of male politics at the centre through an intermediate semi-wild space of female production and reproduction to the bush, home of not-fully-human clients who subsisted on wild food.[17] Jean Comaroff goes so far as to call the contrast between town and bush 'the most fundamental of all oppositions in the Tswana cosmos'.[18] In contrast to the foraging class, oppressed by society and vulnerable to environmental forces, the chief holding court at the centre of town was the richest herder, the most powerful man, and the one expected to control natural forces by providing rain.[19] Although they may suggest an antipathy to the environment, these oppositions cannot be isolated from social power relations to extract thinking about 'nature'. People were more concerned about human social achievements and the ability to overcome natural challenges than they were with non-human 'nature'.

The first phase of the colonial ecological revolution: ecology, production, reproduction and consciousness in Kuruman, 1820s–1884

The foregoing description of relations between people and the environment before the 1820s is rather static. The theory of the colonial ecological revolution does not recognise that tensions could arise from indigenous patterns of production, reproduction and consciousness of the non-human environment, and that these tensions could be a historical force.[20] Static depictions of pre-colonial Africa are an old problem but are in keeping with this theory's portrayal of society as unchanging. It is axiomatic to Merchant's thought that external influence prompted the colonial ecological revolution.[21] Therefore the theory clearly underplays the capacity for change in independent, non-European societies. Related to the stasis critique is the observation that this theory is conducive to a rather 'merrie' portrayal of premodern societies. The field of Africanist environmental history is particularly wary of overly rosy descriptions of old Africa.[22] These observations suggest making modifications to the theory. In Kuruman's history, people's production, reproduction and consciousness made them agents of the colonial ecological revolution. The specific changes of the nineteenth century came through the impact of four categories of outsiders: traders, missionaries, government officials and settlers, but for the first six decades of the colonial ecological revolution, until the 1880s, Tswana people were the leading revolutionaries.

Of the four categories of forces contributing to the ecological revolution, the ecological core exhibits the slowest rates of change. The question whether progressive desiccation has affected this region, particularly since the early nineteenth century, is an old one. In the 1820s missionaries certainly believed they were witnessing dramatic climatological changes.[23] However, a longer-term perspective suggests that this dry period was part of a cycle rather than of progressive change.[24] Even if the environment itself did not experience permanent change, it played a different role after the 1820s than before. The droughts had severe effects across the subcontinent, and hunger and suffering encouraged people to consider new relations with the natural environment.[25] Therefore, even without being changed, the ecological core was an altered force during the colonial ecological revolution as the concentration of settlements in the river valleys increased.

The most dramatic changes of the colonial ecological revolution occurred at the level of production, after missionaries and traders introduced new ways to subsist from the environment. Missionaries and traders from the Cape made first contact with the Tlhaping and Tlharo after 1800. Traders found little success when they sought the most precious commodity, cattle, but purchased natural products, especially ivory, for Cape markets. In contrast to the indigenous customs of environmental management, which valued natural resources less than domesticated ones, traders put great value on ivory, pelts and feathers. Local people responded to this demand and supplied these markets. The result of this transformation of the non-human environment into a commodity was the entry of the cash economy and the depletion of game from most areas of the subcontinent, including Kuruman.[26] As early as 1871 F.C Selous, perhaps the most famous nimrod of nineteenth-century Africa, complained there was little worth shooting in Kuruman.[27] Reports of the total destruction of game were exaggerations: small game certainly survived, and larger animals in the southern Kalahari.[28]

More important than traders as proponents of the colonial ecological revolution were missionaries. The London Missionary Society (LMS) entrenched itself in the region only after the arrival of Robert Moffat in 1821. A man of tremendous energy and remarkable accomplishments, Moffat had worked as a gardener in England and soon took advantage of the water of the Eye, which fed the Kuruman River. Unable to subsist in the indigenous agro-pastoral manner, the missionaries sought an independent and irrigable base. In 1824 Mothibi, the Tlhaping chief, granted the LMS land near the Eye, and Moffat founded a station, where he grew imported crops, maize in summer and wheat in winter. The missionaries' understanding of a fallen creation, that they were called to make the desert bloom, also encouraged irrigation, and they coupled irrigation with belief as part of conversion.[29]

After 1823, conditions of violence and insecurity formerly known as the 'mfecane' created significant numbers of refugees who were more open to Christianity than the established Tlhaping elite had been. When, in the late 1820s, the Tlhaping capital moved to Taung, 120 kilometres east, a population of approximately 800 people remained on the mission station.[30] Moffat may have been magnifying the changes at the mission in his 1842 memoir, but this is his description of the early 1830s:

The ancient ramparts of superstition had been broken through by our converts, and many others, who could see no reason why the production of their fields and garden labour should be confined to...only vegetables cultivated by their forefathers...Ploughs, harrows, spades and mattocks were no longer viewed as the implements of a certain caste, but as the indispensable auxiliaries to existence and comfort. The man who before would have disdained to be seen engaged in such an occupation and with such a tool was now thankful to have it in his power to buy a spade.[31]

Reports from the 1840s and 1850s list a great variety of imported plants: wheat, sorghum, maize, tobacco, rice, potatoes, quince, pomegranates, plums, apricots, pears, grapes, peaches, nectarines, apples, oranges and lemons.[32] Ploughs brought men into the cultivated fields. Beyond a doubt, missionaries had introduced new relations between people and their environment.

As more missionaries arrived and settled at other springs, these changes spread beyond the Kuruman River valley, but they were still of limited significance, for they were confined to converts on mission stations. This changed in the 1850s as non-Christian Tswana first converted to irrigation, and to the use of the plough. Causes for these changes included drought, an epizootic of bovine pleuro-pneumonia (lungsickness), competition for land by settlers from the Transvaal, and the gradual disappearance of wild foods. Also important were centrifugal forces in Tswana society that led ambitious men to break away from the towns and escape chiefly domination. The changes in land use after the 1850s may appear to represent a fundamental shift in production strategy. Certainly, irrigation spread over a wider area, but important evidence shows that these changes were not yet revolutionary. Hoe cultivation by women continued. Cultural and economic factors, including the priority of minimising labour, limited the widespread adoption of intensive cultivation. Producers practised a casual form of irrigation, which supplemented extensive food production.[33] Traders in Kuruman provided opportunities to exchange sheep, goats and cattle for manufactured goods and cash, but the trade did not eclipse local production.[34]

The discovery of diamonds six days' journey south-east of Kuruman in 1867 had tremendous repercussions for the relationship of humans and their environment. The British soon annexed the boom town of Kimberley as part of the crown colony of Griqualand West. The border with Griqualand West ran just 60 kilometres south of the mission, so the colonial economy and politics had increasing effect. Kimberley was an outpost of the world economy, and needed food, fuel and workers. Opportunities for wage earning at mines arose as hunting was dying out in the Kalahari and, in response, Tswana men travelled south to earn cash.[35] Regarding agricultural markets, the Tlhaping at Dikgatlhong, nearer to Kimberley than Kuruman, sold food.[36] It seems, however, that there was no market-producing peasantry in Kuruman. The agricultural trade from Kuruman to Kimberley was practically non-existent, but trade in wood was significant. The Tlhaping provided acacia wood for fuel and mine braces to the markets. The wood trade echoed the trade in ivory, furs and feathers by transforming the non-human environment into a commodity, and exhausting the resource:

> A large trade has been developed in wood. The country is being denuded of its trees and bush to supply the fires in Kimberley and its neighbourhood. And natives in large numbers have been carriers. Every man who has had a waggon and oxen and the inclination has been able to turn in money in this way. Even here, though we are 120 miles from the market, wood waggons have been constantly passing and repassing.[37]

Some of these wagons may have carried food to Kimberley but, like hunting, wood selling provided cash for less labour, less risk and quicker rewards than cultivation.

This preliminary phase of the ecological revolution saw fewer changes at the level of reproduction than at the level of production. This is because of the three activities providing subsistence – pastoralism, cultivation and foraging – the most important, pastoralism, underwent no fundamental changes. It was in this sphere that production interacted most closely with reproduction, supporting biological reproduction by providing calories and brides to the household and social reproduction by providing economic, political and legal power to the man who owned the largest herds. The continuities here were more important than the changes. Cattle remained the repositories of wealth, and stock-keeping still provided a large proportion of the diet.[38] Trade in animal products and wood, being used at the mission by the 1830s, as well as migrant labour made cash available to the region.[39] Cash certainly had the power to transform these relations, but it was used for luxury and supplementary items. There was no dependence on the market economy for subsistence.

The prominence of missionaries in this history suggests important changes at the level of consciousness. The history of Christianity among Tswana-speaking people has attracted impressive scholarship and debate.[40] Important questions are: to what extent was Christianity a hegemonic colonisation of consciousness, to what extent did converts internalise the message, and to what extent did they take the initiative from missionaries in its interpretation? It is likely that associations between the bush and poverty opened people to Christianity, the religion of the river valleys. New relations with the environment were part of the conversion package, and they provide evidence for independent action among converts. For example, Tswana Christians followed the missionary lead in irrigation, but missionary commentary on cultivation practices suggests that they did not believe intensive irrigation to be an imperative.[41] Although Merchant's theory does not recognise it, consciousness can be a force for, rather than just an object of, changing relations with the environment.

The first phase of the colonial ecological revolution thus saw changes in the relationships between humans and their environment. The environment became a commodity to be exchanged for cash. River valleys became a resource to be developed through human labour. Yet, the first 60 years of the ecological revolution in Kuruman reveal significant variation from Merchant's original case. Although Europeans introduced new relations, it is evident that indigenous people willingly adopted them. The fact that poor people and those displaced by violence converted to new uses of the environment before the wealthy and powerful did, strongly suggests that social inequalities motivated them. It is also evident that the people of Kuruman employed new ways to use the environment to their own needs, adapting those changes that suited them. It is important to bear in mind that despite the innovations of this period, pastoralism was still central to society and the diet. The changes of this period occurred through African agency and, as of 1885, they were not revolutionary, but had been gradual adjustments to older patterns. These innovations provided a beginning for the revolution to follow, and continuities between this period and later events impel us to recognise both as phases of the colonial ecological revolution. The case of Kuruman strongly argues for a modification to Merchant's theory to account for the durability of social and cultural forms and also for the agency of people who were colonised.

The second phase of the colonial ecological revolution: ecology, production, reproduction and consciousness in Kuruman, 1884–1903

Indigenous agency is not a strong theme in the second phase of the ecological revolution in Kuruman. After 1884, the ecological revolution shows more similarities with the New England case described by Merchant:

> The colonial ecological revolution in the New England homeland was externally caused and resulted in the erosion of Indian modes of relating to nature. Local ecology on which Indian gathering-hunting and agricultural production depended was disrupted…Biological reproduction was devastated by disease and war, social reproduction by colonial land treaties

that continually reduced tribal territories. The weakening of production was thus reinforced by radical changes in reproduction. With the balance between them destroyed, the ecological core of the Indian way of life collapsed.[42]

These processes – the disruption of production, the endangering of reproduction – occurred in Kuruman as well, and the result was the loss of the ability among Kuruman people to form auspicious relations with their environment.

Although the annexation of southern Tswana lands, including Kuruman, occurred at the height of the scramble for Africa, the catalyst for imperial annexation came from the Transvaal, not from Europe. Expansion by Transvaal burghers into Tlhaping territory had begun already in the 1850s.[43] In 1881 this immigration provoked a violent crisis between Tswana, Khoikhoi and Boer groups competing for land near Mafikeng and Taung, east of Kuruman. The British intervened in 1884, eventually proclaiming a protectorate over what is now Botswana and a crown colony, British Bechuanaland, over the disputed lands south of the Molopo River. From this moment, Europeans had tremendous influence over the laws and practices of social reproduction. It fell to the new imperial government to sort out the conflicting land claims. Imperial land policy in other parts of the world rested on an ideology that superior rights accrued to those who practised a higher – meaning more intensive – use.[44] A land commission appointed in 1886 was instructed to reserve beneficially occupied lands for Africans, but to provide for settlement of 'waste lands' by whites.[45] The result in Kuruman was that the imperial administration recognised and protected what it considered to be the higher form of land use, irrigated cultivation, and ignored, discouraged and hindered the lower form, pastoralism. Unfortunately for Kuruman people, this valuation of land use was precisely opposite to their own. Yet the land policy resulted from a meeting of indigenous practices and imperial ideology. The British were able to promote cultivation at the expense of pastoralism only because irrigation had become part of Tswana land use in the unfolding ecological revolution.

The commission awarded only eight per cent of the total colony to Africans as communally held reserves. In what became the magisterial district of Kuruman there were a total of ten reserves, drawn around springs and along river valleys. The land remaining after the proclamation of the reserves and the recognition of freebooters' farms – that is, 79 per cent of the colony – was declared 'waste land', and made available for settlement.[46] White farmers were not quickly drawn to dry, isolated Kuruman, and land alienation did not take immediate effect. In the first decade of colonial rule, the Tswana people of Kuruman maintained extensive land use. Migrant labour continued, and there was still little trade in foodstuffs.[47]

In the mid-1890s, rapid changes at the level of the ecology occurred. Years of political and environmental trauma began. First, rains failed in late 1894, marking the beginning of a cycle of drought, and very quickly the lack of rain threatened food supplies.[48] Then, in 1895 the Cape Colony annexed British Bechuanaland, bringing a new administration dominated by settler interests. However, the most dramatic blow in this period came with a virgin soil epidemic in a classic case of ecological imperialism.[49] Unlike the human epidemics so devastating throughout other colonised regions, eastern and southern Africa suffered most from an epizootic: the cattle plague, rinderpest.

Rinderpest is a viral disease that strikes ruminants, both cattle and game. The virus is airborne with an incubation period of three to nine days. It is highly contagious and lethal. Morbidity rates run near 100 per cent; mortality rates are around 90 per cent, death coming after a sickness of seven to twelve days. The disease was endemic in Eurasia since ancient times; but it was inadvertently introduced into the Horn of Africa only in 1889 by transport oxen of the Italian army. It swept through east Africa southward, remaining north of the Zambezi River until 1896. Then it spread with remarkable speed through Southern Rhodesia and the Bechuanaland Protectorate, travelling an average of twenty miles per day.[50] These changes were soon felt at the level of production and reproduction. Authorities attempted to control the situation by restricting travel, and by shooting sick cattle as well as healthy herds which had been exposed to the disease.[51] The quarantine of Kuruman stopped wagon traffic and the wood trade, and also slowed food imports, which were important during the drought.[52] Foraging, of course, was a traditional recourse of hungry people during such a crisis. However, annexation to the Cape brought stricter game protection laws.[53]

Despite the hardship, the quarantine measures were well advised, for they delayed the arrival of the plague. It appeared in British Bechuanaland in April 1896, and was in Kimberley by October, but kept on the edges of Kuruman until late in the year.[54] Shooting of apparently healthy cattle caused a rebellion in Taung in December. Fugitives and refugees fled to the remote Langeberg, and government forces followed. In August 1897 Cape forces defeated the rebels.[55] The official estimate of war dead was 1200 to 1500 people. Tragically, the retaliation against those who had resisted rinderpest measures elsewhere finally brought full-blown rinderpest to Kuruman, as the entry of the colonial troops broke the quarantine.[56] According to Cape Colony estimates, the disease took almost 93 per cent of the cattle in the financial division of Vryburg, which included Kuruman.[57] As punishment for the rebellion, reserves in the Langeberg were confiscated and made available for white settlement. In addition, almost two thousand people were sentenced to five years' indentured servitude on western Cape farms. The rest moved to the remaining reserves. As one colonial official put it, 'The one punishment that endures is the loss of their land, for it compels them to scatter and seek a livelihood by honest work.'[58] Even those who did not lose their land found it necessary to increase wage labour during this time, so that in 1898 'most of the able-bodied men' were away working.[59] The combination of rebellion, retaliation, refugee influx and rinderpest had a terrible effect. Households ploughed and irrigated additional land,[60] but irrigated cultivation proved inadequate to replace what people had procured through herding, rainfed cropping and foraging. There were even reports of starvation.[61]

Obviously, production was already in a deep crisis when the next blow came: the Anglo-Boer War. Significant numbers of Afrikaners settled in the Langeberg very soon after its confiscation from the Tswana. In 1899 these Boers rose up in aid of their compatriots in the Boer republics.[62] Already reeling from the decimation of their cattle through rinderpest, violence, land loss and the disruption of rebellion, black people in Kuruman suffered further during the war. The siege of Kimberley cut off opportunities to work in diamond mines from October 1899 to February 1900, and even after the mines opened, Boer raids made travel unsafe.[63] Boer rebels occupied the tiny settlement and mission station in Kuruman on 1 January 1900. The commandos plundered food supplies. Hungry people nearby turned to the missionaries, who feared famine, for support.[64] Liberation by the British came in June, but their troops and horses increased pressure on the food supply. When necessary, the commander of the Kuruman garrison confiscated foodstuffs, and Boer raiders made imports difficult. Throughout 1901 the food situation was still severe.[65] Apart from local violence, other circumstances hindered food production. Rain came too late to sow unirrigated lands in the summers of 1899/1900, 1900/1901, and also 1901/1902.[66] In 1901 locusts took their toll.[67] The British accepted the Boer surrender in May 1902, but the end of the war did not end the food crisis, for the drought continued, and in May 1903, at harvest time, there was again 'a total failure of crops'.[68] It is evident that both environmental and human factors operating in concert created this trauma in subsistence production between 1895 and 1903.

The theory that revolutionary changes arise because of tension at the levels of both production and reproduction holds true here. Production and reproduction were still closely linked, and the collapse of production disturbed reproduction. As in the case of New England, the implementation of colonial law mounted a threat to indigenous social reproduction.[69] However, the most dramatic changes affected biological reproduction, the ability of a society as a whole to reproduce itself. The decline in population figures bears out the reports of famine, death and captivity. The reported population of black people dropped from 12 650 in 1896 to 6280 in 1897.[70] The threat to reproduction demanded response, and an increase in migrant labour was the chief survival strategy. Labour migrancy fulfilled the needs of local households for food, and of the colonial economy for workers. As one official put it: 'In several ways rinderpest has not been an unmixed evil. The wealthy Bechuanas leading indolent lives have learnt the value of labour. The northern locations are beginning to be better tapped, and are becoming what they should be, i.e. valuable labour reserves.'[71] By 1902, 'under ordinary conditions', one-third of the men were away working.[72] Government policy during a serious food shortage in 1903 further promoted migrancy at the expense of local production. M.J. Lyne, resident magistrate of Kuruman after the Anglo-Boer War, repeatedly petitioned the Cape Colony for relief. The Cape government provided feeding supplements for those it considered truly indigent, but halted a local road-building project and declined to provide assistance to cultivated production. Instead, it encouraged men to seek work in Kimberley or on railroad construction elsewhere in the colony. Lyne objected to these solutions because they took men away and lessened their contributions to cultivation, but his objections were unsuccessful.[73] At any rate, migrant labour was supplanting local production. This adjustment supported demographic recovery. The black population rose to 10 630 by 1904, and grew at a higher rate than that of the white population throughout the twentieth century.[74]

The production and reproduction crisis at the turn of the century completed the colonial ecological revolution. New relations with the natural environment replaced the indigenous ones, most importantly in the realm of production. White settlers moved onto the grazing lands and thus claimed the right to the form of production most suited to the Kuruman environment: pastoralism. The intimate interaction between reproduction and production ended when households became dependent upon migrant labour, and the effect was a change in the responsibilities of men and women. Much of the male energy directed toward production and reproduction was now given over to the employer, who did not pay wages sufficient for the reproduction of the workforce. Most costs of reproduction fell therefore to women, who struggled to provide for their families through migrants' remittances, supplementary farming and eventually their own wage labour. The differing effects of this development on men and women are important historical issues,[75] and male and female relations with the environment continued to diverge in the aftermath of the colonial ecological revolution.

Consciousness remains the final consideration regarding human interactions with their environment. More than on the other levels, Merchant's theory on this subject is dependent upon the North American data, and its validity for southern Africa is questionable. As discussed above, missionary conceptions of nature established no hegemony over converts, and this theory is based upon the extension of hegemony. In Merchant's discussion of the ecological revolution, the consciousness of Native Americans is contrasted with its counterpart among western Europeans, particularly the elite classes, in the sixteenth and seventeenth centuries. She postulates that the ecological revolution affected consciousness by replacing indigenous with colonial forms, creating a psychic estrangement from nature: 'rather than an extended consciousness merging with its environment, an autonomous psyche confronted objects outside itself'.[76] She then highlights this alienation as an important aspect in the general theory of the colonial ecological revolution.[77] There are three obstacles to making this argument for Kuruman. Firstly, as we have seen, people there had no intimate consciousness of a non-human world. Secondly, it would be unwarranted to assume that white settlers in all times and places were alienated from their environment. There was no consistent consciousness of nature among colonisers throughout the world.[78] Thirdly, and most importantly, the theory of greater alienation from nature is based on the appearance of a settler population bearing a new consciousness rather than on changing consciousness among one population.[79] Certainly, as in the original case, the entry of settlers introduced new forms of consciousness to the area. However, settlers did not entirely displace indigenous people or their consciousness. Most interesting are issues of how consciousness of the non-human environment changed among the Tswana people of Kuruman, especially as they were affected by Christianity, but the theory has no explanation for these processes.

Assessing the model and theory of the colonial ecological revolution

Southern African environmental history is a young field without established models or theories. Therefore it is essential to look further afield for research questions and paradigms. Merchant's model is important because it reminds environmental historians to look at human relations with their environment at several levels, not limiting themselves to one sort of interaction, such as production or cultural constructions.[80] This is noteworthy, and historians of southern Africa – where the established historiography has very often ignored environmental forces – should consider drawing upon the model. Environmental historians should give explicit consideration to how tensions between the environment, production, reproduction and consciousness give rise to revolutionary changes in human relations with the non-human world.

In addition to the model, Merchant has developed a theory of ecological revolutions to account for changes in human–environmental relationships, relating these changes to the important historical developments of colonialism and capitalism. According to the theory, the interplay of these forces in certain regions of the modern world has brought about dramatic episodes: ecological revolutions. In several instances, the theory will require modification if it is to be useful in southern Africa. Firstly, regarding agency, this theory identifies no indigenous forces for change. The case of Kuruman reveals such forces, and also that indigenous people could adapt to and benefit from the colonial ecological revolution. In Kuruman the examples are strong enough to justify dividing it into two phases, one led by local people, the other by colonial settlers and the government. The second major difficulty involves Merchant's treatment of consciousness. Her assumption of intimate conceptions of the non-human world has little bearing on this case and may not have any bearing on agro-pastoral societies throughout Africa. The last problem arises from the definition of 'colonial', which in Merchant's thought appears to be synonymous with demographic replacement. This is evident in her focus on temperate zones, the discussion of reproductive collapse (as opposed to endangerment and adjustment), the substitution of one consciousness for another, and the narrative's shift to colonial farmers after the completion of the colonial ecological revolution. Southern African societies did not give way to Europeans as those in New England did. Even the Western Cape, the only temperate region in southern Africa, does not qualify as a land of demographic take-over. Despite the forced removals of the apartheid period and the aspirations of some separatist whites, the Northern Cape never came close.

However, the fact remains that practically all of Africa experienced colonialism and that its environmental effects require explication. This exercise suggests that environmental historians should consider several processes: the impact of colonial administration; the effects of natural produce becoming a commodity; the impact of the cash economy (not least wage labour); the relative importance of different methods of production; the level of intensification of land use; and the different relations of black and white, rich and poor, men and women with the environment. Merchant's model will help to frame questions about these processes in different regions of the world.

Chapter Three

White settler impact on the environment of Durban, 1845–1870

Beverley Ellis

The environs of present-day Durban have proved suitable for human habitation for hundreds of years. The first people to settle there permanently were Iron Age farmers, possibly as early as AD 300.[1] Their descendants were joined, in 1824, by a small group of white hunter-traders, and in 1837 this community was augmented by Boer farmers who had emigrated from the Cape Colony. Within the extensive Boer Republic of Natalia that they established, Durban became a tiny town and the only port for the very limited trading activities of the predominantly self-sufficient Boers. The establishment of the Colony of Natal, in 1845, brought control of Durban into British hands, and it remained so for the rest of the period under discussion.

While each phase of settlement mentioned above made an impact on the natural environment of the Durban area, discussion of the environmental changes preceding 1845 lies beyond the ambit of this chapter. It focuses instead on the early phase of colonial rule with the emphasis on the activities of the white settlers, because of their extensive written records. The year 1870 was chosen as an end point because the opening of diamond mines in Kimberley, in that year, stimulated a period of rapid growth in the subcontinent as a whole. In Natal, the rate of economic advance suddenly accelerated, and the settlers began to exploit natural resources far more intensively than they had previously. It would seem, therefore, that 1870 could be seen as a turning point in the environmental history of Natal.

Changes in forces acting on the environment

The community living at the bay between 1845 and 1849 had little impact on the natural environment. Unlike the earliest white settlers, the civilians were not

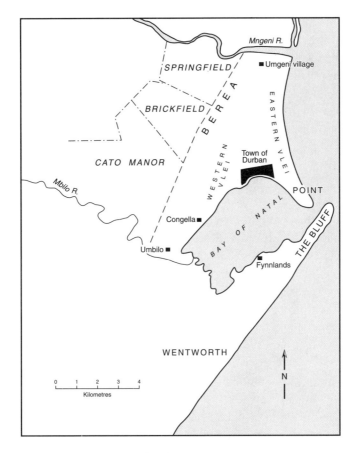

3.1 The Durban town lands

hunting to provide commodities for trade; instead, they were predominantly officials and traders of goods brought into the Colony of Natal. Their demands on the local resources were for domestic purposes only: they needed fuel, food and building materials for the 30 to 40 huts they established on the grassy plain to the north of the bay. Besides the civilian population, there was a small, resident British garrison of the 45th Regiment camped near the bay.

The immigration schemes of the late 1840s and early 1850s brought about 5000 British settlers into Natal. The settlers carried with them their British perceptions and values of the natural environment as well as the skills and technology that would enable them to implement these values. Many settled in Durban, and their arrival had far-reaching implications – both direct and indirect – for the local environment. As the population grew, so too did the physical spread of the town. Its urban growth, which included attaining municipal status, the establishment of a planned infrastructure, as well as some industrial development, was influenced by a settler elite, mainly of wealthy merchants, who controlled the local economy.[2] Under this leadership, Durban became a thriving port and the leading town in Natal, with the range of occupations of the inhabitants reflecting its growing economic diversity.

The influx of settlers caused Durban's white population to grow rapidly in the early 1850s, so that by 1854, when the town was incorporated as a borough, it consisted of about 400 houses.[3] The town lands covered approximately 2901 hectares (7165 acres), with the limits being determined by natural barriers: in the east the Indian Ocean; in the north the Mngeni River; in the north-west the farms Springfield, Brickfield and Cato Manor, bordering the Berea ridge; and in the south the Mbilo River and the bay. However, the government appropriated some of the land for the Admiralty Reserve and for ordnance purposes. This left approximately 2468 hectares (6096 acres) of unalienated land under the control of the town council.[4] The extent of the town lands can be seen on Map 3.1.

As the town council influenced the rate and extent of the modification of the environment within the borough, it is important to consider who held political power in Durban. From Bjorvig's discussion of this, it is clear that political power was in the hands of the white population only and was based on economic wealth.[5] Suffrage was restricted through property qualifications which were even more stringent for those standing as councillors. This ensured that the councillors were wealthy property owners, so the leaders in the economic sphere now became leaders in the local political sphere. They could therefore entrench the existing social order. The town council, however, was still under the jurisdiction of the colonial administration, which could consider long-term changes to the environs of the port, and which could also pass laws to limit environmental exploitation of the area.

With Durban's settler population growth in the early 1850s, it was inevitable that the physical spread of the town would increase. Its expansion was limited, however, as it was flanked to the east and west by large vleis or marshes. Further, the grassy plain to the north of the town was needed for grazing, essential in an era of animal-powered transport. The town council was therefore forced to open up new residential sites at some distance from the town. During the 1850s, lots on the Mbilo River were sold, as were plots at Congella and on the heavily wooded Bluff and Berea. Further localities at Addington and Umgeni Village were first inhabited during the 1860s. The land on the edge of the western vlei was bought up by Indians who had completed their period of indentured labour on the sugar farms of Natal and were now free to settle.[6]

The settlers also demarcated land for recreational purposes in accordance with the British value-systems they brought with them.[7] They laid out several gardens and parks, including the experimental garden and a racecourse at the foot of the Berea. By 1870, Durban consisted of a clearly defined central business district, gardens and parks, and outlying residential areas. There were 870 houses in the borough, housing 3324 whites.[8]

As the major port of Natal, the development of Durban's infrastructure was essential both to the government and to the resident settler elite who had a vested interest in fostering trade. Improvements to the harbour and to all roads leading to the harbour therefore went hand in hand. The government built the main roads – surfaced with stone – that radiated from Durban: Umgeni Road led northwards; Berea Road cut inland over the Berea ridge; while Umbilo Road led southwards. The government also built bridges over the Mngeni River to the north and the Mbilo River to the south-west. Once Durban became a borough, the town council assumed responsibility for making and repairing all roads within it.

In turn, the need to develop good access routes to the bayside necessitated the drainage of the vleis near the town. This made it possible to extend Durban's communication system with the Point, where ships anchored in the deep water on the bay side, so goods had to be transported some distance to and from the town. This haulage was both slow and expensive. In order to further their own ends by making the Durban harbour far more efficient, a group of businessmen formed the Natal Railway Company, which built a short track from the Point to the town, opening it in June 1860. The business sector benefited further in 1862 from the extensions of the line along one of the roads in the town, Pine Terrace.[9] A few years later the government extended the railway to the Mngeni quarry to facilitate the transport of stone to the harbour works.[10]

In addition to these large-scale and very obvious changes taking place in the environment, the settlers were responsible for other, more subtle changes. They needed firewood, building materials and food from the environment, but their greatly increased numbers meant that these demands became heavier. In addition, the population now included skilled artisans and semi-skilled persons, who made a living from using local resources such as shells, thatching reeds, timber and stone. Other commercial ventures included fishing, brick-making and salt-manufacturing.

But the settlers were not the only inhabitants of Durban. Other groups also played a role in changing the environment. Some were entrepreneurs, hawking foodstuffs and building materials obtained from the environment, while others worked in the service sector or were the unskilled, manual labour force of the town. From the 1850s onwards for the rest of the period under discussion, Africans formed about a third of the urban population,[11] but many who were involved in urban life lived beyond the borough limit.

Free Indians also formed part of the Durban population from 1865 onwards. They helped to alter the environment. While many worked in the service sector, others found niches in productive activities such as fishing and market gardening. By 1870 the Indian population numbered 656.[12]

Between 1845 and 1870, Durban was transformed from a tiny settlement of colonial officials and traders into the leading commercial centre of the Colony of Natal. As the size and needs of the town grew, so did production for the local market in the spheres of handicraft manufacture, farming, quarrying, brick-making, fishing, hunting and salt-making. This expansion in the market for commodities caused a concomitant increase in the exploitation of natural resources which, together with the various construction works undertaken by the government and the town council, had an impact on the local environment. The nature and effects of this human activity on the bay environs can be considered under three headings: changes in the landform and mineral resources, in the flora, and in the fauna.

Effects of human activity on the landform and mineral resources

Over the period of 25 years under consideration, settlers made only slight changes to the landform around Durban. In the 1850s they drained the two main swamplands that bordered the settlement of Durban, blocking its access routes. The drainage of the western vlei was accomplished through the cutting and bridging of furrows, but the eastern vlei proved more of a problem. It lay parallel to the coastline and stretched almost across the entire plain between the Mngeni and the bay. The flooding of the Mngeni in 1848 and 1856 enlarged the swamp and made the road from the Point impassable in wet weather. To prevent further flooding, the town council followed the advice of the resident engineer at the harbour, John Milne, and erected an embankment at the head of the vlei above the Umgeni brickfields. Milne's Drain, as it came to be called, was also led out into the bay through Cato's Creek.[13] This scheme effectively drained off water for years and made access to Durban easier. Furthermore, it improved the sanitary condition of the town.

Quarrying activity modified the existing landform in a few places. In the 1840s, the small quantity of stone that was needed for a few public buildings was taken from the nearest available deposits of sandstone on the Bluff. As the town grew in the 1850s, new quarries were opened up within the borough limits and on farms bordering the borough such as on Christopher Cato's farm, Brickfield.[14] Individuals leased the land from the council in order to quarry stone for buildings, paving and for hardening the roads. Small-scale quarrying activity from private quarries continued through the 1860s.

By far the greatest demand for stone during the 1850s and 1860s was for the harbour works that the government embarked on. These focused on stabilising the shifting sands of the Point and deepening the water over the bar at the bay entrance so that larger ships could enter. In 1850, John Milne anchored the sand on the Point by planting Hottentot's fig (*Carpobrotus edulis*) and extending numerous small piers of wattling into the bay. To deepen the water over the bar, Milne proposed creating tidal scour through two stone breakwaters flanking the harbour entrance, the northern one from the Point, the southern one from the Bluff.[15] Criticism of the scheme by the new Lieutenant-Governor of Natal, John Scott, ultimately resulted in Milne's dismissal in 1858. By then, only approximately 137 metres (450 feet) of the proposed 670-metre (2200-foot) northern pier existed, for which about 23 776 tonnes (23 402 tons) of stone had been taken from the Bluff quarries.[16]

In the 1860s, Captain James Vetch proposed a scheme of two long breakwaters, one off the Bluff and the other off the Point, to the north of Milne's pier.[17] Far more stone was needed to begin this ambitious project, but by 1865 the small Bluff quarries were exhausted and so an excellent deposit of sandstone on the right bank of the Mngeni River was quarried. The stone was railed quickly and cheaply to the Point. During 1868 alone, 28 823 tonnes (28 371 tons) of stone were laid in the northern breakwater.[18] Although by 1870 this quarry must have shown signs of heavy exploitation, it remained in use for many years.

Effects of human activity on the flora

The initial impression settlers formed of Durban and its environs was influenced by the apparently luxuriant plant growth around the port. This displayed a mass of green, which was a welcome sight after weeks at sea. On closer inspection the vegetation formed four ecological areas: mangrove swamps, reed beds, coastal forest or bush, and the grassy plain on which Durban itself stood. The settlers cleared vegetation to make way for human settlement, they used it as a source of energy, and also exploited certain species selectively as the raw materials of building and specific manufacturing activities. Each of the ecological zones was affected in a different way.

Along the Mngeni and Mbilo rivers lay extensive reed beds of tambukie grass (a general name for several species of *Cymbopogon*, *Hyparrhenia* and *Miscanthidium*). These beds were harvested by local Africans for thatching reeds for their huts throughout the period under discussion. In addition to this domestic consumption, some Africans gathered and sold or bartered reeds as a commodity to whites.[19] Settlers used them for partitions, ceilings and fences, as well as cheap roofing material that was suitable in the warm climate. Thatching provided a livelihood for both European and African craftsmen. In the 1840s and 1850s most houses in Durban were thatched, but as from 1861, the use of the combustible reeds as roofing material by the white inhabitants was prohibited by a building by-law.[20] Alternative roofing material such as tiles, slates, shingles and corrugated iron had to be used instead. Despite all the years of exploitation of the reed beds, it is unlikely that they would have been much depleted by 1870, as the reeds would have regrown rapidly after each harvesting.

The sandy plain on which Durban was sited was covered with coarse grass, dotted with clumps of wild date palms, wild bananas and wild fig trees. Although we have no direct evidence to show that Africans used the plant resources of this particular zone, it was certainly typical of the areas from which they would have collected grass for mats and the stems of wild dates for brooms for their own use and for sale to the settlers. As with their cutting of the thatching reeds, their exploitation of local resources was intensified because of the demands of the townspeople for these commodities. Hawkers sold their wares around Durban, charging 1 shilling for mats and 3 pence for brushes in 1850.[21] While vegetation such as the coarse grass used for mats would have regenerated rapidly, the wild date palms would have grown far more slowly. A record of the mid-1860s gives an indication of the effects of the destruction of the palms, for it stated that 'as the natives make brooms of the stems, it is now seldom found of any great height'.[22]

The third ecological area to be discussed is that of the mangrove swamps. Early records show that both red and white mangrove trees grew abundantly at the bayhead and on the islands. Being so close to the town they formed a ready supply of accessible timber so that for much of the period mangrove poles were used in the construction of houses, fencing, bridges and jetties. White mangroves in particular also provided a fuel supply for the bayside industries of both salt-making and lime-burning, which drew on the abundant supply of shells found at the water's edge. In the early 1850s lime-burners operated in the vicinity of Cato's Creek and later at Congella too, where a short-lived saltworks was established in 1857.[23] In order to cut mangroves from within the Admiralty Reserve, the lime-burners needed permission from the resident magistrate.

The result of this exploitation was soon clear. While both the written and visual records indicate that in the early 1850s mangroves grew thickly around the bay,[24] by the mid-1860s little of the mangrove forest remained. A Durban resident recorded that few trees of any size were to be found in the bay.[25] The colonial engineer himself noted the scarcity of red mangrove within Natal in 1867.[26] As it was needed for use in the harbour works, this shortage may well have prompted the publication of a notice in 1869 which prohibited the destruction of any trees, bush or underwood from the islands of the bay or within a distance of 46 metres

(150 feet) of the high-water mark, unless with the permission of the Harbour Conservancy Board,[27] which had been formed in 1867.

Thick coastal bush, as it was known locally, covered the Berea and the Bluff, as well as the dunes from the Point to the Mngeni. While we have little information on settlers clearing for urban development, we know far more about them cutting bush when the timber was needed for a specific purpose. Timber was much in demand for housing, furniture and wagons, which is why the thickly forested Berea lots were considered the most valuable of all the town lands.[28] The bush also supplied fuel, required for domestic, military and industrial purposes.

When the settlers first arrived, they could cut fuel freely from the local bush, provided they kept off government land. Once the borough was proclaimed, the council limited bush-cutting from the town lands to that needed by white families for their domestic use. Most settler families employed servants who collected firewood as part of their domestic duties. There were no officials appointed to check on the cutters so the limits imposed on their activities were purely theoretical. It was only in 1863 that the town council really took steps to limit bush-cutting. It agreed to a bush-cutting licence fee of £2 and upwards per acre, with the price being determined by the council in each particular case.[29] By 1870, when the white population stood at 3147, the amount of firewood cut each month from the town lands for domestic consumption must have been considerable. There are no records concerning the amount of fuel, if any, cut from the town lands for the personal use of the employed servants.

The fuel requirements of the military camp at Port Natal also had to be met from local resources. In 1857, for instance, its daily consumption of fuel was approximately 313 kilograms (690 lb), apparently supplied by private tender.[30] It is most likely that the fuel was cut in the vicinity of Durban, thereby contributing to the denuding of the bush.

Local reserves of wood were also used as fuel for the light industries of lime-burning, salt-making and brick-making. Up until 1855 firewood could be collected from the land around the town, but thereafter it was necessary to obtain a permit from the council to cut wood for industrial purposes. As has been discussed already, the lime-burners drew their fuel supplies from the mangrove swamps close to their works, as did the saltworks at the west end of the bay. The brickyards, by contrast, were positioned at several places: Greyville, the foot of the Berea, behind the Berea, and at the Mngeni. They were all established in the early 1850s and remained in operation throughout the period under discussion. Certainly, by 1859 the brick-makers were having difficulty in obtaining fuel, which caused them to increase their prices,[31] but we do not know whether the problem lay in obtaining permits to cut fuel or in a lack of suitable fuel.

As the local bush contained tall forest trees it was a source of good timber. Yellowwood, knobthorn, stinkwood and red milkwood trees were felled by settlers to provide timber for furniture and shop fittings. Milkwood was also felled to build small vessels, while yellowwood and essenwood timber made good planking. These last three were used, together with numerous other types of timber, in wagon-building.

Settlers were able to draw on this local resource of timber to earn a living. The burgess's roll of about 240 people in 1855 listed two wagon-makers, three coopers, two sawyers, a cabinet-maker, three wheelwrights and a ship's carpenter. Ten years later the number of producers who needed timber as a raw material was still about the same, although the white population of Durban had increased by about 2000 people. The wagon-making business was important because until the railway was opened up from Durban to Pietermaritzburg in December 1880, the wagon was the most common form of transport between the two towns.

For the government, timber was a vital resource that might be needed at any time for government building operations. The government therefore attempted to protect the forests on government ground by issuing certain regulations. The first of these was promulgated in 1849,[32] and it forbade tree felling on government ground in or near Durban, without the special permission of a magistrate.

Further government notices issued in the early 1850s restricted the cutting of timber from government forests. In terms of an official proclamation of September 1853,[33] timber could no longer be removed from Crown land unless a licence of £2 per saw per month was paid. The fact that a man who earned a living cutting and selling timber for buildings was apprehended and told to obtain the necessary licence[34] shows that the authorities in Durban were concerned to implement the new legislation, although no officials had been appointed to enforce it.

Once the borough was formed in 1854, the town council took over control of timber cutting on the town lands. To a certain extent this enabled forest conservation measures to be practised. For example, in 1863 the council passed a resolution aimed at protecting particularly large trees on the town lands from being felled.[35] As there was only the superintendent of police to implement these regulations, besides fulfilling all his other duties, it is likely that much illegal tree-felling occurred.

Given that Durban's white inhabitants made a marked impact on the timber resources of the area, all the government's regulations mentioned above were ineffective in the long term. Whereas in 1850 there were plenty of timber trees in the neighbourhood, with red milkwood in particular being plentiful, after fifteen or so years of heavy exploitation few large trees, not even red milkwood, were left standing near the town.[36] The forests had therefore diminished rapidly through the selective felling of favoured species. As no effort was made to cultivate seedlings of these particular species, they were permanently eliminated. Their removal also affected the forest microclimates, for most of the trees felled for timber belonged to canopy species.

As the variety and supply of timber on the Durban town lands diminished, timber merchants were faced with two choices: they could import timber or obtain indigenous timber from the forests of the Natal Midlands. The fact that there were ten saw mills operating in the Midlands in the 1860s proves that these forests were not yet exhausted, but the transport costs to Durban were so high that the merchants found it was cheaper to import timber. [37]

Records throughout the period show that deal, spruce, yellow and red pine, and other softwoods and hardwoods were imported from Prussia, Sweden, England, Australia, India, North America and the Cape.

The settlers not only destroyed indigenous vegetation, they also deliberately introduced other plant species into Natal. In Durban, the amateur botanist Robert Jameson imported Australian prairie grass (called *Bromus schaderie* in those days) in 1869.[38] He immediately offered it to the town council to stabilise the sand towards the racecourse. The grass also provided a good horse and cattle feed.

Effects of human activity on the fauna

In 1845 a wide variety of fauna still found suitable habitats in the environs of Durban, in the sea and bay, the rivers, reed swamps, the grasslands and the coastal bush. As the settlers expanded the built-up area, they caused some animal species to withdraw from the locality of their own accord. Through this process alone the composition of the local fauna would have changed over time. However, in addition, certain species were actively preyed upon by the human population for food, sport, trophies and collecting purposes, besides being killed in defence of lives and property. Consequently, the fauna around Durban decreased in number and variety throughout the period under discussion.

The carnivores which were feared the most were the lion and leopard, for they were considered to be dangerous to persons and their livestock. The settlers therefore attempted to eliminate these animals from the environs of the town. Lion seem to have moved away from the settlement fairly early on, for the last record of a lion in the vicinity dates from 1854.[39] Leopard, by contrast, were still found near Durban in the late 1850s,[40] but no record of their presence there was found for the 1860s.

There were numerous herbivores in the habitats around Durban in 1845 including elephant, buffalo, antelope (bushbuck, reedbuck, grey and red duiker), hippopotamus, monkeys and bush-pigs, to name only the more obvious ones.

Unfortunately, settlers destroyed many of the buck and the larger animals, gradually eliminating them from the area.

Hippopotamus were shot because they destroyed settler gardens in their nocturnal wanderings. The nearest hippopotamus to Durban in the 1850s were those left in Sea Cow Lake, north of the Mngeni. Buffalo and elephant were killed mainly for sport by the settler elite and officers of the garrison. In the 1840s there were herds of these animals in the thick forest of the Berea, and in the Mngeni bush.[41] Over the next ten years they must have been killed off and driven away by sportsmen, for there are no known records of these animals being in the vicinity from the late 1850s onwards.

Other herbivores, particularly buck, were shot for food. Although this must have been a relatively common occurrence in the 1850s, when many of the settlers were struggling to survive, there are very few records of it. One statement dates from 1850, when game was still plentiful in the bush: buck-meat was a common article of diet, varied occasionally with bush-pig.[42] Certainly by 1859 the game had been considerably thinned off near the town.[43]

In 1866, through the efforts of a group of sportsmen, Natal's first game law was introduced. As elsewhere in Africa, the Natal law restricted the hunting of certain animals, listed in Schedule C, to the ruling class.[44] Other animals were protected during closed seasons: partridge, pheasant, guinea fowl, ostrich, buffalo and most buck commonly found. The game law allowed resident magistrates to issue shooting licences; holders of these licences were then free to shoot where they liked during the open season, except on private land. At Durban, the town council issued special regulations regarding shooting on the town lands.[45] These laid down that there would be no shooting on the Berea between the Mngeni and the Mbilo rivers; whereas for ten shillings a year, persons over the age of sixteen could get a permit to shoot on the Congella flats, the vleis, the racecourse and the back beach bush near the Point.[46] Although this attempt by the council to control hunting seems to have arisen from concern for settler safety, it would have had the effect of slowing the destruction of game on the town lands.

The activities of the settlers also led to the diminution of the bird life in the town's environs. In 1845 pelicans, flamingos, hadedahs, cranes, egrets and spoonbills flocked to the bay and the islands. The grasslands, reed beds and thick bush all teemed with birds. As the town grew and the vleis were drained, the size of the feeding places for wild duck and snipe were reduced, while suburban development on the Berea and the Bluff disturbed the bird life through forest clearance.

Settlers diminished the bird life further by deliberately shooting birds. For the immigrants of 1850, the blue and green pigeons from the coastal bush were a source of food.[47] In an era when interest in museums and zoological gardens in

Western Europe was burgeoning, birds also brought in revenue for a few settlers who collected them to send overseas.[48] This activity continued throughout 1845–70. Birds were also killed for sport, with the islands of the bay being popular hunting haunts.[49] The parks proclaimed by the council were too small to provide an adequate refuge for fauna, and public awareness of the diminution of the bird life came too late. While it is not possible to pinpoint exact dates in this process of change, it is clear that the early settlers were responsible for much of the destruction of Durban's bird life.

There were two species of reptiles that were preyed upon – for different reasons – by local settlers. On the one hand, turtles were a good food source and references relating to their presence in the bay or their capture exist throughout the period under discussion,[50] indicating that settler exploitation did not eliminate the turtle population. Crocodiles, on the other hand, living in the reeds of the alluvial flats, were shot because they posed a threat to the safety of people crossing rivers and livestock drinking at the water's edge. With the increase in traffic to the bay during the 1850s, the appearance of crocodiles became more rare.[51] There seem to be no records of crocodiles being sighted near Durban in the 1860s. Presumably by then they had either been destroyed or moved away from the settlement.

As with the turtles, the fish in the bay and off the coast were a source of food for the settlers. Numerous records attest to both the variety and the quantity of fish in the bay in the 1850s and early 1860s, with the most common fish being rock-cod, springer, mullet, Cape salmon, shad, stumpnose, bonito and albacore. Despite the richness of these resources, few whites earned a living as fishermen in the 1850s because, though prices were good, customers were scarce and scattered.[52] Some Africans also caught and sold fish: in the late 1840s Mnini's Thuli people conducted a steady trade in fish, worth between £100 and £200 per annum, with the settlers.[53]

In the 1860s the scale of exploitation of fish resources increased considerably. This was partly because the importation of Indian labourers into the coastlands created a far greater demand for fish as food, as it formed the staple diet of the labourers. More people were therefore able to earn their living from fishing. In 1865, for example, there were ten white fishermen fishing in the bay.[54] A small fishing company, the Birkenhead Industry, operated off-shore from the Bluff from 1862 until 1868 when it collapsed because of the death of one of the partners.

The year 1866 saw a number of free Indians becoming a new group of fishermen at the bay. As fish formed such an important part of their diet, it was not surprising that many Indians went to the bay to fish. Almost immediately, protests appeared in the local newspapers because the small size of the mesh of the Indians' fishing nets trapped many fry.[55] Since about 70 nets were in daily use,[56] the long-term consequences for the fish supply could have been serious.

The government reacted promptly to the settler complaints. It appointed a Conservancy Board in May 1867, consisting of the surveyor-general, the collector of customs, the port captain and the colonial engineer. Because of the Board's recommendation, a law concerning fishing in the bay was gazetted in October 1867.[57] The law did not, however, provide for the appointment of special officers to enforce it. As the members of the Conservancy Board were all officials in full-time employment, it is unlikely that they had the opportunity to apprehend many offenders. According to the law, a fisherman needed a licence costing £1 to use a net or a fish trap. Such licences were to be issued by the resident magistrate. As the law did not stipulate the size of the mesh of fishing nets it was duly repealed, and a revised law, Law No. 8 gazetted in September 1868, took immediate effect. This law laid down the minimum size of the mesh when wet, and the length of the net, but we have no records to show whether the law was implemented or not. This, however, seems unlikely as, once again, there was no special officer appointed to apprehend offenders, although the fact that 22 people took out fishing licences in 1868[58] indicates that some fishermen regarded the law seriously.

Smaller animals such as molluscs and arthropods were also utilised by the settlers. As limestone was scarce around Durban, the deep banks of shells washed up on the shore were valuable because they were easily collected and burned by lime-burners to make lime for use as mortar.[59] Shells were also removed from the bay islands when some visiting ships in the late 1860s used them as a more lucrative form of ballast than sand: they were sold once the ships reached England.[60]

Living molluscs and arthropods in the bay and along the coast were also preyed upon by humans. Crayfish, mussels, crabs, oysters and shrimps were caught by both Africans and white fishermen as food for the white settlers.[61] The fishing law of 1867 made some attempt to control this activity by making a licence costing ten shillings necessary for shrimp fishing. It seems likely that this financial burden would have discouraged Africans from continuing in the trade. Despite the exploitation by humans, there is no evidence to suggest that the supply of shellfish had been adversely affected by 1870.

Conclusion

From the early 1850s onwards, Durban's population grew rapidly and the effects of exploitative human activity became more noticeable. The heavier demands of the bigger population increased the scale of exploitation, while the range of demands on the environment also expanded.

After 25 years of colonial rule, the landform of Durban showed several signs of settler activity. Perhaps the most obvious change would have been through the drainage of the large vleis. The demand for stone for the harbour works, buildings and roads had caused quarries to be opened up and worked, first on the Bluff, and then at several sites within the borough. The most noticeable quarry in 1870 would have been at the Mngeni, for the government had the capital to finance the labour and technology required to shift large quantities of stone. By 1855, the shoreline of the bay side of the Point was more firmly established, while the entrance to the bay was deeper. The marine side of the Point looked much as it had in 1845, except that the two unfinished piers extended from it.

The natural vegetation had been greatly interfered with. The settlers had introduced Australian prairie grass and they had destroyed much of the indigenous bush as residential sites were cleared and fuel cut. The demand for fuel had become heavier over the years, with the growing urban population and the development of fuel-burning industries. This fuel was cut from the coastal bush and the mangrove swamps. While it cannot be estimated to what extent human exploitation had diminished the bush cover, we do know that by 1870 most of the mangrove trees that had once formed a dense growth around the bay had been cut down. The need for timber for buildings, wagons and furniture had led to selective exploitation of the trees around Durban, thereby reducing the forest cover and altering the forest composition.

The faunal resources of the bay area had clearly been both diverse and vast in 1845. Early settlers were able to eliminate those species they feared, while preying on others for food and sport. As a result, over a period of 25 years they destroyed large numbers of animals and reduced the number of species found there. While the turtle, fish and shellfish resources seem to have been unaffected by settler exploitation up to 1870, it was evident that the Durban area was no longer the sporting field it had once been when elephants browsed on the flats,[62] for the bird life and game had diminished most markedly.

Some of the changes caused by humans were evident to the government and colonists. Where these were disadvantageous to the white population, as in the destruction of valuable resources, steps were taken to control the damage. The government promulgated laws to protect timber, fish and game, but neglected to appoint officials to enforce the laws. When the town council took control of the town lands, it also made regulations concerning the exploitation of fauna and flora in the municipal area, but again provided no effective means to ensure its regulations were obeyed. Despite such limited attempts to control the exploitative activity of the settlers, the environment of Durban had been greatly and irreversibly altered by 1870.

Chapter Four

'The titihoya does not cry here any more': The crisis in the homestead economy in colonial Natal

John Lambert

The grass is rich and matted, you cannot see the soil. It holds the rain and the mist, and they seep into the ground, feeding the streams in every kloof …

Where you stand the grass is rich and matted, you cannot see the soil. But the rich green hills break down. They fall to the valley below, and falling, change their nature. For they grow red and bare; they cannot hold the rain and mist, and the streams are dry in the kloofs. Too many cattle feed upon the grass, and too many fires have burned it. Stand shod upon it, for it is coarse and sharp, and the stones cut under the feet. It is not kept, or guarded, or cared for, for it no longer keeps men, guards men, cares for men. The titihoya does not cry here any more.[1]

Although written in 1946, Alan Paton's contrasting image of well-tended, white-owned farms and the arid, devastated, African-occupied Ndotsheni reserve would have resonated with any observer of early twentieth-century Natal. In 1916, Maurice Evans had painted a similar picture of African reserves 'scratched with the plough, unmanured, weeded in slovenly fashion and yielding scanty and irregular crops'. To Evans, Africans were the worst agriculturalists and most wasteful occupiers of land in the world.[2]

Evans's observations were widely shared by settler society, and even Paton, perhaps unconsciously, suggests that the devastation of the valley of Ndotsheni was caused by a 'backward' people. This chapter examines why homestead modes of agriculture and stock-keeping – perfectly suited to pre-colonial conditions – struggled to maintain their viability when faced by growing land shortage and settler hostility.

The pre-colonial homestead economy

During the pre-colonial period the African inhabitants of the region evolved a homestead economy suited to the climatic and environmental conditions of south-east Africa. The basic unit of this economy was the *umuzi*, a homestead under a head, the *umnumzana*, in which all members were subordinate to his authority. This authority was passed on to the chosen son of his chief wife, and the continuation of his lineage ensured the material, social and spiritual well-being of the *umuzi* members.[3]

Each *umuzi* consisted of a central cattle kraal surrounded by huts or households belonging to the wives, dependent relatives and widowed mother of the head. The eldest son seldom left his father's *umuzi*, and the younger sons generally stayed until after they had married a second wife. The *umnumzana* controlled distribution of the resources within the *umuzi*, set aside gardens for his wives and his sons' wives, and allocated cattle for the use of each household and as *lobolo* (bridewealth) to enable his male dependants to marry. In return, he was entitled to receive produce and labour services from the inhabitants of each household. He also had considerable legal authority over his dependants and was responsible to his chief for their good behaviour.

Within each *umuzi* there was a sexual division of labour. Men were responsible for the husbandry of livestock, building and maintaining huts and cattle kraals, digging grain pits and clearing the land for cultivation. Women and girls were responsible for agricultural production, domestic labour, thatching huts and portering. In the manufacturing field, there was also a sexual division between men, who produced wooden and iron articles and baskets, and women, who made pots and mats.

For all its generally heavy rainfall and comparatively rich vegetal cover, Natal's environment placed certain restrictions and limitations on the inhabitants of the *umuzi* and on the homestead economy in general.[4] The best endowed of Natal's regions is the narrow coastal strip with high rainfall, abundant rivers and streams, and fertile soil. It is not suitable for livestock, however, and cattle diseases such as redwater and gall sickness were endemic in the region in the nineteenth century. Africans living on the coast had to move their cattle inland during the summer.

The interior of Natal consists mainly of a broken and rugged terrain dissected by major rivers such as the Thukela, Mzinyathi, Mngeni, Mzimkhulu, Mnambithi (Klip), Mtshezi (Bushman's) and Mpofana (Mooi). These rivers cut out deep gorges and form great river valleys, climatically hot and humid and with shallow soils unsuitable for agriculture and susceptible to erosion. This terrain experiences marked dry seasons followed by severe storms in late summer, which exacerbate conditions of erosion by washing the shallow soils into the rivers where they drain away to the Indian Ocean.

The Drakensberg highlands region is too cold and broken for either agriculture or livestock to prosper, while the coastal hinterland and the Thukela valley have a low annual rainfall averaging 600–700 millimetres and frequent summer droughts. With broken ground and, in the early nineteenth century, a thin grass cover vulnerable to erosion, the coastal hinterland and Thukela valley are generally not conducive to either agriculture or cattle-keeping. The lands in the Thukela valley in particular are generally exceedingly steep and broken, being described in the mid-nineteenth century as 'worthless as the sands of Arabia'; a more broken, worthless region could hardly be found'.[5] Both, however, are in close proximity to lands which, at the time, were wooded or had a palatable grass cover supporting an abundance of game and on which stock could graze throughout the year.[6]

Climatically and environmentally, one of the most suitable regions for habitation is the narrow mist belt stretching north of the coastal hinterland from approximately Ixopo in the south-west through Richmond and Pietermaritzburg to Greytown in the north-east. With soft, mist-like rains, soils conducive to agriculture and excellent grazing, the mist belt is ideal for livestock. Much of the remainder of Natal consists of the open savannah lands of the interior. While not suitable for intensive agriculture, they generally provide lush, well-watered pastures ideal for livestock. Both sweet- and sourveld grasslands are to be found which provide year-round grazing.

The diversity of environmental conditions and the fact that Africans in pre-colonial Natal could move their homesteads and cattle with relative ease to take advantage of the different conditions, meant that there was little continuity of settlement except in riverine areas. Shifting cultivation was followed whereby land was cultivated for as many years as it remained fertile. It was then allowed to revert to bush while trees would be burned in a new area and vegetation cut back for new gardens. Cattle were moved between sweet- and sourveld grasslands to take advantage of winter and summer grazing. Through centuries of experience of the vagaries of the region's climate and the infertility of its soils, the inhabitants had evolved a subsistence agricultural economy suited to the region's environmental conditions.[7]

The homestead economy was affected by years of drought when food shortages could cause considerable suffering, but in most years the inhabitants enjoyed a balanced diet which ensured a healthy existence. From the cattle herds, milk provided an important protein. Seldom drunk fresh, it was curdled and fermented in a gourd or sack and, as *amasi*, was consumed by adults, children, and particularly by new-born babies and by boys at puberty. Protein was also provided by groundnuts and beans and, on the coast, by fish. Carbohydrates were supplied by sorghum, maize, pumpkins and sweet potatoes. These also supplied bulk and were supplemented by wild fruit and veld vegetation, game and game birds. Other than milk, the most important of these foods were maize and sorghum. These complemented each other, as sorghum is resistant to drought while maize grows more quickly and is less susceptible to bird damage. Sorghum, consumed usually as beer, *utshwala*, was exceptionally important both in social intercourse and as a form of social control: refusing to allow young people to take part in public beer drinks was one of the ways in which the *umnumzana's* authority was asserted over junior members of the *umuzi*.[8]

The African diet and the sufficiency of food varied according to the seasons. In spring the veld provided natural vegetation, herbs, berries, and wild melons and roots. During spring and the first half of the year, when maize and sorghum were harvested there was generally sufficient food to provide two meals a day in all but the most arid areas while the digging of grain pits meant that there was surplus grain to consume during the 'hungry season', from June to October. In situations of serious shortage the wider kinship system also provided mechanisms such as the *ukutekela* (the obtaining of food from other *imizi*) and *ukusisa* (the placing of livestock in the care of a dependant, who is then given certain rights of usufruct) customs to provide assistance.

The upheavals in Natal in the 1810s and 1820s commonly known as the *mfecane* would have modified the homestead economy: firstly, by forcing many Africans to seek shelter in the more arid and broken coastal hinterland and Thukela valley and, secondly, by draining cattle from *imizi* as tribute to the Zulu state. By the 1830s, under King Dingane kaSenzangakhona, conditions began to revert to normal, with chiefdoms returning to settle in Natal and with the king providing lands for previously dispersed chiefdoms such as the Nadi and Mphumuza.[9]

The early colonial homestead economy

Further changes occurred with the arrival of the Voortrekkers in the late 1830s. Also a pastoral people, the trekkers sought the savannah lands of the interior which were favoured by the Africans and began carving out large farms for themselves. The presence of the trekkers' herds, especially after large-scale confiscations of royal cattle from Zululand, put pressure on the grazing requirements of the *imizi* while the civil war between Dingane and his brother, Mpande kaSenzangakhona, saw a large influx of refugees into Natal. Entire chiefdoms such as the Thembu, Chunu, Mthethwa and Qwabe moved into the lands west of the Thukela valley, increasing conditions of population pressure.[10] After the annexation of Natal to the British Crown in 1843, this influx gathered momentum and by the 1850s over 100 000 Africans were estimated to be in the colony. While many *imizi* were remote from centres of white settlement, those close to the newly established towns and villages seized the opportunity to supply their needs. Even as early as the 1820s, Africans who had sought the protection of the hunter-traders at Port Natal had adapted their economy to meet white needs. In return for land and cattle from the traders, they had supplied game, fish and produce.[11] By 1850, the settler James Methley was writing of 'potatoes of several kinds, Indian and kaffir corn, beans, fruits and a variety of other vegetables' being sold by Africans who, 'having no European competition to contend with, are beginning to find that the trade of a market gardener is one of the most lucrative'.[12]

In 1847 a Location Commission was appointed to inquire into the best way of governing the African population. Realising the colony's dependence on African produce, the commissioners recommended the establishment of reserves in which an African peasantry could develop.[13] Their recommendation came to nothing. In order both to prevent an exodus of Voortrekker families and to have land available for British settlers, the administration set aside reserves mainly in regions unsuitable for white settlement. With few exceptions the reserves were in the coastal hinterland, the Thukela valley, or the Drakensberg foothills, lands which, as seen above, were generally not conducive to either agriculture or cattle-keeping. Even in the 1850s, the great block of reserves established in eastern Natal, the Impafana, Tugela, Umvoti and parts of the Inanda, could not provide the agricultural or grazing needs of their population.[14]

Despite the intention to settle all Africans in reserves, the administration did not have the resources to remove *imizi* off private and Crown lands. Before the 1880s, no official attempt was made to distinguish between Crown and reserve lands, and many African *imizi* were located on Crown lands. Many also maintained their *imizi* on settler lands, either because the homesteads predated the arrival of the whites or because the settlers allowed Africans to live on their farms provided they agreed to conditions of labour tenancy, supplying labourers from their *imizi* for six months a year at a nominal wage and often with a range of extra conditions; these could include the requirement that at periods such as weeding and harvesting all inhabitants had to provide labour *gratis*.[15]

During the early colonial decades, labour tenants could enjoy considerable benefits, the most important being the ability to move livestock to take advantage of seasonal grazing. Few stock-farmers practised winter feeding but instead held both winter- and summer-grazing farms and allowed their tenants to move their cattle between them. Also important, as stock-farmers cultivated very little of their land, their tenants had access to sufficient land for their own gardens. By the 1880s, however, as stock-farmers began cultivating more land themselves, so they needed more labour, which created considerable friction within labour tenant *imizi*. Because the farmer contracted with the *umnumzana* for labour, dependent homestead members deeply resented what they saw as enforced labour. And, as farmers needed extra labour at the same time that it was required within the *umuzi*, homestead agriculture suffered and tenants frequently had to send their sons out to work to supplement their income.[16]

An alternative to labour tenancy was rent tenancy on absentee-owned farms. A continuing depression in land prices in Natal until the end of the 1870s saw land speculators encourage Africans to establish *imizi* on their lands from which they drew rentals. Many such farms were in fertile areas, such as the mist belt and coastal strip, that were also close to markets. In addition, as the price of maize rose steadily until the 1880s, rents could be met through grain sales.[17] And, while land prices remained low and there was little profit to be made from improving farms, few landowners limited the stock owned by an *umuzi* or restricted access to arable land.

Many *abanumzana* were therefore able to use the colonial presence to build up their herds. By 1869, the first year that cattle statistics were gathered in the colony, Africans owned an estimated 334 563 head, with each hut in the colony averaging five head. Overstocking was resulting in the reserves, where a delicate balance existed between cattle numbers and the condition of the veld. Restricted access to land meant that herds were being grazed on the same grass cover throughout the year, causing a rapid degeneration of the veld, destruction of the top soil and a deterioration of the herds, making cattle more susceptible to drought and disease.

It was not only livestock holdings which were expanding. With official and commercial encouragement homestead agriculture expanded as well, from an estimated total acreage of 90 057 reaped by Africans in 1867 to 279 298 in 1882.[18] In both years, well over half the acreage was under maize and many *imizi* were able to meet taxes and rentals by expanding maize production for the market. Supplying maize to the market required little adaptation to homestead agriculture. *Imizi* continued to be based on primary production and subsistence cultivation. The colonial presence had, however, created conditions which, even in the early years of white settlement, militated against a continuation of the pre-colonial lifestyle. This lifestyle depended on unrestricted access to land, the very condition the colonial presence was destroying. Particularly in the Thukela valley, many *imizi* could not cultivate at all and had to subsist by bartering stock for grain or by sending men out as migrant labourers.[19]

An adaptation of traditional cultivation practices was accordingly imperative if *imizi* were to continue to be self-supporting, to say nothing of supplying the market. But to a conservative rural society, innovation was suspect and tended to occur only when encouraged by strong financial incentives. Homestead Africans in divisions close to the Durban and Pietermaritzburg markets were far more receptive to innovation than were those in outlying divisions and were more speedily drawn into a cash economy.[20] In general, even in *imizi* whose inhabitants were prepared to innovate, maize sales remained the most important source of money. The demand for maize and the increased price buyers were prepared to pay for it, combined with the labour-intensive nature of growing most other cash crops, discouraged diversification. This concentration on maize, however, created a potentially dangerous situation in which most *imizi* depended entirely on maize as a cash crop.

The crisis facing the homestead economy

By the late 1870s, both the growing African population and the increased production of maize were contributing to a shortage of land. African numbers had experienced a threefold increase since the late 1840s, with just under half the approximately 300 000 Africans in Natal living in the reserves. Many chiefs were now finding it very difficult to allocate land to *abanumzana*, grazing was becoming restricted and many reserve inhabitants were 'at the end of their tether as far as cultivation goes'.[21] Access to non-reserve land was also becoming more restricted as more white settlers immigrated into the colony and as sons of the original pioneers required farms for themselves. By the end of the decade, absentee landowners such as the Natal Land and Colonisation Company began selling off their better-placed lands or increasing rentals. As a result, rent tenants were being evicted or marginalised on poorer arable and pastoral land.[22]

To try to meet the growing demand for land, not only from Africans but also from settlers, the administration began auctioning Crown lands in 1882 under extremely generous terms of payment. Africans proved enthusiastic purchasers but an agricultural depression in the mid-1880s saw many lose their lands.[23] In addition, many squatters on Crown lands were evicted by the new purchasers or left when the purchasers imposed rentals or labour services on them. Africans who were evicted, or who left their lands to avoid labour services or rentals, had a limited choice of new lands. Where possible they moved onto remaining Crown lands or onto private lands. Yet few of the remaining Crown lands were suitable for agriculture or pasture while increased rentals or labour demands on privately owned lands made these unattractive.[24]

Most were reluctant to move onto reserves because of the limited land available or because they did not want to fall under chiefly control. Despite this, the shortage of alternative land meant that many had no choice.[25] The result was increasing over-population in virtually all the reserves, and forced settlement on lands which could not provide sufficient crops for even their existing populations.[26] The growth of the African population in the reserves saw a decline in the number of acres available to each hut. Between 1884 and 1891, the number of reserve huts that paid taxes increased from 39 913 to 50 092, while the average number of acres available to each hut declined from 55.1 to 43.9. In the arid Inanda, Umvoti and Tugela reserves the decline was even more serious, from 42 to 34.9 acres per hut.[27] By the 1890s, the homestead economy in the reserves was becoming increasingly unable to cope with the stresses arising from dwindling land resources and growing population numbers.

These conditions meant that shifting cultivation, admirably suited to conditions of abundant land, could seldom be practised. Instead, *imizi* inhabitants had to cultivate exhausted gardens or more marginal lands, and the quality and quantity of their crops declined.[28] The growing number of *imizi* with ploughs (by 1893 Africans owned 17 672 ploughs)[29] was also encouraging cultivation of poorer soils and steep slopes, but these lands yielded smaller returns and were rapidly exhausted. The American scholar W. Allan points out that it takes anything up to twenty years for the fertility of such soils to be restored.[30] Africans, compelled to find new ground for gardens and grazing, were ploughing up young trees and bushes, thereby accelerating the degradation of the environment.[31] The situation was particularly serious in the sweetveld areas where the destruction of the woodland removed the semi-shade necessary for the veld's survival.[32]

Although all categories of land were affected, the overcrowded reserves suffered most. By the late 1880s, the once heavily wooded Zwartkop reserve was left with only a few isolated clumps of trees.[33] Over-cultivation and the destruction of forests and bush cover created perfect conditions for erosion, particularly in the rugged reserves of the coastal interior and the Thukela valley. Ironically, the one innovation widely accepted by homestead Africans, the plough, further accelerated erosion. Palmer and Parsons point out that in southern Africa deep ploughing has had disastrous ecological effects, opening up the 'topsoil (only a few inches deep) to be dried by the sun…Few African soils have the chemical properties to sustain continuous cultivation, and continuous deep ploughing has been responsible for turning cultivable soils into sun-baked powder.'[34] In addition, women and children were often unable to hoe and weed the larger ploughed fields properly, with the result that their crops suffered from unavoidable neglect.[35]

The ecological pressures on the reserves were compounded by a sharp rise in cattle numbers. Despite lungsickness and redwater in the 1870s, African-owned stock numbers increased during that decade from an estimated 334 563 in 1869 to 384 557 in 1882. During much of the 1880s, the colony was remarkably free of cattle disease and enjoyed relatively wet summers with only localised droughts. Because of this, *umuzi* cattle numbers continued to increase, reaching 494 382 by 1896.[36] Magistrates' reports frequently refer to the difficulties Africans were having in finding suitable pasture lands. Not only were they having to graze a greater number of cattle on a steadily shrinking land resource, but the herds were also having to compete with a rapidly increasing number of goats, a sign of the growing impoverishment of many *imizi*.

Under these conditions, cattle were becoming a liability. D.I. Bransby calculates that cattle require between ten and twenty acres of grazing per head to obtain optimum results in the climatic and ecological conditions of the Thukela valley reserves. During a dry season this can rise to as high as 62 acres.[37] No figures are available for cattle holdings in the reserves before 1896 but in that year the 281 399 acres of the Inanda and Umvoti reserves, which fell within the Mapumulo and Indwedwe divisions, carried 56 000 head.[38] Thus each animal had an average of only 5.02 acres. The result was an unremitting decline of the veld, cattle condition and milk production. Cattle deterioration was worse in winter, so that by the planting season oxen were of little use for ploughing. By the 1890s, and particularly during a drought cycle from 1888 to 1893, winter stock losses were becoming severe, a situation which was exacerbated by the encroachment of gardens onto the sourveld as reserve Africans attempted to raise sufficient crops.[39]

In earlier years, Africans in drought-stricken areas could move their livestock to lands less affected. The absence of adequate surveys and fences had made this possible even when settlers moved into an area. This was more difficult by the 1890s after the introduction of a more systematic surveying of the colony's lands and, more detrimentally for Africans, the introduction of the Dividing Fences Acts in 1887 and 1889. By the early 1890s the colony's farms were rapidly being fenced.[40] Africans now often found themselves barred from traditional rights of way, many of which had long been used to drive stock between different grazing lands. As a result, optimum use of seasonal grazing was becoming impossible, and overgrazing and grassland destruction were becoming endemic. In more arid reserves, much of the sweetveld grass was beyond recovery.[41]

During the drought years, many Africans faced destitution because of crop failures while in the more arid reserves chiefs warned of starvation amongst their peoples.[42] Many *imizi* survived by selling stock, often at ridiculously low prices; in Ixopo, for example, a mare and foal were sold for four bags of maize in 1892.[43] Homestead inhabitants were also eating more drought-resistant sorghum rather than maize, leading to an unbalanced diet. Sorghum has a relatively low protein and amino acid content, and an over-reliance on it can lead to protein-deficiency diseases such as kwashiorkor, particularly in children. In addition, because it ripens later than maize, the period of seasonal hunger became longer and its effects more acute.[44]

The monotony and shortcomings of a grain diet were exacerbated by the serious decline in the colony's game. More intensive grass burning to refertilise the soil drove game birds away from the *imizi*. Buck were not only becoming more scarce throughout the colony, but official restrictions virtually prohibited Africans from hunting those that remained.[45]

By the 1890s, rather than adapt agricultural practices to cope with overcrowding and limited resources, many *imizi* were making ends meet by selling stock or by sending men out as migrant labourers. Few were prepared to emulate Indian cultivators who used the same gardens for years by rotating legumes and grain crops. Eric Hobsbawm's general explanation seems valid for Natal: pointing out the extent to which nature's threat dominates peasant communities, he argues that to people with few resources, the potential risks of innovation appear greater than the possible gains.[46] In a situation of land shortage and drought, such as in Natal in these years, these risks became more marked. Despite seeing their market for maize steadily captured by settler and Indian suppliers and a drop in the price they were receiving, grain cultivation still seemed a more sensible option than trying to diversify.

The growing reliance on migrant labour was causing social dislocation within the *imizi*. While the men were away, the work they performed was neglected or was performed by women, upsetting the sexual division of labour in the homestead and causing considerable resentment particularly amongst younger women. And often, when the men returned, having tasted the freedom of working away from the restraining influence of the *umuzi* and wider kinship group, many were reluctant to conform to social conventions. By ignoring restrictions such as those on the drinking of beer, they were effectively challenging the authority of the *abanumzana*. Their attitudes had a ripple effect on other groups within the *imizi*. Complaints from African elders about the insubordination of young men and women[47] and of growing squalor within the *imizi* became common while attempts to enforce patriarchal authority frequently led to both young men and young women deserting the *imizi* completely and moving to the towns and to gold and diamond mines.[48]

During these last decades of the nineteenth century, Africans were faced not only by deteriorating ecological conditions but also by growing official indifference to their well-being. With the colony relying increasingly on white and Indian farmers for produce, the administration no longer felt obliged to encourage homestead production. At the same time, as Natal moved towards the attainment of responsible government in 1893, so more attention was paid to the wishes of the settlers and particularly to the demands of farmers to reduce competition from African cultivators. After 1893, homestead Africans could expect little official sympathy. On the contrary, they were confronted with growing hostility, increased taxation, and a barrage of legislation designed to undermine their independence.

It was in a situation such as this that the homestead economy faced its greatest challenge in the second half of the 1890s. A succession of natural disasters occurred: a continuation of the droughts which had gripped the colony between 1888 and 1893, a locust plague in 1894–1896 and, most devastating of all, rinderpest which paralysed the homestead economy between 1897 and 1899. With the lives and customs of homestead society so intimately bound up with cattle-keeping, rinderpest dealt a blow to the homestead economy from which it never completely recovered. To quote the magistrate of Weenen, George Adamson:

> Old headmen and fathers would cry like children, as I saw them, at the sight of their cattle and calves, their sole asset upon earth which they had watched for years grow and increase before their eyes, drop down and die by scores before them, cleaning out the coveted collection of a lifetime in fewer hours than it had taken them years to acquire them, the food for their children, and the wives for their young men taken from them without power of rescue... To say that the consequences of this scourge have been the disorganization of their social system and the disaster of their domestic is only to briefly compass the evils which its advent has entailed. Cattle being the basis of all their social contracts and ceremonies, and money being in their eyes an impossible substitute, I do not think it can be adequately appreciated by Europeans what the force and effect of these enormous losses to the Natives really mean.[49]

The process of rebuilding herds was painfully slow. Some *imizi* were able to use the boom conditions caused by the Anglo-Boer War to rebuild herds partially, but the process was interrupted in the early 1900s by a recurrence of rinderpest and then by a devastating outbreak of east coast fever. Africans were never again to have the large herds of pre-rinderpest days. This had enormous consequences for homestead society.[50] Despite their reluctance to accept *lobolo* in any form other than cattle, by the twentieth century goats and cash payments were being taken. Most Africans were also finding themselves excluded from the distribution of resources within the wider kinship unit, which even as late as the early 1890s had helped to hold homestead society together. This served to cement Africans into a position of dependency on the settlers. With their chiefs and *izinduna* unable to supply their needs, many Africans had no choice but to turn to farmers, traders or touts for the resources they needed to survive. In the process, the ties binding members of kinship groups together were further weakened, while the ability of *imizi* to function independently of migrant labour was made well-nigh impossible. This struck at the very basis of the *umuzi* and accelerated a process of proletarianisation in African society.

This process was hastened by the fact that, by the early twentieth century, few lands remained in Crown or absentee hands and the great majority of homestead Africans were either labour tenants or crowded onto the reserves. As farmers cultivated far more of their lands now than had been the case in the nineteenth century, labour tenants found the size of their gardens reduced and were allowed to graze only a small number of cattle.

As congestion grew on the reserves, so the destruction of the natural vegetation and soil erosion increased. Soil exhaustion and erosion seriously hampered African grain cultivators: between 1902 and 1904 *imizi* production was half of what it had been in the early 1890s. Africans supplied only 38 per cent of Natal's maize crop and their sorghum crop had also declined.[51] They were finding it difficult meeting their own food requirements, let alone supplying the market.[52] With grain, meat and milk now in short supply, and with the depletion of traditional stand-bys such as natural vegetation and game, Africans throughout the colony were experiencing food shortages. In general, Africans had too little to eat, and what they did eat provided a starchy and unbalanced diet.

Purchases of food only partially remedied the problem. The district surgeons' reports reflect a deterioration in health caused by overcrowding, bad diet and malnutrition. As overpopulation reduced access to fresh water, typhus and dysentery spread, while cramped conditions in many huts encouraged tuber-culosis. Intestinal complaints and enteritis were also becoming common.[53] Children continued to suffer the most, and malnutrition undermined their resistance to disease. In 1905 the district surgeon of Estcourt reported on the number of infant deaths caused by the milk shortage and estimated that African mothers lost on average two out of three babies through abdominal complaints.[54]

By the early twentieth century, although most Africans would have retained some access to land and, through this, access to at least some of the resources controlled by kinship groups, few would have lived in *imizi* with sufficient resources to provide for any but their most basic needs without cash from migrant labour. Many *imizi* had broken up completely through the ravages of rinderpest or as a result of evictions from private lands. Their inhabitants had either sought refuge with relatives or drifted to the towns. Even for those Africans who were able to recreate a semblance of homestead life elsewhere, the impact of their removal from land intimately associated with their past and with ancestral spirits would have involved a traumatic change of lifestyle, one to which it would have been difficult to adapt. In many of the *imizi* which continued to exist, the orderly pattern of a cattle kraal within a circle of huts had disappeared,[55] reflecting the breakdown of control within them. Gardens of stunted grain crops, choked by weeds, and grasslands eroded away and robbed of the nutrition necessary to support cattle, bore eloquent witness to the environmental crisis faced by the homestead economy.

The native affairs official James Stuart was only too aware of this crisis. In a moving account of the disaster that had overtaken homestead society, he described the average *umuzi* as 'a mere shelter from the sun, rain and wind and cold…filled with nothing else but distressed and careworn creatures whose constant solicitude are [*sic*] the next year's taxes or rent'.[56]

Chapter Five

'I can see my old *umuzi* where I now am. I had fields over there, but here I have none': An ecological context for *izimpi zemibango* in the Pinetown district, 1920–1936

Jabulani Sithole

This chapter explores an environmental context for violent conflicts – the *izimpi zemibango* – which erupted amongst the abaMbo of the Umlazi location in the Pinetown district in the 1920s and 1930s.[1] While causes for conflict are complex, almost invariably a resource crisis creates conditions for tension to degenerate into violence. The *imibango* (disputes) over succession in the Umlazi location provide a case study of tension that was pushed into violence by a whole range of causes including a resource crisis. This happened when a boundary line which had been lying dormant since the nineteenth century became disputed from the early 1920s onwards.[2] My analysis will show that the failure of the provincial Native Affairs Department (NAD) officials to act decisively and impartially on the boundary dispute of the 1920s resulted in the confluence of a long-simmering succession dispute within the main Mkhize chieftaincy and disputes over land. It will also show that the re-opening of the succession issue in 1928, and the subsequent failure of the NAD to demarcate clear chiefdom boundaries for the chiefdoms of the main Mkhize chiefs, Thimuni and Nkasa, triggered off a series of *izimpi zemibango* within the Umlazi location.

Trends in the historiography of conflict and violence

Several perspectives on what causes outbreaks of violence have emerged in the historical literature which deals with conflict and violence, but I should like to limit my focus to only three in this chapter. The first perspective presents Africans as intrinsically violent, and dismisses all manner of conflict within and between African communities as 'faction fights'. This view was developed initially by

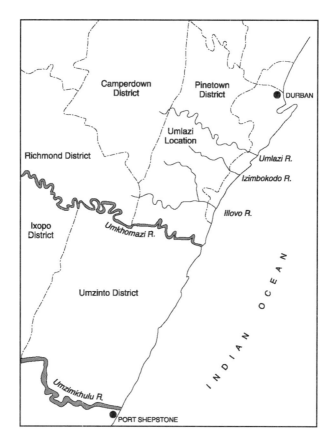

5.1 *The Umlazi location*

colonial officials and anthropologists during the early colonial period in Africa. Writing for metropolitan and settler audiences, and seeking to justify colonial conquest and violence, colonial officials presented African societies as intrinsically violent.[3] The officials of the successive native administrations in South Africa embraced these views as did settler writers whose novels written during the late nineteenth and early twentieth centuries portrayed African characters as innately violent.[4] These views had a huge impact on how the NAD officials perceived conflict within African communities.[5] The apartheid state also lurched onto this tradition during the 1980s, and labelled the state-sponsored vigilante violence as 'black on black' violence. The problem with this view is its assumption that a natural tendency towards violence exists amongst Africans.

Following closely on the heels of the 'settler-inspired' explanations of violence is a second perspective, which attributes all forms of violence to colonial conquest and imperialism. This view was common amongst South African intellectuals linked with liberation movements, and usually writing from exile from the late 1960s onwards. They presented the turn to armed struggle during the early 1960s as a natural, inevitable option. They argued that the apartheid state had turned violent against popular opposition, giving the liberation movements no option but that of reinvoking violence. What seems clear is that while colonial and settler thinking tended to dismiss Africans as intrinsically violent, anti-colonial thought tended to present imperialism and settler rule in the same way.[6] This apportioning of blame does not help us to understand what causes the outbreaks of violence.

Recent scholarship within South Africa and abroad has recast explanations of violence in terms of material deprivation. These works constitute the third perspective in this chapter. Clegg and Lambert have argued that there were increased possibilities for violent conflicts in Natal and Zululand during the nineteenth century when chiefs lost control over land resources. Colonial officials deepened *imibango* between chiefdoms by allocating land which had traditionally been occupied by one chiefdom, to another chiefdom.[7] This land allocation exerted pressure on the occupants of land which was ceded, thus hastening the outbreak of violence. Elaborating on the above framework, Beinart has warned against an analysis which claims that material crisis was a sufficient reason for the outbreak of violence. He says material deprivation only provides an underlying reason for discontent, and for actions based on that discontent. His essay has been helpful in highlighting that violence does not break out whenever conflict develops.[8]

Crummey also maintains that more than just the material crisis context is required to explain why violence only occurs at certain times and not at others.[9] If the material crisis conditions do not automatically give rise to the outbreak of violence, what does? Byerley has identified three key prerequisites for the outbreak of violence, namely human agents who agitate for violent confrontation, the existence of a feeling of discontent, and 'trigger' events.[10] Homer-Dixon et al. have added an environmental dimension to the analysis of what causes the outbreaks of violence.[11] They contend that environment is one variable in a series of economic and social factors which can become a major source of social disruption. With these points in mind, let us explore the extent to which competition over scarce land resources was a key factor which pushed tension into violence in the Umlazi location.

Population and environmental pressures in the Umlazi location

It is necessary to retrace our steps to put the conditions of the 1920s and 1930s in a slightly broader historical context. The Natal reserves were established in the middle of the nineteenth century as a feature of the colonial land and labour policy. They later became political and administrative control mechanisms for the Natal provincial government.[12] The reserves had been extensively incorporated into the regional economy as suppliers of male migrant labour by the 1920s. Industrialisation stimulated a high demand for African labour in Natal's towns, especially Durban. The emerging manufacturing sector, centred primarily in the Greater Durban region, was one of the branches of the Natal economy which relied heavily on African labour. The newly employed workers were kept as migrants through compounds and hostels policies, and through continued access to land in the reserves. The proximity of the Umlazi location to Durban encouraged the phenomenon of migrant labour.

African workers who could not be accommodated in the Durban hostels and compounds settled in the nearby Umlazi reserve. This reserve was densely populated by 1921 but it continued to attract Africans from further afield who wished to be near the labour market. The population of the Pinetown district increased from 22 894 in 1921 to 54 442 in 1936.[13] Approximately 35 000–40 000 of these people were living in the Umlazi location.[14] This gave rise to overcrowding and land shortage. Land shortage was partially a result of natural population increase: between 1916 and 1936, for example, there was a 54 per cent increase in the Natal reserve population. Despite the rapid growth, the boundaries of the reserves stayed the same as in the nineteenth century.[15] Land shortage also resulted from the fact that the Umlazi location was one of the dormitory centres from which the rapidly growing city of Durban drew much of its labour.[16] The overcrowding that occurred was harmful to the natural resources of the Umlazi location.[17]

The soil texture of the Umlazi reserve varies from thin and sandy loam on the hillsides to deep red and black alluvial soil in the lower-lying areas. Rainfall is generally good,[18] and the area is well watered, being intersected by a number of streams and rivers. While the climate, soil and topography rendered the area suitable for intensive farming, the maintenance of soil fertility was a major concern. Failure to maintain soil stability renders grass cover and bushes – especially on the steep slopes – vulnerable to permanent damage. Original grass had been superseded by the tough wire grass, *Aristida junciformis* (*ingongoni*), by the 1920s.[19] This was caused by overpopulation, heavy grazing and the indiscriminate burning of grass. In the past, factors such as accessibility to water and wood resources had contributed to the choice of the best land on which to settle. Now, however, the worst lands were often overcrowded while the best lands were occupied by a privileged few such as the ruling chiefs and *izinduna*.[20]

The natural forests of the Umlazi reserve comprise thornveld and valley bushveld, but these were on the verge of extinction by the 1920s. The population growth meant that an increasing number of people cleared the forests in search of land on which to settle and for firewood. The affluent families also cleared indigenous bushes because they were beginning to grow valuable wattle plantations.[21] By the 1920s the environmental pressures had begun to create scarcity and frustration in the Umlazi reserve areas.

East coast fever, a tick-transmitted disease that affects only animals belonging to the bovine family, also exerted pressure on the reserve communities.[22] Heavy cattle losses were suffered as a result of the frequent outbreaks of east coast fever in the Natal districts of Camperdown, Pinetown and Richmond. Cattle decreased from approximately 63 713 in 1925 to 55 381 in 1933 in these districts.[23] The southern Natal districts, where there were high concentrations of African-owned cattle, were severely affected.[24] The reserve community was stratified into relatively affluent and poor groups by the 1920s, and cattle ownership was distributed along these lines. It is therefore possible that cattle losses affected these social classes differently. This loss of cattle and the destruction of crops by locusts strained the already overcrowded Umlazi reserve.[25] It was against this background that a boundary which had been lying dormant since 1864 suddenly became disputed in the 1920s. The NAD's handling of this dispute provided a link between land disputes and the disputed succession within the main Mkhize chieftaincy.

Land and succession disputes in the Umlazi location, 1920–1931

The boundary disputes began when the subjects of an acting Mkhize chief, Bhinananda Mkhize, lodged a complaint of land encroachment with the NAD against commercial farmers who owned sections of the farm Valsch River in 1921 (Map 5.2).[26] Meanwhile, one of Bhinananda's subjects, Msuthu Mkhize, also laid complaints of land encroachment with G.L. Kirby, the inspector of locations, during 1922 and 1923. Mkhize accused a farmer, Robert Bell, of cultivating the reserve dwellers' grazing land, and of impounding their cattle when they were grazed on it.[27] The NAD authorised Kirby to investigate the reserve dwellers' complaint and he found that someone had tampered with the beacons on the boundary line.[28]

Kirby's report persuaded the NAD to order the surveyor-general, J.L. Lewis, to conduct further investigation. He established that the beacons of the farm Clifton were incorrectly erected by a state surveyor named Fannin in the nineteenth century. Consequently, surveys that were conducted several years after Fannin's work were misleading. Owing to this error, the commercial farmers were cultivating parts of the reserve lands. The commoners were denied the use of land which stretched from the eastern beacon G of the farm Valsch River, through to

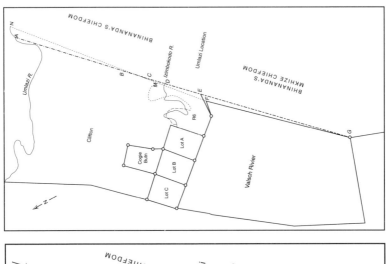

5.3 Survey of lands, Clifton and Valsch River

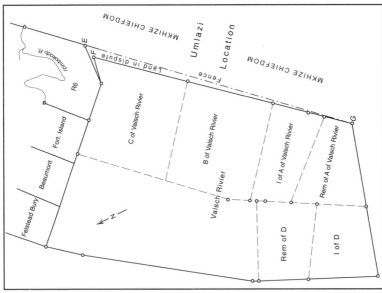

5.2 Valsch River lands

beacon N of the farm Clifton (Map 5.3). But they never campaigned for the rectification of this matter until they experienced overcrowding during the 1920s.

Once the NAD officials had learnt that the reserve dwellers' complaints were correct, they opened negotiations with the commercial farmers over the disputed land, and simultaneously harassed and victimised certain articulate individuals amongst the reserve dwellers, seeking to isolate them. While the chief native commissioner (CNC) was exploring options of negotiating the disputed boundary with the commercial farmers during 1924 and 1925, at the same time he suppressed any campaigns for land by the reserve dwellers. At first, he requested that the commercial farmers take full responsibility for the expenses of relocating the boundary fence to its correct position. Many commercial farmers rejected the request and denied that they were encroaching on the reserve land. They threatened the state with litigation should it alter the boundaries that were adjacent to their farms.[29] When the provincial and national NAD officials realised that the farmers were determined to challenge them on the matter, they surrendered the disputed land.[30]

At a time when the CNC was involved in negotiations with the commercial farmers, he isolated the abaMbo complainant, Msuthu Mkhize, for victimisation. He ordered Kirby to investigate possible charges against Msuthu which could justify his removal to a site deeper into the location where he would cease to be a source of friction.[31] Kirby found no incriminating information against him. He uncovered, however, that Msuthu was a highly respected member of the Mkhize ruling family. He was a special assistant to ex-chief Tilongo, and there were claims that he had been Tilongo's senior messenger to Dinuzulu, head of the Zulu royal family, during the Bhambatha rebellion.[32]

In the absence of sufficient reasons to justify the eviction of Msuthu from his site, the NAD officials passed on the responsibility for his removal to the state-appointed acting chief, Bhinananda. The reserve dwellers were annoyed when Bhinananda ordered Msuthu to transfer his *umuzi* to a new site away from the disputed land. Bhinananda's action against Msuthu tarnished the image of the state-appointed chiefs since the commoners lumped him together with more compliant state-appointed chiefs. The commoners' bitterness against Bhinananda, and their desire for hereditary rule, coincided with the death in 1926 of Sikhukhukhu.[33] He was one of the two Mkhize chiefs who were sentenced to life imprisonment on St Helena in 1906. The NAD's handling of the land disputes, and Bhinananda's role in it, linked scarce land resources and the succession dispute. It also set the scene for a different kind of state intervention in the 1930s, which was to produce more explosive and tense results. Let us retrace the origins of this succession dispute in order to understand how the land disputes of the 1920s fed into it.

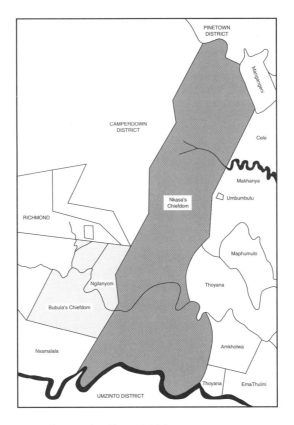

5.4 Nkasa's chiefdom, 1930

The making of a new set of boundary disputes in the 1930s

Sikhukhukhu and Tilongo were the sons of chief Ngunezi. The state had recognised them as co-chiefs over the abaMbo after the death of Ngunezi in 1894.[34] They were charged with sedition during the Bhambatha rebellion, deposed and sentenced to prison terms on St Helena.[35] The main Mkhize chieftaincy was fragmented and placed under state-appointed chiefs: Bhinananda, Ntiyantiya, Maguzu, Mguquka and, lastly, Bubula, who had previously served as *ibambela* (regent) for Sikhukhukhu.[36] Sikhukhukhu and Tilongo were released from St Helena in 1910 and allowed to return to Natal to live as commoners away from the Umlazi location.[37] The state banished Sikhukhukhu to the Dumisa chiefdom in the Umzinto district, and Tilongo to Somahashi's location in the New Hanover district. Tilongo died in 1919 and Sikhukhukhu in 1926.[38] Their sons, Nkasa and Thimuni respectively, became new rallying symbols for the reserve dwellers during the 1920s. The commoners campaigned for the recognition of these two sons as chiefs.

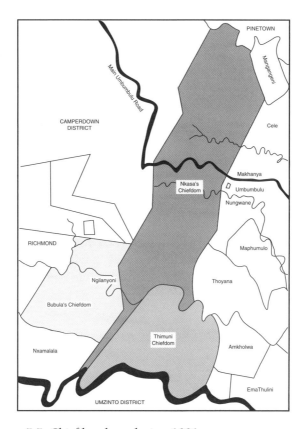

5.5 Chiefdom boundaries, 1931

Their campaigns coincided with the state's retribalisation policies. Retribalisation was a national social and political initiative that was designed to shore up South Africa's 'tribal' order in the context of urbanisation and class-based resistance politics of the 1920s and 1930s.[39] The convergence of interest between the NAD and the reserve dwellers resulted in the re-opening of the succession issue in 1928. The first Board of Inquiry was appointed to investigate ways of resolving the succession dispute. It recommended that the NAD should appoint only Nkasa as the main Mkhize chief. The NAD confirmed Nkasa's position in April 1930 (see Map 5.4). In making these decisions it undertook not to interfere with Bubula's position during his lifetime out of gratitude for his loyal service,[40] and it only deposed Bhinananda, Maguzu and Mgadlela.[41]

The followers of ex-chief Sikhukhukhu challenged the appointment of Nkasa as the only hereditary Mkhize chief. A total of 1100 heads of *imizi* campaigned for the recognition of Thimuni as a chief over the people who were formerly loyal to his father. The huge number of Thimuni's supporters forced the CNC, Pringle, to reconsider the sole appointment of Nkasa. He overturned the decision of his predecessor, and appointed Thimuni as co-chief in 1931. Pringle convened a meeting to demarcate chiefdom boundaries (Map 5.5). He then ordered the commoners to transfer their *imizi* to the chiefdoms of their respective chiefs within two years. He ruled that on the expiry of the period, the people who had not moved their *imizi* would automatically become subjects of the chief in whose chiefdom they were living. This was a recipe for disaster because almost all of Nkasa's followers were in Thimuni's territory, while 75 per cent of Thimuni's supporters were living in Nkasa's chiefdom.[42]

The reserve dwellers were required to transfer their *imizi* at a time when the NAD was unwilling to restore the reserve land which the commercial farmers were cultivating illegally. They were also forced to leave their sites during a period of social and economic hardship caused by natural disasters such as drought and famine. Official records suggest that the economies of the southern Natal districts had reached new crisis levels. These economies had to contend with additional strains when there was an influx of evicted farm tenants from the commercialising farms, and during the Great Depression.[43] For example, the native commissioner (NC) for the neighbouring Umzinto district, F.S. Heaton, informed the CNC that people were eating leaves in order to survive in some chiefdoms of his district.[44]

The followers of Thimuni and Nkasa responded differently to the order to relocate their *imizi*. Thimuni's supporters were unanimously prepared to move over to their chief's territory. They considered the government's recognition of their leader as a chief a truly remarkable achievement since the government had left Thimuni's father, Sikhukhukhu, in the cold for more than three decades when it refused to recognise him as a chief. However, Nkasa's people simply ignored the order, and simultaneously attacked Thimuni's followers to prevent the transfer of *imizi*. Meanwhile, Nkasa's supporters were annoyed by the NAD's retraction of its earlier decision of recognising only Nkasa as the main Mkhize chief. They consequently boycotted the occasion for the installation of Thimuni as a chief. A stalemate developed when none of Nkasa's men moved from Thimuni's chiefdom. On the expiry of two years not a single transfer had been effected.[45] The determination of the NAD to enforce the orders for the transfer of *imizi*, despite this opposition, pushed the succession issue into violence. The *izimpi zemibango* happened in two phases. The first occurred from March 1932 until December 1933, and the second from August 1934 to about June 1936.

Fighting broke out in March 1932 and minor skirmishes occurred throughout the year. The police narrowly averted a fight by approximately 200 men in April 1933. One of Thimuni's followers, Mfanekiso Shezi, was the first person to die. Nkasa's followers stabbed him to death when they attacked Thimuni's main *induna*, Mahleka Shezi, and his companion, Mfanekiso, in December 1933.

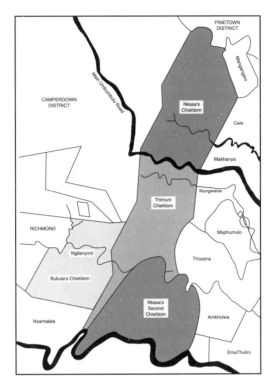

5.6 Thimuni chiefdoms, 1934

Mahleka narrowly escaped death. Thimuni's supporters retaliated, and killed one of Nkasa's men.[46] Two people died and fifteen others were wounded. The small number of deaths suggests that the reserve dwellers were using violence as a political strategy to force opponents out of specific territories.

The continuing incidents of violence forced the NAD to review its 1931 chiefdom boundaries in April 1934. It appointed a second Board of Inquiry to carry out this review. The board granted Thimuni one chiefdom, which was sandwiched between Nkasa's two chiefdoms, in August 1934. It made the main road a boundary between the chiefdoms of Thimuni and Nkasa (Map 5.6).[47] The board was insensitive to the prevailing resource crisis because it once more required people to relocate their *imizi*. The abaMbo were unhappy with the decision but they could not influence it since they were told that the meeting was convened strictly to announce the board's recommendations. When it became clear that there was no possibility of negotiating the chiefdom boundaries, the *izimpi zemibango* broke out again.

More violence erupted from 3 August 1934 onwards. Fighting broke out on either side of the main Umbumbulu road to Pietermaritzburg and also erupted at

Ngilanyoni. More than 600 huts were burnt down and twenty people died.[48] The high number of deaths is an indication that the reserve dwellers' aim during this period was to kill their adversaries. Women and children were also subjected to physical assaults. If ever there was a set of social rules which guided conflicts between chiefdoms, and which prohibited attacks on women and children, such rules never applied to conflicts in the Umlazi location. It seems as if the depth of hatred which was beginning to manifest itself between the followers of Thimuni and Nkasa blurred distinctions between male and female targets.

Violence subsided for a while between October 1934 and February 1935 as a result of NAD-brokered peace meetings.[49] However, conflict resurfaced in February 1935 at Ngilanyoni, and fighting erupted in the vicinity of the main Umbumbulu road in June and September 1935. Nkasa's followers attacked one of Thimuni's supporters. The NAD responded in at least two ways to the renewed conflict. Firstly, it reduced the size of Bubula's chiefdom and allocated his former territories to Nkasa and Thimuni[50] (see Map 5.7). The reduction of the size of Bubula's chiefdom did not bring an end to conflict. Instead, it created more of a financial and social burden for the already distressed reserve communities because many people were instructed to transfer their *imizi* from Bubula's chiefdom. Tension could have been minimised had the NAD deposed Bubula and placed his subjects under Thimuni. After all, Bubula had ascended to the Mkhize chieftaincy as the *ibambela* for Thimuni's father, Sikhukhukhu.

Secondly, the NAD set up an inquiry to investigate what had caused the outbreak of violence in 1935. The inquiry established that many *imizi* on either side of the main Umbumbulu road were situated too close to the boundary. It then instructed the owners of these *imizi* to transfer them deeper into their respective chiefdoms. This decision caused more resentment among the reserve dwellers, and the burning of huts resumed in 1936 and continued on either side of the main road in June 1936. The NC for the Pinetown district facilitated peace meetings between Thimuni, Nkasa and their followers during June and July 1936.[51] It is not clear why the *izimpi zemibango* subsided shortly after these meetings, but it is possible that the NC for the Pinetown district brokered a satisfactory land deal between the Mkhize chiefs and their followers.

Understanding the commoners' participation in the *izimpi zemibango*

Why were the male commoners so ready to participate in the fights? Let us try to find answers to this question through a brief analysis of the possible reasons for the male commoners' participation in the fights in the Umlazi reserve.

The threat to land and property drew the reserve dwellers deeper into the succession dispute. The story of the disputed succession within the main Mkhize

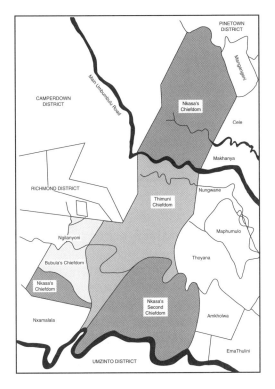

5.7 Bubula's chiefdom reduced, 1935

chieftaincy was essentially a tale of shifting boundary lines for the Umlazi reserve dwellers. They witnessed at least four alterations of chiefdom boundaries between 1930 and 1935. It was quite common practice for the NAD to give the reserve dwellers a period of two years to transfer their *imizi* to the territories which had been allocated to their respective chiefs. They made this ruling in November 1931, in August 1934, and again in August 1935. The constant shifting of boundaries shows that when making the decisions to alter the boundaries, the officials neglected the interests of the reserve dwellers, who were badly affected.

The decisions of the officials when allocating boundaries caused social and economic difficulties for the reserve dwellers. Several orders for the transference of the *imizi* to new sites came at a time of social and economic distress during the early 1930s. The succession dispute began not only to affect the 'Mkhize aristocracy', but to impact negatively on the lives of the commoners. A number of reserve dwellers were forced to cede their allegiance to chiefs whom they sometimes despised, just because they could not afford to relocate their properties within the usual two years. This created a fairly explosive situation when people who did not see eye to eye were forced to live side by side. The

Umlazi reserve dwellers also experienced difficulties during the transferring of the *imizi* because the reserve was overcrowded by the 1930s. These conditions prompted the commoners to participate actively in the fights which broke out in the Umlazi location from March 1932 until June 1936.

Some commoners were more concerned with survival than with loyalty to the Mkhize chiefs during the conflict. Albert Mkhize, for example, informed the NAD in 1934 that he did not mind which chief ruled him as long as he did not lose his property.[52] Testimonies to the NAD inquiry in 1935 also reflected similar sentiments. For example, Joyise Shange testified: 'I removed from the Nungwana side when the main road was made a boundary. I can see my old *umuzi* where I now am. I had fields over there, but here I have none. I now live in the *umuzi* of Cabajana Shange with my wife and six children. I do not work as I have chest trouble.'[53] Resentment led to the outbreak of *izimpi zemibango* in 1936. This is an indication that some commoners were participating in the fights because the succession dispute had begun to affect their access to land, which was an important resource for their livelihood.

The NAD's insensitivity to land shortages was partly responsible for the commoners' participation in the fights. It took Harry Lugg, Chief Native Commissioner for Natal, a long time to acknowledge that land shortage was one of the sources of conflict. He tried to attribute violence in the Umlazi reserve to the failure of Thimuni and his *izinduna* to control their followers and on excessive drinking of *utshwala* (beer). Only the reports of the NC for Pinetown forced him to admit that land shortage was also a source of conflict. His admission changed very little because he did nothing about the problem. The Secretary for Native Affairs (SNA), Smit, also made a vague promise to the abaMbo in 1935 that the government was going to find a solution to the problem of land shortage in Thimuni's chiefdom.[54] When Thimuni followed up Smit's promise, Lugg ordered Thimuni either to reduce the size of land which individual families within his chiefdom were occupying, or step down as a chief so that an efficient man could take control of his chiefdom.[55] This official attitude to land shortages limited chances of resolving boundary and land disputes amicably.

Conclusion

This chapter has several implications for our understanding of violent conflicts within the African communities. It has demonstrated that the constant shifting of chiefdom boundaries, and the insensitivity of state officials to land shortage, prompted male commoners to participate in the fights. It has suggested that a resource crisis may give rise to conditions in which conflict deteriorates into violence. The chapter has also shown that we can best understand what causes the breakdown of peaceful resolution of conflict if we analyse specific case studies of violence instead of relying on untested and superficial generalisations such as 'faction fights'.

In the case of the Umlazi conflict, deliberate use of violence as a political strategy was obvious in the different stages of conflict. The differing patterns of human deaths confirm that violence was used as a political strategy by the reserve dwellers. They turned violence on and off like a tap, and they were able to transport it from one part of the reserve to another. What seems clear about this use of violence is that the anger of the participants in the fights was misdirected because the state officials, who deepened conflicts by failing to demarcate clear chiefdom boundaries and who were insensitive to land shortages, were not subjected to any attacks. The reserve dwellers vented their anger on one another, and certain chiefs took advantage of this.

Chapter Six

Environmental origins of the Pondoland revolt

William Beinart

The revolt in Pondoland in 1960 was one of the most intense political conflicts in the South African countryside during the apartheid era and indeed during the century as a whole.[1] In itself it presented no major threat to the South African state, despite the fact that it was one of a number of African protests, in urban and rural areas, at the time. Nevertheless, alongside the earlier rebellion in Sekhukhuneland, it achieved a relatively sustained level of organisation.[2] The rebels in Pondoland were largely rurally based men, most of them with experience as migrant workers, who opposed government policy in South Africa's homelands. From March 1960, they attempted to neutralise state intervention by attacking its local African agents.

Those seen to identify with the government were hauled before rebel courts, homesteads were burnt, a few were killed and many forced to flee. Illegal committees were formed and large popular gatherings held on isolated hilltops in Bizana and Lusikisiki districts. The state reacted with force: one crowd at Ngquza hill was fired on in June 1960, with considerable loss of life; an army operation rounded up thousands of rebels, including the leaders, by the end of the year. Without firearms, and with very limited support from urban organisations, the popular movement had no further means of resistance.

Pondoland was part of the Transkeian Territories, the largest single block of land left under African occupation following the conquest of South Africa and a key element in South Africa's homeland policy. The rebellion was restricted largely to eastern Pondoland, then home to nearly 300 000 people, an area perceived of as among the most traditionalist in the Territories, where rural smallholder production had to some degree survived alongside migrant labour.[3] In many senses the rebellion was a final outpouring of anger against external rule which had transformed African societies and was now seen to threaten their remaining rural base. My argument in this chapter is that in Pondoland, at least, conflicts over the control of natural resources, and their political legacy, while not the only cause of revolt, contributed very significantly to the deterioration in relations between the local Transkeian state and its subjects.

Environmental explanations have not been absent from analyses of the rural conflicts and disturbances in South Africa during the two decades after the Second World War. It is widely accepted that they were precipitated not least by new forms of state intervention: rehabilitation schemes and Bantu authorities. Betterment or rehabilitation schemes had been formulated by the government during the late 1930s, but implementation was largely delayed until the post-war era when sufficient funds and manpower became available.[4] The policies were designed by officials to benefit the hard-pressed environment of the African reserves as well as to underpin denser settlement in these segregated zones. They aimed, ambitiously, to transform settlement and land use throughout these areas, by villagisation of scattered homesteads, reorganisation and fencing of arable plots and grazing areas, as well as culling (compulsory sale) of livestock where carrying capacities were deemed to be exceeded.

Many rural people perceived Betterment as a threat to their way of life and to the remains of their economic independence. Even though relatively few families in the Transkei relied on rural production alone, the bulk of homesteads still attempted to generate income from agriculture alongside wages from migrant workers. Implementation had begun in the Libode district of western Pondoland in 1947, and while little attempt was made to extend the scheme to the con-servative districts of eastern Pondoland before 1960, the threat of these policies was a factor in the revolt.

My argument here, however, is that the unease about state intervention in Pondoland had deeper roots than this specific set of policies. Since the early years of Cape rule in this, the last annexed area of the Colony (1894), conflicts had simmered over the management of land and natural resources. Subjecting natural resources to some measure of central control has been an important element in the establishment of most states and, possibly, in the formation of colonial states in particular. Such interventions have been designed to regulate use, to privilege access for particular, often dominant, social groups and, in some cases, to conserve resources; they have sometimes cut across existing patterns of resource use and conceptions of legitimate access. Although relatively little of the land occupied by Mpondo people was alienated, a wide range of new laws and proclamations began to govern, among other things, land occupation, forests, pasture management and burning, hunting, noxious weeds, movement of stock, and soil erosion.

The impact of such regulations varied in relation to particular resources and the local political balance. Because the state was often acting through intermediaries such as headmen and chiefs, these issues could become highly politicised in the local community and were frequently bound up with conflicts over incumbency of such political offices. These were not entirely new problems for the chiefs, in that the functions of chieftaincy had always included some regulation of natural resources, but they took on new dimensions in the colonial context. This chapter traces two environmental conflicts over a longer period in eastern Pondoland and links them with disputes which helped to precipitate the revolt. It focuses on locust eradication in Amangutyana, Bizana district, in the 1930s, and coastal forest protection in Lusikisiki.

Locusts and headmen in Bizana

The Amangutyana area of Bizana was critical in the politics of the district and eastern Pondoland as a whole in 1960. The leading rebel spokesperson, Solomon Mbambeni Madikizela, came from this sub-chieftaincy and it was the site of the central rebel meeting point through much of the revolt, Ndhlovu hill. One of the leading pro-government men, C.K. (Columbus) Madikizela, father of Winnie Madikizela-Mandela, and Minister of Agriculture in the first phase of Transkeian self-rule from 1963, also had his base there.

The Amangutyana chief Madikizela had moved into independent Pondoland after the annexation of the southern part of Natal in 1866. Like other immigrant chiefs who had large followings but were not of the Mpondo royal lineage, he retained a good deal of separate power and authority. The Amangutyana chieftaincy was divided into three locations when Pondoland was annexed in 1894. Government policy was ambivalent in respect of chiefs. In line with established Cape practice, each location, a subdivision of the new magisterial districts, fell under a government-appointed headman. But the government largely recognised established patterns of authority by appointing chiefs as headmen, paying a higher rate to more senior chiefly headmen, and acknowledging that chiefs who formerly controlled more than one location would continue to influence neighbouring headmen.

Madikizela's son Langasiki was recognised and paid by the government as a senior headman, and referred to as a chief; two of his sons were later appointed headmen in the neighbouring locations. But Langasiki was among the most reluctant to buckle down and bear the authority of the new state. He took a leading role in confronting the veterinary authorities during the crisis triggered by the introduction of compulsory dipping to combat east coast fever (c.1909–13).[5] He also attempted to assert his rights against the Mpondo paramountcy and alienated that potential source of support. Because of this history, the magistrate of Bizana recommended that recognition of the Amangutyana chieftaincy be

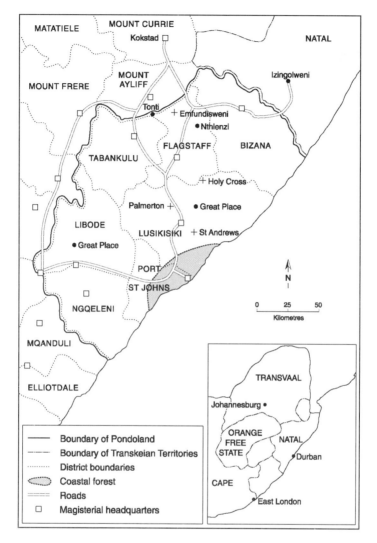

6.1 Pondoland after 1910

Source: adapted from Beinart, W. 1982. *The political economy of Pondoland 1860–1930*. Johannesburg: Ravan Press.

terminated when Langasiki died in 1926.[6] Langasiki's preferred heir, appropriately named King Langasiki, apparently the son of his twentieth wife, was still a minor.

The magistrate's argument was not directly approved. The authorities accepted that the man appointed as headman during the minority of King Langasiki would in effect be a regent, or a caretaker for the chief. But his court was not recognised to try civil cases by the government under the 1927 Native Administration Act, and when King Langasiki eventually succeeded as headman of the central Amangutyana location in 1933, his conduct was subjected to close scrutiny by officials. He was in a particularly difficult position because he had become the symbol for the reassertion of the waning authority of chieftaincy. The issue on which he and his councillors chose to take a stand was the locust eradication campaign of 1935.

Locust swarms of various species were a recurring feature of South African ecology. In 1934–35, the Transkeian Territories were particularly affected by the red locust, although brown locust swarmed in many other parts of the country in that year. Usually, locusts hatched and swarmed in large numbers when a drought was broken, although by no means after every drought; serious red locust invasions were relatively infrequent. Nevertheless, they were particularly serious in the wetter, eastern, arable zones of South Africa because they could compound the impact of drought by devastating crops after the rains came. Hatchings often coincided with the wetter, warmer months of the growing season in summer rainfall areas such as the Transkei. In the mid-1890s, devastating locust swarms had, following a drought, accompanied the rinderpest epidemic in the Transkei, and helped to push men from Pondoland into migrant wage labour.

By the 1930s, systematic research and experimentation had established that poisoning of hoppers before they swarmed was the most effective measure to combat plagues, although it was by no means foolproof. A Union-wide administration under the Department of Agriculture supervised eradication at the cost of hundreds of thousands of pounds in locust plague years. During 1934–35 £1.3 million were spent, over half the total departmental budget.[7] Legislation and proclamations required both private landowners and headmen in African reserve districts to assist the locust officers.

The cycle of locust swarms, egg-laying and hatching in 1934–35 followed the breaking of major droughts in the early 1930s. Drought and depression made these years particularly unfavourable for livestock owners throughout South Africa and millions of animals were lost. Rainfall in the eastern Pondoland districts was among the highest in the country, but even they were affected by the drought: small stock (sheep and goat) holdings fell from about 920 000 to 640 000 between their peak in 1930 and 1934.[8] The years of 1933 and 1934 also saw the first significant downturn in cattle numbers after nearly two decades of continuous growth following the introduction of compulsory dipping in the 1910s. The price of animals and animal products fell during these depression years. Imposition of restrictions on stock movements to control diseases was all the more resented: 'we trade in cattle', King Langasiki told the magistrate of Bizana, 'and though we are able to pay our taxes, our existence depends on them'.[9]

Against this background of heightened sensitivity to stock losses, residents in King Langasiki's location had apparently obstructed the work of a locust officer. The chief signed a letter to the magistrate in February 1935 noting that they were 'aware of the dangers of the voetgangers [hoppers]', but against the use of poison.[10] Events were seen as sufficiently serious for the chief magistrate to drive from Umtata for a public meeting in the location with Langasiki and six other neighbouring headmen. C.K. Madikizela, an educated member of the district council, emerged as one of the chief spokespeople.

We Pondos are frightened of locust poison – we are very suspicious. Our stock will die if locust poison is used on the location commonage. We would like to know if there is no other remedy for the destruction of this pest. We asked our magistrate to first allow us to use our own methods of destroying the hoppers…When hatchings took place we employed our own methods. We Pondos maintain, Sir, that our methods of destruction have proved effective, more so than locust poison. I will say that our methods of destruction do not destroy our cattle.[11]

As in other such conflicts, there were a number of layers to the dispute. Mpondo spokespeople were basing their argument on their experience of the government eradication campaign in the previous year, 1934. They maintained that poison was not very effective because it had failed to destroy all hoppers immediately and hatchings had recurred in 1935. Secondly, they argued that the operation had been careless. Red flags were to be hoisted when poison was laid, so that livestock could be stopped from straying into the area; this had not been effectively done and they cited specific numbers of cattle killed. People also wanted to be paid more if they were to work on the government programme.[12]

Clearly white officers from outside the Transkei, working with inexperienced local men, may have made mistakes and, unaccustomed to the etiquette of Transkeian administrative interaction, handled objections brusquely. Locust work in the depression years attracted unemployed whites who were sometimes quickest to defend their racial status. However, a locust officer explained that in 1934, they were compelled to work at night in order to deal with 'flyers' and although they had tried to publicise their work, this might have been the root of misunderstandings. Officials also suggested that flags placed by locust teams were deliberately removed by people wishing to hamper them.[13] Moreover, some leeway had apparently been given to local headmen to organise eradication themselves, as long as the results were open to inspection by the locust officers. Such inspection had allegedly been hampered in the case of the Amangutyana locations.

In this context the argument that local methods were more effective than poison served both as a statement of resistance and as a belief based on experience. A headman recalled that during the locust invasion before rinderpest in the 1890s, 'we worked ourselves and overcame them ourselves'; 'the natives did good work then' and the locusts had gone: 'We use flat pieces of wood in destroying these hoppers, we all sit down on the ground and wipe them out. We also surround them, make fires, and burn them. No hoppers get away. Where hoppers are in short grass, the women collect old thatch grass and burn the hoppers. We also boil water and burn them.'[14]

Magistrates countered these arguments by asserting the government's authority, affirming the superiority of the state's methods, and emphasising the necessity of successful eradication everywhere in the country to prevent swarming. Although the Transkeian style of paternalistic rule, which placed considerable reliance on consent, was under some strain in the inter-war years, some care was taken to persuade opponents of the virtues of poison and inadequacy of beating.[15] Nevertheless, when the district locust officer and his team arrived again in Amangutyana, most people refused to assist him. As a result King Langasiki was suspended and subsequently dismissed as headman. He was replaced by another member of the Amangutyana royal lineage, Meje Ngalonkulu. Ngalonkulu had competed for the headmanship before Langasiki was appointed and had received a minority vote in the show of hands which magistrates usually sought when a replacement was being considered. Ngalonkulu was seen to be more sympathetic to the government.

Although sporadic opposition was also evident in Zululand at this time, there was no general resistance to locust eradication.[16] Subsequently, locust eradication ceased to be an important issue in Bizana. But the relationship between the dismissal of King Langasiki in 1935 and the Pondoland revolt in 1960 is direct. Headman Meje Ngalonkulu survived in office over a deeply split location until 1960, with the support of C.K. Madikizela and the minority of 'progressives'. The deposed King Langasiki lived there throughout and the rights of this senior branch of the Amangutyana royal lineage continued to be asserted: 'representations on these lines', a magistrate commented, 'seem to have become a hardy annual'.[17]

The chieftaincy dispute was exacerbated by the attempt to introduce a tribal authority in the three locations in the 1950s. Meje Ngalonkulu was also known to support rehabilitation. The combination of environmental conflict and chieftaincy dispute remained potent. When the rebellion broke out in March 1960, Ngalonkulu was one of the first headmen targeted and he was forced to flee. When he explained the conflict to the authorities, he started with the locust eradication incident in 1935.[18] (Ngalonkulu was reinstated as headman in 1961, when the rebellion had been quelled.)

Coastal forests in Lusikisiki

Rainfall in a narrow belt along the Pondoland coast is particularly high – over 1000 mm per annum – and it sustained lush subtropical forests which penetrated some distance inland, especially in the sheltered river valleys and on sea-facing mountain slopes. Earlier perceptions by botanists of forests extending continuously to the midlands of the Transkei and Natal up to about the sixteenth century, before they were cleared by African settlement, have been strongly questioned.[19] Moreover, even the coastal strip was not uniformly forested. At least by the nineteenth century, and probably before, the section of the coastal plain at Lambasi and Mkambati was largely grassland.

Nevertheless, even if the historical extent of forested land on the east coast has been exaggerated, there had been considerable clearing by the end of the nineteenth century to produce, on their margins, the patchwork of arable plots, pastures, homestead settlements and woodland that characterised the area. It is hard to overestimate the centrality of trees and woodland to many pre-industrial societies. In Pondoland trees provided fruit, shade, medicines, materials for building, for sticks and weapons, for a wide range of household implements and, above all, firewood. Forests were used for hunting and the collection of honey. As important, trees often had to be cleared for pastures and plots; ash provided a valuable fertiliser for new fields. Population and settlement grew quickly in the twentieth century so that many of these uses intensified. Ploughs, sledges and ox-draught significantly enhanced capacities to extend cultivation, and forests came under considerable pressure. Clearings were made within the forests for the cultivation of well-hidden plots of dagga (*Cannabis sativa*). The damp forest margins provided, along with the grassland plain at Lambasi, dry-season winter pastures for cattle herds from the interior.

By the time of annexation (1894), the Cape colonial government had already evolved wide-ranging policies of natural forest reservation and afforestation. Both of these strategies implied removal of settlements from proclaimed zones. South Africa had relatively little indigenous forest cover; the Pondoland coastal forests were already recognised as among the largest and densest. A branch of the forestry department under a conservator of forests had been established in the Transkei in the 1880s and its work included the demarcation of forests. Following various delays, the process began in earnest in Pondoland in 1908.[20] Beacons were first placed to mark the boundaries of the main coastal forests, Egoso and Ntsubane; officers then named 66 smaller forest patches for reservation. Legislation was tightened in the Union-wide Forest Act 16 of 1913. At the same time, regulations provided for further wooded areas to be proclaimed under the control of headmen, who could allow some use but not clearing.

State control of forests not only implied the removal of rights of access, but also supplanted the earlier regulation by chiefs. Similar disputes over who was to control the resources of Pondoland arose over the small pockets of land appropriated by the state and over hunting.[21] The issue became so sensitive that the Union's chief conservator of forests travelled to Lusikisiki district, seat of the Mpondo paramount chief, to negotiate in 1914. He made limited concessions. Two significant patches of forest were placed directly under the responsibility of the paramount chief, Marelane. Any removals from demarcated forests were to be made gradually and sympathetically. Legislation provided that forest boundaries should be set twenty yards beyond the edge of forests, to protect them against fire and casual use. It was agreed that this yardage would not be insisted on if it involved moving homesteads. The blurring of boundaries was a significant political victory for the paramount chief and led to considerable confusion in enforcement after 1915.

Throughout the inter-war years, small encroachments took place into reserved forest areas; but magistrates, who worked closely with chiefs and headmen on such questions, tended not to take harsh action. By contrast, forestry officials found this approach frustrating. Not only was Pondoland judged to have particularly valuable forests, but it still seemed relatively under-populated compared with the rest of the Transkei. Foresters argued that there was sufficient rich grassland soil to cultivate outside the forests. Here, at least, they felt it should be possible to pursue the major aims of forestry policy: long-term enhancement of timber resources, and protection of rare species and of watersheds.

In 1934, following a discussion in the Transkeian Territories General Council about the possibility of fencing forest reserves, a detailed record was made of all homesteads (86 with 333 huts) within proclaimed forest boundaries in Lusikisiki.[22] About half of the huts, many of them in smaller new homesteads, were noted as built since demarcation. In 1936, the forestry department in the Transkeian Territories affirmed that arable land was not to be allocated closer than twenty yards from the edge of demarcated forests but tried to extend the rule for homestead sites to not less than two hundred yards. Effectively, the understanding reached with the paramount chief in the 1910s was rescinded. Alarm about the state of Transkeian forests led to arguments for further restrictions on access in 1939.[23]

As noted above, by no means all the forested areas in the Transkei were state reserves under the forestry department. Some of the more dispersed woodland was left under the authority of chiefs and headmen; this amounted to about 5000 hectares within Lusikisiki district in the inter-war years. The regulations governing headmen's forests, restated in 1932, recognised the importance of woodland resources to rural African people and tried to distinguish between use and clearing.[24] Headmen had a duty to protect 'timber trees', which could only be cut with the permission of a magistrate.[25] Headmen also had to 'conserve for public benefit' all vegetation but could give permission for the cutting of non-protected species. People could remove dry firewood, bark and twine without permission as long as it was for their own personal use and not for sale. Headmen were expressly forbidden to charge a fee.

After the passing of the Native Trust and Land Act of 1936, the possibility arose that headmen's forests would be taken over and administered centrally by the government.[26] But state control and further exclusion from such scattered patches of forest would have required heavy expenditure. Staff shortages during the Second World War precluded any action and undermined control even in state forests. By 1945, the forester at Ntsubane, one of the two major reserved areas in coastal Lusikisiki, despaired of the situation, arguing that forests were being extensively destroyed to clear arable lands. Even large trees were being burnt out by the stacking of brushwood against their trunks.[27]

Government responses in the next decade, while within the scope of existing legislation, should be set in the context of a more muscular approach to conservation of natural resources following the Second World War. It was signalled by the passing of the Soil Conservation Act (1946), the proclamation of a New Era of Reclamation (1945) in the African reserves, and the beginnings of systematic implementation of Betterment and rehabilitation. At the same time, oral evidence suggests that many new families were moving into the more sparsely populated coastal locations; they were an internal Transkeian frontier. In 1946, the district forest officer from Kokstad bemoaned 'the devastation' in the headman's forest in one coastal location. He estimated that there alone 170 hectares had recently been cleared for plots, 'which will produce a magnificent crop for two years, a poor one for two more years and will have been washed to sea leaving a few rocks and some rubble to mar the face of the earth in the fifth or sixth year'.[28] The headman concerned avoided a meeting with the police and forestry officers.

The national director of forestry called for action in 'the broad national interest'.[29] In 1946 and 1947, forest officers brought over 100 cases before the magistrate at Lusikisiki.[30] In the case of the headmen's forests, however, the magistrates found that they had little legal power to convict, except where cases involved cutting of timber trees and protected species. Headmen who were brought to court generally testified that they had been given permission. The magistrate argued that the foresters' initiative had been counterproductive as headmen gained a far clearer idea of their legal position. Headmen were reported to have told the people that they could effectively issue licences.[31]

The position changed in 1949 when a new, robust magistrate took office, travelled through the coastal forests and, alarmed about deforestation, decided to put into practice the long-established, little-enforced policy of removal. There was a further motor to bureaucratic action. Along the coast to the north-east of the forested area stretched the Lambasi coastal plain, which had for many years served as a winter, dry-season grazing ground where neither residence rights nor cultivation was supposed to be permitted. The magistrate who worked in Lusikisiki up to 1932 claimed that this understanding was in fact enforced by the administration up to that date. Seasonal grazing camps could be erected, but 'the few natives who slipped in occasionally and established themselves were compelled to remove'.[32] Part of the area was reserved for the Mkambati leper hospital between Lusikisiki and Bizana districts.

From the late 1930s and even earlier in Bizana, however, the coastal grassland plain had attracted settlement.[33] Homestead sites were built along stream banks in declivities so that they were not easily visible from the main transport routes.[34] In 1948, removal of homesteads in Lambasi within eight miles of the coast was authorised; the magistrate argued that 'it was essential from the soil conservation angle'.[35] But a constable reported that about one-third of the 145 families involved refused to move, despite the promise of alternative sites.[36] The Lambasi headman requested that the width of the exclusion zone should be reduced to six miles. Protests over the threat of removals from Lambasi grazing lands were soon linked with the closing of headmen's forests in more westerly coastal locations. In 1949 and 1950, forest rangers were assaulted in Bizana.[37]

In deputations to the chief magistrate, customary rights were invoked: 'the reason why we fetched you is that we were born in the forests and then they were demarcated. God made them for us and then you came and took them. We had our old kraals there.'[38] Such resources, it was claimed, belonged to the people, represented by their chiefs. Mnqingo Pikani, who emerged as the most forceful spokesperson, noted that people were being arrested simply for going into the headmen's forests and had been prosecuted 'for removing old stumps'.[39] Demands took shape around requests for dismissal of the new, activist magistrate and his style of 'forced administration'.[40]

The chief magistrate made it clear that the issue at stake was the clearing of land and new settlement in headmen's forests, not an absolute ban on their use. He agreed to stop removals until a further survey had been made and, in a rare concession to popular representations, the magistrate was moved. In 1950, a special commissioner was appointed to investigate land occupation in the coastal areas; he too met with 'passive resistance'.[41] In 1951, officials again attempted to initiate removals with some success; alternative sites were generally found. But one sub-headman refused to go even after he was prosecuted.[42] Foresters trying to explain the position were met with 'considerable hostility' and noted that force would probably have to be used: 'once the natives get into the Reserves they remain there however much they are prosecuted by this Department, and when they have been...fined they appear to think that they have paid for the right to occupy the area'.[43] It was rumoured that the area was being surveyed for rehabilitation.[44]

A meeting in 1952 ended in defiance.[45] The magistrate accepted that removals would only take place if alternative sites were available, but insisted that the survey of coastal locations should proceed so that a fair solution could be found. (Survey did not here imply exact measurement of all sites, but a record of all homesteads and their arable holdings.) In effect, the protesters were arguing that they did not want an overall record made on the basis of which officials would then decide which homesteads to remove. Peasants recognised that state knowledge could be translated into state power.[46] Mnqingo Pikani, using the insulting term 'mlungu' for white men, argued that following the threat of forest removals, rehabilitation and fencing, the survey was the last straw: 'The "Mlungu" came here and found us here – we agreed to his coming and to live peacefully. We now object to this survey and we oppose it. This we do not want – we don't want the [measuring] chain (Applause). The "Mlungu" may just as well shoot us now.'[47]

The politics of chieftaincy again intruded into natural resource disputes. Botha Sigcau, the paramount chief, had been installed in 1938 by the government, overriding strong popular support for an alternative claimant, Nelson Sigcau. Their political rivalry, focused around issues of legitimacy and attitudes to state intervention, did not subside in ensuing decades. Botha's attendance at the meeting was inflammatory; when his spokesperson accused protesters of behaving like children, there was uproar:

> Mnqingo gets up and loudly shouts for his horse and adds that he is a busy man and cannot waste time...In the meantime Mnyungula Maqutu wearing blankets and dancing to a war-cry into the arena made towards the Chief, jumped into the air in front of the Chief and bared his backside to the Chief and the Officials at the meeting, at the same time stabbing a short assegaai into the ground. The war-cry chant was taken up by many at the meeting as they broke up in disorder and a large gathering followed Mnqingo away from the meeting place where they mounted and rode away in column.[48]

The *Torch*, newspaper of the radical Unity Movement, which had close links with the Cape African Teachers' Association, concluded that 'the masses of Pondoland are ripe for the ideas of the Liberatory Movement'.[49] The chief magistrate decided on a show of force, and in August 1952, 300 police were sent into the coastal locations of Lusikisiki. Men gathered on the hills and lit fires; women sounded the war cry. But ultimately, armed resistance was avoided. Mnqingo Pikani, after initially ignoring a summons, was arrested, convicted and deported to another part of the country.

Yet the issues were not resolved. Throughout the 1950s, control of coastal homestead sites and arable plots, as well as intrusion in forest reserves, remained a major problem for the government. Towards the end of 1959, the Bantu affairs commissioner (formerly magistrate) of Lusikisiki inspected the coastal forests to find further recent 'damage'.[50] 'The Headmen are absolutely unable to control these forests,' he concluded; '"high" forest trees 3 and 4 foot in diameter are being destroyed and these include sneezewood, yellowwood, red milkwood.'

> The native residents of the area are recalcitrant and aggressive. They say the forests are theirs...and also that they have worked on European farms where the owners destroy indigenous forest with impunity. Many of them own illegal firearms and...since my assumption of duty here there have been three shooting affrays between bands of Forest Guards and organised hunting parties.[51]

A black forester had been crippled, another killed and his assailant sentenced to death. The chief regional forest officer felt that any attempt to enforce stricter protection would possibly lead to 'open rebellion and bloodshed'.[52] Similar disputes in the Bizana district were one of the main triggers for the Pondoland revolt early in 1960, and some of the coastal locations of Lusikisiki were important areas of resistance.

Conclusion

A full analysis of the background to the Pondoland revolt would require more extensive discussion of social and economic change in this African reserve in the era of apartheid, of the role of migrant workers and wider African nationalist ideas, of generational and gender conflicts, of the new Bantu authorities, and political tensions between chiefs, educated modernisers and traditionalists. Yet evidence of disputes over the regulation of natural resources recurs in a variety of contexts. An understanding of the sequence and logic of these conflicts is important in explaining the deeper origins of the rebellion as well as some of the immediate precipitating events.

Chieftaincy remained so central an issue in environmental politics, partly because many rural people felt that chiefs and headmen should to some degree protect them against the central state, rather than act as its agents. Headmen who were too closely aligned with the magistracy could attract intense popular suspicion. Moreover, chiefs and headmen still played a significant role in regulating and controlling access to the natural resources which were so central an element in rural life.

Recent literature on forestry has highlighted the potential of decentralised strategies in providing for timber and fuelwood requirements in rural communities where demand remains high.[53] In this respect the Transkeian administration was inventive from early in the twentieth century, recognising the authority of local headmen over some woodland and forest patches, and attempting to facilitate sustainable use. Decentralised plantations of exotics, largely for local use, were also an element in Transkeian forest policy. The intensity of conflict in the 1950s arose not least from the failure of these strategies in the face of rural demand for land, wood and local control.

It should not be assumed that African rural communities' requirements for these natural resources necessarily outpace their capacity to regenerate them. Research in other parts of Africa has argued powerfully that rural people can afforest rather than deforest their surroundings.[54] Human settlement necessitates transformation of natural environments that need not also result in degradation. Certainly people in the coastal locations of Pondoland planted fuelwood trees around their homesteads, notably the exotic black wattle, as well as fruit trees and shrubs for fencing. Nevertheless, the evidence does suggest a breakdown of controls over headmen's forests, which were effectively reserved for local communal use. Rural spokespeople openly admitted that they were destroying forested land, and asserted their right to do so; peasant communities do not always work with general concepts of resource conservation. These questions remain of great moment in the coastal Transkei, following the recent legal claims to, and invasions of, reserved areas such as Mkambati and Dwesa.[55] The central government's capacity to reserve and protect sensitive natural resources is no less contested in the new South Africa.

Chapter Seven

The emergence of privately grown industrial tree plantations

Harald Witt

I can think of no better way of showing confidence in a country than to embark on a large scale forestry investment. (C.M. Engelhard)

No development in South Africa is possible without timber. In fact no human life is possible in South Africa without timber. (The Farmer Show Supplement)

The foundations of the large-scale and highly profitable commercial tree plantations[1] in KwaZulu-Natal have their origins both in the initiatives of private agriculture and in the state forestry sector. The early development and prosperity of privately established wattle plantations, and the culture of tree-growing that evolved from it, contributed significantly to the successful establishment of future commercially grown tree plantations. Yet, for a long time, the private sector did not adequately provide the timber that had become identified as a national priority. The efforts of state foresters paved the way for future private commercial tree-growers by experimenting with and introducing a greater variety of economically viable tree species. The state also actively encouraged and assisted the private sector to participate in the establishment of commercial plantations.

At the turn of the previous century most of the locally harvested wood from tree plantations was utilised in the mining industry or consumed as fuel. In Natal, wattle producers met much of this demand although, increasingly, eucalypts were grown for the same purpose. Other wood, timber and related product needs were imported. As the South African economy modernised and diversified, local demand grew and became more specialised, resulting in a greater dependence on imports. This growing reliance on imported timber drained foreign exchange reserves and increased the vulnerability of the South African economy to international fluctuations in the supply of commercial tree products. This was highlighted by the isolation experienced during the two world wars.

In an attempt to make South Africa independent of the international wood and timber markets, the state embarked on an extensive tree-growing programme, and encouraged private landowners and farmers to do likewise. In Natal, where tree-growing was dominated by wattles, progress was relatively slow. Potential commercial tree-growers had little incentive to enter into competition with the comparatively cheap timber imports of the established chain of importers and distributors. Furthermore, the long-term nature of commercial tree-growing profits discouraged private growers.[2] Ironically, during the periods of trading isolation, the few alien commercial timber trees that had been planted locally, realised exceptionally high levels of profit. This precipitated a growing momentum in tree-crop farming in Natal and Zululand, which accelerated in the late 1940s. The period after the Second World War also witnessed the diversification of private tree-growers into softwoods, linked to rapid development of wood and timber processing industries that subsequently catapulted the KwaZulu-Natal region into the foremost tree-growing region in South Africa.

Early experimentation

As with most alien plant species, there is uncertainty as to when the large variety of alien commercial timber trees, which now dominate the natural and agricultural landscape of Natal and Zululand, was first introduced into the region. Private tree enthusiasts did not necessarily keep records, and the officially recognised dates reflect data from formal conduits of plant distribution, rather than informal and spontaneous plantings. It is not inconceivable that seeds from introduced tree species may have accompanied early white settlers in the early nineteenth century. What is certain is that, as early as 1846, J. Dicks had planted an assortment of acacias and gums in the Howick area.[3] In 1862, travellers to Pietermaritzburg pointed to the presence of 'tall gum trees'.[4] John Shedden Dobie, who travelled extensively through South Africa in the early 1860s, also reported on the presence of 'tall gum trees' on several of the Natal farms.[5] Although these introductions by 'tree enthusiasts' undoubtedly contributed to the introduction and propagation of a variety of alien tree species into Natal, it was organised institutions such as botanical gardens that established the foundations of a commercial tree-growing industry in a more systematic manner.

Botanical garden staff initiated a more rigorous and scientifically based introduction of, and experimentation with, introduced tree species. Unlike the Cape, where botanical institutions were only established a century and a half after initial European occupation, the Botanical Gardens in Durban (1851) were established within a decade of the annexation of Natal. This greatly facilitated the movement of alien plant species, including trees, within Natal, the Empire and the world. The Durban Botanical Gardens, for example, distributed thousands of *E. globulus* trees throughout Natal in the late nineteenth century.[6] In 1874, the Botanical Gardens in Pietermaritzburg were established, and by 1880 they could offer the tree-planter five varieties of *Eucalyptus* and five varieties of pine.[7]

Spurred by the successful propagation of 'useful and ornamental trees' in the Colony, these official conduits were readily duplicated by the private sector, often with equal, if not greater, success.[8] By the late nineteenth century there appear to have been at least four privately owned nursery gardens near Pietermaritzburg. According to Sir H. Bulwer, these sent out between 200 000 and 300 000 young forest trees a year, excluding the numerous fruit and ornamental trees.[9] These nurseries dealt primarily with eucalypts and wattle trees, with one nursery claiming to have access to 94 varieties of eucalypts. These nurseries were considered to be 'great benefactors to the Colony', and distributed trees and seeds to 'neighbouring countries and even to Delagoa Bay and the East Coast'.[10]

Despite the successful distribution of introduced trees, it is difficult to measure the exact extent and economic importance of early commercial tree-plantings. It is equally difficult to differentiate between wattle plantings and other commercially grown timber trees such as pines, eucalypts and poplars. As Hutchins commented, many trees were planted around homesteads and in arboreta, not as tree crops.[11] Newspaper reports in the late nineteenth century would occasionally report on the success of local tree-growers who owned plantations with thousands upon thousands of trees – 10 000 acres of gums and wattles.[12] Yet it is likely that such reports were slightly exaggerated, not only in terms of the extent of the plantations themselves but also of the weighting given to eucalypts. In 1902 there were already 34 574 acres of wattle in Natal and 1075 acres in Zululand, yet large-scale plantings of other tree crops remained scarce. According to Sim[13] during his early inspections of 1903–4, there were:

> practically no trees from Hilton Road upward anywhere except at Howick (Sir G. Hutton) and Tweedie Hall (Mr I. Morton) and practically none downward to the coast, trees not having been procurable. About Greytown and Krantzkop there were more trees, for Mr. Handley Senior at Hallcare, Greytown had raised many trees and distributed them singly at high prices, and these scattered widely, had produced many self-sown seedlings...[14]

In Zululand, Sim claimed that the 'only Eucalypt I saw were a few in Eshowe and an Avenue of *Eucalyptus citerciodora*[15] at Dunn's house in Emoyoni'.[16] A more realistic appraisal of non-wattle plantations came from Hutchins, who, a few years later, estimated the area of private plantations in Natal 'at not less than 5,000 acres', composed mainly of eucalypts.[17] This dearth of trees was an issue which individuals such as Sim and Hutchins, and the state, wished to address quickly. Unlike wattle, which had gained in economic importance in the late nineteenth century, the marketing of other commercial tree species is harder to trace. Although the mines and sugar mills consumed vast amounts of commercially grown wood and timber, consumption figures did not always differentiate between wattle, eucalypts and other hardwoods. The volume of local wood fuel consumption is also unrecorded unless transported by rail.

State participation in extensive tree-growing in Natal only began on a systematic basis at the turn of the century, and even then was hindered by financial difficulties. Building on the foundation of the Botanical Gardens, state foresters began to experiment with a variety of species. Methods of soil preparation, planting distances and other silvicultural techniques were tried out and adopted or abandoned. Under trying conditions, state foresters in South Africa worked impressively to fit introduced tree species to different localities.[18] In addition, the state investigated the various 'pests' and diseases that affected the introduced trees and how these could best be combated. At a later stage the state conducted a series of fertiliser experiments, while simultaneously laying down regulations for the control of the fire regime.[19]

The inability of many eucalypt[20] species to be cultivated on a viable basis in Natal and Zululand was primarily due to climate, unpredictable weather patterns and local variations in rainfall, temperature, altitude and soil types.[21] The only species that thrived reasonably well was E. saligna, which, by the 1930s, had begun to dominate the hardwood plantations in Zululand and the Natal Midlands. Yet even this species was occasionally susceptible to the vagaries of nature and the detrimental impact caused through the involuntary exchange of plant and animal matter. The latter led to the unintentional introduction of the Eucalyptus snout-beetle (Gonipterus scutellatus) from Australia in 1916.[22] The beetle caused extensive damage to the foliage of eucalypts and by the mid-1920s had become cause for national concern. To control the snout-beetle, a variety of methods was attempted, including the burning of coppice and the dusting with arsenical insecticide from aeroplanes.[23] Owing to the expense incurred and lack of success, together with an escalation in concern, biological methods of control were investigated, and in 1927 a mymarid egg parasitoid (Anaphoidea nitens) was introduced with great success.

As with the eucalypts, it was the state that conducted the majority of the early experiments to determine which softwoods would be the most suitable for Natal and Zululand. Although private landowners had been quick to cultivate wattle trees, and readily accepted eucalypts as an additional or alternative tree crop, they were reticent when it came to softwoods and, by 1926, only 690 acres of pines had been planted by private farmers in Natal. This does not suggest that pines were not planted as landscape modifiers or as ornamentals, yet prior to the Second World War there was little economic incentive for private landowners to cultivate such trees.

The responsibility for determining which pine species were most suitable for Natal and Zululand was therefore left almost entirely up to the state. Many of the initial trials were conducted at Cedara, where a variety of species that had been grown successfully in the Cape was planted.[24] None seemed to flourish locally, especially in state plantations along the Zululand coast, where their weakened condition made them more susceptible to diseases.[25] Additional species, better suited to local conditions, were required, and at the insistence of Hutchins, new varieties were introduced from Mexico and Arizona between 1906 and 1917, including *Pinus patula* and *P. caribea* (often mistakenly referred to as *P. elliotii*). Many of the newly introduced species were initially tried in other regions, and it was only in the late 1910s and early 1920s that these species were planted more extensively in Natal.[26] *P. caribea* (or *P. elliotii*) soon replaced *P. roxburghii* in the earlier established state plantations, while *P. insignis* was the species most favoured by private tree-growers.[27] As plantations increased, the susceptibility to outbreak of diseases or attack by 'pests' increased, and those species that appeared excessively vulnerable were rejected. In Natal, *P. insignis*, *P. pinaster* and *P. canariensis*, for example, were highly susceptible to Diplodia dieback, a fungal disease.[28] This disease also led to the abandonment of *P. radiata* in other summer rainfall areas.[29] By 1941, *P. patula* was considered to be no longer resistant to Diplodia and was often replaced by *P. elliotii*, which had until then grown more rapidly and yielded a larger volume of sawn timber per acre than any other species on the Zululand coast.[30]

In addition to the various fungal diseases, pine trees in Natal were occasionally susceptible to defoliation from moths such as the pine tree emperor moth (*Nudaurelia cytherea capensis*) and the pine brown-tail moth (*Euproctis terminalis*) which had been introduced from the United States. In general, however, once specific eucalypt or pine trees had been matched to a suitable environment, there were few if any factors, except climatological, that impeded the propagation of such trees. The lack of natural controlling factors facilitated the spread of trees from cultivated plantations into more pristine environments.

Incentives and encouragements

In Natal, a major initiative to encourage the planting of commercial tree species came through the introduction of tree-growing competitions. These were based on competitions in the Cape in 1884–85, when the Cape government offered prizes for the planting of commercial tree species.[31] The results in the Cape had been disappointing and the competition was abandoned in 1901. This poor response, however, did little to dampen the enthusiasm for similar competitions in Natal.

Although Natal forestry officials, such as Schoepflin, had endeavoured to encourage private landowners to grow trees commercially,[32] the first real initiative in Natal appears to have come from organised agriculture. Shortly after its inception, the Durban and Coast Agricultural Society offered a medal for the best essay on tree-planting for the coastal district. This particular competition was won by M.S. Evans, who subsequently tried to encourage tree-planting by offering prizes for the best plantations in the Pietermaritzburg–Richmond area.[33] Although no specific entries for the competition were received, several farmers were enticed to plant a variety of commercial tree crops.[34] In October 1903, Evans took up the issue again at the Farmers' Conference in Pietermaritzburg. On this occasion a total of £500 was made available for the 'best plantation of forest trees planted'.[35] Once again the response was disappointing, with only one entrant, A. Sclanders of Kelvin, Glen Isla in Weenen County, entering the competition.[36] Various tree enthusiasts ensured that the interest in tree-planting was kept alive in Natal. One such enthusiast was O. Hosking, who at the 1909 Farmers' Conference, moved to submit a resolution to the Royal Agricultural Society, which would draw the government's attention towards the distribution of advice on tree-growing other than wattle. It was suggested once again that the Farmers' Union should start the movement by offering prizes.[37] Additional prize money came from the Natal government, which provided £1000 for the competition.[38]

The aim was to grow trees of commercial value, with the final objective being to establish a Colony that would become a timber-growing country.[39] Natal was divided into three sections: coast to 2000 feet altitude,[40] 2000 to 4000 feet; and 4000 feet and above, with each section resulting in a first and second prize of £80 and £20 pounds respectively. The minimum requirement was a five-acre plot with at least 600 trees. The details of tree-planting competitions until 1924 are given in Table 1.[41]

The competition, according to forestry officials, had a 'considerable influence in stimulating public interest in afforestation'.[42] As Sim argued in his unpublished autobiography, this meant that up to 1923, the government had facilitated the growing of 2550 acres of commercial tree plantations for a mere £1500.[43] In other words, these plantations had cost the state ten shillings an acre compared to the average cost of £36 per acre on state plantations. This acreage excluded competitors who never bothered formally to enter the competition, as well as the corporation

Table 1: Tree-planting competitions in Natal, 1910–29

Competition	Year	Plots	Farmers	Acres
1	1910–15	31	18	155
2	1911–16	66	25	330
3	1912–17	28	15	140
4	1913–18	15	12	75
5	1914–19	38 (26)	19	190
6	1915–20	35 (24)	17	175
7	1916–21	60	12	300
8	1917–22	– (55)	–	–
9	1918–23	–	–	–
10	1919–24	53 (54)	19 (21)	265
11	1920–25	79 (90)	26 (23)	395
12	1921–26	55 (55)	9 (9)	275
13	1922–27	28 (38)	6 (6)	140
14	1923–28	22 (25)	4 (4)	110
15	1924–29	(3)	(9)	–

plantations at Pietermaritzburg, Newcastle, Greytown, Estcourt, Vryheid, Durban and Harding. If these plantations were included, and a waste factor of 25 per cent was introduced, the final figure would have been closer to 4000 acres.[44]

Although it was slow, forestry officials appeared to have been more than satisfied with the manner in which farmers, and public bodies, had embraced planting. Even during the First World War, forestry officials remarked on the increase in sales of such trees, especially of eucalypts, and estimated that in 1916 farmers in Natal planted more than one million timber trees.[45] Forestry officials and private enthusiasts also diligently continued to support the competitions. In the 1932 annual report of the Department of Forestry, the chief conservator reiterated that he remained convinced that 'Private afforestation can be encouraged considerably by means of awarding prizes or bonuses for afforestation competitions…Carried out carefully and subject to suitable conditions, this scheme will certainly help to improve the resources of the country.'[46]

Participation in the sponsored tree-planting competitions, however, continued to decline. In an attempt to resuscitate the competition a new subcommittee was appointed in 1932 and a £100 fund was introduced. The new subcommittee consisted of Hunt Holley, G.A. Wilmot, I.J. Craib and T.R. Sim.[47] Yet, as the *Cape Times* lamented, year after year national tree-planting campaigns and other spectacular means of tree-growing were put forward but to no avail.[48] Although the growing of wattle was never included in the competition, it is interesting to note that a close parallel existed between successful wattle growers and the emerging growers of commercial tree plantations. Even the 1932 competition subcommittee was still dominated by personalities with a strong history of involvement in the wattle industry. Hindered by a lack of archival material, it is difficult to set a time-scale for the expansion of wattle farmers and wattle companies into the commercial tree-growing industry. Sim, for example, describes how the Town Bush Wattle Syndicate extended operations by leasing 300 acres from Grey's Hospital. These lands were planted with E. saligna before being transferred to the Pietermaritzburg Town Board for revenue.[49] Unfortunately these transactions were not dated, although they probably occurred before 1910.

By 1915, many of the famous wattle-growing farms such as Harden Heights, Buccleuch and Cramond had entered commercial tree plots in the tree-growing competition.[50] Birnam Woods Limited, managed by Robert Dunlop, who was also the secretary of the Wattle and Timber Growers' Association, won the twelfth competition in 1927. Second was C. McKenzie of Richmond, who was also a prominent wattle grower.[51] The 1941 plot winners of the short-term competition (1938–41) were, in order of success, the Harden Heights Wattle Company, Major F.K. Lawson, Harden Heights Wattle Company and, in joint fourth place, the Clan Syndicate, Holly Brothers and L.E. Tulley. Entrants to the long-term competition (1936–56) were R.F. McMillan, N.F. Küsel, J. Crowe, Holley Brothers, and E.T. Hill & Sons.[52] The majority of these names were synonymous with the development of the wattle industry, illustrating the pivotal role that wattle farmers played in laying the foundations of private commercial tree-growing in Natal and Zululand.

Theoretically and practically, the emergence of wattle growers as pioneers in commercial tree-growing comes as no surprise. As tree growers, wattle farmers were naturally well placed to experiment with other tree crops. The majority of the successful wattle farmers were also progressive and innovative rural entrepreneurs. They were farmers at the cutting edge of the rural transformation in agriculture in the Natal Midlands, and therefore aware of emerging markets.

The experience gained from the marketing of wattle wood, to mining companies as mining props or to sugar mills for fuel, had given wattle farmers insight into the future potential of commercial tree-growing. The distribution patterns established by wattle-growers also gave them a competitive edge in the timber market, ensuring that the planting of commercial trees was an economically viable option to them. As Sim pointed out, these companies were formed for the express purpose of grinding out dividends; scenic beauty was only a by-product.[53]

In relative terms, however, the participation rates in the tree-planting competitions were not spectacular. In fact, as indicated in Table 1, between 1910 and 1920 an average of only eighteen farmers competed every year. These came out of a total of 8978 farms that existed in Natal and Zululand in 1921, although admittedly not all farms were suited to the growing of commercial trees, or were even occupied.[54] Unfortunately, the number of entrants in competitions beyond 1924 could not be found, yet there is little evidence to suggest that the number of competitors increased. Furthermore, as the majority of entrants were already successful wattle-growers, it is questionable whether the competitions managed to instil or broaden a tree-growing culture in Natal and Zululand. It did, however, create an awareness of the potential of commercial tree-growing.

As the successful wattle-growers contributed much to the introduction and organisation of the competitions, there is little doubt that this handful of progressive farmers was committed to the ideal of transforming Natal into a 'timber-growing country'. The evangelical enthusiasm of the farmers was probably motivated by the desire to convert unproductive and inaccessible land into productive farmland, thereby taming the natural environment and maximising agricultural profits. Consideration also needs to be given to a variety of environmental, philosophical and conservational factors that continually influenced attitudes towards land use. The participation of these farmers in the competitions was seen by them as a catalyst which would, hopefully, inspire other farmers to convert to commercial tree-growing. On a personal level, although the prize money was a sweetener, it was probably less important than prestige and peer-group recognition.

Despite this commitment, even the most successful wattle-growers were susceptible to market fluctuations. These fluctuations may explain the decline in the number of competition entrants in the 1920s. Initially, the large number of entries in 1910–11 was indicative of the general enthusiasm for tree-planting. This enthusiasm was seen as justified during the timber famine experienced between 1914 and 1918. The economic depression after the First World War contributed further to the continued interest in the commercial planting of trees, as wattle-bark sales suffered and farmers converted to long-term investment crops to bypass the immediate impact of the economic depression. Yet once wattle-bark prices improved, farmers refocused their energies on wattle, leading to a decline in interest in commercial tree-growing. In addition, during the early 1920s, the forestry settlement programme initiated by the state was expanded, greatly increasing the area under commercial tree plantations. The much publicised programme may have convinced farmers that future market demands would be met by the state, which was also considered to be in a better position to carry the risk of long-term investment. This also coincided with the state's commitment towards planting 15 000 acres of trees annually. A further consideration is the coming to power of the Pact government in 1924 and its greater emphasis on agriculture. Farmers, secure in the knowledge that they were now assured of more state support, may have calculated that it was easier to continue farming with less risky traditional crops.

Although the prestige and material incentives provided by the competition could be assumed to appeal also to less successful farmers, this evidently was not the case. The reasons for this probably varied. Some farmers may have had little desire to subject themselves to the rigours of examination and competition. Others may have lacked the financial or labour resources to implement the silvicultural techniques needed to impress judges. The competition, as noted above, was also dominated by individuals or syndicates that were familiar with tree-crop agriculture. Less experienced farmers may have been discouraged from entering. Furthermore, the long-term nature of tree-crop farming should not be forgotten, as it was generally the more successful farmers who could afford to invest in long-term ventures. Other impediments, such as the shortcomings of transportation and marketing structures, must also be considered.

To encourage these marginal farmers to plant trees, forestry officials and private tree-growing enthusiasts such as Sim resorted to propaganda. Essentially this took on a three-pronged discourse. On the one hand, many of the propaganda strategies that evolved originated in the environmental and ecological debates which emerged in the late nineteenth century. In many instances, large-scale tree-growing was advocated as the only solution to impending ecological and environmental disasters, jeopardising the continued existence of civilised habitation in Natal and South Africa. The public were constantly reminded of horror scenarios such as the threat of the advancing desert; a life without rain; the terror of a changing climate; the drying up of water resources; and the repercussions resulting from too much sun. On the other hand, these visions were accentuated by concerns that international timber supplies, on which South Africa depended, were about to be exhausted. This would cause the fledgeling South African economy to stagnate and remain undeveloped, unless local commercial tree plantations were established. Finally, propaganda promoting extensive tree-growing was not limited exclusively to the realm of pending doom but also attempted to promote an alternative, positive vision. Propagandists emphasised the physical and aesthetic improvement of the landscape. The potential of commercial tree-growers to accumulate wealth was publicised. Timber farming was depicted as an occupation of relative leisure, and tree-growers praised for their sense of patriotism. As the environmental aspects of the tree-growing debate warrant a much broader platform for discussion, only the last two forms of propaganda will be discussed below.

Despite the convincing arguments put forward by the ecological prophets of doom, there were sufficient contradictions in the speculative theorising to undermine the thrust of these controversial principles. The same could be said for the timber famine theorists, although the isolation experienced in 1914–18 and 1939–45 was very real, and did serve to remind the South African public of their vulnerability to international markets. To wean South Africans off their preferred taste for imported timber and other tree products, and to encourage development of local commercial tree-growing, this vulnerability was accentuated by claims that commercially harvested forests in the major forested regions were disappearing. As a result, South Africa would inevitably experience a permanent timber famine.

Although the threat of a timber famine appeared to dominate the South African tree-growing debate in the inter-war years, reference to such a threat had come earlier. Shortly after arriving in Natal in 1902, Sim warned that 'the prospect of a timber famine is not so far off as many would suppose'.[55] A few years later, in 1908, F.J. Stayner delivered a speech to the Dundee Farmers' Association in which he stated: 'The fact that before many years the world will be confronted with a timber famine does not impress Natalians as it should, but it will assuredly be a serious matter. The timber producing countries are rapidly working out their forests and prices have risen…'.[56] The theme was later taken up in the *Natal Agricultural Journal* when a correspondent, referring to the London *Times*, pointed out that there would be a world depletion of timber in 25 to 30 years. According to the report, supplies in the United States and Canada would soon be exhausted, while the most 'accessible timber on the shores of the Balkans' had been used up and 'internal supplies will be gone in less than 30 years'.[57] Similar speculative reports of the pending crisis continued to appear, and it was not uncommon to hear that supplies of softwood timbers in Europe, with the exception of Sweden and Norway, 'would be totally exhausted in the next eighty years', or that accessible timber supplies in the United States would be exhausted within fifteen years, with comparable supplies in Canada lasting only another twenty-three years.[58] This imminent crisis of a global timber famine had also been widely discussed at the 1920 and 1923 British Empire Forestry Conference, and it was for this reason that South Africa had been encouraged to produce its own timber supplies. It was also from these conferences that many of the statistics emanated that would form the basis for future timber famine debates.

To emphasise the emerging crisis, the Department of Forestry published a set of statistics to illustrate the global condition of the timber industry. According to the department the utilisation of softwoods in Europe in the early 1920s exceeded the annual increment by 2250 million cubic feet. In the United States, it was estimated that softwoods would last only another 25 years and that standing timber was being cut at four times the estimated annual growth.

Originally, there had been 822 million acres of timber trees in the United States. By the mid-1920s only 463 million acres remained of which 137 million were virgin timber. These remaining forests were being harvested at 5.5 million acres per year and, as a result, the United States was already dependent on Canada for two-thirds of its newsprint. In Canada itself, however, forests were also being rapidly depleted, exacerbated by wasteful processing.[59]

The threat of a timber famine was articulated by newspapers such as the *Natal Farmer* and the *Natal Witness*. Occasionally the papers carried articles which claimed that world softwood supplies would only be sufficient for another 60 years, or that accessible stands of virgin softwoods would only last another 37 or 25 years, depending on which source was to be believed.[60] When these predictions were combined with fears about climatic change and advancing desert, any patriotic or concerned farmer would have been foolish not to be convinced that a secure future lay in the planting of trees.[61] To Sim, the timber famine was 'no scare bogey; it is a definite result of world wide causes which cannot be checked'.[62] Sim claimed that demand for wood and timber in Natal was sure to increase, while the supply from timber-exporting countries was 'rapidly decreasing'.[63] South Africa therefore, Sim continued, had a 'duty to produce the timber it will require and to proceed rapidly, even at high cost, rather than be destitute when the shortage becomes acute'.[64] Several years later, prior to the 1935 conference, R.S. Troup, who was professor of forestry at Oxford University and director of the British Imperial Forestry Institute, made similar suggestions. He claimed that the world's annual consumption was 50 per cent greater than annual production and that imminent world shortages would be severely felt in South Africa. It was therefore crucial, Troup stressed, that South Africa become more self-supporting.[65]

As South Africa was generally a tree-poor country, it was fairly obvious that some planting of commercial timber plantations would have to take place to supplement the meagre local resources and to decrease dependency on imports. Within this context, the threats of an international timber famine were manifestations of a genuine concern yet, simultaneously, they could be and were manipulated as a propaganda tool, to create fear and generate a patriotic tree-growing sense of duty. Furthermore, the fears of timber famine were often associated with future consumption, which heightened the anxieties of local consumers. Such predictions were often distorted by inaccurate assumptions that did not take into account the realities of global production and consumption. In Canada, for example, the average volume of timber used in a timber-frame house fell by 50 per cent between 1920 and 1960. In the United States the total sawn timber used for all purposes decreased by 53 per cent from 1900 to 1955.[66] Although partly offset by the increase in population, future consumption figures had to take potential declines into consideration, and the rise of alternative materials.[67]

The major incentive to farmers and landowners came in the form of guaranteed profits from the conversion to, or investment in, commercial tree-growing. Farmers had to be convinced that the long-term investment in trees would pay dividends. As risk was spread over a longer time, final dividends would have to compensate for this accumulated risk. Again, it was Sim who emerged as the most vocal advocate of the material benefits of commercial tree-growing, especially the planting of eucalypts.[68] For several decades, Sim had been the great champion and promoter of the Australian wattle. By the 1920s, however, his enthusiastic support had shifted to the promotion of eucalypts that had become 'a more valuable product'.[69] As evidence, Sim claimed that 'Ranching returns, say 20s per acre per annum profit; mealies yield £2 per acre profit on suitable soils; wattles, £3 per acre profit per annum where all goes well, and saligna ten to twenty pounds per acre per annum ... under these circumstances who does not prefer saligna?'[70]

Further to enrich the attraction to farmers, Sim appealed to the emerging class of rural capitalists. In 1902 he had pointed out that 'those who plant now' would enjoy advantage in future when they would be recognised as being first in the field.[71] Sim also argued that when he had first advised Natal farmers to plant black wattle, those who had taken his advice had become not just successful, but prominent public figures in Natal, while many of those 'who did not follow that advice have since been labouring on government relief works'.[72] According to Sim the 'look-ahead men who are planting saligna to-day are the coming leaders of public opinion'.[73] However, to avoid the ignominy of 'relief works', commercial tree species, preferably eucalypts, had to be planted on a large scale:

> not by the dozen or by the acre as has happened in so many object-lesson plots through the country during the past two decades, but by the hundred acres or the thousand acres for therein lies the foundation of that great industry which is rapidly coming wherein the cultivation and utilisation of saligna timber will amass the fortunes of many, at the same time employing as many Europeans, natives or Indians, and thereby helping to make South Africa a white man's country.[74]

The motivation of profits and prestige, together with the environmental benefits which could accrue to timber farmers, was not the only reason why farmers were encouraged to convert. If Sim is to be believed, the particular life-style of a commercial tree-farmer was one many farmers would have aspired to: 'A Zululand patriot swelters in the tropical heat bossing coolie sugar hands while he might just as well sling his hammock in the saligna plantation and await developments.'[75]

As was the case with many other extravagant proposals that sought to promote the benefits of extensive tree-growing, forestry officials never publicly corrected or contradicted the popular myths that circulated in tree-growing circles. Occasionally the department recognised the need for 'careful' propaganda so as not to undermine wattle, sugar and other agricultural sectors in Natal. Also, commercial tree-growing did not always dominate the promotional platforms available. For example, in June 1927, the *Natal Farmer* predicted that wattle prices would continue to increase, and that farmers who had planted gums and pines would 'wish they had not wasted this land'.[76]

The promotion of commercial tree-growing in Natal and Zululand prior to the Second World War met with reasonable success. By 1926, there were already 16 522 acres of privately owned eucalypt plantations in Natal and Zululand, and this expanded to 38 307 acres in 1937. During the same period, the size of private conifer plantations increased by an astronomical 440 per cent, albeit from a low base of 690 acres, to 3729 acres. These areas, however, still paled when compared to the extensive wattle plantations that consisted of 359 164 acres in 1937. In its 1931 annual report the Forestry Department commented on the 'fair progress' being made by private tree-growers in Natal.[77] Officials noted that preference was generally given to eucalypts, and mention was made of 'the remarkable instance' where a 'single individual' at Kwambonambi had a *E. saligna* plantation which covered 3000 acres. This in all likelihood was the plantation of Major P.M. Rattray. The success of the Rattray plantation soon encouraged other landowners and companies to plant commercial timber trees, and by 1937 there were almost 20 000 acres in the Kwambonambi district.[78]

The gradual increase in tree-farming was not entirely unexpected; as the *Cape Times* pointed out in 1935, South Africans were 'as a nation, somewhat more appreciative of the value of our trees than we used to be. It would be strange if we were not, considering the variety of occasions on which afforestation is recommended as a certain cure for a number of our ills.'[79] Despite this, it was still apparent that individuals felt the state should be responsible for the large-scale planting of commercial trees. As the *Natal Witness* cynically remarked in a preview article to the 1935 Empire Forestry Conference, foreign delegates would discover the 'pleasant and trouble-saving' system established in South Africa, where everything was done by the state. This attitude, continued the *Natal Witness*, could not persist. If 'every farmer, every landowner, "did his bit" in planting trees, the solution of their present difficulties would be immeasurably hastened'.[80]

Mining and timber

A major stimulus to the establishment of plantations was a growing demand for mining timber (Table 2). Initially, indigenous trees had met this demand, but as these were denuded, private landowners as well as mining companies set about establishing an alternative, reliable source of timber. In the early 1880s, the first such plantation was laid out at Braamfontein, north of Johannesburg. A few years later, the state made its first contribution to the mining industry by making timber available from the state plantations at Kluitjeskraal, in the Cape. This plantation supplied the diamond fields of Kimberley from 1897.[81] By 1909, mining houses were planting trees on their own lands, mainly in the eastern Transvaal. These, together with state and private plantations found within a 400 kilometre radius of the mines, satisfied the initial demands for mining timber.[82]

Wattle and other commercial tree-farmers in Natal, who had struggled to penetrate the lucrative mining timber market, were given a boost in the mid-1920s when the snout-beetle invaded Transvaal eucalypt plantations, affecting mine-prop supplies in the province. Natal farmers were encouraged to use this convenient misfortune to penetrate and dominate the mine-prop market on the Rand. As Sim argued, if mines could not depend on a reliable supply of timber, they may 'turn a new corner'.[83] Many wattle farmers in Natal had a long-established association with the mines and welcomed the opportunity to expand their existing niche. Yet the 1920s coincided with the harvesting of many of the eucalypt plantations established after the First World War by non-wattle farmers. The threat of additional competition did little to appease traditional wattle-growers, who sought to discourage the emerging class of non-wattle tree farmers from entering the mining timber market. It therefore comes as little surprise to learn that Robert Dunlop, Secretary of the Wattle and Timber Growers' Association, felt that the cutting of valuable young eucalypts for mine props, was an economic mistake and that they should be left to grow, 'owing to the increasing cost and world shortage of commercial timber'.[84] Table 2 shows the increasing demands of the mining industry for timber.[85]

Although the gains made from the increase in Natal's market share of mine-props were partially undermined by the Great Depression and the gold standard crisis, the situation rapidly improved once South Africa left the gold standard in December 1932. The mining boom that followed coincided with the growing realisation by mining authorities that Zululand, Natal and the northern and eastern Transvaal were far more suitable for the growing of short-rotation mining timber than the areas in close proximity to the mines. Initially the wattle sector had provided a substantial proportion of the required mining timber, yet as more and more private capital was invested in the growing of eucalypts, this proportion declined steadily.[86] As the mine timber market was highly competitive, tree growers sought to maximise yields in the shortest possible time. Tree-farming rapidly became a more sophisticated process demanding a wider range of inputs and greater application of established silvicultural techniques. It was soon acknowledged that no 'other sphere of applied botany has played so direct a part

Table 2: Demands of locally grown hardwoods by Transvaal gold mines

Year	Total value (£)	Total volume (cu. ft)
1911	250 000	–
1920	500 000	–
1930	647 000	14 090 000
1932	732 000	15 225 000
1934	916 000	17 790 000
1936	1 244 000	22 310 000
1938	1 625 000	29 590 000
1960	5 372 674	–

in the establishment of the gold-mining industry' as the tree-growing sector.[87] Eucalypts grown specially for use as mine-props were planted as short-rotation crops. Tree spacing was less important, which allowed eucalypts to be planted close together to maximise production per acre. These denser plantations had a significant effect on soils, groundwater and local biota.

The intensive extraction of groundwater was exacerbated by the short-term nature of the crop, which curtailed the development of true forest conditions. Undergrowth could not establish itself, and the possibility of soil erosion increased dramatically. In environmental terms, this form of intensive tree-crop farming was the most devastating within the commercial tree-growing sector.[88] Despite the inevitable competition from concrete and steel, timber maintained its strategic importance to the mining industry. In 1959, 28 per cent of national roundwood production, mainly from *Eucalyptus* plantations, was consumed by the mining industry.[89]

The Great Depression also precipitated two fundamental changes in the sector. Owing to allegations by the private sector that the state had deliberately kept timber prices below market prices, to enable it to dominate the mining timber trade, a commission of inquiry was established in 1936 to investigate these claims. This commission concluded that the future supply of mining timber would be left to private growers, and by 1950 the state had withdrawn almost entirely from the production of mine-wood. This is indicated by the fact that between 1926 and 1960, eucalypts in state plantations in Natal decreased from 40 per cent to 12 per cent. The Great Depression had also exposed the dependence of wattle and eucalypt farmers on the gold mines, forcing tree farmers to weigh up an alternative tree crop. To many, as the *Farmer's Weekly* correctly pronounced, there was 'Gold in Pines', and many farmers re-evaluated their earlier reluctance to cultivate pines and began to invest in this tree crop.[90]

Despite the impressive developments in the growing of eucalypts and, to a lesser degree, pines, tree-farming in Natal prior to the Second World War still consisted largely of wattle. The foundations of a commercial tree-growing sector had, however, been laid, and as officials noted, the 'Department and the public were doing their utmost to accord afforestation its rightful place in the development of South Africa'.[91] Yet South Africa still relied heavily on imports, even wood used for boxes, a demand which could easily have been satisfied locally. This dependence was highlighted during the Second World War when South Africa's economic isolation had seen timber imports drop substantially. As the national demand for timber and other tree products now had to be satisfied by domestic production, a mini-boom resulted – a boom characterised by excessive profits, high earnings and little capital investment. National production increased from 250 000 cubic feet, in 1938, to 9 818 000 cubic feet in 1945, an increase of some 2000 per cent.[92] These figures included the exploitation of isolated woodlots, firebreaks and other irregular sources of timber, which were harvested in a desperate attempt to meet demand.

The impressive financial performance of timber during the Second World War proved to be an enormous incentive to private capital, which began to invest heavily in commercial tree-growing in the post-war period. Yet despite the 'relatively successful' participation of some private growers in planting softwoods, some commercial growers bore the marks of 'untrained, sometimes unimaginative, and often haphazard management'.[93] According to the South African Forestry Association, many fundamental but avoidable mistakes had been made as private growers rejected direction from skilled professionals and paid little attention to site quality, suitability of species, fire protection and the general management of plantations, in the quest for quick profits.[94] Although the focus of the association's comments was on softwoods, the position would have been similar in the rest of the sector. Mismanagement may have exacerbated the general fire hazard, while impacting on and altering soil structures on lands not suited to tree-planting, thus rendering them unsuitable for other land-use activities. The association did, however, add that the position was beginning to change, which was probably due to the emergence of the larger companies which typified the growing agro-industrialisation of the timber industry in the post-war period.

After the Second World War

As with wattle-growing, the increasing importance of commercial tree-growing led to the formation of numerous smaller companies such as the Enon Forestry and Springbok Forestry. Yet the ownership of commercial tree plantations became increasingly concentrated and, by the 1930s, HL&H and NTE had emerged as the single largest tree cultivators.[95] Both companies had, in the past, invested heavily in the wattle industry and continued their interests in wattle-growing and -processing. Yet the importance of eucalypts and pines resulted in a gradual shift by these companies into the cultivation of these species. This shift accelerated in the post-war years, which also witnessed the emergence of a new player in Natal's tree-growing sector – the South African Pulp and Paper Industries (SAPPI) – which moved to Natal in the 1940s.[96] The growing dominance of these three companies in the tree-growing sector was reflected in the related processing sectors.

Not only did the presence of processing industries ensure a secure market for tree farmers, but they simultaneously created a growing demand for tree products. It has been argued that this latter stimulus contributed to the rapid growth of commercial tree-growing in Natal, rather than actual demand.[97] In Natal, the major tree-product consuming industries to emerge in the 1950s were the SAPPI paper factory at Mandini, and the SAICCOR rayon pulp factory at Umkomaas, which began operating in 1955. The SAPPI mill, producing kraft and newsprint, consumed approximately 1.5 million cubic feet of *E. saligna* and just over 4 million cubic feet of pine annually.[98] Shortly after being erected, the SAICCOR plant required 6 million cubic feet of *E. saligna* per annum.[99]

Other major industries included the African Building Board factory (Timberit) at Canelands and the Masonite factory at Estcourt. Timberit, which by the mid-1960s was considered to be the sixth-largest hardboard manufacturer in the world, was reliant on large quantities of *E. saligna*. The Masonite factory consumed more than two million cubic feet of wattle timber and a substantial amount of pine timber annually in its production of fibreboard.[100] Other less prominent yet equally important industries, which relied on tree products as a raw material, were the Lion Match Factory and South African Board Mills, both in Durban.[101] In addition, there were numerous furniture and box-making factories, impregnating plants, and the sawmills themselves, which provided the sawn timber utilised in these industries as well as construction timber. C.E. Lack, the conservator of forests in Natal, estimated that by the mid-1950s, approx-imately ten million cubic feet of pine timber and twenty million of eucalypt timber were being produced annually in Natal, most of which was processed locally.[102]

The large-scale capital investment in these wood-consuming industries was indicative of recognition of the province as a tree-growing region. In their turn tree growers, assured of a ready market, transferred this security into higher levels of commercial tree-growing. Other factors, such as the crisis experienced by the wattle industry in the 1950s, had also contributed to the increasing emphasis by tree farmers on the planting of alternative industrial tree crops. World shortages in the supply of softwoods in the 1950s and 1960s fostered further growth of the sector in Natal and South Africa. Expansion was also facilitated by the mechanisation of the agricultural sector. This enabled tree farmers to clear and prepare extensive areas, while easing the harvesting and transportation of this bulky crop.[103]

In Natal, the total area under eucalypts and pines increased from 42 000 acres in 1937 to 103 000 acres in 1950, to more than 230 600 acres in 1959. An important development in this expansion was that the share of softwoods, out of these totals, increased from 9 per cent to 34 per cent and then to 42 per cent. Although it was often argued by forestry officials that tree-growing was ideal for 'otherwise useless' land, a large proportion of these new plantings occurred on land suitable for pastoral and arable farming. As successful timber production is mainly limited by rainfall parameters, the high-rainfall areas of the Natal Midlands were ideally suited for commercial tree-growing. The Midlands were, however, also ideal milk-producing areas, and tree-growing was therefore seen as a 'serious threat' to the dairy industry. This threat, according to Lack, was aggravated by 'wholesale and indiscriminate afforestation', without specific long-term planning or a greater emphasis on mixed farming.[104] The other area ideally suited to pines and eucalypts was the coastal strip along the Zululand coast, where the climate and rainfall level are particularly suitable. Unlike the Midlands, however, the initial expansion of the tree-growing sector into this region did not result in direct competition with other sectors of agriculture.[105] The particular coastal strip favoured by timber growers was generally narrow, although it reached a width of 80 to 100 kilometres in the Ubombo and Ingwavuma districts. As the soils along the coast are generally unsuitable for other forms of agriculture such as sugar cane, which is grown further inland, commercial tree-growing was able to expand unchallenged.[106] This rapid expansion soon led to Kwambonambi being known as the '*Eucalyptus saligna* growing belt'.[107]

Although competition for land, from tree-growing enterprises, was a major concern for the traditional stock and crop farmers in Natal, the environmental and aesthetic implications of large-scale tree-growing continued to raise the hackles of these farmers. It was primarily the competition for water supplies that galvanised rural resistance against the commercial tree-growing sector. This is perhaps best illustrated by the controversy surrounding the drainage of the Umvoti vlei by the Lion Match Company in the late 1940s, which provided a major catalyst for rural frustrations. In many ways, the controversy also reflected the growing tensions between small-scale tree-growing farmers, sugar farmers and the larger tree-growing companies. It was also indicative of the growing party politicisation and expediency of broader environmental issues.[108]

The Umvoti vlei, however, was certainly not the first wetland to be dredged and drained for agricultural purposes in Natal – and, unfortunately, it was not the last. Yet the controversy was symbolic of the state's tendency to broaden the scope of its conservation measures and recognise the potential threat of tree-growing to the environment, rather than viewing it as a necessary ally in the conservation struggle. In the face of an expanding state and private commercial tree-growing sector, this position was not always free from contradiction or public scepticism; nor was the question of vlei drainage only focused on the Umvoti area. In southern Natal, for example, the MP for the South Coast claimed that eucalypts were being planted in vlei lands which could be used for the growing of rice.[109] Altogether, there were 10 000 acres of the 'most fertile land' which were going under eucalypts; a situation which led D. Mitchell to ask, 'How far is it in the national interest to allow the use of these lands for commercial farming for the purpose of supplying raw material to the rayon and pulp factories when we are looking to … greater production of food?'[110]

Although the anxiety over the loss of grazing and other agricultural land may have precipitated local fears of an impending food shortage, they did little to halt the advance of tree monocultures. In many instances, the increase in food production and agricultural productivity also deflected these concerns in the post-war period. Agricultural research, mechanisation, improved infrastructure and the sustained support of the state ensured that transformation in the agricultural sector continued after the war. Through legislation such as the Marketing Act of 1937, farmers were often guaranteed a set price for their produce. This price stability for certain products contributed to rapid, sustained increase in agricultural production, and also to the non-viable and destructive use of marginal lands. Nevertheless, these conditions would have done much to allay the fears of a food famine induced by the expansion of tree-growing.

The prolific increase in privately grown plantations after the Second World War inevitably also gave rise to two related and contentious debates within the sector. One was the production of a surplus, which was exacerbated by the second issue, the lack of an adequate marketing system. Dr I.J. Craib had already warned in 1939 that there would be a phase when 'the market will not readily absorb the maximum potential volume of locally produced commodities'.[111] In 1941 the *Farmer* called for more systematic control and survey of the timber-growing sector, warning of the dangers of over-production and the potential threat of a drop in prices.[112] In addition, the wattle sector had struggled for many decades to market the wood and timber produced in its plantations. These warnings and experiences, however, appear not to have slowed the prolific increase of plantations.

A position of over-production was finally reached in the 1950s, when the thinnings of plantations grown since the Second World War began to flood the market. Over-production of wood and timber was set to continue. In the late

1950s, it was estimated that surplus production accounted for a further 50 million cubic feet of log volume, for which a market would have to be found 'during the next quarter century'.[113] Alarm among many of the private commercial tree farmers that no markets could be found for their product led to the formation of the South African Timber Growers' Association (SATGA) in 1956. SATGA committed itself to solving this particular problem, although it was also concerned with competition from imports, which continued to dominate local markets in the timber and related product trade. SATGA recognised that, to plan with greater certainty, more accurate data on the extent and size of plantations were required. But it was only with the passing of the Forest Act of 1968, which replaced the 1941 Act, that the Department was empowered to collect information on plantation areas and timber consumption. It also empowered officials to impose penalties on timber growers or timber processors who failed to submit the required details.[114] Up until this time, forestry officials had planned and promoted in an environment that was devoid of accurate data. This lack of planning was subsequently reflected in the chaos that characterised the wood and timber processing industries during the 1950s.

The apparent unity among tree growers was short-lived. Discord emerged between tree farmers and the larger growers-cum-manufacturers with vested interests in the timber-producing and wood-processing complex. These tree industrialists eventually formed their own association, the Forest Owners' Association (FOA). The split resulted primarily from an insistence by SATGA on forming a selling department for all members, notwithstanding existing commitments.[115] Other points of disagreement revolved around sectional voting rights, although, as the *Financial Mail* noted, a more fundamental point of dispute pertained to the question of timber and fibre prices.[116] Small growers believed that processors were paying them unreasonably low prices while rapidly increasing their profits, allowing for higher levels of capital investment in the processing sector. Processors, in turn, argued that an increase in the material costs would price them out of the emerging export market.

In 1960, the state controlled 105 039 acres of eucalypt and pine plantations in Natal, a mere eleven per cent of the total, with a further 34 533 acres in the African reserves. Privately owned commercial tree plantations totalled 205 322 acres, which excluded the formidable 601 000 acres of wattle plantations. Private farmers and the larger companies, therefore, controlled more than 85 per cent of the area under tree crops in Natal. On a national level the total capital investment in tree-growing and the related processing industries in 1960–61 was R380 million, which was approximately one-tenth of the total investment in agriculture. A substantial and increasing proportion of this investment would have been in the province of Natal. Between 1946 and 1960, the national value of gross output in the timber industry increased at a compound rate of 12 per cent a year while in 1960 a total of 52 000 individuals were employed in the industry.[117]

The accelerated expansion of tree-growing in the 1950s was due to a variety of reasons. Unlike the conditions that followed the First World War, the South African economy was now far more developed, with a growing manufacturing and industrial sector. In addition, the pioneering and experimental plantings of the state and a core of progressive farmers had ensured that the risk of tree-growing had decreased substantially. Through trial and error, suitable species had been selected and appropriate silvicultural methods established.[118] The foundations had been successfully laid, and the growth of commercial tree-growing was a natural step in the broadening natural resource base of an industrialising economy.

Furthermore, the factors always retarding the industry – lack of adequate infrastructure, the dearth of local saw-milling facilities, labour shortages, prejudice against local timber – had been addressed by the state and almost entirely eliminated. In this sense, the role of the state had shifted from that of innovator in the timber industry, to its facilitator. Unlike wattle, however, the cultivation of pine, and to a similar extent eucalypts, had become a mass-production business requiring formidable resources of capital, technical and managerial resources, and control over the market – a requirement best suited to the large agro-industrialists rather than small growers. With the diversification of the South African economy, commercial tree-growing moved away from simple mine-prop and sawn-timber production, towards satisfying the needs of the more sophisticated wood-, timber- and fibre-consuming industry in South Africa, and the global market.

Chapter Eight

Technology and ecology in the Karoo: A century of windmills, wire and changing farming practice

Sean Archer

[An] old South African farmer…when asked whether he had seen any changes on his farm over his lifetime, replied, upon serious reflection, 'I think the rocks are growing'.[1]

This chapter raises a research question which has not received attention previously.[2] What was the effect on land use in the Karoo, and thus on its ecosystem, of two technical innovations in the late nineteenth century: windmills to pump underground water for consumption by domestic stock; and wire fencing for controlling the grazing patterns and grazing intensity of that stock? By every historical account farming practice changed radically once these new methods of production were in place. In most areas the old shepherd-plus-kraaling procedure disappeared from commercial stock-raising by the second decade of the twentieth century. The new production system comprised the enclosure of farm boundaries, the internal division of grazing land into camps, free range within them, and the provision of artificial watering points where natural sources of water were inadequate.

Understanding how these new techniques affected land utilisation, and specifically the productivity and resilience of plant communities, is a preliminary to identifying the causes of long-term trends in the Karoo's environmental history. The hypotheses examined here are that these innovations led to more continuous utilisation of the vegetation in a given location, higher stocking rates and, during drought episodes, lower animal mortality with less stock trekking into other regions. Biodiversity loss accelerated, and in consequence the integrity of the system altered decisively. Thus it was an open question at the end of the twentieth century whether a return was possible to the density, composition and stability of the vegetation recorded by observers in early colonial times.

To date, the historical literature on the Karoo does not contain a direct study of technological change in stock-farming. This chapter is not yet a study at the scale required. Its purpose is to pose a range of questions, to suggest relevant tendencies in the record of veld conditions during the last century, and to identify a conceptual framework within which to consider the Karoo as an ecosystem. For this purpose it draws upon ideas in ecology perhaps not familiar to historians. The factual material cited, particularly the quotations from documentary sources, is intended as preliminary support more than sufficient evidence. A realistic research effort will require a larger geographical scale and greater time depth.

The Sneeuberg is the main region of interest in this chapter (see Figure 8.1). Running approximately west to east for 200 kilometres, this mountain range straddles the northern half of the Graaff-Reinet magisterial district and portions of Murraysburg, Richmond, Middelburg, Cradock and Pearston. However, some farm-level information and some illustrations have been drawn from the area of lower altitude south of Graaff-Reinet town, which has a lower mean rainfall and, in the pre-windmill days, fewer sources of surface water. Here the land area required to support a 'small stock unit' (sheep, goat, ostrich or springbok) is greater, but offset in part by the larger size of the average animal.

Two vegetation systems intersperse and overlap in this region, depending upon altitude and location on the west–east continuum. These are the Nama Karoo and Grassland biomes.[3] Gradients in their associated micro-climates, particularly in rainfall and temperature, create a gradient in growing conditions.

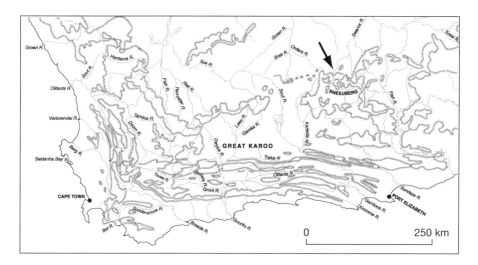

8.1 The Karoo and Sneeuberg

Source: Acocks, J. 1979. The flora that matched the fauna. *Bothalia* 12:676.

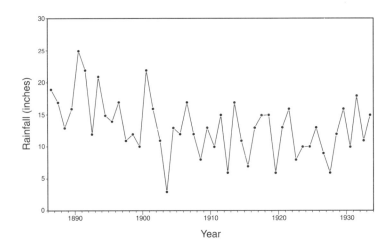

8.2 Rainfall, Nieu-Bethesda, a village situated in the centre of the Sneeuberg

Source: compiled by A. Erlank, Municipal Offices, Nieu-Bethesda.

8.3 Sneeuberg landscape near St Olives, Eastern Cape

Source: Timm Hoffman.

But such heterogeneity of the bioregion can be turned to advantage in posing the broad questions of this first study, in that the major changes in farming practice that occurred with the introduction of windmills and fencing wire had an even greater effect in the Nama Karoo veld where the water resource constraint was more acute. That proposition applies to the lower, and thus warmer and drier, valleys and gravel plains called the Camdeboo in the eighteenth century. These historical place-names can be confusing. Today the inhabitants of Graaff-Reinet apply that name to one specific locality below Toorberg, a prominent mountain in the range. The high inter-annual variability of the rainfall in this region is illustrated in Figure 8.2 that straddles the period containing the changes in technology under discussion. The mean annual rainfall recorded between 1886 and 1933 was 13.54 inches (344 mm). Yet by itself this average is of limited significance for vegetation composition and ecological characteristics, given the striking fluctuations from year to year.

Ecological perspectives

The choice of a conceptual framework on which to base an examination of land degradation in arid areas is integral to current research work on grazing systems. Even a historical perspective must take note of the main issues in contention in order to pose the right questions. New strands of thinking about this problem elsewhere, for example Africa further north, Australia and the western United States, have striven to keep pace with recent developments in ecology. These debates are ongoing, but the principal themes in the literature provide the context for this discussion.

The plant succession or climax theory of vegetation change was formulated in 1899 and elaborated later along with a wider public exposure through the writings of Clements after 1916. A highly influential set of ideas, it was in dispute from the beginning, concerning the kinds and mechanisms of succession and interpretation of the observational evidence. For example, to infer temporal succession from the comparison at a single point in time between spatial zones in which plant communities have experienced differing histories of disturbance can yield indeterminate and even conflicting inferences about vegetation stages. Furthermore, the occurrence of 'retrogressive succession...in which many of the processes normally associated with conventional succession are set in reverse' was not accorded much attention before the 1960s.[4]

Applied to grazing land, the succession model predicts that changes in plant composition and structure and in processes at ecosystem scale, caused by exposure to domestic stock, can ultimately be reversed by their removal from the land. With sufficient time and normal climatic events, plant communities return along a number of dimensions to their climax phase. By presumption such a state is stable in the accepted sense. 'A system is deemed stable if and only if the variables all return to the initial equilibrium following their being perturbed from it. A system is locally stable if this return is known to apply only certainly for small perturbations and globally stable if the system returns from all possible perturbations.'[5] Thus, change in dimensions such as plant mass, coverage and species diversity is perceived in this framework to be linear, continuous and reversible along the relevant scale.[6] For resource management the production problem translates into the search for strategies that will result in sustainable yields at intra-climax equilibria. Expressed in economic terms, the goal is the optimal trade-off between production of animal off-take (numbers, sizes, secondary outputs) and consumption of biomass, a balance that has to be maintained continuously over time. 'Under the range succession model the object of management is to choose a stocking rate which establishes a long-term balance between the pressure of grazing and the successional tendency.'[7]

Implicit in much of the older literature was the presumption that plant succession along a continuum occurred in all systems under regular climatic conditions, so abiotic differences such as the level and variability of rainfall were not obstacles to the fit of the model. With succession thinking in the air, and without delving far into the older documentation on Karoo grazing land, it is possible nevertheless to find a number of sceptical statements about the feasibility of restoring its veld cover to its presumed state before colonial settlement:

> The deterioration in the vegetal covering which is closely connected with the operations of the small stock farmer in the drier parts of the Union, has been shown to be due mainly to kraaling, scarcity of drinking places and overgrazing ... Where the extent of the reduction of [plant] cover is serious, the loss of moisture due to the increased run-off and evaporation may become so great that the total amount available will be insufficient to support the original vegetation. When such a condition is reached, rapid deterioration results, unless other contributory factors, which man may control, are made more favourable to recovery.[8]

> Apart from the destruction of the vegetation ... that is ascribed almost wholly, and directly, to the work of man, the evidence available in respect of the three most significant trends of vegetal change, namely, the invasions by Karoo vegetation, thornscrub and vegetation of the Fynbos type, as well as the failure of prolonged efforts in the False Karoo to restore the vegetation to a semblance of its former condition (or at least sufficiently to stabilise the soil) by any method of grazing control, or complete protection,

clearly indicate a disturbance of the available moisture supplies, and, more specifically, a reduction in either the effectiveness or quantity of available summer moisture.[9]

Throughout the Karoo and the southern margin of the thornveld...the deterioration of the plant cover and the concomitant soil erosion have proceeded beyond the critical stage when prolonged resting might have permitted recovery and restoration of the original vegetation...the critical stage is reached when the plant cover, particularly the grasses, is just able to protect the soil against erosion. Deterioration beyond this stage leads rapidly to soil depletion that makes impossible the restoration of a plant cover comparable with the original veld (even if grazing is suspended entirely)...[10]

At the eastern end of the Escarpment, one can still see the black humus topsoil disappearing and form some idea of the luxuriance, quality and carrying capacity of the original veld; elsewhere there is only subsoil and an occasional handful of topsoil left to indicate that there was such a soil and such a vegetation...The essential difference between the original state of the karoo veld [before the onset of commercial grazing] and its present state is that then the spaces between the bushes were still occupied by topsoil, held in place by grass, bulbs and the roots of annuals, no matter how short the grass may have been nor how often the annuals themselves may not have been there.[11]

None of these statements refers directly to succession thinking as such, although in this and other writings Acocks alludes often to climax states of plant communities. But their import for that model is clear: if their judgements are empirically supportable then these writers were questioning, intentionally or not, a central implication of succession ideas. This is the prediction of a reversal up the continuum of successive vegetation states when the identified cause of degradation, heavy stocking, is removed. The broad reasons for the scepticism expressed in these quotations are the degradation of topsoil leading to its physical loss, and decreased efficacy of a given quantity of rainfall due to reduced vegetation cover and smaller seed beds. The common inference they drew was that these would block the linear trend of the Karoo vegetation in returning to its climax condition even if domestic stock were removed.

In what respects the succession framework is incomplete and inapplicable, and thus by itself not adequate as an interpretation of observed change, is still not agreed. But there are suggestions in the current literature that draw upon observations and efforts to conceptualise differently the dynamic properties of an ecosystem. An alternative perspective is emerging on long-term trends in grazing systems.[12] Thus for the present purpose, whether the effects of the drilling, pumping and fencing technologies introduced into commercial farming in many parts of the world after about 1880[13] are better viewed in the old or the new framework is a pertinent question.

Certain writings on arid grazing lands now favour the 'state-and-transition' or 'billiard-ball' model as potentially a better fit than Clementsian succession or as, at minimum, a supplement to it. This set of ideas starts with a number of objectives, the most notable being the following (given that this is a historical study, the aim is to convey the flavour of alternative proposals that may illuminate ecological change in the Karoo, not to provide a full account of current debates):

– To allow for the episodic character of changes in species composition is essential because 'both the establishment and mortality of plants is generally a function of a very particular set of conditions, which may only occur in association with "rare" events'.[14]

– Vegetation states are best characterised as discrete and locally stable, but not necessarily globally so, in the sense of 'stability' defined above.

– Transitions between such states can cross successional thresholds when 'induced by natural episodic events such as fire or by management actions such as grazing'.[15]

– Once thresholds are crossed, succession may not be reversible within time periods significant to management, and in the absence of intervention through investment of resources in reclamation of biotic components (for example, plant eradication and re-seeding) and abiotic components (for example, damming water courses and mechanical ripping of the subsoil on bare surfaces) of the ecosystem.

– Grazing lands conceived as 'ecosystems do not have single equilibria with functions controlled to remain near it'.[16]

– 'Policies and management that apply fixed rules for achieving constant yields (e.g. fixed carrying capacity of cattle or wildlife, or fixed sustainable yield of fish or wood), independent of scale, lead to systems that increasingly lack resilience, i.e. to ones that suddenly break down in the face of disturbances that previously could be absorbed.'[17]

– It follows that command-and-control management, while it might generate short-term economic gains, will also increase the vulnerability of a system like grazing land 'to perturbations that otherwise could be absorbed. [Thus] any move toward truly sustainable human endeavours must incorporate this principle or it cannot succeed.'[18] By hypothesis, the new technology facilitated such production methods by farmers and other land resource managers in the Karoo.

In summary, this state-and-transition model aims to allow for 'alternative stable states, discontinuous and irreversible transitions, non-equilibrium communities, and stochastic effects in succession'.[19] One of its principal implications is that higher environmental quality is not likely to be achieved by simply eliminating the proximate cause of retrogression; for example, in the case of the Karoo not only by removing all livestock, but also requiring active restoration. Metaphors and diagrammatic presentations of these ideas typically use ball-and-topography analogies to show how an ecosystem, like a ball, can flip from one locally stable state to another if taken beyond a stability threshold by the slow accumulation of perturbations or disturbances.[20]

An application of non-equilibrium concepts to the understanding of grazing systems in African arid zones has emerged in the last decade.[21] The main proposition in the paradigm case of non-equilibrium is that where rainfall is highly variable over time the link between vegetation state and grazing pressure is weakened. It is of secondary importance, in the limit of no importance, in determining the density and species composition of plant cover, and therefore of the ecological status of arid grazing land. Under such climatic conditions 'fodder is scarce because there is too little rain rather than too many animals. Moreover, major droughts are frequent enough and herd recovery is slow enough that livestock numbers are never given an opportunity to approach ecological carrying capacity.'[22]

By hypothesis, vegetation adapts to climatic disturbance and acquires resilience that enables plant communities to endure. Management (or development) decisions then also change, away from the intra-climax phase targeting of the rival model. Under such variability and unpredictability in the production environment 'conventional development procedures are destabilising influences in ecosystems which are dominated by stochastic abiotic perturbations'.[23] Instead, resource managers maximise returns by pursuing opportunistic strategies. In the real grazing systems from which the non-equilibrium model is derived, there is considerable spatial and temporal variation in forage availability, so managers split livestock into small groups that range over large areas tracking pulses in vegetation growth, manipulate herd structure to meet subsistence requirements and to minimise risk, and maintain reserve areas for periods of severe scarcity.[24]

Whether state-and-transition will prove a perspective superior to succession in the long term remains to be seen.[25] But it does direct attention to two key implications in the case of the Karoo. Firstly, if the main contention of the non-equilibrium model is correct, then grazing by domestic livestock, and by inference by game herds earlier, has had a much more limited effect on the land's productivity of edible biomass than has been presumed hitherto. It would follow that the *rate* of decline in plant densities, species diversity and soil integrity was much lower when graziers were less constrained spatially and temporally by the entrenchment of individual property rights. That would have been so in the countless centuries of game migration and transhumance by Khoikhoi herders, and later by nomadic *trekboere* of the eighteenth and early nineteenth centuries. Thus the role played in ecological change by the institution of private exploitation rights for grazing on designated land units, even before enclosure by fencing, requires emphasis in a historical explanation.

Secondly, the pursuit of stability in production conditions by land managers, through the radical changes wrought in grazing practice with the new technology of windmills and wire, may mean that the major phase of degradation took place more recently than previously presumed. If correct, then compared with the shepherding form of grazing, all these innovations led to greater constancy and more unremitting pressure on vegetation and landscape by domestic stock, because the new practices raised profitability via increased numbers per land area. How this became apparent (and how rapidly) to the individual decision-taker, the farm-owner or his manager, as distinct from a collective group under communal tenure which is the paradigm underlying the non-equilibrium model, must be a research question for a larger-scale study.

Technological change

When the first windmill and wire fence appeared in the Sneeuberg is not known. On a farm for which documentation exists – Wellwood – north of Graaff-Reinet, the first wire fence was erected in 1877 and the first windmill pumping from a borehole into a constructed reservoir dates from September 1905.[26] Another source confirms for the 1870s that farmers were investing in wire fencing and even in 'pumps driven by wind to raise water for their flocks'.[27] Civil commissioners of the Cape government confirm the existence of 'windmill pumps' at that same date in the more arid western Karoo, in Victoria West and Calvinia.[28]

Whether these were locally made windmills or imported ones of the kind described below remains to be established. A 'Halliday Standard windpump' erected in Hopetown in 1874 is the earliest recorded example of an imported windmill from the United States.[29] It was constructed of wood rather than steel and its location is also in the western Karoo, where sheep rangelands are hotter, drier and contain less surface water than the Sneeuberg. Other early mill installations were in the Little Karoo region and the Graaff-Reinet district, both of which contained large ostrich feather industries during the boom years before 1914.[30] It is plausible that high profits from feather sales provided ready investment funding for windmills. It is tempting further to speculate that the new technology in stock-raising moved from ostrich to sheep production when their relative profitabilities tilted that way with the collapse of feather prices. However, this awaits detailed research.

According to Rolls, 'the first big wire fenced paddocks in Australia' were erected in 1856 at Burburgate in New South Wales.[31] A plausible inference is that Karoo fencing was later in coming. One reason for later innovation was the lower cost of Karoo farm labour relative to Australian, so a technology such as self-sufficient camps which saved on shepherding activity was a more appealing investment in Australia. In addition, the larger scale of average grazing units in Australia, with the lower financial risks that big sheep stations entailed for raising funds, would have projected profitability gains from investment with higher certainty than in South Africa. By the time the Select Committee on Fencing held hearings in 1889, considerable quantities of fencing were already erected 'in the Karroo districts' as well as Grahamstown, Queenstown and elsewhere, areas for which witnesses led evidence.[32] The first agricultural census of 1918 lists 15 000 farms 'wholly fenced' and 13 000 'partially fenced' out of 31 000 farms in the Cape Province. For the Union of South Africa as a whole the same fencing categories are 38 000 and 30 000 in a total of 76 000 farms.[33]

Initially both windmills and wire were imported, principally from the United States. Import statistics of fencing wire measure the trend in the volume of fencing constructed in the early years of the century. In 1906, 13 400 tons were imported into the Cape, rising to 35 800 tons in 1911 and a peak of 47 600 tons into South Africa as a whole in 1928. Large quantities were shipped in during the 1920s to make up for the decline in import volume during the First World War.[34] From 1922 barbed wire imports were categorised separately, and remained much larger than smooth fencing wire until local production began after the mid-1930s, reflecting farmers' perception of its greater effectiveness.

On windmill totals, census and import figures show the broad trend. The 1904 Cape census contains the first mention of them. 'The omission of wind motors and water wheels in [the previous census of] 1891 would seem to imply that they did not exist in any appreciable number at that time. There are 1,275 of the former, and 364 of the latter in use in the Colony at the present time [1904].'[35] Windmill imports in value terms (pounds sterling) are recorded in foreign trade statistics from 1909 onwards. Using a price deflator to remove the changing *value* of the currency – with 1909 as the index base of 100 – imports amounted to £27 000 in that year, rising to £72 000 (an index of 267) in 1913,

£78 000 (289) in 1920, £129 000 (478) in 1929, and £104 000 (385) in 1948. Import *quantities* would be more enlightening but are not available. Local manufacture for the domestic market expanded rapidly after the Second World War, so import value totals ceased to be a reliable measure of farming investment in windmills and therefore of the spread and density of stock watering points. Another data set confirming this trend is the recorded windmill numbers on South African farms, derived from agricultural census sources: 44 000 in 1926, 101 000 in 1946 and 151 000 in 1955.[36] These figures are acceptably comprehensive because annual census returns by farmers in earlier years were reputedly encouraged by local authorities and the police in rural areas through an arrangement with the census authorities. Technology has evolved further in recent times, towards solar power and submersible pumps in boreholes as the electricity grid spread into Karoo districts during the 1980s and 1990s. But the bulk of artificial water sources for livestock in these areas is still supplied by the windmill.

Windmill technology has absorbing historical interest in its own right. Vertical or tower windmills, with the rotor turning in a vertical plane, are believed to have entered Europe from the Middle East after the Crusades. The 'earliest authentic mention of a windmill in western Europe yet discovered is in a deed, reliably dated as c1180…' pertaining to an abbey in Normandy.[37] Its symbolic role in later medieval times is striking. Then it performed an intellectual and cultural function similar to the robot and computer in the industrialised societies of the twentieth century:

> In the middle of the fifteenth century, while the first wave of European world conquerors was growing up, artists suddenly and incongruously clothed the allegorical representation of Temperance, then generally considered the greatest of the seven Virtues, with a panoply of the new technology: on her head she wore that triumph of machine design the mechanical clock; in her right hand she held eyeglasses, the chief new boon to the mature literate man; she stood on a *tower windmill*, the most recent form (it appears in the 1390s) of the most recent power machine. The late Middle Ages considered its advancing technology profoundly virtuous, a manifestation of obedience to God's command that mankind should rule the Earth.[38]

But the windmill which altered stock-farming so radically in the arid parts of the world was the steel mill, developed in the second half of the nineteenth century to meet the requirements of ranchers and railroads on the Great Plains of the United States.[39]

What was needed was a mill which would have good low-speed torque for starting, be able to keep on running in relatively light winds, face those winds from whatever direction they came, and cease to operate if the wind became too strong...Therefore the Americans had to evolve a self-regulating windmill which could be left to fend for itself and operate even in the worst of their winters.[40]

Besides the basic design, the other accomplishment was mass production of standard interchangeable parts, transportable in knocked-down form for erection on site by labour with no specialised mechanical skill. Often farmers themselves assembled the windmill on the ground and then simply pulled it upright onto its four foundation blocks. Large-scale manufacture commenced in 1862,[41] and an 'estimated 6.5 million machines were sold between 1880 and 1930'.[42] Aermotor, made in Chicago and considered in the Karoo to be the best quality mill because many still operate there, is recorded as having 'over 800,000 windmills in service by the middle of this century'.[43] The import figures cited earlier confirm this dominance of American manufacturers in the South African market: up to the Second World War about 80 per cent of the total supply came from them.

A number of interesting issues not pursued in detail here can be noted for later research. Firstly, the coming of wire and windmills to the Karoo can be viewed as an example of 'induced innovation'. New technology and new institutions respond to changed circumstances, in this case to an increased demand for mutton with the sudden rise in immigration and urbanisation. Within three to four years of the diamond fields opening in 1870, sheep prices in the Karoo doubled,[44] yet under the old production system of shepherding and kraaling, output in animal numbers marketed could be expanded only marginally. So farmers searched actively for ways to raise the productivity of their land, and investment in artificial watering points and the fencing of grazing camps now looked profitable and affordable.

Secondly, diffusion of an economically superior technology is never instantaneous, but more 'typically follows an s-shaped or "sigmoid" curve, such that the adoption rate is initially slow, then faster, and then slower again as saturation is approached'.[45] This probably had little to do with negative ecological effects that might have been anticipated from the new grazing technology, but it is interesting to enquire why there was initial reluctance to invest in devices that intensified production on a given area of land. By 1903 Graaff-Reinet farmers were convinced enthusiasts for the new water sources:

Mr Rubidge [said] ... had boreholes Nos I and III not been the success they are, should have had to remove most of my stock. Mr Burger added his testimony to the great value of boreholes for stock purposes, he had two boreholes and an open well, at which holes he had to water three thousand small stock, together with a few head of cattle and ostriches. He used one hole for his own stock, a neighbour using the other for his thousand head of stock... he believed that enterprise in this direction would decidedly pay ... certainly as far as stock was concerned. Two of his neighbours were joining him in sending off an order for a jumper drill... Mr Spence's experience had been practically the same. If he had not gone in for boring he would have lost his cattle... Mr Lee said he had a government drill on his place and had put down two holes. Every pound that he had expended as his share had saved him 10 worth of stock. (Hear hear).[46]

Thirdly, windmills and wire fencing constituted large investments for individual farmers. For example, a new water point required a borehole, a windmill, a reservoir, lengths of galvanised iron piping, and a number of watering troughs. To estimate the average price of a windmill during the relevant period is not straightforward. The only import quantity data to match with data on prices is that available for 1931–32, when the average landed price of a windmill is calculable as £27.[47] Being depression years this import price was cyclically low, as well as below the retail price actually paid by farmers. So, although confirmatory evidence has still to be sought, a windmill was a substantial investment cost relative to other farming inputs such as land, livestock and the labour required under the old as well as new systems.

From environmental as well as political economy perspectives, the methods used to finance these investments and the distribution of them between large- and small-scale farmers warrant research attention. Firstly, the magnitude of the increase in stocking after introducing camps and artificial water sources is likely to have been linked inversely to farm unit size. By hypothesis, smaller farmers – smaller than the average by size of land holding – had to stock more heavily thereafter because the new investment was a heavier overhead cost burden. Secondly, during income declines caused by downward price fluctuations in wool, meat and ostrich feathers, as well as by droughts, smaller farmers were less able to tolerate lower livestock levels when struggling to maintain income. The fortunes of such farmers and white *bywoners* (sharecroppers) preoccupied policy-makers during the period under discussion. For instance, a major term of reference given by government to the 1923 Drought Commission was to investigate drought effects upon the number of poor whites on the land. Under the shepherding system of extensive grazing, many farms contained outlying *veeposte,* or stock-posts, to which animals returned at night. Because they were often manned by *bywoners*, the new technology made these people redundant and helped to push them into towns and cities. Thirdly, the process of land consolidation into larger units and fewer owners could have been accelerated. Scale economies in raising finance for new techniques made it cheaper for already above-average-sized farmers, and the higher capital value of land embodying such investments in watering points and camps provided security for borrowing on mortgages. By this route the owner could acquire additional land from other farmers, or from the state in western parts of the Karoo during the early decades of the century.

What the net environmental consequence of these differences was between large and small farms concerning the advantages of the new techniques is unknown at this stage. What is clear is that the progress of land consolidation in the Karoo, and therefore ownership concentration, occurred parallel with investment in the new technology in the first half of the century.[48] But what the causal connection is between the two is not known. In the semi-arid areas of Australia, the 1950s was the peak for these investments, although it seems that ownership and management units there even decreased their size in contrast to the South African trend. But the high point of investment activity is likely to have been at broadly the same time in the Karoo because the underlying reason was the same – the Korean War boom in wool prices that generated spectacular increases in farm income.

It was not until the 1950s that very large numbers of water points were established because a series of favourable seasons and high wool prices gave [Australian] pastoralists surplus cash to invest in capital improvements. During this period, property sizes were reduced and fencing of paddocks reduced average flock sizes from the thousands seen in the early part of the century, to a few hundred. Smaller flocks placed less stress on individual watering points and some degree of land rehabilitation was begun.[49]

The [South African] sheep farmer in general made full use of the prevailing favourable wool, pelt and meat prices to stabilise the industry [in the early 1950s] ... The remunerative income of sheep farmers once again enabled them to improve their camping and to apply better veld management ... Although extensive progress in veld management cannot be reported generally, individual farmers have attained phenomenal success. A fairly general awakening to the fact that camps should periodically be rested is, however, noticeable. Farmers are realising more and more that well managed veld ensures a stabilised form of income notwithstanding the uncertain rainfall.[50]

Farming practice

The shepherding system existed for millennia before land was fenced and water supplied artificially. There may have been no other way to manage domestic stock, whether the objective was subsistence or commercial production. For example, 'Before Burburgate was completely fenced [after 1856], seventeen shepherds had charge of the sheep in flocks of a thousand to fifteen hundred,' we are told about the first sheep station to be fenced in Australia.[51] By Karoo standards, where the family farm was still the norm, these Australian flock and farm units were very large and yet the same basic method of operation was applied. The South African version of shepherding and stock outposts has a lengthy history, in that the practice arrived in the Western Cape 2000 years ago, having taken a further 6000 years to travel down the continent from North Africa.

> Sheep farming may have preceded the introduction of cattle by several hundred years [with evidence from] the site of De Kelders near Gansbaai...of the early herding communities using a stock post system to disperse their flocks and culling upwards of 75% of lambs as in modern market-orientated sheep farming...In the new colonial order that emerged...elements of Khoikhoi plant and animal lore, nomadism, and veld management practices were integrated with and facilitated the expansion of the European farming frontier.[52]

Numerous references to the shepherd-and-kraal system before farms were fenced took it for granted, and some stating explicitly, that it was an inefficient practice. The reasons given were broadly the same: it wasted the animal's energy to be herded out in the morning to pasture and home at night to the kraal; dust and manure entered the wool; infections and parasites were easily transmitted between individual sheep, flocks and farms; there was erosion and soil compaction by hoof action, as well as intensive grazing of areas around water sources and kraals; and stock suffered high mortality rates through their direct dependence on the diligence of the shepherd, which was sometimes not forthcoming.[53] Fencing promised advantages under all these heads, but specifically it would allow a higher stocking rate. Evidence by witnesses to the 1889 Select Committee appointed to inquire into the Fencing Act is unambiguous and a representative source:

> 121 Do you think that it would pay to fence any kind of land? – Yes, and I think that the poorer the veld the better it would pay. 122 How many sheep could you graze on a morgen of land in your district [Queenstown]? –

Three. 123 Where you require two morgen of land for one sheep [as in the Karoo] do you think that it would pay to fence such land? – Yes, it would pay the owner of such land better than it would pay me, because sheep tramp about the country, and have to be brought home every night. In a few years the farmer, instead of having to take two morgen of land for one sheep, would be able to double his stock... 126 Will you again state the advantages of fencing? – Yes, in the first place it assists in finding out any stock which may have been stolen, seeing that the thief must either destroy your fence or go out at your gates. In the second place, it allows your stock to run at large, owing to which they are healthier and produce better wool. In the third place, there is returned to the soil a great deal of that which is now wasted and injurious to the homestead – I allude to the manure – and this increases the productiveness of the farm, and enables you to raise more stock; and you also save in the number of [shep]herds who look after your stock... 171 Are the advantages of fencing great? – The advantages of fencing are very great. It increases the amount of stock which land can carry, it prevents the spread of contagious diseases amongst animals, it checks thieving, and civilizes the country, as there can be nothing worth calling a farm until the country is fenced and the farmer has his stock thoroughly under control.[54]

The aim of the research in this chapter is simple: to ask whether and how investment in wire fencing and windmills intensified the ecological degradation of Karoo grazing land. But evidence bearing on it directly is not abundant. Commentators at the beginning of the process assumed the new technology would be profitable because it would *improve* the veld cover, and therefore raise carrying capacity, in the long term through associated changes in farming practice. This presumption can be tested only by consulting farm-level evidence on production procedures and perceptions of resource managers. But the evidence is sometimes ambiguous. For example, an entry in the Wellwood farm diary for 23 October 1926 expresses concern about the effect of the new camp system on the physical condition of the sheep and, by extension, on that of the veld. But it is not clear what the farmer expected realistically could have happened under the old shepherding system with similar adverse climatic conditions:

Sheep averaged 9 lbs 6 oz wool – usual average other years $12\frac{1}{2}$ to $14\frac{1}{2}$ lbs. This quite lowest av[erage] in my records. Under old herding conditions never had such weak yield from good sheep. I gather from this the new knowledge that under free run [inside a camp] a sheep can be made to exist and survive in such a condition of starvation that wool is not produced, whereas under old system of herding the misery of the animal would have ended at commencement of short rations. The lesson learnt is whether this forced salvation of the animal is not going to cause complete demolition of pastorage. (1926 was the record rainless summer.)[55]

Other sources put a figure on the expected increase in the carrying capacity of grazing land. Looking ahead in 1896, 'our idea is that a well-paddocked farm will carry more than one-third more stock and in better condition'.[56] Looking back in 1923 the Drought Commission considered this estimate of the increase in carrying capacity to be a lower bound:

[It] is eloquent corroboration of the evidence of those witnesses who told your Commission how the internal fencing of their farms had so improved their veld as to enable them to carry from 33 per cent to 75 per cent more stock …Evidence showed that, by the adoption of the principle of free ranging [inside camps] an increase of 75 per cent of stock was carried on a certain farm without damage to the veld, which, on the contrary, actually improved. Similar evidence was received also from other farmers.[57]

Environmental change

All environmental historians have to decide which is the relevant past of a habitat, landscape or region, and where in that past baselines have to be established for the purpose in hand.[58] This is not an issue to be approached as a simple preliminary before the real business of historical inquiry. For the research project described here, starting with the emergence of the camp system of grazing over two to three decades, the question has still to be settled. We require a historical reference point for environmental quality in the Karoo, and this in itself is a major task. Two complications have to be noted. Firstly, available secondary sources are sufficient to establish that well before the new camp-grazing practices were instituted observers believed that 'overstocking' was causing deterioration of the veld cover. For instance, writing about the Middelburg magisterial district, which includes part of the Sneeuberg and Colesberg immediately to the north, two Civil Commissioners had the following to say in 1875:

This district [Middelburg] has been celebrated for its sheep walks, but owing to its being overstocked and successive droughts, the capabilities of the pasturage have been reduced. Formerly two sheep could be kept on a morgen, now there is scarcely food enough for one. Enclosing [fencing] would, to a large extent, improve the veld by allowing the sheep to sleep out.

> When sheep were first introduced in this district [Colesberg] the pasturage consisted chiefly of grass and sweet bush, but now the 'bitter bush' and intoxicating melicae, or 'dronk-grass', are spreading in every direction, the former, being of a nauseous character, enjoys immunity and is only eaten by sheep when in blossom, or in cases of dire necessity. The valuable schaap-bosch *Pentzia incana* and other sweet shrubs are gradually disappearing in some parts.[59]

Secondly, in current research on the timing and extent of change in plant composition and 'desertification' in the Karoo, no consensus has emerged. One recent proposition is that the long-term compositional change in the eastern Karoo, 'a broad ecotone between grassland and shrubland vegetation' with the bushes gradually predominating, was already in progress *before* settlement by colonial graziers.[60] Were this the case, then the intensified pressure on the veld a century later, through camp fencing and provision of artificial water sources, would be a new impetus added to a shift in plant composition and density already in progress. Also significant is the qualitative change in grazing patterns that occurred with the incursion of domestic stock in greater numbers when the *trekboere* arrived to displace Khoikhoi nomads: 'Wide-spectrum grazing, which was a result of the range of grazing habits exhibited by the mixed populations of indigenous animals, was replaced by narrow-spectrum grazing by only a few species of animals. Browsing game were either eliminated or relegated to a secondary role because of the predominance of grazers over much of the country.'[61]

If a long-term alteration in these botanical dimensions was already under way, this is intriguing but would not be unique to colonial settlement in the Karoo. Human impact within the sequence of identified causes leading to degradation in the arid lands of the western United States was like a catalyst or trigger within the changes already ongoing, according to one argument. 'This interaction of climatic, geomorphic, and biological factors has been summarized as a "trigger-pull": long-term climatic trends were already underway when cattle arrived to serve "as the trigger-pull that set off an already loaded weapon."'[62] The classic problem of distinguishing between 'slower' and 'faster' variables in the environmental equation arises here. It is not clear under which head forcing the pace of environmental change through new technology is to be classified. Like the farmers who made production decisions in the past with environmental consequences, we observers are inclined to overlook or underweigh outcomes that are less perceptible, familiar and predictable because their cause and their effect are separated by intervals filled with short-duration climatic events. Technological innovations in the middle-distance past – two to three human generations back in the present case – probably have ecological consequences observable only after a considerable time lag. They may be a 'latency phenomenon' accumulating over substantial periods of time, so that the underlying relationships are neither linear nor gradual, but rather spasmodic and prone to flip, as postulated in the state-and-transition model.[63] If so, the changes in technology under discussion would be slow variables rather than fast ones such as drought events, price movements or financial variables such as interest rates.

If the initial research work reported here reaches established conclusions, these should have a bearing on the broader debate concerning Karoo environmental change that goes back to writings by botanists such as Acocks and other commentators nearly a century ago. There are no such results to report yet. But certain distinctions and hypotheses suggested by informants in the Karoo and by the literature on grazing systems are relevant preliminaries to a full historical account.

'Overstocking' is too blunt and ambiguous a concept for understanding how ecological changes have occurred in the past. A number of separate dimensions and practices under that heading have to be distinguished. Defining 'carrying capacity' is a related issue, with its own diversity of meaning and a set of conceptual links with 'sustainability'. Much in these discussions is too abstract and unsettled to be useful in a historical paper. Yet a great deal hinges on the distinction between economic and ecological carrying capacities, not least because it illuminates the possible divergence between individual and communal objectives and between privately efficient and socially inefficient actions in production. This is taken up at the end of this chapter. Here we suggest the minimal distinctions that need noting when devising a baseline to identify the various dimensions of grazing pressure.

Overgrazing pure and simple is livestock numbers per unit area of land per extended time period, so high as to cause 'vegetation change that is deleterious to future animal production'.[64] As said already, the task of choosing an acceptable beginning point – using some plant status yardstick – should be tackled in any historical study, however rough such measurement. But land ungrazed by domestic livestock is extremely rare in the Karoo, and grazing trials in the twentieth century provide evidence of ambiguous relevance to the pre-camp composition of the veld, so what that composition was in different regions is not known with confidence. But what is seldom questioned anywhere about plant communities exploited over lengthy periods of time for commercial production is that, as in Australia, 'very heavy grazing results in a decline in the number of species, a reduction in abundance of the remaining species and dominance by a few species'.[65]

In the Sneeuberg region much debate has concerned the extent, though not the direction, of shrub intrusion within the 'pepper and salt' composition of bushes and grasses, to use Acocks's phrase. This may well have reversed on individual farms in recent times – after the Second World War – with the growth of veld awareness, but the longer-term trend of bush encroachment has certainly fitted international patterns.

> Displacement of grasses by woody plants over the past century has been widely reported for arid and semiarid rangelands...Available data indicate these directional shifts in life-form abundance have been: (i) rapid, with substantial changes occurring over 50- to 100-year time spans; (ii) non-linear and accentuated by episodic climatic events (droughts or above-normal rainfall); (iii) locally influenced by topoedaphic factors [for example, soil slope, elevation, orientation, degradation and displacement]; and (iv) non-reversible over time frames relevant to management.[66]

Continuous grazing practices are livestock consuming plant dry matter on the same unit area of land without seasonal variation or rotation. In other words, there are no rest periods during which domestic animals are denied access to the biomass produced by plants.

Grazing during and immediately after drought is a further dimension of overstocking. This is particularly the case where livestock are sustained by supplementary feeding from outside the grazing unit, or are reintroduced into an area from elsewhere immediately after a drought is broken by rainfall sufficient to initiate regrowth in plants, which are then promptly grazed.

Locally concentrated grazing occurs in the vicinity of homesteads, kraals and water sources as the direct result of management practice. In general this was associated with the shepherding system, and such concentrations were predicted to lessen with the switch to free-range camps containing dispersed stock.

Grazing animals harvest plants non-randomly, so *selective grazing* occurs when the most palatable plants are enabled by climate and management to be eaten at a higher rate than the average on a unit area of land. 'Preferential utilization of plants which vary in their palatability or sensitivity to defoliation can *directionally* alter the nature and intensity of plant competitive interactions and influence population dynamics and hence species composition.'[67] The proportion of preferred species in the composition of plant communities at any one time depends on a range of locational determinants in addition to stock numbers. Principally these are mean rainfall and variability, but also altitude, soil texture, moisture retention, gradient and orientation. For example, north-facing slopes in the Karoo are generally hotter and drier than slopes in other directions, depending on altitude. Given these, 'it is the defoliation management to which the [plant] community is subjected which largely determines both the relative abundance of the individual species and their productivity ... These influences are magnified by differences in the defoliation treatment applied to different plants when grazing is selective.'[68]

These distinctions bring out the complex patterns of botanical composition and herbage quantity and quality, particularly regarding time lags and threshold effects, that could have followed the new wire and windmill technology. Even with the benefit of hindsight we do not know the time profiles of the physical and chemical processes at different hierarchy levels that govern the behaviour of dynamic systems such as the Karoo veld. It is not surprising, then, that decision-takers on the ground – farmers in the main – in the past made choices under high levels of uncertainty. They acted on information premises far from complete or uniform. A contemporary observer appreciates this directly when consulting the opposing sides amongst farmers on the effectiveness of rotational grazing schemes, whether associated with Acocks's recommendations on non-selective grazing or the related set of guidelines termed 'holistic resource management'.[69]

The same decision-problem faces resource managers elsewhere in arid and semi-arid zones. They all strive to maximise the chances of survival and profit in a complex arena in which environmental effects are imperfectly known, specifically 'the resilience of the ecosystem to disturbance and the socio-economic constraints of being able to regularly and quickly manipulate livestock numbers'.[70] As already argued, commercial graziers in arid areas such as Australia and the south-western United States probably faced these decision-problems earlier, because labour was more scarce and the unit scale of operation was larger, so the attraction of a technology promising economy in labour input was stronger. The following Australian account could fit the Karoo:

> The arrival of exotic livestock changed this [Aborigine fire-stick] system of land management irrevocably. Initially, stock numbers increased at a remarkable rate. Overstocking was the inevitable outcome. Typically, an El Niño drought would lead to a complete removal of grass and ground cover, huge stock losses would follow and a swing to a La Niña wet period would foster shrub seedlings and sucker regeneration. This pattern has been repeated at intervals throughout the whole period of occupation by Europeans and their livestock. However, provision of stock watering points, fencing, better adapted livestock and road transport has helped mitigate the effect of drought on livestock production.[71]

The remainder of this section summarises the main themes in the responses of current land-resource managers in the Karoo to questions about the effects on veld cover and composition following adoption of the camp system. Few farmers now living experienced the transition to the new technology, but their answers are informed hypotheses to investigate in a longer-term research agenda. Permission to identify individual informants amongst Sneeuberg farmers and other respondents still has to be negotiated.

Firstly, another technological innovation suggested by respondents that should be brought into the discussion is the railway, which arrived in the region at the beginning of the period under study. The line from Graaff-Reinet to the north was completed in 1898. It had reached the town from Port Elizabeth in 1879 but went no further for twenty years, to the frustration of commercial interests who believed the district failed to benefit fully from the diamond fields boom in the national economy. The suggested ecological consequence of the northern line opening was that farmers were able, during extended dry times, firstly, to import supplementary feed supplies, principally maize from the Free State; secondly, to send their animals to other regions for the duration of the drought; and thirdly, after sufficient rainfall had broken the drought, to purchase new livestock supplies in other areas and rail them back to the Karoo.

According to the testimony of Graaff-Reinet farmers, such new strategies for coping with drought led to earlier and heavier grazing of the regenerating veld. In addition, state policies for drought relief came to include railway rebates and subsidies for the transport of fodder and livestock to and from drought-stricken areas. This was an outcome of the 'politically dominant rural electorate' that existed until the political changes of the 1990s:[72]

Rebates of 50 per cent on the railage of local maize consumed in the Union …and 25 per cent on the transport costs of stock feed to drought-stricken areas are granted. In the case of the forward transportation of stock from drought-stricken areas to better grazing a rebate of 37.5 per cent is allowed which is born by the Central Government, plus an additional 50 per cent contributed by the Railways Administration, with the result that the farmer pays 12.5 per cent only. No charge is made by the Railways Administration in respect of the return transportation of livestock.[73]

Secondly, initially farms were only boundary-fenced, so that an attenuated version of the herding system survived for a while inside such enclosures, in sheep-farming areas particularly where jackal and lynx predators caused substantial losses and so necessitated the continued use of shepherds. But with the internal subdivision, through additional watering points from windmills and jackal-proof fencing, the free-range camp system came fully into being. Contemporary farmer respondents assert that the original objective was to include a variety of vegetation types within each separate camp in order to provide a range of alternative food sources for stock in different seasons. This increased the opportunity available for herbivore preference; that is, the process of selective grazing, and probably thereby the pace at which veld composition changed towards fewer plant species and greater homogeneity in ecological functions.

Thirdly, the existence of camps made proper rotation of stock feasible for the first time, and facilitated therefore a decrease in the practice of continuous grazing per unit area irrespective of season or climate. Theoretically this is true, but in fact the initial philosophy amongst graziers, although what proportion of them is not known, was one of no rotation on the grounds that sheep and cattle would thrive best when they became thoroughly familiar with their own camp environment.

Fourthly, greater numbers of watering points, or *suipings*, more dispersed in free-range camps, led to lesser concentrations of stock, but it also allowed more sustained grazing during droughts, so that fewer animals died. This means that the veld cover then suffered greater stress, *ceteris paribus*, than was likely to occur under the old herding system with its higher stock mortality. Sufficient evidence for this suggested difference between the old and the new practices, if observed by farmers at the time, has still to be assembled. An example of what is required is the 1926 entry from the Wellwood farm diaries quoted earlier.[74] This hypothesis about drought effects under the camp system is supported by a recent Australian study:

> Artificial supplies of water have become so common and reliable in the arid and semi-arid zones that the term drought has taken on a functionally different meaning. Water is available ad libitum to most mobile vertebrates … Now, grazing animals do not abandon land that was once naturally waterless, but continue to graze the perennial vegetation that survives during long dry periods. But because the vegetation does not grow very much without rainfall, perennial grasses and palatable shrubs can be removed over large areas.[75]

Despite the early predictions of higher stocking rates, as in the Drought Commission report of 1923, and the fact that stock numbers nationally did peak in 1930,[76] the net effect of the camp system on the magnitude of 'simple' overgrazing, defined earlier, remains ambiguous as a single cause. But it seems clear that the new grazing method did provide farmers with scope for manoeuvre to expand the stocking rate in the short term to take advantage of increased demand for mutton and wool. This occurred for instance during the mining boom commencing in the 1870s, the rapid economic growth of the 1930s after South Africa's departure from the gold standard, and the Korean War wool price rises of the 1950s. Conversely, the same new opportunity to raise numbers existed if falling prices of farm outputs put pressure on farm livelihoods, as is documented for Australia.[77]

Fifthly, a more subtle possibility is that the camp system caused greater degradation through mistaken 'light' stocking, because it accentuated the inherent tendency towards plant selection by animals as described above. According to one informant, when herded under the old grazing scheme stock were more hungry at the start of each day, having spent the night shut up in a kraal for between ten and fourteen hours, depending on the season. They were then shepherded to the water and most convenient grazing areas in a relatively tight group and not allowed to wander. The upshot could have been that animals grazed less selectively:

> You can see this behaviour when we open the gate, under Acocks [rotation system], to begin grazing another camp... When fencing came in, the stock were left in the camp day and night; they could thus wander where they wished, eat what took their fancy, and this led to selective grazing... On [the farm I inherited] was a camp of about 200 morgen that my dad said was solid rooigras [*Themeda triandra*], with just a footpath in which they used to ride their bicycles. 'What happened to the rooigras I don't know, because all we kept there was a horse or two', said my dad. Now that's not overstocking, but severe overgrazing [of selected plants]. Try and tell that to these scientists! (Sneeuberg farmer, written response.)

Finally, termites common in the Karoo are contended to have played a role in the changing composition of the veld from grass to shrubs. Although not directly linked to the introduction of the camp system, it has been argued from evidence for the western Karoo north of Ceres that when their staple, the grass component, diminishes, termites turn to roots of shrubs for their food sources. They thereby accelerate the destruction of vegetation cover and thus accentuate the shift towards diminished density independently of current grazing practice once the trend is in progress towards increased shrubbiness at the expense of grass (Cape Town informant).

Conclusion

This chapter has outlined initial findings concerning the environmental impact of new forms of technology adopted in the Karoo in the closing decades of the nineteenth century. It is the first stage of work on a larger scale which seeks greater depth of evidence on the questions posed here. What is striking is the dimensional complexity and time depth involved.[78] We are dealing with communities of organisms that interact internally while responding to external biological and physical events, such as rainfall, grazing and management strategies. So it is no wonder that we do not yet possess the source materials for a 'reasoned history' of environmental change in the Karoo. But it would be a mistake to be inhibited until such time as the multiple disciplines required can be marshalled to answer these questions.

Three broader comments will add final perspective. These concern the limits on the information available to resource managers and observers, both then and now, as well as the incentives and socio-economic constraints which they faced. Firstly, there is the challenge to explain why private owners adopted practices which led in most cases to the accelerated destruction of their greatest asset, the natural capital of their land. This was not an 'unmanaged commons' in that no land in this region of the Karoo was in the relevant period a common property resource, as conventionally understood. Such a resource is one where users are co-equal in their rights to use it, and from which potential users who are not members of the group of co-equal owners are excluded.[79] Since permanent settlement commenced at the end of the eighteenth century, private property rights attached to land titles have allowed free disposal by inheritance or sale.

Succeeding generations of owners bequeathed to their heirs capital assets in land which they believed to have retained their economic value, or even increased in value with prior investment in the technology discussed here. This was because ecological damage through biodiversity loss and soil destruction did not manifest itself in economic terms, specifically not in resource prices that reflected fully the opportunity costs, being the value of productive uses forgone. In general, decision-takers on the land did not receive the signals necessary to react in the ways required to conserve ecological integrity. Nor did they have individual incentives to obtain information about the ecological value of their capital. By inference, the mix of market forces and state policies failed, and failed dismally with the new techniques of grazing, to reflect the flows and accumulation of costs stemming from the managerial decisions on land use. This information deficiency was historically not unique to the Karoo by any means, and there are highly likely to be political economy reasons as well for the retention of what is a perverse system:

> The reason it [sustainable use of biodiversity] has not been more widely adopted is ascribed very clearly to 'perverse incentives', that is, to being made relatively uncompetitive through the use of tax breaks, subsidies, price

controls and distorted property rights. The underlying reason for many of these perverse incentives is to ensure that control of the resources is retained by those in charge, so that they can more easily appropriate the profits.[80]

This directs attention to the probability of conflict if private users of natural resources are to be compelled in the future to take account of the social costs of their actions. This would arise because of the difference between their goals as enterprises, being economically sustainable land use, and the regional or national goal of ecologically sustainable management to maintain functions such as water quality, biodiversity, aesthetic values, and non-consumptive activities. At the latter scale, larger than the single ownership unit, multiple land uses that require such functions, for example tourism, are apparent but may not be perceived at the scale of the individual land holding.

What institutional reforms will best achieve this in the Karoo are not simple to forecast. After eight or more generations of commodity production for the market it would be surprising not to find presumptions and mindsets similar to those identified in the United States. There the arid and semi-arid West has a shorter history of commercial stock-raising than the Karoo, but the ecological movement is undoubtedly more powerful. Yet today 'even if there is no ecological justification for livestock grazing in some areas there is a strong cultural tradition supporting it'.[81] This means that 'an important role, perhaps the most important role, for conservation biologists is to find ways to protect biological diversity on lands that are being managed to achieve other objectives'.[82]

The second point of perspective concerns the state-and-transition model and the non-equilibrium hypothesis already discussed. If these are valid, then how is our perception of the Karoo ecosystem, as exemplified in the Sneeuberg region, affected by them? One implication of these paradigms is that, viewed in this manner, such a system modifies its own possible states as it alters over time, a process known as hysterisis. Thus its history, the path it followed up to the present, determines directly what future states are open to it. For instance, at distinct values of variables such as grazing pressure on an increasing path the system may jump (or flip) into a new state. Once there, it will not revert back merely by adopting the opposite strategy of decreasing this pressure, as commentators such as the Drought Commission quoted earlier sensed to be the case. For instance, states of the Karoo ecosystem that result from the removal of livestock may be quite different from their starting character because of soil loss, the presence of exotic species, interference with natural fire regimes, or for other reasons producing hysterisis effects still to be identified. Thinking along such lines in the context of this research work, one can ask whether the adoption of windmill and wire technology forced the pace of degradation and loss of resilience so far and so fast that the system has flipped? If so, the return of the Sneeuberg environment to an approximation of its structural and functional condition before the damage was done may not be possible, and it would be prudent to acknowledge this possibility.

On the question of whether the north-eastern reaches of the Karoo fit the non-equilibrium end of the typology of grazing lands in which there is weak animal–plant interaction, there is neither the evidence nor the space for an adequate discussion here. It is enough to note the generalisations (1) that all ecological systems fall somewhere on a continuum from equilibrial to non-equilibrial; (2) that translating metaphors for system behaviour (quoted throughout this chapter) into testable hypotheses for field use by ecologists is not an easy task; and (3) that major conceptual and methodological questions about the rival paradigms of arid and semi-arid grazing lands remain to be resolved.[83]

Thirdly, there are suggestions in the literature, and in what can be interpreted as the first moves by resource managers, that 'sustainable habitation' be substituted for direct use of the land as a new goal in regions of the world where conventional agriculture is perceived by many people as failing to meet their needs. The proposal is that a complex of mixed land uses will diminish the productive significance of grazing by one or only a few herbivore species. Diversity in herbivore populations would not only exploit the vegetation heterogeneity but also broaden the consumptive (hunting and culling) and non-consumptive (tourism) optional uses of the habitat as a whole.[84] There is observable evidence that this process has commenced in the Karoo, although still on a minor scale. Commercial hunting, private nature reserves and tourism are income-generating activities pursued there in the past two decades for hard-nosed economic reasons. The *real* price of wool (removing the effect of inflation), still the main marketed product and income determinant of the region, is at a historic low at the moment, so farmers have had to seek alternative land uses as a survival strategy.[85]

These are all ambitious issues to raise. But they do not imply that ecological restoration should be demoted to being a secondary goal until we can explore them fully. What they do is bring to the fore the realisation not only of the amount of investigative work to be done, but rather of the kinds of social adaptations referred to earlier. If Australians are deliberating seriously about the desirability of decreasing the number of artificial water sources in their arid regions, then it is feasible that South Africans might come to think along the same lines for the same ecological reasons. This will require a new 'governing myth' for the Karoo, as it is labelled in one American case study: 'The emergence of social learning as an approach to the Columbia [River] can be understood as a change in governing myths, a shift in the way people imagine their place in the natural landscape they inhabit.'[86]

Chapter Nine

'Our irrepressible fellow colonist': The biological invasion of prickly pear (*Opuntia ficus-indica*) in the Eastern Cape, c.1890–c.1910

Lance van Sittert

The European Diaspora which followed in the wake of the 'great discoveries' of the fifteenth century is an acknowledged watershed in both the natural and social sciences. For the former it marks the collapse of previously discrete bio-geographical realms and the onset of an ongoing process of human-induced and -facilitated 'biological invasion' of 'natural ecosystems' world-wide.[1] Social scientists too regard it as heralding the start of the military, economic and cultural invasion of 'indigenous societies' by Europe and their forcible incorporation into the emerging capitalist global economy.[2] In a bold but flawed attempt at interdisciplinary synthesis, Alfred Crosby coined the term 'ecological imperialism' and argued that Europe's 'portmanteau biota' of plants, animals and pathogens was more important than its technology in facilitating the conquest and settlement of the 'Neo-Europes' of the temperate zones.[3]

Although natural science acknowledges human agency, and social scientists biological agency in the making of the modern world, neither are entirely comfortable with these admissions. Natural scientists treat human agency as an unwelcome extraneous variable for which the evidence is incomplete, qualitative and immune to experimental manipulation. Consequently, humans' role in abetting or combating biological invasions is widely acknowledged but otherwise ignored in a search for the physiological, demographic and genetic characteristics of the 'ideal invader'.[4] Conversely, biological agency readily suggests environmental determinism to practitioners of disciplines wedded to the notion that human beings make their own history, albeit not in conditions of their choosing. Hence Crosby's subordination of biological to human agency, stressing translocation and environmental disturbance by the latter as the key determinants of biological invasion. The result was a naïve biological Eurocentrism that denied any reciprocal invasion of Europe by plants, animals and pathogens from the colonies in order to preserve the cherished primacy of human agency in the historical narrative.[5]

The respective biases of disciplinary praxis have effectively foreclosed any critical engagement by either discipline with the concepts borrowed from the other. For social science practitioners, this requires, firstly, recognition of the culturally determined nature of all 'biological invasions'. The notion that Europeans encountered pristine nature anywhere in the 'new worlds' has been thoroughly discredited and the hand of the indigene everywhere revealed moulding, with fire, spear and hoe, of ecosystems blithely assumed by the first European observers to be 'natural'.[6] In southern Africa evidence of *Homo's* hand can be traced back 1.5 million years through an archaeological record littered with extinctions and alien introductions, and ecosystems adapted to fire.[7] Secondly, if notions of 'natural' ecosystems are illusionary, so too is the quest for their nemesis, the 'ideal invader'. Instead of a fruitless search for innate biological qualities of effective 'invaders', the term itself might be more usefully regarded as just one in a lexicon of cultural labels used to denote an organism whose presence out of place in a particular time conflicts with the perceived interests of human health, subsistence, profit or aesthetics. Thus yesteryear's beneficial import becomes today's 'invader', and the anthropomorphic death sentence of 'vermin' and 'weed' is even-handedly pronounced over alien and indigenous species alike when and wherever they threaten human interests.

Biological invasions are thus intrinsically historical processes primarily shaped not by the biology of the invader, but by the shifting cultural values and practices of the invaded society, as demonstrated by the prickly pear (*Opuntia spp*) 'invasion' of the Eastern Cape c.1890–c.1910. The historical context can be written shorthand as colonial and capitalist, but to reduce opuntia to just another example of the inevitable environmental despoliation caused by humanity's Faustian pact with Mammon is to risk being boring and simply substituting economic for biological determinism. In a recent critique of the prevailing utopian Luddite orthodoxy in the environmental history canon, Frank Uekoetter proposed an alternative 'organisational approach' in which 'the definition of an environmental problem always results from the perception of a divergence between objective natural conditions and certain political, economic or cultural norms and values'.[8] The historian's task, he ventured, was to explain how such problems come to be perceived and defined, constituencies mobilised for and against reform, decisions made and implemented, and the consequences of action assessed. In short, just as there is no pristine 'nature' for natural science to defend against invasion, so, Uekoetter suggested, there is no objective 'interest of nature' against which environmental historians can measure humanity's use of natural resources now or in the past.

Genesis

Few plants, other than domestic crops, have tracked the European Diaspora as closely as the more than 120 species of platyopuntias, or 'prickly pears'. Members of the Cactacea family native to the Americas, the peculiar physiology of *Opuntia* (hereafter, simply 'opuntia') was conventionally explained as a series of evolutionary adaptations to aridity. Jenzen, however, has made a compelling case for the role of an extinct Pleistocene megafauna in moulding opuntia's morphology and distribution, a niche now filled by imported European herbivores after a hiatus of 10 000 years.[9] Opuntias were also extensively harvested and cultivated for food, ritual and other uses by pre-Columbian human inhabitants for 9000 years before the arrival of Europeans. The Aztecs are reputed to have founded their capital on a site indicated by a vision of an eagle perched on an opuntia and prized the plants as hosts for the cochineal scale insect from which they extracted a rich red dye. Columbus took opuntia plants back across the Atlantic to establish plantations in Spain and the Canary Islands, which supplied Europe with carmine dye until their ousting by cheap annaline dyes in the nineteenth century. From Spain, opuntia spread eastwards through southern Europe (Italy, Sicily and Greece) and, following the expulsion of the Moors in 1610, North Africa and the Levant to India.[10] From the Indian subcontinent, the plant is purported to have made its second transoceanic crossing in the late seventeenth or early eighteenth century, in the holds of Dutch East Indiamen, to the newly established refreshment station at the Cape.[11]

There opuntia's armoury of sharp spines recommended it to beleaguered Dutch colonists as a 'living fence', but it remained a garden curiosity in the agrarian south-western Cape, where it never spread far from human habitation. This awaited opuntia's transport into the more favourable pastoral environment of the eastern Cape Colony. According to settler oral tradition collected in the 1890s, a farmer called Van der Berg journeyed to Cape Town from his farm on the Camdeboo and returned about 1750 with two opuntia leaves, which bounty he shared with at least one of his neighbours.[12] Other anonymous introductions followed, and by the 1770s travellers to the region reported the 'cactus' being used by settlers both as a 'living fence' and to distil a home-made brandy.[13] Opuntia's escape from domestic captivity was abetted by its fortuitous introduction into a favourable environment coinciding with the historical moment of overlay by an expanding colonial frontier.

The Eastern Cape is a loosely defined 'region of transition' lying between the Gamtoos and Kei rivers and Great Escarpment and Indian Ocean. The chief physiographic features are bisection on an east–west axis by the mountain chains of the Cape Folded Belt, the remnant escarpment or 'Winterberg–Amatola line' and Great Escarpment, and on a north–south axis by the deeply trenched courses of the Gamtoos, Sundays and Fish river systems and their myriad tributaries. The climate is transitional between year-round and summer rainfall regimes and the vegetation shades from Karoo into grassland moving west to east. The Cape Folded ranges cast their rain shadow over the heart of the region up to the foot of the Winterberg–Amatola line, and 'the Intermediate Lands…are thereby robbed of a great deal of the precipitation which they would probably receive but for this shadow effect'.[14]

The Eastern Cape was also a cultural 'transition zone' between indigenous hunter-gatherers, pastoralists and farmers, and European colonists. The latter began arriving in the region in numbers in the late eighteenth century and fought ten 'frontier wars' against the indigenes between 1778 and 1878 to roll the colonial boundary back to the Kei River. This process was accompanied by wide-ranging transformations in the regional environment. Scorched earth was an integral part of the military campaigns which levered Africans off their land, and pushed the colonial boundary steadily northwards. In their wake, the land was converted to private property and seeded with European settlers, stock and crops, swiftly enmeshed in a widening commercial web of credit, roads and (later) railways centred on the new market towns of the interior and Port Elizabeth.[15]

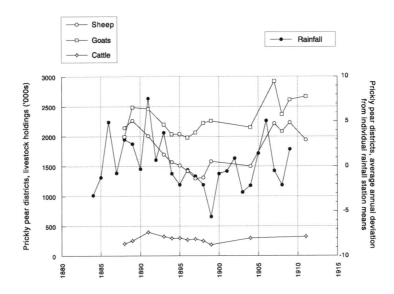

9.1 Eastern Cape prickly-pear districts: stock-holdings 1888–1910, and average annual deviation from mean rainfall, selected stations 1884–1909[16]

The cornerstone of this economy was small-stock farming with woolled sheep and goats – more than three million animals by the mid-nineteenth century – whose selective grazing, daily 'tramping out' and nightly kraaling rapidly stripped the land of its original vegetation cover and initiated widespread soil erosion.

Opuntia was imported into the heart of the arid swath of territory between the Cape Folded Belt and 'Winterberg–Amatola line' in the mid-eighteenth century where it encountered a similar environment to that which it had adapted to over the *longue durée* of evolutionary time in the Americas. These adaptations included minimal investment in structural tissue and root systems, the development of flattened photosynthetic stem portions (cladodes) instead of leaves, and use of crassulacean acid metabolism (CAM) to fix carbon at night with a minimum of water loss. This enabled opuntia to propagate itself vegetatively by means of its cladodes and survive extended periods of severe water stress. Thus the cladodes remembered by the oral tradition made the long journey from Cape Town and took root in the Camdeboo, where their descendants maintained themselves through subsequent droughts which native plants survived only in seed form.[17]

The time lag between introduction and spread of an alien species has been variously ascribed to genetic, demographic and environmental factors, but only impressionistic accounts can be gleaned from the historical record. These suggest opuntia 'did not make much progress except as a cultivated plant' before the mid-nineteenth century. It was missed more often than recorded in the wild by visiting botanists and landscape artists and ignored by legislators, who identified *Xanthium spinosum* (burrweed) as the main alien botanical threat to commercial stock-farming in the Colony as late as 1860.[18]

When opuntia did start to flourish beyond settler gardens, farm yards and fence lines, it did so on the rising tide of human and animal traffic inundating the region – the multiplying flocks' daily tramp from kraal to veld and back, the quickening pulse of commerce along expanding road and rail arteries, and the secret beat of baboons, *bywoners* and black squatters – and everywhere seized the ground denuded, eroded, compacted or neglected by the teeming throng. By 1889 H.A. Bryden, evoking the landscape of an Eastern Cape farm, could no longer overlook opuntia, denouncing it as 'that Mexican marauder' which 'propagates and spreads itself with alarming readiness…and once it attains a strong hold…is well-nigh impossible of extermination, neither fire, poison, nor the knife effecting its downfall'.[19]

In its native America, opuntia benefited from the spread of commercial livestock ranching through increased seed and cladode dispersal and the suppression of competitors by trampling, overgrazing and fire, which enabled it

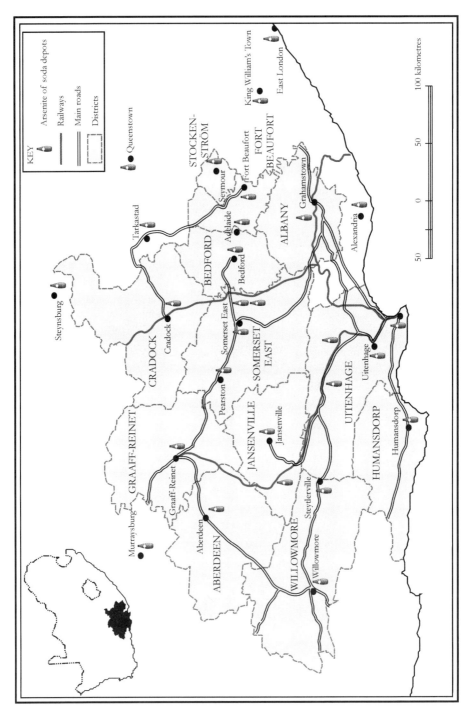

KEY

Arsenite of soda depots
Railways
Main roads
Districts

100 kilometres

Queenstown

King William's Town
East London

STOCKEN-STRÖM

Seymour

Fort Beaufort
FORT BEAUFORT

Grahamstown

Tarkastad

BEDFORD

Adelaide

ALBANY

Alexandria

Steynsburg

Bedford

CRADOCK

Cradock

Somerset East

SOMERSET EAST

UITENHAGE

Uitenhage

GRAAFF-REINET

Pearston

JANSENVILLE

HUMANSDORP

Humansdorp

Jansenville

Murraysburg

Graaff-Reinet

Steytlerville

Aberdeen

WILLOWMORE

Willowmore

ABERDEEN

9.2 *Eastern Cape 'prickly pear districts', c.1895*[20]

to expand its range rapidly, especially during periods of drought.[21] In the Eastern Cape, opuntia was reportedly able to grow in any soil, on rocks and 'almost anywhere where it is not wanted, from a galvanised iron roof downwards' and its advance was often imperceptible.[22] Noted one early inquiry, 'the plant…after having been for many years in a district, seems to obtain a complete mastery, although in the first instance no fear whatever is entertained respecting it'.[23] This insidious spread could accelerate sharply during periodic drought crises when opuntia advanced from the margins to colonise and suppress the sweet veld prized by stock-farmers.[24] 'Some plants will grow for a number of years and there will be no signs of their spreading over the neighbouring land', reported one farmer, 'but a time comes which seems favourable to the plant and then it spreads with great rapidity.'[25] Frost alone checked its inexorable march at the Winterberg–Amatola line and made it 'essentially the weed of the Karroo, of the dry bare uplands and of dry climates'.[26]

Here opuntia 'spread…systematically over the face of the country', became 'a characteristic feature of the landscape' and undisputed 'lord of the soil' by the end of the century.[27] The siting of farms along watercourses throughout the region allowed cladodes to spread independent of human agency, surfing rivers swollen by seasonal floods to new localities downstream. Thus the 'great flood' of 1874 was blamed for spreading it from Cradock down the Fish River such that the confluence of the Baviaans and Fish rivers was reportedly an 'impenetrable jungle' of opuntia by 1890.[28] Nor did the plant depend solely on its cladodes for propagation, but produced an annual crop of seeds densely packed in fleshy pear-shaped fruits attractive to wild animals, domestic stock and humans alike. By this means it spread far beyond the confines of farms and river courses to all corners of the countryside. Frugarious birds, baboons, monkeys, wild pigs, porcupines, dassies and even jackals were reportedly fond of the fruit and excreted seed over a wide area, opuntia clustering under trees and dotting krantzes wherever wild animals laid up. Farmers responded by destroying its accomplices out of hand, particularly the baboon.[29] Despite this, the plant crossed fence lines, rivers and mountain ranges in the guts of its animal consumers, germinating from seeds softened by ingestion and embedded in dung to appear in new areas far distant from its known range.[30] The vast multitude of settler domestic animals – horses, cattle, sheep, goats and ostriches – also acquired a taste for opuntia fruit and helped to spread its seed over the veld, outspans and road networks, where it sprouted 'from the droppings of cattle as thick as grass'.[31] During droughts stock gorged on opuntia for want of other grazing and officials identified the 1859 drought as marking the onset of opuntia's rapid spread, owing to the fact that 'fences were not in vogue at the time, and stock had more liberty to roam over the country, and in their travels deposited the seed in their excreta'.[32]

Although 'utterly despised' by the colonial bourgeoisie, who deemed it 'a disappointing *morceau* when all is said and done', opuntia fruit was widely consumed as an exotic import by their fellows in England – 'The oddity of the fruit provokes English curiosity, and the cool watery sweetness with a mingled flavour of cucumber and melon prevents it being set down as insipid' – and as a summer staple by settlers and blacks in the Eastern Cape where its harvesting and sale was a major source of seasonal employment.[33] In the process, cladodes and seed were spread far and wide. Farmers were reported to 'go four or five hours to farms to get the fruit, with which they make a kind of preserve for eating purposes and they take the fruit away in wagon loads... by that means the seeds are taken to the farmer's own homes'.[34] In addition, 'coloured people cut off the leaves with the fruit on them and carry them to gather off the fruit; and wherever the leaves are left they grow' and 'The blacks wander around from farm to farm selling the fruits to farmers at sixpence a hundred. The fruit and skin and seed are thrown anywhere, and if the ground is rich the young plants soon grow up.'[35] By the early 1890s opuntia was synonymous in the minds of progressive farmers and state officials with 'kraals and native huts', and said one settler, 'Where ever the Kafirs live there you will find the prickly pear taking root.'[36] Railway workers were the other favourite culprits, accused of 'gathering the fruit and by means of trolleys and other means running bags of fruit up and down the rails, and so spreading the prickly pear to another part of the country'. As a result, opuntia could be found clustered around 'platelayers cottages' and all along the Graaff-Reinet–Uitenhage line.[37]

Opuntia's biological endowment of drought resistance, vegetative propagation and extensive seed dispersal facilitated its metamorphosis from a 'very good servant' in the West to 'an extremely hard and cruel master' in the East, but always in the shadow of settler disturbance of the Eastern Cape environment.[38] By the end of the nineteenth century this shadow had lengthened sufficiently for even settlers to detect the dark pall they everywhere cast over the land. The president of the Upper Albany Farmers Association, T.T. Hoole, warned his fellows in 1904 that

during the last thirty years certain districts have entirely altered in appearance and have depreciated in every way as stock farms; properties that were at one time covered with succulent herbage, and capable of carrying large herds of stock, are now growing bitter karroo and poisonous plants and unable to carry one half of their former stock ... The effect of this pernicious system [of stock-farming], if continued for another fifty years, will result in turning what may be a prosperous district into a howling wilderness ...[39]

As progressive farmers became increasingly aware of their own hand in the gradual transformation of the landscape around them, so opuntia intruded from the margins to the centre of Hoole and his ilk's troubled gaze. Glimpsed through this lens, with its particular distortions of race, class and profit, opuntia no longer appeared as a curiosity or occasional summer bounty, but a direct menace to the very foundations of an already depressed pastoral economy; burdening farmers with the escalating costs of stock losses and eradication, discouraging and corrupting black wage labour, and swelling the ranks of poor whites by eroding land values and carrying capacities.

Panic over the pear

Organised and influential, progressive farmers' 'constant agitation' over opuntia reverberated through parliament in the early 1890s, articulated by Eastern Cape members – themselves stock farmers – in freely mixed moral (evil), medical (infection) and military (invasion) metaphors.[40] They urged the colonial state to take immediate action against opuntia to save the pastoral economy from the threatened ruination of its stock-holdings, labour and pastures and protect the nascent class and racial hierarchies erected on this foundation. W. Gerard Hobson of Jansenville district reckoned 'the prickly pear pest ... the third worst curse our colony is suffering from' after scab and veld deterioration caused by 'kraaling' stock against the 'carnivora plague' and F. Douglass, a member of parliament, warned that, if unchecked, opuntia 'in a very few years ... would have half the farming population in the country in a state of poverty'.[41]

Progressive farmers claimed, firstly, that opuntia not only supplanted the Karoo vegetation but caused widespread injury and frequent death to their domestic stock which grazed it with great relish during droughts and the annual fruit season. The spines and acidic succulence of the cladodes mutilated and purged already weakened cattle, sheep, goats and ostriches, while the fruits' covering of fine hairs 'scoured out' the digestive systems of healthy animals with often fatal consequences.[42] They conservatively estimated the annual stock lost to opuntia at a round £200 000, but hastened to stress that to this must be added the indirect costs of the plant's demoralising effect on labour and destruction of carrying capacity and land values in the region.

Opuntia, they maintained, allowed blacks and poor whites to elude wage labour for half the year by harvesting and selling the fruit crop.[43] Hundreds went out into the countryside each summer for this purpose from Graaff-Reinet and at Jansenville: 'The prickly pear is a staple article of diet for the natives during certain times of the year ... whole families often going together to gather the fruit

...either for their own use or to sell to the village inhabitants'.[44] The cheap and abundant fruit was also prized by blacks and poor whites for brewing 'villainous compounds' which were consumed at 'drunken orgies' and rendered them unfit for labour.[45] Meanwhile, 'vagrants', 'squatters' and 'wandering natives' took up permanent residence in the opuntia thickets, subsisting on the fruit and stock theft. The thickets along the Plaat and Vogel rivers were reportedly a 'nest of thieves' where rustled stock from Cradock and surrounding areas were hidden and butchered in partnership with 'mean whites'.[46] '[S]o suitable and safe an asylum does this jungle offer', said one official of the numerous opuntia thickets throughout the region, 'that when within its boundaries these thieves can practically defy detection as there they can live for weeks on their plunder and the fruit of the plant, or if necessary on the fruit alone.'[47] In the opinion of progressive farmers, 'The Kafirs and the poor whites are the people who are the friends of the prickly pear...where the prickly pear grows there they live.'[48]

Lastly, opuntia cut deep into the material base of the settler economy – land – rendering it unfit for pastoral farming. In its spreading wake, the carrying capacity and market value of private farms and public land collapsed – by up to three-quarters in the worst-affected areas – and owners and occupiers were literally forced off by the plant's advance.[49] '[I]f the owner of a place does not take out a prickly pear on that place', warned one, 'the prickly pear is sure to take him out in course of time.' Those who ignored or delayed heeding this advice found that the cost of eradication soon exceeded the declining value of their land.[50] Debt, subdivision and tenancy also sapped the means and incentive of many farmers to resist.[51] Some attempted to eke out a living by harvesting the fruit and leasing the land to black squatters, but others 'trekked' or abandoned farming for itinerant employment in the rural economy. Reviewing more than 30 years of farming in the Jansenville district in 1898, C.G. Lee recalled:

> farms that used to carry one sheep to the morgen, and even more than that. They cannot now carry anything at all. People cannot farm, and the places are practically abandoned. They have left off trying to cope with the prickly pear, and they are living from hand to mouth, going from bad to worse, and becoming degenerated. Many of them are Europeans...who now have to work for somebody else...they are going out as herds, and are doing fencing work for other people.[52]

Progressive farmers saw in poor whites' complicity in the illicit opuntia liquor and stock trades further evidence of their 'degeneracy' and deemed them 'a threatening danger to the country' by the close of the nineteenth century.[53]

For all these reasons progressive farmers maintained 'the time has now come for the state to associate itself with the private individual in endeavours to exterminate the Prickly Pear' by passing a law which made eradication compulsory and provided for state financial and labour assistance to the needy and expropriation of the indifferent.[54] The existence of 'a certain class of people who cannot see their own interest, as is proved by the objections to the Scab Act' made such drastic measures necessary, they maintained, for 'If one man cleans his land and his neighbour does not, all his labour is lost' and recalcitrants, 'when they are compelled to do what is necessary for their own interest … afterwards see the benefit'.[55] 'A law on the subject was very much wanted', explained one Legislative Council member, 'if it was only for protection from people who would not do anything without a law.'[56] These same people's votes also influenced field cornets and divisional councils to render unpopular permissive legislation – such as the abortive Xanthium Spinosum Act and relevant sections of the new Divisional Councils Act – dead letters.[57] Responsibility thus rested squarely on the colonial state to deal with opuntia's menace to the commercial stock industry in the same way as the phylloxera threat to Western Cape vineyards – by enacting compulsory legislation and voting generous financial assistance.[58]

Opuntia's genetic mutability and popular utility, however, combined to frustrate all attempts by progressive farmers to spur the colonial state to legislative action. When refracted through a Linnaean prism, 'prickly pear' yielded a seemingly infinite spectrum of subtle variations which defeated the best efforts of botanists and lawyers at complete description. The opuntia family's 'great readiness to hybridize among themselves and produce cultural varieties' was well known from their long cultivation as curiosities in Europe, spawning a 'very intricate and unsatisfactory' botanical literature marred by 'great confusion in the nomenclature' and a profusion of species 'described as new which are probably only varieties or abnormal forms of the same species'.[59] Similar confusion reigned at the Cape where local botanists could agree on neither the number nor identity of naturalised opuntia species.[60] One frustrated official feared 'there would be no end of inventing new names for this variable plant, and certainly no practical advantage could be gained by it', and 'fail[ed] to see that even from a botanical point of view we are justified in South Africa in recognising more than two varieties'.[61] He thus proposed jettisoning professional botany's Tower of Babel for the simple folk-botanical dichotomy of 'doornblad' ('thorn leaf') and 'kaalblad' ('naked leaf') to designate in law the plant species intended by the state for destruction.[62]

The naming of opuntia in the rural patois, however, reflected not only long intimacy, but also the plant's multiple utility within the rural economy, contrary to claims by progressives that 'vermin, thieves, and destructive animals...are the only live creatures that benefit by the prickly pear'.[63] Wrote one Somerset East farmer: 'I get on very well with the prickly pear. I feed cattle, horses, and ostriches and all animals therewith in times of drought, and I can send you samples of vinegar, sugar, syrup, and dried prickly pear all made from the fruit; and I am of opinion that there is nothing better in this country.'[64] 'Doornblad' varieties, being better armoured and bearing sweeter 'pears' than the 'kaalblad, were prized for quick-growing live fences and windbreaks as well as their fruit'.[65] The fruit, in addition to being eaten fresh and preserved, was used to produce alcohol, yeast, vinegar and syrup. Officials familiar with this bounty marvelled at the 'light and delightful perry...distinct from the Kaffir-beer'; yeast 'specially convenient in its mode of use, keeping well and producing excellent bread and cakes'; vinegar 'clear brown piquant with a distinctive but pleasant taste'; and syrup comparable to commercial golden syrup or molasses, requiring 'the addition of a little chicory or ginger – to destroy the wild flavour' and noted for its laxative properties.[66] By contrast, 'kaalblads' or less thorny opuntia hybrids were cultivated for their hardiness and succulence throughout the Karoo to provide winter fodder for cattle, ostriches and pigs and emergency grazing for sheep and goats during droughts.[67] The cladodes were harvested, stripped of their light thorn cover by hand or machine, and mixed with small quantities of grain to combat the plant's diarrhoeic effect. An opuntia diet allegedly maintained stock in good condition – pigs fattened, cows continued to produce milk and ostriches raised chicks – through periods of otherwise fatal dearth in natural grazing.[68]

For all these reasons a cross-section of settler opinion within and beyond the Eastern Cape regarded opuntia as 'more of a necessity than an evil' and was implacably opposed to any legislation compelling its eradication.[69] The member of parliament for Richmond, A.S. le Roex, for example, cultivated opuntia as fodder for his ostriches and pigs, and harvested the fruit for drying and the manufacture of vinegar and syrup. 'I would not be agreeable to have the pear taken out where I live under any circumstances', he bluntly informed a parliamentary select committee. 'It is a plant that is worth a great deal.' His sentiments were echoed by other Karoo farmers-cum-parliamentarians.[70] Proponents of the 'kaalblad' even went so far as to assert that it was the original form of opuntia and the 'doornblad' a 'degenerated' local 'sport'.[71] They wondered, 'If a number of lazy farmers had allowed wild oats to get the upper hand in some of our grain-growing districts down West, would that be sufficient reason to pass a law that no more oats were to be grown in the Colony?' and appealed to 'legislators [to] eradicate the thorny prickly pear if they like, but *give us a chance* with the thornless'.[72]

Parliament was only too happy to grant their request. The deep division among white farmers over opuntia and a conservative estimate of £500 000 to eradicate it from half a million morgen in the Eastern Cape effectively killed support for compulsory legislation among members fearful of the political and economic repercussions of such action.[73] Thus in 1906 the Director of Agriculture again refused a Prickly Pear Act on grounds that 'it would be a hardship to farmers…and unfair towards the general taxpayer'. The preferred alternative of legislators and civil servants in Cape Town was to devolve responsibility to the countryside by placing permissive legislation in the dead hands of local authorities even less willing or able to grasp the nettle than the centre. The noxious weed provisions of the 1889 Divisional Councils Act were twice amended and extended to native locations before 1910, but still only mentioned the old enemy *Xanthium spinosum* by name and left it to divisional councils to request the Governor to declare additional plants weeds.[74] Very few bothered before the 1900s and then only three, two bordering the prickly pear districts, proclaimed opuntia a noxious weed.

Instead, official attention shifted decisively away from devising legal mechanisms for compelling eradication to discovering ways of cheapening its cost. Conventional wisdom held that 'the spade and the pick-axe alone could do the work', but the high cost of labour – 'anywhere from 5s to £5' per morgen depending on the terrain and degree of infestation – made manual eradication ruinously expensive.[75] The development of commercial 'scrub exterminators' to combat opuntia in Australia held out new hope of a cost-effective means of eradication and parliament promptly voted funds for the Department of Agriculture to test their effectiveness under local conditions.

Poisoning the pear

Manually eradicating opuntia from a farm was a laborious process stretching over several years.[76] 'The bulk of the labour is in cutting the trees and the leaves', reported one farmer, 'because prickly pear is a big plant. It is very heavy, and every portion of it has a leaf and a stem as well.'[77] Under optimal conditions individual opuntia could grow to twice the height of a man and weigh up to a ton. Stumps and roots also had to be 'grubbed up' to prevent their putting out new growth. Burying, though preferable, was seldom practical owing to the hard Karoo soil and the dismembered plants were instead piled in heaps on beds of kindling and left to rot.[78] When terrain and transport allowed, huge stacks, containing 40 to 50 Scotch cart loads, hundreds of yards in length and tens of feet high were built.[79] These heaps had to be tended to clear cladodes rooting round the edges, and smaller piles regularly turned to ensure decomposition. It took up to three years for opuntia's succulence to drain away in death and the heaps become sufficiently desiccated to burn. The final immolation returned the site to productive use, but care had to be taken not to incinerate any fruit, as fire stimulated seed germination and rendered the area unusable for several more seasons until all the new plants spawned by the conflagration had been eradicated in their turn. Once cleared, constant vigilance had to be maintained and the process repeated at regular intervals to prevent opuntia from re-establishing itself on a farm.[80]

The labour intensity of the eradication process made it so expensive that even wealthy farmers balked at the prospect. 'On one occasion, when I found that on one of my farms the prickly pear had taken root and was spreading', explained one, 'I tried to bargain with a party of natives to clear it, but found that they would not do it under three times the value of the land.'[81] Unable to afford cash wages, poor farmers were forced to depend on 'families of natives who for clearing a fixed extent of land are allowed to locate on various parts of the farm with the right of grazing their stock'.[82] All requests for cheap convict labour were refused and, in desperation, many farmers experimented with available toxins – including salt, oil of vitriol, creosote, caustic soda and 'sundry carbolic sheep-dip preparations' – to poison opuntia, but with little success.[83] The 'germs of life' proved extremely difficult to extinguish in a plant known colloquially as 'Kan niet dood' ('cannot kill') for its remarkable 'virility'.[84] To stock farmers, already making increasing use of poison to control ticks, acari and carnivores threatening their flocks, a chemical 'scrub exterminator' promised freedom from the crippling labour costs of 'grubbing up' and a return of land to grazing in a matter of months rather than years by destroying the plant *in situ*. No poison ever delivered on this claim, however, and the few that came close threatened to destroy not only opuntia, but all attendant land, livestock and labour into the bargain.

The first remedies were imports: R.J. Murchison of Melbourne's 'Scrub Exterminator', fresh from purported triumphs over opuntia in Australia and India, and a range of British-manufactured garden weed killers (Smith's 'Perfect' Weed Killer, Eureka and Atlas).[85] Despite the high hopes of members of parliament and best efforts of the Department of Agriculture, the latter was forced to concede glumly in 1893 that 'none of the solutions used and applied … possess … any material advantages as regards destructive merits over the usual method of eradicating the plant viz. uprooting by manual labour'.[86] Although the poisons usually managed to destroy existing plants, they seldom killed all the cladodes, which were shed in response to chemical attack and generated new opuntia, often in even greater numbers than before.[87] Official investigations did, however, reveal white arsenic to be the 'active principle' in the imported specifics and arsenite of soda as a cheap and effective substitute which destroyed felled opuntia within weeks and reduced the labour costs of eradication by up to half.[88] The publicity given arsenite of soda by the settler press, official journal and evangelising work of the local agricultural assistant, A.C. MacDonald, saw it eagerly embraced by wealthy

9.3 Grubbing out opuntia[89]

farmers as the panacea for opuntia.[90] 'The labour saved by the use of the chemical can hardly be conceived,' wrote one early convert, 'besides which your land is saved from being cut up by the carting process, as of yore.'[91] 'The Government extirpator is one of the greatest helps our colony has had,' another enthused, adding 'or rather it will be in a few years if the Government import large supplies.'[92]

The Department of Agriculture began importing arsenite of soda direct from the Apothecaries Hall, London, in 1893, relying on eliminating middlemen and a preferential shipping rate to distribute it to Eastern Cape farmers at half the cost price of £25 per ton. Variations in the annual budget and a 'spasmodic and very erratic demand' made supply and distribution 'irregular and unreliable' and five years later it was reported that arsenite of soda's 'benefits have been comparatively small and wholly inadequate to the requirements of the case'.[93] The showcase successes of progressive farmers were not emulated and did little to check opuntia, which gained ground everywhere during the dry 1890s, overwhelming ordinary farmers too enfeebled by recession and drought to either afford arsenite of soda or otherwise resist opuntia's spread. Indeed, many relied on opuntia as a makeshift fodder, refusing to poison it and even cultivating the plant for feeding purposes. In a desperate bid to stanch the spread of opuntia and haemorrhaging of whites from the land, the colonial state commenced distributing arsenite of soda 'gratis' in 1899.[94] Applicants were restricted to a maximum of five cases (675 lb) for which they had to arrange transport from the depot, sign a guarantee to use the chemical only on opuntia infesting their land as directed, and report progress before receiving any additional supplies. By year end, 60 tons of arsenite

Table 1: Cape colonial state arsenic of soda purchases, 1893–1910[95]

Year	Tons	Estimate (£)	Expenditure (£)	Receipts (£)	Price (pence per lb)
1893–94	26	1000	1006	34	2.5
1894–95	30	1000	880	122	22.5
1895–96	17	600	537	448	2.5
1896–97	0	350	218	338	2.5
1897–98	20	1000	762	311	2.5
1989–99	40	1000	1589	–	free
1899–00	52	2000	2195	–	free
1900–01	40	4000	2336	–	free
1901–02	0	2500	41	–	free
1902–03	20	1500	846	–	free
1903–04	90	1500	1769	–	free
1904–05	70	1500	1584	–	free
1905–06	20	1	1674	626	2.57
1906–07	?	1500	402	?	2.57–2.58
1907–08	?	1	1511	?	3.75
1908–09	?	1000	?	?	3.75
1909–10	?	1000	?	?	3.21–2.94
Totals	425+	£21 452	£17 350+	£1874+	

of soda had been distributed on this basis – nearly two-thirds the amount sold at half the cost price over the previous five years.[96]

Arsenite of soda – 'a most virulent poison' – was potentially as lethal to farmers' land, livestock and labour as the intended target, opuntia. The Department of Agriculture alone distributed sufficient by 1910 to prepare around ten million gallons of poison. Quality was variable and storage a major problem – the dry powder being liable to explode when damp, and liquid poisons to settle out of solution and corrode their drums, which were notorious for leaking.[97] Arsenic caused 'considerable injury…to thorn trees, shrubs, and herbage' surrounding opuntia thickets or heaps, and officials claimed farmers were inclined to 'waste it on the veldt', blighting the very land they were trying to reclaim for productive use.[98] The side-effects on livestock could be equally severe, but fatal poisoning was only rarely diagnosed owing to crude autopsy techniques, manufacturers' spurious disclaimers and the stigma of 'carelessness' attached to such admissions.[99] Labour too was extremely vulnerable to poisoning and, although arsenite of soda was most effective when the 'sap was rising' in opuntia, one farmer warned his fellows to '*On no account* allow men to work with the arsenite of soda in the summer, although it kills more readily then, it will also poison the men, the spray vapour rises from heaps and gets into workmen's eyes and onto their hands and faces, consequently your men are all disabled for weeks'.[100] Symptoms included severe skin burns – 'a painful and unpleasant rash, developing into yellow watery pustules' – suppurating finger nails and asphyxiation.[101] The only known prophylactic was 'aprons of canvas, well rubbed with fat, and the hands and arms... similarly protected', and milk was the only antidote.[102] The number of fatalities is unknown, but the cause of a 'boy's' untimely death was unlikely to be more accurately determined than that of livestock, where economic self-interest at least ensured a more than casual concern.

The hidden costs of arsenic of soda were ignored by the state and stock-farmers committed to waging all-out chemical warfare on opuntia. At the end of 1899 one official gleefully reported that Eastern Cape farmers – 'who have been handicapped so unfairly by the Prickly Pear incubus, perhaps for half their lifetime' – had at last 'caught on' to arsenite of soda and 'everywhere I was besieged with questions as to what I had observed of successes against the pear plague in places where I had been to ... The interest in the matter was very general, and so lively as to show that there is every intention on the part of the questioners to turn the experience of their neighbours to account.' The results were reportedly everywhere visible:

> The traveller by rail through the Midlands can see for himself in every direction piles of the extirpated pear heaped up to rot and dry off, after having been killed by the exterminator; and for miles where the land used to be so thick with this plague that it could not carry stock, there is absolutely not a living prickly pear to be seen.[103]

Such triumphalism proved premature, however, as the South African War and post-war depression first blunted and then forced the abrupt termination of the chemical campaign against opuntia by a cash-strapped colonial state in 1905.[104] A Boer guerrilla passing through the Camdeboo in 1901 was forced to traverse a 'terrible cactus-belt that girdles the foot of the mountains' comprising 'a veritable forest of this vile growth, standing twenty feet high in places'.[105] Required to once more purchase their arsenite of soda – initially at cost price – farmers simply refused, forcing the Department of Agriculture to hastily reinstate its old policy of selling the chemical at half the cost price. The scrapping of the 100 per cent subsidy and subsequent price increase in arsenite of soda brought a host of local folk poisons onto the market masquerading as 'scrub exterminators'. Each bore the name of its 'inventor' who kept his 'recipe' a closely guarded secret and hired a lawyer to try and extort financial rewards, endorsements and other concessions from the state.[106] The 'preparations' came in a variety of forms, strengths and applications but, like their predecessors in the 1890s, all shared the same 'active principle' – arsenic – combined with a bewildering array of other substances intended as much to create a distinct brand identity (red oxide) as enhance their efficacy (caustic soda), the latter often being impaired by the former. All shamelessly repeated the hoary old boast about destroying opuntia *in situ* at lower cost than arsenite of soda. The result was often acrimonious wrangling between inventors over ownership and officials over the effectiveness of the new specifics.[107]

By 1910 the Department of Agriculture had tested more than ten new 'scrub exterminators' in the hope of discovering 'a remedy simpler, cheaper and more effective than the present process', only to report despondently that 'The experiments have brought to light no talisman for extirpating prickly pear, but have clearly demonstrated the superior efficacy and cheapness of Arsenite of Soda'.[108] Despite holding its own against all competing 'proprietary preparations', the 'Government exterminator' remained so 'laborious, slow and expensive' to use that – even when free – it seldom paid to clear land for grazing.[109] The search for a chemical talisman to the opuntia chimera thus continued, and in 1910 the Department of Agriculture went so far as to purchase the 'secret' recipe of one proprietary preparation following a successful trial and publish it in the official journal.[110] The Department's main role, however, was to protect farmers from unscrupulous snake-oil salesmen by conducting field tests to refute their often outlandish claims and confirm the superiority of arsenite of soda.

Utilitarian visions

Not everyone, however, regarded opuntia as an evil to be exorcised from the land and alternative schemes proliferated for 'turning the tables on the erstwhile plague' by utilising the plant to rehabilitate the rural economy or as raw material for new colonial industries.[111] The immigrant German horticulturist H. Fehr planted thousands of opuntia on his farm in the King William's Town district from the mid-1890s and blamed the prior failure to cultivate opuntia for its fruit on 'extreme carelessness, the South African habit to leave things alone to get on as best they will or can, a happy go lucky' and boasted that 'With a penknife 10,000 O[puntia] can be kept in order the first 4 or 5 years and guided exactly as wanted'.[112] Such optimism was shared by other eccentrics and charlatans alike, spawning a host of commercial propositions similar to Fehr's. Some – such as grafting vine stocks onto opuntia stumps, using opuntia for the manufacture of soap, paper, brandy and industrial alcohol, or employing opuntia to control soil erosion – received short shrift, but others, to convert opuntia into fodder, garnered considerably more attention.[113] Part of the reason was environmental: the drought conditions prevailing throughout the Eastern Cape during the decade 1894–1904 made opuntia a vital 'famine food'.[114]

Thus an Albany correspondent reported in 1895 that 'The plant has now become almost indispensable to the farmers, especially during the present drought, tons of leaves being used to feed ostriches, cattle, and pigs...several farmers are cultivating the Kaalblad for use in dry weather'.[115] The same was true in Oudtshoorn where, five years later, 'farmers offered a shilling for a bag of leaves and could not get them at that, whilst many sent their mule and ox wagons long distances to get leaves...several have decided to plant it now they have discovered its value in time of drought'.[116] By the end of the drought decade even the Department of Agriculture was reluctantly forced to concede that 'This plant makes such excellent stand-by fodder it seems a pity that someone does not go in for propagating the spineless variety with a view to its permanent establishment as a crop'.[117] Opuntia's succulence may have given it a biological advantage over indigenous vegetation during droughts, but it was the utility of succulence to beleaguered stock farmers that facilitated its speedy proliferation under such adverse circumstances.[118]

Farmers, although traditionally hostile to the notion of 'working for their cattle', increasingly cultivated fodder crops such as lucerne and clover and were keen to find a crop capable of withstanding drought.[119] The government botanist, Peter MacOwan, who described opuntia as 'our irrepressible fellow colonist', proposed they look no further than the 'Opuntiaries of the Midlands' and claimed that, by adopting the preparation methods pioneered by Australian and American stockmen, it was possible to 'clear a depreciated, pear-curst piece of land, and raise a mob of cattle at the same time' without recourse to arsenite of soda.[120] Subsequent analysis confirmed what farmers already knew – that opuntia was more than ninety per cent water and little else – but as one official pointed out, 'There is plenty of it to make up in quantity for any deficiency of quality, and the problem is, how to render these hundreds of thousands of tons of stock-food available for that purpose instead of it remaining a source of ruinous loss and endless expense incurred in its destruction.'[121] The solution was left largely up to individual farmers and, while the majority continued to strip cladodes of their thorns by manual and mechanical means, a few innovators experimented with steam-cooking, brazing and ensilage techniques learned from abroad via the official journal.[122] With the return of the rains in the mid-1900s, however, official and popular interest in opuntia fodder dissipated in the continued search for a chemical talisman to the bane of the Midlands.[123]

Nature and culture

Opuntia's designation as a threat to commercial stock-farming at the Cape was neither instantaneous nor unanimous, but rather a gradual transformation from utility to weed as the plant traversed space (west to east) and time (seventeenth to nineteenth centuries), entering new natural environments (Karoo for Mediterranean) and economic arenas (market for subsistence) more conducive to its rapid spread. Even then, its definition as 'evil' reflected class and regional biases not shared by either the rural poor of the Eastern Cape (whether black or white) or stock farmers above and west of the Winterberg–Amatola line who prized and frequently cultivated the plant for subsistence and fodder. This division and widespread non-compliance blunted official extermination efforts and left the matter unresolved by the end of the colonial period. Thereafter, opuntia's location on the cultural continuum between 'weed' and 'crop' continued to shift; in the direction of extermination when new biological (*Cactoblastis cactorum*) and chemical (DDT) controls were discovered,[124] and of domestication during periods of severe economic stress when the plant was socially rehabilitated as drought fodder and, most recently, employment provider and cash crop.[125]

This explicitly cultural explanation for opuntia's spread has been privileged over alternative 'biological' and 'apocalyptic' readings to make two basic theoretical points about environmental history's strengths and limitations as an interdisciplinary enterprise and practice as history.[126] That tireless crusader for an interdisciplinary and activist environmental history, Donald Worster, has recently hailed the field as 'a small doorway' in 'the wall that separates nature from culture, science from history, matter from mind' and called for 'genuine dialogue and a new openness in all the disciplines' arising out of the current tentative 'conversation' between science and history.[127] While crediting science with making historians 'see beyond the realm of culture', Worster urges science to reciprocate by 'historicising' its praxis and model of nature as well as recognising the need for historians to help it see beyond the realm of nature.[128] This is a bold but disingenuous challenge which denies both 'the truly profound methodological differences between the two cultures' and its own ideological commitment to an ecocentric notion of nature 'for itself'.[129]

Certainly, prevailing scientific theories of 'biological invasion' discount both humanity's role in such events and the way the events themselves are culturally determined. As Crosby reminds us, 'Weeds are not good or bad; they are simply the plants that tempt the botanist to use such anthropomorphic terms as aggressive and opportunistic.'[130] This theoretical blind spot is particularly problematic in ex-colonial societies such as South Africa where the extent of recent human disturbance of the natural environment is widely acknowledged and hotly debated by scientists, and a recent botanical review of the subject found 'it...difficult to discriminate between the effects of human activity and other historical factors on the one hand and the role of ecological interactions on the other in determining the patterns and rates and invasions by introduced plants'.[131] In this context, environmental historians' glib presumption of interdisciplinary competency and spurious claims to unique intellectual or moral vantage points on the spectacle are unlikely to further the 'conversation' with science.[132] A more useful approach would be to take the 'methodological differences between the two cultures' seriously and admit the limits of the historical record, which does not permit a 'biological' reconstruction of opuntia's spread at the Cape. Science's methodological requirement for quantification and prediction can, however, be nuanced and enhanced by incorporating qualitative historical data (for example, socio-economic indicators or folk botanical classifications) into scientific models of 'biological invasion'.

There is also a rich irony in Worster lecturing scientists that 'what we mean by nature is inescapably a mirror held up by culture to its environment, a mirror reflecting itself', while seeking to rally them in defence of biodiversity and sustainable development against the prevailing 'world view of materialism'.[133] The latter is no less a cultural construction of nature than the scientific models Worster berates for their ignorance of history, although it deceitfully 'pretends to define ecological problems purely from the standpoint of nature'.[134] As critics of ecocentricism have pointed out, 'unless one adopts a mystical or religious standpoint, there is always a human interest behind the attitude that nature should be left out there "for itself."'[135] Worster's position is both dishonest and innately hostile to science as the handmaiden of materialism and thus unlikely to promote interdisciplinary exchange through his 'small doorway' when what is being sought is not conversation, but conversion.

A more useful basis for meaningful dialogue would be the materialist position that humanity's lot is to simultaneously participate in and seek to dominate nature. Here all talk of harmonious coexistence is utopian and what has to be decided by all historically existing human cultures is the appropriate form of transforming nature. It is in this context alone – not in reference to some external standpoint of nature – that environmental problems arise. 'In the process of coping with them it is likely that the problems will not be abolished completely but only reduced, transformed and displaced. It may also be the case that the cultural forces shaping the perception of these problems will change. Consequently the definition of what counts as an ecological problem will change.'[136] Uekoetter's organisational model attempts to operationalise this theory by abolishing all ecocentric shibboleths and encouraging environmental historians to practise what they preach by historicising humanity's relationship with the non-human world.

C h a p t e r T e n

Fire and the South African Grassland Biome

John McAllister

Almost as indispensable as oxygen and water in making life on earth possible grass is the source of most of our food and covers one quarter of the earth's land surface.[1]

The South African Grassland Biome covers an area of 343 216 square kilometres or 27 per cent of South Africa. It is of major importance to the stock-farming industry in South Africa. The entire Maize Triangle falls within the biome, with 34 000 square kilometres being planted to this crop. South Africa's major gold and coal deposits are found there. The biome supports the highest urban population density in South Africa and includes the large urban areas of the PWV (Pretoria–Witwatersrand–Vereeniging) complex, the Witbank–Middelburg coal fields of Mpumalanga, Bloemfontein and the gold fields complex of the Free State, and Pietermaritzburg and the Newcastle–Ladysmith complex of KwaZulu-Natal. The eight power stations on the Mpumalanga highveld alone produce 70 per cent of South Africa's power requirements.[2] Most of the 15 000 square kilometres planted to alien trees in South Africa comprise transformed grasslands.[3]

Earlier grassland researchers in South Africa would have us believe that the vegetation in the South African Grassland Biome would revert to that of its neighbouring biome were it not for the management practices implemented by 'Man' from the San hunter-gatherers to modern-day farmers. In other words, these practices have resulted in grasslands invading formerly afforested or wooded areas.[4] Over the past decade, however, there has been a growing school of thought that maintains that the grasslands are, in fact, an ancient vegetation form that covered as much as 60 per cent of Africa. The forests and present-day 'savannahs' have in fact invaded these grasslands and are still in the process of doing so.[5] Fire in particular plays a major ecological role in the Grassland Biome.

It has done so since at least the Pleistocene[6] and probably a good deal earlier.[7] Authors in the past believed that these fires were anthropogenic in nature, whereas today many researchers believe that they are primarily a result of climatic conditions. In view of the importance of the biome to South Africa this chapter examines the validity of these opposing views. In order to enter into the debate on fire in grasslands, one needs to have an understanding of the causes of major fires within the biome.

Anthropogenic fires

Fire may have been used by australopithecines in southern Africa 800 000 years ago.[8] Primitive humans probably refined the use of fire into an art – an art that 'was not only used for very definite purposes that were valuable to them, but was virtually necessary for their existence'.[9] From evidence gleaned at hearths associated with Early Stone Age artefacts at sites in Zambia and the former Northern Transvaal (Kalambo Falls and Makapansgat respectively), it can be inferred that fire was used as a tool (for clearing fields or for attracting wild animals) in southern Africa to some extent by Early Stone Age peoples.[10]

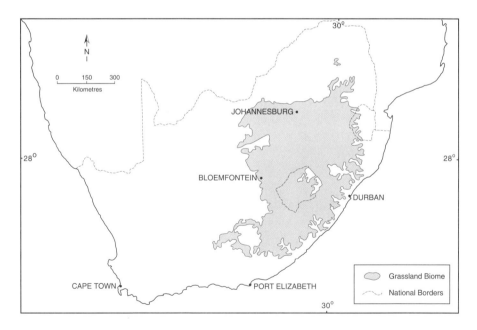

10.1 The Grassland Biome

Source: adapted from Rutherford, M.C. and Westfall, R.H. 1986. Biomes of Southern Africa: an objective classification. *Memoirs of the Botanical Survey of South Africa.* 54: 1–98.

However, no such evidence could be found at other Early Stone Age sites in southern Africa.[11] This could indicate that while fire was used as a tool during the Early Stone Age it was used more prolifically by the Middle Stone Age. Burning would have been carried out by these early hunter-gatherers wherever and whenever there was sufficient accumulation of combustible fuels, that is in seasonally dry grasslands or savannahs.[12]

There is much evidence to show that fire has been used as a tool by Stone Age peoples as part of their hunting techniques or to improve the quality of edible plants in grasslands and open savannahs. There is, however, no evidence that these peoples manipulated the production of combustible fuels. These anthropogenic fires occurred mainly as substitutes for lightning or physically induced fires.[13]

There were Iron Age farming communities in the Grassland Biome from about AD 1000. Burning was probably carried out by these farmers in much the same way as their Stone Age predecessors, but the new grass growth obtained after a fire was used to provide grazing for domestic stock rather than to attract wild game to the area.[14] Burning in the winter rainfall region by white settlers dates from 1652, but burning by colonial farmers in the grassland and savannah biomes of the summer rainfall regions only commenced after settlement of the Eastern Cape by the 1820 Settlers and of the Orange Free State and Transvaal by the Voortrekkers after 1836.[15]

Lightning as a causal agent of fires

Evidence of lightning-induced fires in South Africa is conflicting. Some authors consider that lightning plays or has played a significant role as a causal agent of fires in grassland.[16] The South African Secretary for Forestry supplied Komarek – an American researcher into fire and its effects on natural vegetation – with figures showing that eleven per cent of plantation fires in the South African Grassland Biome between 1957 and 1970 were caused by lightning. Komarek felt that there would have been even more lightning-induced fires had the vegetation still been natural grasslands.[17]

By contrast, other authors consider lightning to be insignificant in causing fires in the biome.[18] Nevertheless, it would seem that lightning-caused fires are more common in years of good rainfall than in dry years, with fires being more common in spring in wet years and during early summer in dry years.[19] The importance of lightning-induced fires in South Africa may well be obscured by current land use and management practices.[20] In contrast to the South African evidence, reports from the United States Forestry Service indicate that as much as 90 per cent of all American forest fires between 1945 and 1966 were caused by lightning: there were between 700 and 2700 lightning-caused fires per annum during this period in these forests alone.[21] The incidence of these fires would be expected to be far higher in the savannahs and grasslands of Africa, but it is kept low by heavy stocking rates of domestic animals, which reduce the body of combustible fuel.[22] In a study conducted to establish the relationship between vegetation and lightning strikes it was found that the highest density of lightning ground-strikes (up to a mean of 16.2/km²/year) occurs on the higher-lying grasslands.[23] This is closely followed by other grasslands, which suggests that the potential for lightning fires must be relatively high in the Grassland Biome. The results also correlated well with the importance of fire, or the lack of it, in the other South African biomes. Late spring and the summer months of November and January have the highest incidence of lightning strikes.[24]

There is little evidence of other physical factors leading to combustion of vegetation and thus being a cause of fires. As there is no current volcanic activity in South Africa, this cannot be a source of fires in the country at this time. Edwards notes fires caused by rock falls in the mountainous areas of the Cedarberg and the Drakensberg, but feels that fires caused by rock falls are limited to such areas and this factor is unlikely to be a significant cause of major fires in the Grassland Biome.[25]

The argument for anthropogenic fire being the controlling factor

As mentioned before, many authors on the biome considered that the South African Grassland Biome was seral to the neighbouring Savannah (open wood-land or bushveld), Fynbos (macchia), Forest and Karoo (arid scrub) biomes. According to these authors the Grassland Biome comprises, for the most part, a collection of fire climax grasslands where, should fire be excluded, the natural succession would progress towards the vegetation of another biome. The majority of these authors imply that anthropogenic fires are of overwhelming importance to the continued existence of the biome.

Grassland veld types were separated into 'pure' and 'false' grassveld types. 'Pure' grassveld types were climatic climax grasslands, whereas the 'false' grassveld types were kept seral to savannah by fire and other human activities.[26] On the black clay soils of the former Eastern Transvaal, which had been protected from fire and grazing for fifteen years, the succession was from a *Themeda triandra*-dominated grassland to one dominated by *Setaria nigrirostris* (another grass species).[27] The study plots were near the towns of Bethal and Standerton in a veld type known as Veld Type No. 52 – *Themeda* Veld. This veld type was considered to be a 'pure' grassland that was not seral to any other vegetation type.[28]

The Grassland 'Formation' – called thus as it was argued that the grasslands could not form a biome as they were artificially maintained as grasslands by anthropogenic fires – was divided into two major divisions: climatic climax grasslands and fire climax grasslands. These divisions were further apportioned into a number of subdivisions: high- and low-altitude climatic climax grasslands, fire climax grasslands of potential forest areas (again further subdivided into high- and low-altitude areas), and potential Savannah areas.[29]

In the early 1980s the Grassland Biome Project study area was defined. Here it was stated that even the 'pure' grasslands of Acocks should not be considered to be climatic climax grasslands. It was argued that the *Themeda-Festuca* Alpine Veld (Veld Type No. 58) represented a fire climax vegetation seral to heath. The fact that highveld grassland, protected from fire and grazing, becomes moribund rather than advances successionally to a woody community should not necessarily be attributed to climatic limitations. 'Given a source of seed,' it was argued, 'and usually with disturbance to the soil drainage pattern, woody plants grow.' Thus these grasslands, too, were kept in a seral state by anthropogenic fire.[30]

The mid-1980s saw another grassland classification. It was suggested that five categories of grassland existed based on the successional status of the vegetation: Afro-Alpine grass-heath communities; montane forest-grassland communities; grassland communities of potential savannah areas; vlei (wetland) communities; and arid to semi-arid grassland communities. Of these only the last was considered to be a 'true' or climatic climax grassland. The first four categories were thought to be seral to various other biome communities as follows:

– The *Afro-Alpine grassland* was seral to an Alpine fynbos community of *Erica-Helichrysum* heath.
– The *montane forest-grassland* was seral to forest, and fire played a major role in maintaining the grassland. Both forest and fynbos were confined to refuge sites and this was taken to indicate that the natural succession, in the absence of anthropogenic fire, would be to fynbos or forest. In the southern parts of this area it had been shown how fire could be used to control invading fynbos.[31]
– The *grassland of potential savannah areas* was seral to savannah and includes Acocks's 'False Grassveld Types'.
– The *grassland of vlei communities* was considered to be seral to 'hydrophytic' woodland communities.
– The *semi-arid grasslands* were the only grasslands recognised as climatic climax grasslands and even here some were considered seral to savannah or karoo.[32]

The invasion of the Dohne Sourveld (Acocks's Veld Type No. 44b) in the Eastern Cape Province by fynbos was considered to be the result of incorrect veld management and was cited as an example of how the exclusion of fire resulted in grassland reverting to fynbos. It was felt that the elimination of controlled burns for management, together with overgrazing the grassland, had allowed the veld to revert to fynbos.[33] One reported case of grasslands reverting to savannah comes from the 1920s. The Springbok Flats north of Pretoria were formerly grasslands with *Acacia* species dotted here and there. The area supported large herds of springbok – a typically grassland antelope – which now no longer occur there. While there were still areas of open grassland on 'the Flats' in the 1920s these were rapidly being invaded by *Acacia* species. This was attributed to plant succession and the exclusion of fire mostly by the European farmers who had recently settled the area. Prior to this, it had been the practice of the African communities to burn the area on an annual basis. The grassland here could apparently not survive without anthropogenic fire and reverted to a savannah.[34]

Much evidence was presented to show that grasslands would revert to forests if anthropogenic fires were excluded. Two grassland veld types, the Highland Sourveld and the Dohne Sourveld (Veld Types No. 44a and No. 44b), were included under the category 'Temperate and Transitional Forest and Scrub' as they were considered to have been 'forest and scrub forest' as recently as AD 1400. They had been transformed into grasslands through anthropogenic fires.[35] It was widely felt that fire confined forest and fynbos vegetation to refuge sites in the Natal Drakensberg area. This was purported to be a direct consequence of management fires that were set during winter when the vegetation was tinder-dry. The resultant fires were of such a high intensity that they damaged the woody vegetation and thus artificially prevented it from recolonising the grassland.[36] A commission of inquiry held in 1923 had condemned burning in catchment areas, and consequently fires were artificially excluded from many of these areas between the mid-1920s and the early 1960s. By the end of this period the virtual exclusion of fire from the Drakensberg catchment areas had resulted in an expansion of the area covered by woody plant species.[37] This was seen by some as proof that these seral grasslands should be forested areas.

While it was realised that many of the current doctrines were not compatible with a growing body of evidence and research, it was still felt that there was a climatic climax in 'pure' grasslands and a 'biotic' climax in 'false' grasslands. 'False' grasslands were maintained as grasslands through 'biotic' factors such as grazing and anthropogenic fires.[38]

The argument for fire being a *climatically* caused controlling factor

The Grassland Biome of today was likely to have been far more extensive in the Pleistocene. While some areas of the Grassland Biome may well have supported forests during the wetter periods, the 'temperate mixed grassland' of southern Africa would have expanded greatly during these periods. It was likely that during the drier periods of the Pleistocene the same grasslands would have retreated to the montane grasslands of the Drakensberg.[39] Although he was a protagonist of the theory that South African grasslands were maintained by anthropogenic fires, Acocks himself suggested that the invasions of fynbos and Karoo vegetation into the grassveld were the result of the farming methods employed. Nowhere is it stated that these invasions were caused by the exclusion of fire. On the contrary, much mention is made of the excessive use of fire as being a contributory cause to veld degradation; that is, contributory to the degradation of existing grasslands by invasive woody vegetation rather than the expansion of artificially created grassland.[40]

Killick emphasised that natural fires had been a factor in the grassland environment 'ever since the climate induced a dry season'. This precluded the presence of forest in the Highland Sourveld as suggested by Acocks.[41] Any theory concerning the presence of recent continuous forest in this veld type 'faces the difficulty of explaining the widespread, almost ubiquitous distribution of *Themeda triandra*, a grass with poor powers of dispersal'.[42] This grass species occurs in the Grassveld, Savannah, Nama Karoo and Fynbos biomes, but *not* in the Forest Biome. It is postulated that the widespread occurrence of this grass species may be an indication that the extent of the Grassland Biome was once far greater than it is today, as suggested by Cooke.[43]

Remains of typically grassland animals as old as 8000 years have been found in the floor deposits of caves in the Natal Drakensberg in Acocks Veld Type No. 44a: Highland Sourveld. It seems strange, to say the least, that typically grassland species such as Grey and Redwinged Francolins should have centred their distribution on what was, according to Acocks, forest or scrub forest only 600 years ago.[44] Archaeological studies in the Transkei in Acocks's Veld Type No. 44 (Highland Sourveld and Dohne Sourveld) showed the claim that the grassland vegetation here is human-induced to be unfounded.[45] This veld type coincides largely with Tainton's high-altitude fire climax grasslands, which he maintained were seral to forest.[46]

During the mid-1980s it was at last demonstrated that climate and climatically induced fire, not anthropogenic fire, is the controlling factor determining the extent of the South African Grassland Biome. A biome was defined as being the largest land community unit recognised at a continental or subcontinental level, mappable at a scale of no larger than 1:10 million, distinguished from other biomes *primarily* on the basis of dominant life form(s) in climax systems and *secondarily* on the basis of major climatic features and not an unnatural or major anthropogenic system. For the primary separation of South African biomes on the basis of dominant life forms, Rutherford and Westfall made exclusive use of vegetation and used the following life forms:

- *phanerophytes,* which have elevated bud-bearing shoots exposed to the atmosphere;
- *chamaephytes,* which have bud-bearing shoots close to, but above, the soil surface;
- *hemicryptophytes,* which have bud-bearing shoots at the soil surface;
- *cryptophytes,* which have the bud-bearing shoots below the soil surface; and
- *therophytes,* which are annual plants that survive the unfavourable season in the form of seed.

On this basis seven biomes were distinguishable in South Africa, these being:

- Forest Biome, where phanerophytes are dominant;
- Succulent Karoo Biome, where chamaephytes are dominant;
- Grassland Biome, where hemicryptophytes are dominant;
- Desert Biome, where therophytes are dominant;
- Savannah Biome, where phanerophytes and hemicryptophytes are co-dominant;
- Nama Karoo Biome, where hemicryptophytes and chamaephytes are co-dominant; and
- Fynbos Biome, where chamaephytes, hemicryptophytes *and* phanerophytes are co-dominant.

There was no biome where cryptophytes were a dominant, or even co-dominant, life form.

Rainfall, both the annual total and the seasonality of that rainfall, and temperature were found to be the most important climatic factors influencing vegetation growth and development. Computerised rainfall data from the Weather Bureau in Pretoria were available for 1755 stations for a twenty-year period throughout South Africa. The following calculations were made for each of these stations:

- mean annual rainfall;
- the percentage of mean annual rainfall that fell during winter (April to September inclusive);
- the mean summer rainfall (October to March inclusive) and;
- the Summer Aridity Index (SAI) – essentially the $\log_n$ of the sum of the mean monthly precipitation during the four hottest months of the year.

Suitable temperature data for a period of eleven years were only available for 105 stations in South Africa. For each of these stations they determined the identity of the four hottest months and calculated the mean lowest minimum temperature for the coldest month and the mean daily minimum temperature for the coldest month. By plotting each 'rainfall station' on a matrix of SAI and percentage winter rainfall (a climagram), it was possible to graphically correlate the biomes described above. On this basis, however, the Grassland Biome still appeared to fall within the confines of the Savannah Biome. However, when the 'temperature stations' were plotted on a matrix of mean summer rainfall and mean lowest minimum temperature for the coldest month, the Grassland Biome separated out clearly on the graphic correlation and at last there was a 'coherent explanation for these areas in southern Africa'.[47]

The origin of the Grassland Biome

Acocks felt that it was reasonable to suppose that before grasses had evolved, some form of fynbos performed the function of holding soils together in the more erodible areas. With the advent of the sward-forming tropical grasslands, fynbos was pushed back into its strongholds in the winter rainfall areas, which were less favourable to grasses.[48]

The above supposition notwithstanding, it was not until Rutherford and Westfall demonstrated that it was climate that determined the extent of South African grasslands, that the Grassland Biome was recognised as a fully fledged biome in its own right in South Africa. Prior to that it was considered to be some sort of 'Cinderella biome' seral to every neighbouring biome and maintained as such only by frequent anthropogenically ignited fires raging through the area. There may have been a global climatic change about three million years ago (that is, the beginning of the Pleistocene) that favoured the development of trees in what were pure grasslands at the time; that is, a wetter climate with less dramatic temperature extremes. This allowed the spread of trees across much of Africa. The famed African savannahs are thus probably no more than grasslands invaded by trees.[49] The fact that the majority of the large mammals here are grazers rather than browsers appears to bear this out. The South African Grassland Biome has many endemic species.[50] With twelve bird species endemic to the biome it is one of the largest centres of bird endemism in Africa and is internationally recognised as an Endemic Bird Area.[51] It seems difficult to believe that these species would be endemic to an area that was under constant threat of being changed into an uninhabitable zone were it not for the beneficence of humans and their agricultural activities.

A far more plausible explanation is offered by Komarek. Lightning-induced fires were common in the Palaeozoic, Mesozoic and Tertiary eras. He suggests that while the forest fires in the Mesozoic would have had little influence on current vegetation of the Earth, fires in the Tertiary 'would help us to understand the origin of the vast number of species that today seem to depend on fire'. These species had already evolved by the time anthropogenic fire became any sort of a factor in the Earth's ecosystems. They were, however, eminently placed to take advantage of the additional opportunities offered by humans.[52]

Flawed conclusions of some earlier researchers

The conclusions drawn by some previous grassland researchers would seem to have flaws. Galpin's conclusions regarding the Springbok Flats ignored the fact that the area had become heavily over-utilised by humans. Overgrazing together with the transformation of farming activities from ranching to crop production was the most likely main culprit for the encroachment of the Springbok Flats by *Acacia* species, not the lack of anthropogenic fires. It was reported that only a small fraction of lightning ground-strikes were responsible for fire ignition in South Africa.[53] This was taken as evidence that lightning was not a major factor causing wildfires. A more likely reason seems to be that fuel loads are lower in most South African biomes now than they were before wild ungulates were replaced by domestic livestock.[54] In the semi-arid conditions such as those pertaining in Africa, 'even an extremely light stocking of domestic livestock (one cow per square mile) is enough to inhibit such [lightning-ignited] fires'.[55] Furthermore, controlled burning frequently takes place before the advent of the spring rains. This often tends to prevent the build-up of the fuel loads necessary for the later ignition of the vegetation by lightning.[56] These factors may well account for the conflicting evidence for lightning fires in South Africa. The inhibition of lightning fires may also be responsible for the apparent inability of climatic conditions alone to control the encroachment by other biomes on the grasslands of Africa in general and South Africa in particular.

Thirty years of annual winter and spring biennial burning – the most likely time of year for lightning-ignited fires in the past – in the catchment grasslands of the Cathedral Peak area of Natal resulted in no significant change in the veld condition.[57] The area concerned is classified as Highland Sourveld (Veld Type No. 44a) and *Themeda-Festuca* Alpine Veld. The first was considered to be seral to forest by many researchers, including those involved in this study. The second was considered to be a 'pure' grassland by some,[58] but as seral to fynbos or heath by others.[59] The mere exclusion of fire in the highveld grasslands of South Africa often results in the formation of dense stands of moribund grasses rather than any progression towards a woody community.[60] On a study plot at Frankenwald, near Johannesburg (Veld Type No. 61 – Bankenveld, a 'false' grassland supposedly seral to savannah),[61] it was found that, after 22 years of protection from fire and grazing, the 'Trachypogon-Other Species' grassland had been replaced by *Stoebe vulgaris* – a woody species with fynbos (macchia) affinities. There were no signs of a succession from grassland to savannah. The researcher could find no sign of 'historical evidence of a more widespread scrub forest and no record of scrub destruction by Man [sic]'. He felt that the description of the woody species in this veld type as scrub relicts was unjustified.[62] Interestingly, *Stoebe vulgaris* is known by South African stock farmers as 'bankrupt bush' and is widely regarded by them as being a consequence of overgrazing.

Many other conclusions relied on the artificial exclusion of fire from naturally fire-prone areas. One such conclusion was that forest and fynbos vegetation was confined to 'refuge sites' in the Natal Drakensberg area by fire.[63] These researchers came to this conclusion in spite of their recognition that it 'appears that fire must be absent for at least several decades before grasses are entirely replaced by woody vegetation'. Later researchers found that the development of woody plant species in the Drakensberg catchments after 30 to 40 years of protection from fire proved that these grasslands are kept in a seral state. They also found that while the amount of woody vegetation had increased, there had been a reduction of grass basal cover, an accumulation of dead fuels and concomitant increases in fire hazard and reduced water yields.[64] The fact that it was unlikely in the extreme that, in this lightning-prone environment,[65] the area would not have burnt naturally without the intervention of humans was ignored.

Another such conclusion was that most lightning-induced fires in the Drakensberg, before the advent of modern humans, would have occurred between October and March, with a peak in January. It was concluded that most lightning-induced fires would have taken place near the peak of the thunder-storm activity. It was felt that management technique of burning during late winter and early spring was in fact favouring the maintenance of seral grasslands as the woody component of the vegetation would have been less susceptible to fire. Based on this conclusion it was recommended that a programme of summer burning be instituted in certain areas within Giant's Castle Game Reserve to encourage the growth of woody vegetation there.[66] This conclusion and the consequent recommendation were based on the incidence of electrical thunderstorms, not on the recorded incidence of lightning-induced fires. It ignored the fact that the researchers' own data indicated that there was a high incidence of thunderstorm activity coupled with a relatively low incidence of rainfall during September to October. While the majority of thunderstorms do indeed occur during January, this period coincides with the peak of the rainy season. The vast majority of storms would be accompanied by heavy downpours. It seems likely that any lightning-induced fires at this time would be doused by rain before they could be of any major significance. In addition the vegetation would be green and moist, and therefore unlikely to burn over very large areas.

Thunderstorms in the beginning of the season would be quite another matter, however. Many of them would be dry storms and the vegetation would be highly flammable. In fact, earlier researchers concluded that Killick (1963) felt that most lightning-induced fires in the Drakensberg occurred during spring before the first significant rains started; that is, when the grass is tinder-dry. Such fires would have been hot and would have resulted in 'clean' burns. Following such a fire the build-up of fuel would be insufficient to allow for the supposed cooler fires during the immediately following summer.[67] Little cognisance seems to have been taken of this in later research except to dispute the fact that woody plants in this area are 'more resistant to fire in summer than in winter'.[68]

Given these flawed conclusions it was hardly surprising that it was found that after only three recommended summer burning treatments there had indeed been minimal damage to the woody species, but the herbage yields and composition of the grassland had deteriorated markedly.[69] Research in the 1980s confirmed that burning the veld after the commencement of the growing season had a detrimental effect on the grass sward, particularly on *Themeda triandra*.[70] In an attempt to justify some of the above conclusions, Mentis and Huntley claimed that Schulze and M[c]Gee found that Holdridge Life Zones for southern Africa indicated that the climax vegetation for *all* South African grasslands would be forest, ranging from wet through moist to dry forest.[71] Schulze and M[c]Gee point out, however, that the criteria of annual temperature and precipitation, as used in determining the Holdridge Life Zones, are perhaps too coarse to delineate vegetation zones. They conceded that any relationships between the distribution of vegetation and the Holdridge indices were purely fortuitous.[72]

The effects of fire on grass and other vegetation

South African forests are intolerant of burning and developed in areas where the incidence of lightning ground-strikes was low. Grasslands had, by contrast, developed in areas where the incidence of lightning ground-strikes was the highest in the country.[73] Figures supplied by the Secretary for Forestry showed that a significant proportion of the plantation fires between 1957 and 1970 were lightning-ignited fires.[74] The implication would seem to be that these grassland areas are *not* suitable for forest development, be it natural or human. Research on the effects of fire intensity showed that while fire intensity had almost no effect on the recovery of a dormant grass sward, it had a devastating effect on the recovery ability of the bush component of an Acocks's False Thornveld – a veld type of the Savannah Biome.[75] Winter or early spring burns, before the onset of the growing season, had little or no effect on the recovery of the grass sward, but did affect the bush component of the veld in the Eastern Cape Province.[76] The highest incidence of dry thunderstorms and lightning ground-strikes in the Grassland Biome occurs precisely at this time.[77] These would have resulted in hot, lightning-ignited fires which would have kept the woody vegetation at bay, but would have had no effect on the grass component of the Grassland Biome.

While the vegetation in the Fynbos Biome requires fire for its long-term survival, the frequency of these fires should not be more than once every fifteen to thirty years. Frequent burning results in a reduction in fynbos species and an increase in grass species.[78] There is a fairly low incidence of lightning ground-strikes in this biome.[79] Fynbos invasion of grassland is favoured by heavy grazing and the consequent scarcity of fuel to carry intense fire.[80] It is suggested here that this lack of fuel is the root cause of the invasion of the Grassland Biome, rather than the exclusion of fire *per se*. The lack of fuel precludes the occurrence of fire which is necessary for the stimulation of grass growth, and this allows the growth of other plant forms. 'Follow-up burns' after an original treatment to eradicate invading fynbos in the Amatole Mountains resulted in the successful eradication of that fynbos.[81] Under a natural fire regime, combined with 'rest periods' that would have resulted from migratory game movements, lightning would no doubt have produced the same or similar results.

In contrast to the other biomes, winter and spring burning was found to have little or no effect on grassland canopy cover. Canopy cover was in fact up to 40 per cent lower throughout the growing season in a grass plot that was burnt after sixteen years of protection from fire than in plots burnt annually in winter and biennially in spring. Canopy cover was up to twenty per cent lower in the case of a summer burnt plot. It was also found that burning during winter or spring did not result in accelerated soil losses due to erosion, nor did it have any adverse effects on stream flow.[82] Edwards found that biennial or triennial spring fires resulted in the best vegetation cover in the Drakensberg.[83] This coincides fairly closely with the late winter and early spring fires suggested above, and is supported by earlier research.[84]

Mean annual rainfall has been linked to the occurrence of fire. The incidence of fire was found to increase with annual rainfall of more than 235 mm and did not normally occur in areas with a lower rainfall than this.[85] There is a positive correlation between mean annual rainfall and the grass fuel load.[86] There is also a similar association between annual precipitation and the frequency of lightning ground-strikes in South Africa, thus demonstrating once again the importance of the association between grass and lightning.[87] In almost all of the grassland veld types *Themeda triandra* features high on, if not at the head of, the list of climax grass species. It was found that there was a decrease in both *Themeda* and basal cover in summer-burnt veld when compared to spring-burnt veld. This seems to indicate that *Themeda* and other plants providing basal cover and thus protection against erosion in the relatively high rainfall grassland areas have evolved under a regime of spring rather than summer lightning-ignited fires. It is also noteworthy that these researchers found that the species composition was ecologically less desirable in summer-burnt veld than in veld burnt during spring. Similar results indicating the detrimental effects of summer burns in grasslands were obtained by other researchers.[88]

Conclusions

That fire is of cardinal importance in the South African Grassland Biome is undeniable. It is indisputably one of the major factors responsible for maintaining the biome in its present state. To imply that anthropogenic fires are the reason for the existence of the South African Grassland Biome, however, is a distortion of the facts. Climate, particularly low temperature extremes and the occurrence of frost, plays a major role here. These low temperature extremes result in the production of moribund grasses and the concomitant build-up of the heavy fuel loads. This build-up in turn allows fire to play its role in maintaining the biome in a state of relative stability. Climatically (that is, lightning-) ignited fires in the past, at the end of the dry season, would have ensured that these heavy fuel loads burnt with sufficient intensity to curb any attempted invasion of the grassland stronghold by woody plant species.

It is suggested that, prior to the influence of humans, the extent of the Grassland Biome was determined by the sufficiency of summer rainfall followed by winter droughts, the severity of minimum temperatures – that is, the general presence or absence of frost during the coldest season – and dry electrical storms. These are all elements of climate. The summer rainfall encouraged the growth and regrowth of hemicryptophytes. The severe frosts killed off the aerial growth of these hemicryptophytes and created much highly inflammable material. These high fuel loads were ignited by lightning prior to the advent of the main rains during the next summer. With the advent of humans these fuel loads were lowered by the implementation of various veld-management practices and the fire-adapted species of these grasslands had no option but to be 'ready to seize the … opportunities offered'.[89]

Chapter Eleven

Wakkerstroom: Grasslands, fire and war – past perspectives and present issues

Elna Kotze

There are a few striking things about the Wakkerstroom area. The first is the landscape, which is quite different from the savannah or Karoo, which are more generally associated with Africa. This is a landscape of rolling green hills, dotted with wetlands of varying shapes and sizes and intersected by many meandering streams and rivers. It is no surprise that there are flocks of sheep and herds of cattle. The second striking thing is the seemingly pristine nature of the landscape. The water runs clear, the air is crisp and clean, and there is no industrial activity to be seen. You need to look closely for the subtle signs of environmental damage: the scars – now grassed over – that wagons left in their struggle up steep slopes; the presence of trees – sometimes in great numbers and mostly exotic – in places where no tree would naturally grow; the unnaturally straight line of encroaching *Leucocidea*; the discovery of an opencast coal mine in a secluded valley.

The beauty of the area enchanted me when I first came to Wakkerstroom; then I became fascinated by the interaction of people and this particular environment. An internationally renowned photo-journalist, Janet Jarman, summed it up: 'This is the most fascinating place. Such incredible eye candy and such hard burning issues. What a combination!' This chapter is an attempt to explain, very briefly, the origins of both and thereby illustrate the necessity for a comprehensive environmental history of Wakkerstroom and how that can establish a basis for devising strategies to meet the challenges of the present.

The origins of the high montane grasslands

As discussed by John McAllister in Chapter 10 of this book, the South African grasslands are thought to be of very ancient origin, dating back to well before the break-up of Gondwanaland.[1] They are now an endemic relict of a biome that once covered 60 per cent or more of the continent.[2] Their peculiar climate, particularly in winter, is a major factor accounting for their continued existence. According to Moll, there is evidence to show that 'the soils were such that woody plant growth was inhibited. However, with the disturbance of the soil through erosion, grazing and cultivation – the factor(s) inhibiting woody plant growth – have been altered.'

To understand the climate, the soils and the distinctive landscape we need to start with the geology of the district.[3] The Wakkerstroom district occurs on soils formed from the sedimentary rocks of the Karoo System with dolerite intrusions and basalt and rhyolite extrusions.[4] The age of this system is some 120 to 300 million years and was deposited just before Gondwanaland broke apart. The Karoo System is composed of four layers of which three occur in the Wakker-stroom district. The youngest of the three occurring here is the Lower Beaufort and at places like Majuba it is up to 280 m thick.[5] It forms most of the high ground in the district from Majuba to KwaMandlangampisi and is mostly found above the 1850 m contour. This layer is reasonably resistant to erosion. Beneath this layer is the Upper Ecca, which is found mostly between the 1600 m and 1850 m contours and consists mostly of blue-gray shale interspersed with thin sandstone strips. This layer is highly erodable and thus does not form any topographical landmarks, and is mostly deeply eroded and covered with *ouklip*. This layer occurs under Wakkerstroom town and most of the district to the west of the escarpment. The third layer – the Middle Ecca – is the thickest and consists of alternate layers of shale, sandstone, mudstone and coal. It is only exposed at the lower-lying areas east of the escarpment and to the south where the Slang River has cut a deep-enough bed. As the Karoo System underlies most of South Africa, it is this layer that forms the basis of the South African coal industry.

The breaking apart of Gondwanaland was accompanied by huge volcanic eruptions that covered the Karoo sediments. In areas of the Drakensberg this layer is thousands of metres thick. It also penetrated the sediments and formed horizontal sills and vertical dykes. Evidence of these dolerite intrusions can be seen everywhere in the district, as they are highly erosion resistant. Most high ground is the result of a dolerite cap, as are most of the spectacular cliffs and virtually all the waterfalls, both characterised by the column structure of dolerite, very different from the smooth nature of sandstone cliffs or overhangs. The formation of the Drakensberg range also created a continental divide. In the Wakkerstroom district this divide is marked by the Langberg, which lies north of the town. Wakkerstroom is 1760 m above sea level and most of the surrounding area lies above 2000 m with the top of Ossewakop, the hill behind the town, at 2156 m. This relatively high altitude gives rise to a temperate climate and shortened summer growing season. Winters are dry and cold, often with severe frost and occasional snow. These cold, frosty winters favour the specially adapted grasses[6] and bulbs over trees. The district occurs in an area with a relatively high summer rainfall, mainly between 750 and 1200 mm.

The present topography is the result of processes of erosion that have taken place since before Gondwanaland broke up. Less resistant sedimentary rocks were selectively eroded and washed away by rivers; thus, for example, the Lower Beaufort series is now confined to high-lying islands where dolerite caps provided a measure of protection against erosion. KwaMandlangampisi, an impressive inselberg to the east of the escarpment, is the most isolated of these islands and its very thick dolerite cap protected it from erosion by the Mabola and Pongolo rivers. The dolerite sills and dykes have also affected the course of rivers in many ways. Where rivers cut through thick dolerite sills they create a high-sided canyon-type topography. The Slang River below Zaaihoek Dam is a good example. Where, however, the river cuts through softer sedimentary rocks, as does the Utaga River around Wakkerstroom, wide shallow valleys are created. Most of the larger wetlands in the area have probably also been created by a dolerite sill. The Wakkerstroom wetland was formed by a dolerite sill crossing the uThaka River near the KwaZulu-Natal border and slowing the flow of the river. This slower flow enabled the deposit of sediments which in turn slowed the flow even further to the extent that the river began meandering, creating oxbows in places. The Slang River at Groenvlei is another example of this kind of effect of a dolerite sill. Its exaggerated snake-like meanders gave the river its apt name.

At the farm Tafelkop to the east of Wakkerstroom the escarpment is descended by a pass called Kastrolnek. It is the watershed between the Assegaai River and the uThaka River. This ridge also forms the border between 'true' grassland (Veld Type No. 57 – North-Eastern Sandy Highveld), which lies to the west, and 'false' grassland (Veld Type No. 63 – Piet Retief Sourveld) to the east. They are termed 'false' grassland because Acocks believed that because of the warmer climate to the east of the escarpment the vegetation would become bushveld if fire were to be excluded from the system and climax vegetation were allowed to develop.[7] There are sheltered areas just east of the escarpment in which extensive acacia savannah has evolved where this process can actually be observed. The Langberg north of Wakkerstroom forms the border between the North-Eastern Sandy Highveld (Veld Type No. 57) and the Themedaveld Transition (Veld Type No. 54), which becomes Themedaveld (Veld Type No. 52) further west.

It is necessary to explain the concept of 'sweet' and 'sour' grasses further as it is of major importance in understanding settlement patterns and determining the human impact on grasslands. Generally 'sweet' grasses are palatable and high in nutrients throughout the year. 'Sour' grasses, by contrast, are palatable only during the growing season and lose much of, if not all, their nutritive value after flowering.[8] Management practices on sour grasslands include extensive burning at various times of the year in order to induce new growth. The use of fire as a management tool in the sweet grasslands is for the most part restricted to getting rid of excessive moribund growth. Both the geology and climate play important roles in determining whether the grasslands are sweet or sour. On the nutrient-rich soils overlying the Ventersdorp Supergroup the grasses are generally sweet. On the nutrient-poor soils derived from sedimentary rocks of the Witwatersrand Supergroup and the Karoo System in the higher-rainfall areas of Mpumalanga and the Free State, the grasses are generally sour.[9] High rainfall has the effect of leaching out nutrients and lowering the pH of the upper levels of the soil.[10] Sour grasslands thus occur in the higher rainfall areas and sweet grasslands occur in those parts of the biome with a lower annual rainfall. The sweet grasslands are generally more prone to the effects of injudicious burning, overgrazing and trampling than the sour grasslands. Frost also plays a role in determining whether the grasslands are sweet or sour. As a protective mechanism against heavy frosts, grasses translocate nutrients from the leaves and stems to the roots during winter and are unpalatable and low in nutritive value during this period; sour grasslands are more subject to winter frosts.

Apart from the obvious fact that grasses are the dominant plant group, a further characteristic of many of the flowering plants which abound in grasslands is the presence of underground storage organs which help them to survive fire and frosty winters.[11] Floral biodiversity is high with far more species per unit area than the Fynbos Biome (81 species per 1000 m^2 versus 65).[12] In healthy grasslands only one species in six is a grass.[13] Fire and frost generally restrict shrubs and trees to protected kloofs and rocky areas.

Since time immemorial, fire and grazing have played a major role in the maintenance of grasslands. Komarek quotes many sources to show that lightning-induced fires were common, particularly in Africa, in the Palaeozoic, Mesozoic and Tertiary eras.[14] The host of specialised fauna and flora found in the biome are all fire-adapted and many have been shown to be dependent on fire for their continued survival.[15] Encroaching forest, savannah and fynbos are kept at bay by fire where the grass fuel load is high enough. Where the grass layer has been damaged by heavy grazing pressure, fires cannot occur and these other vegetation types encroach and often become problematic to stock farmers. Manry and Knight calculated the average annual number of lightning ground-strikes per counter measured by 353 lightning-flash counters situated throughout South Africa.[16] The highest density of lightning ground-strikes (up to a mean of 16.2/km^2/year) occurs on the higher-lying grasslands. Evidence of lightning-induced fires in South Africa is conflicting. 'Modern' authors such as Manry, Knight and Komarek consider that lightning-initiated fires, together with dry, frosty winters, are the root cause of grasslands. Forests and savannahs have invaded the African grasslands and are still doing so. Komarek cites figures showing that eleven per cent of plantation fires in South Africa between 1957 and 1970 were caused by lightning. He feels that this figure must have been far higher when the vegetation had been natural grassland. By contrast, 'classical' authors such as Roux, Edwards and others consider the South African Grassland Biome to be artificially maintained by human-caused fires and that if left to nature it would 'revert' to forest, fynbos or savannah.[17] Trollope and Komarek indicate that the importance of lightning-induced fires in grasslands may well be obscured by current land use and management practices.[18]

That fire is of cardinal importance in the grassland is undeniable. It is indisputably one of the major factors responsible for maintaining the biome in its present state. McAllister feels that climate – particularly low temperature extremes and the occurrence of frost – plays a major role here.[19] These low temperature extremes result in the production of moribund grasses and the concomitant build-up of heavy fuel loads. This build-up in turn allows fire to play its role in maintaining the biome in a state of relative stability. In the past, climatically ignited (that is, lightning-ignited) fires at the end of the dry season would have ensured that these heavy fuel loads burned with sufficient intensity to curb any attempted invasion of the grassland stronghold by woody plant species. The extent of the Grassland Biome was determined by the sufficiency of summer rainfall followed by winter droughts, the severity of minimum temperatures and dry electrical storms – all elements of climate. The summer rainfall encouraged the growth and regrowth of hemicryptophytes. The severe frosts killed off the aerial growth of these hemicryptophytes and created much highly inflammable material. Lightning prior to the advent of the main rains during the next summer ignited these high fuel loads.

All the above factors contribute to the rich diversity of fauna and flora that occur in the Wakkerstroom area. Because the Grassland Biome in Africa is now confined to South Africa many of these species are endemic to South Africa. Twenty-nine bird species found in the Wakkerstroom area are endemic or near-endemic to South Africa. Of these, six species that birdwatchers from around the world come to Wakkerstroom to see – Bald Ibis, Blue Crane, Whitewinged Flufftail, Rudd's Lark, Botha's Lark and the Yellowbreasted Pipit – are ranked as globally threatened by BirdLife International. This is why this area is classified as an Endemic Bird Area (EBA) in urgent need of conservation by BirdLife International, the advisers on matters relating to birds to the International Union for Conservation of Nature and Natural Resources (IUCN), the world's pre-eminent and oldest conservation organisation. Six mammal species found in this area are endemic or near-endemic to South Africa and nine mammal species here are included on the South African Red Data List. Two butterfly species that are endemic to the Mpumalanga Grassland Biome and are on the South African Red Data list are found in the Wakkerstroom area. Two butterfly species (*Aloeides merces* and *Dingana alaedeus*) only occur on the farm Tafelkop.

The advent of people

The presence of many caves containing rock paintings in the Wakkerstroom area indicates that San hunter-gatherers utilised the area, possibly for many centuries.[20] Although there is no proof, it would be reasonable to speculate that the grasslands here were subjected to burning by these early hunter-gatherers wherever and whenever there was sufficient accumulation of combustible fuels, for instance, in late winter or early spring before the first rains.[21] McAllister[22] cites Hall, who in turn cites various authors (Burchell, 1822; Marshall, 1976; Schapera, 1976) to show that fire was used as a tool by hunter-gatherer people as part of their hunting techniques or to improve the quality of edible plants in grasslands and open savannahs. There is no evidence that these peoples manipulated the production of combustible fuels.

While the hunter-gatherers had a high degree of mobility, their movements were, to an extent, cyclic. There were often definite seasonal movements in pursuit of the migrating animals and other resources. As the grasses in the high-lying areas were palatable only in spring, animals would move to these areas until the grazing lost its palatability and return to their winter grazing areas, and the hunter-gatherers would follow. The implications are that in the summer rainfall areas such as the Grassland Biome the incidence of anthropogenic fires would have occurred more frequently during spring in the high-lying areas and during autumn and winter in the low-lying areas. This would encourage fresh grass growth and so attract game when productivity was low. The frequency of anthropogenic fires would have depended on how often these Late Stone Age peoples visited or revisited the area. In high-lying sandstone areas with plenty of caves, a suitable microclimate would have been created to encourage these nomadic peoples to return year after year. It is reasonable to suppose that, under these conditions, the immediate surroundings of these caves would be burned almost annually. In the low-lying areas rock shelters do occur, but far less frequently than in the high-lying areas. It is inferred from the numerous scattered finds of stone artefacts that – probably as a result of the more benign climate – these communities often made use of temporary camps or shelters here and that there was no need to return to the same sites year after year. For this reason it is felt that anthropogenic fires would have been far less frequent in the low-lying areas than in the highlands. Based on management practices seen in the

Wakkerstroom area today, the burning regime imposed on the grasslands here was probably much the same as that of the Stone Age hunter-gatherers: late winter–early spring in the high-lying areas and autumn–early winter in the low-lying areas.

McAllister cites Hall as proof that there were Iron Age farming communities in the Grassland Biome from about AD 1000.[23] Burning was probably carried out by these farmers in much the same way as their Stone Age predecessors had done, but the new grass growth obtained after a fire was perhaps used to provide grazing for domestic stock rather than to attract wild game to the area.

The abundance of grazing and water has been the determining factor in the human settlement and utilisation of the area. Large herds of game would originally have attracted utilisation, whether by Stone Age or Iron Age peoples. The inclement winter climate of the montane grasslands was, however, not conducive to permanent settlement. This led to a seasonal habitation of the area. The blank one encounters on most anthropological maps regarding this area could be due to a lack of research. Our hypothesis is that – especially in so far as Iron Age people are concerned – the area would only have been utilised as a summer grazing area for their cattle and possibly as summer hunting grounds. This is based on the fact that the later European settlers treated the area in much the same way. Transhumance was in fact necessary for the survival of cattle and hence of the Nguni society and economy.[24] It was so essential that when climatic and demographic factors impacted on the practice in the beginning of the nineteenth century, it contributed to the events known as the *mfecane* ('the crushing'). The battle for trade with the Portuguese at Delagoa Bay was the other contributing factor.[25]

The turmoil to the east, the present Swaziland area, and the south-east in what was later known as KwaZulu had far-reaching effects on the Wakkerstroom area. At the end of the eighteenth century Jobe of the Mtetwa died and Dingiswayo, who had fled into exile, returned and displaced his brother as ruler. Dingiswayo had spent some of his time in exile with the Hlubi, who were at the time settled on the upper umZinyati (Buffalo) River to the south of Wakkerstroom. This sojourn so impressed these hosts that when the later ruler, Langalibalele, was born in 1818, the same year that Dingiswayo died, he received two names. The one, Langalibalele ('scorching sun'), was given because the area was gripped by a crippling drought, and the second was Mtetwa in honour of Dingiswayo. The Balele Mountains to the south of Wakkerstroom carry his name, thus indicating his area of abode. This same Langalibalele was displaced by the *mfecane* and subsequently settled by Sir Theophilus Shepstone in the foothills of the Drakensberg, where he later led a rebellion, was sent to trial, and subsequently banished to Robben Island.[26] Enough remnants of the Hlubi returned in later years for this history to be alive in oral accounts.[27]

In the 1760s the brothers Ludonga I and Dlamini – sons of Ngwane I – were in conflict. Ludonga decided to leave and look for a place further afield in which to settle. After many travels he settled in a cave at Mhlongamvula, which is one of the peaks in the KwaMandlangampisi massif. The San hunter-gatherers who were in occupation retreated as they were heavily outnumbered. Ludonga fathered Mavuso, who in turn fathered Ludonga II, the father of a man who is a local legend, Shabalala, also known as Mandlangampisi – originally Mandla-angangawempisi, 'he who is as strong as the hyenas'.

The last person who defeated the Zulus was Mandlangampisi. The indunas for Shabalala's tribe were Malinga, an *induna* of Zwane, Ngema and Mnisi, the indunas of Yende. The wars between the Zulus and Mandlangampisi took place between 1852 and 1854. One big battle was fought at Mhlongumvula. When Mandlangampisi's people saw the Zulus approach they retreated into the cave. The Zulus had no intention of fighting – they were merely exploring the area. When they entered the cave they could only enter one by one and those in front were killed without those following realising what was happening. This happened because the Swazis thought the Zulus had come to fight. During this battle Hlomendlini was born and got his name from the battle which was 'fought whilst in the house'. The remainder of the troops went back to Zululand. When years passed and the others had still not arrived, Mpande sent a large contingent to go back to the area where they had last been seen (the cave) and to engage a Zulu ceremony hoping that the smell of meat and the sound of the ceremony would entice their comrades to come and investigate. Nobody realised that the Swazis had killed them. They were therefore relaxed during this ceremony and their weapons unguarded. The Swazis ambushed them and then used their own weapons to engage battle.

When word reached Mpande he sent a request to Hlomendlini to train Mpande's troops, as he was such a brave and strong man. Whilst Hlomendlini was in Zululand, Mandlangampisi died. The regent in Hlomendlini's absence was Zwane. White settlers came looking for land and offered to acknowledge Zwane as the legitimate ruler if he would give them land. He refused and pointed out that the legitimate ruler was presently in Zululand. Whilst Hlomendlini was in Zululand he had an altercation with one of the troops he was training and broke his back. Mpande sent him home. He was accompanied to Mhlongumvula by some of the Zulu including Mthonga – the king's son who fled Zululand because the king's second wife (the mother of Cetshwayo) was plotting to kill him, the first-born son, in order that her son would inherit the throne. A white settler (farm-owner) gave him permission to settle on his land. Because so many people came from Zululand to see him he was told to leave and he settled in the Wakkerstroom area on a piece of land later known as Saxony. His second wife lived next door on what became known as Nogwaja's farm. He also spent a lot of time at Ophondweni on the Volksrust road (also referred to by some oral accounts as eSikhaleni). He died at Nogwaja's farm and was buried there; some oral accounts refer to the same place as KwaMgilikidi.[28]

After the Battle of Blood River in 1838 and the subsequent death of Dingane in 1840, Mpande became ruler of Zululand with the help of the white settlers. In acknowledgement for this help he granted them the right to settle on the upper umZinyati River. This was formerly Hlubi territory and temporarily a seemingly empty landscape in the wake of the *mfecane*. After the annexation of Natal and the defeat of the Voortrekkers in June 1842 at the Battle of Congella, many of the pioneers left Natal and moved to the Free State and Transvaal. Swart Dirk Uys (from his black beard and hair), brother of Voortrekker leader and hero Piet Uys, also left and settled in the Utrecht–Volksrust area.[29] In 1853 the town of Utrecht was founded, and in 1854 a written agreement was entered into between Mpande and the white settlers for the right of settlement in an area that became the Utrecht district. It is fair to assume that this right to settlement was interpreted broadly and that a wide area around the present towns of Utrecht, Wakkerstroom and Volksrust was settled by white pioneer farmers. In 1859, President M.W. Pretorius and the Revd van der Hoff decided that Potchefstroom was the centre of too large a district and therefore instructed Uys to search for a suitable site for a town.

His choice of site, which was to become the town of Wakkerstroom, was totally dictated by the magnificent wetland – so much so that from its inception to the present day the wetland in its entirety has lain within the municipal boundaries of the town. The main body of the wetland is some 650 ha in extent and some 9 km long. This makes it one of the largest of its kind in the former Transvaal. It is classified as a priority wetland of KwaZulu-Natal, lying as it does right on the Natal border.[30] The motto on the town's coat of arms, *Inter Flumina ad Montes*, 'between rivers and mountains', was the town fathers' affirmation and acknowledgement of the resources which brought them here. The values of 150 years ago hold true to this day. The uThaka River which feeds the wetland and runs through the town has a history of never having dried up, even during very big droughts (1907, 1933 and 1982). Many settlements depended on the river as a reliable water source. In big droughts people came from very far to get water from this river and therefore it was called uThaka – 'something special that people depend on'.[31]

Near the present Dirkiesdorp is an area known as KwaNgema. It had its origins in the mid-nineteenth century when Yende was given the right of settlement in this area by Mandlangampisi. Ngema was one of the indunas who had come from KwaZulu with Hlomendlini and he ended up staying in Yende's area. Ngema was literate and was therefore appointed as secretary to Yende. He was supposed to write a letter to Pretoria asking for the land to be registered in Yende's name. Instead, he wrote requesting the registration in his own name and thereby got the land, which became known as KwaNgema. The result of this treachery is still felt in the tensions between the KwaNgema residents and those at Driefontein, where the present Yende resides. Driefontein was founded in the early 1900s when local black leaders were given land by the government. It was historically one of the only areas where blacks could own land and it played a prominent role in the apartheid era when the government tried to relocate its residents to the homelands. It is estimated that 40 000 to 50 000 people live in the township, but all of the land is owned by approximately 320 families (who own 8 morgen each). They earn income by renting land to the other inhabitants. The community is extremely poor and the majority of citizens who do not own land are supported by the pensions received by older members of the family. Small farmers in the community own an estimated total of 2000 head of cattle. The cattle graze on the small, sub-leased plots and in the streets. There is a high demand for land access and community development.

In 1861 white settlers were given the right of settlement to a large area around the mPivane and Blood rivers in exchange for the return of Mpande's son Mthonga. What is not clear is whether the white settlers were able to keep their side of the bargain and, if so, how one explains the oral tradition that Mthonga continued residing in the Wakkerstroom area until his death.

The other settlement that had a significant influence on this area was that of German missionaries from the Hermannsburg Mission Society. The first of these missionaries arrived in Durban in 1854, setting up the mission Hermannsburg near Kranskop. A second group arrived in 1859 when it was decided to extend mission activities into northern Natal. In 1860 two mission stations – Entombe and Ekhombela – were started. Then a financial problem led to the decision to release the colonists from their contracts and allow them to build their future independently. In 1863, the first three families moved to the Ncaka region and by 1869, when all the colonists had gained their independence, quite a number had joined them and Luneburg was founded.[32] They obtained a concession from the government in the Transvaal to harvest the timber in the indigenous forests. The Ncaka escarpment receives as much as 1200 mm of rain per annum and the protected kloofs and southern slopes boast some spectacular indigenous forests. Unfortunately, one particular forest, Zuurbron, was totally decimated by this harvesting. Only single huge forest trees bear testimony to what must have been a significant forest a century ago; there are reports of the birds collected here in 1904 by Captain Grant for the British Museum which would have needed a sizeable forest as habitat.[33]

The role that grasslands played in the Anglo-Boer War has yet to be appreciated. In his journal on the war Deneys Reitz writes about the troops mustering in this district days before war was declared and estimated the number at 15 000.[34] If it is taken into consideration that each horseman had at least two horses and added to that is the fact that 'the meat supply consisted of an immense herd of cattle on the hoof', it is clear that adequate grazing was a prerequisite. Reitz states further that the two republics had mobilised 60 000 to 70 000 men, most of them on the high montane grassland of the eastern Free State and what was then southern Transvaal. Could the need for the British to import vast amounts of fodder for their horses have had anything to do with the fact that they were, in the beginning at least, concentrated in what the Boers would have referred to as 'winter grazing areas' at the beginning of October? These vast amounts of fodder left a legacy of Scottish Thistle, 'khaki-bush' and Cosmos. Though the last has become the symbol of the highveld, all three – but particularly the first two – cause farmers (and gardeners) great problems.

White farmers, the majority of whom are third- and fourth-generation, dominate the present freehold agriculture tenure. The average size of a farm is between 800 and 1200 ha although there are, of course, farmers who have much larger holdings. All the early farmers had 'winter' and 'summer' farms; the former in the lower-lying areas of KwaZulu-Natal, the latter on the highveld. This practice was only changed when either economic factors or the number of sons led to denser settlement patterns and different sons inheriting the 'summer' and 'winter' farms. To the present day the more affluent and successful farmers have huge landholdings distributed between 'summer' and 'winter' areas. There are still sheep-trekking roads in use: these are rights of way across farmland which are fenced-in narrow corridors, to facilitate moving huge flocks of sheep, sometimes across distances up to 100 km. The change in this type of landholding only became prevalent after the 1933 Depression. It would seem that it was beneficial in that grazing lands were left to rest for long periods of time. Since it changed there has been enormous pressure on the grazing, exacerbated by economic, political and climatic pressures. Presently the area is primarily a stock-farming area, and crop-farming is limited to small patches of subsistence crops planted by labour tenants and larger patches of maize and monoculture grass planted by the farmers as winter fodder. This became necessary as farmers settled permanently in this district with no 'winter' farm to go to. On the farm Tafelkop good veld management is evidenced by a photograph used by Acocks[35] – taken in 1945 – to illustrate Veld Type No. 57. Comparing this photograph to the same view today shows an unchanged landscape except for a few more large boulders fallen from the cliffs above.

This district was unfortunately the heartland of the labour-tenancy practice. This practice, much as in feudal Britain, determined that a labourer has the tenancy right to a piece of land for his homestead and some maize lands. This would usually be an average of some 3 to 5 ha. He would also be allowed a certain number of cattle – typically about ten. These privileges were in lieu of any wages, and in return he, his wife and children would be bound to deliver a negotiated form of service. The practice of rotating labour six-monthly was prevalent – one of the family would work for six months and then be replaced by someone else from the family. Over time this has changed on most farms in all sorts of ways. Paying of wages is now more the rule than the exception and the rotational system has also been abandoned on most farms. Both these changes came about as a greater appreciation for the skills and qualities of certain individuals were recognised by the farmer, and as South Africa's political dispensation has brought other pressures to bear.

In spite of an auspicious start, Wakkerstroom landed in an economic backwater. The main cause can be found in a fateful decision regarding the planned Port Natal–Pretoria railway line that was to follow the logical route through Wakkerstroom. The town fathers decreed otherwise in fear that the chickens would stop laying, cows would not give milk, and their wives and daughters would suffer bad complexions.[36] This is possibly the first Environmental Impact Statement in Wakkerstroom's history, and the question does arise whether we are any more accurate today. The railway was then routed via Charlestown, a small settlement on the Natal–Transvaal border and this led to the establishment of Volksrust and its subsequent growth – to the detriment of Wakkerstroom.

As the economy steadily declined, those who could not or did not want to move to the cities and larger towns turned to what could at best be described as a little better than subsistence agro-economy centred mainly on cattle. The wetland became an even more important resource base. Much of the winter–summer farming mindset of the farming fraternity was shared by the smallholders and cattle-owning townsfolk. In other words, people kept stock numbers commensurate with that mindset and not geared to being permanently in an area previously regarded as unsuitable for winter stock-farming. Provisioning for winter was at best a haphazard affair and by the end of August every year stock-owners turned to the wetland for relief. If this was burnt during July it ensured a 'green bite' from mid-August until the veld had recovered sufficiently – usually two to four weeks after the first rain, which should fall around the end of September but can stay away until December. It is reported that in the 1933 drought the wetland supported more than 2000 head of cattle for more than a year. People did not burn the wetland that year – they baled it.[37] The poor inhabitants of eSizameleni, and many in Wakkerstroom, utilised the wetland in other ways, and the hunting of waterfowl and collecting of eggs persist to this day, as does fishing for the pot in the river and dam above the wetland. Collecting dung as an energy source is still prevalent, as is the cutting of reeds for reed walls in the gardens and courtyards of residents' houses.

When my family moved to Wakkerstroom in 1989 with a vision of a tourism future for the town, we were enthralled by the natural beauty and tranquillity of the area and the immense potential, particularly in the 'birding' market. We set about establishing a guest house, much to the bemusement and amusement of the locals. The feasibility of an economy built on birds was proved when the empty and derelict houses in town started filling with enthusiastic 'birders' who saw the economic sense in investing in a holiday property so close to Gauteng that it could be utilised every weekend if they so wished. The political instability and unrest merely fuelled the interest in a safe, quiet retreat. In 1992 a second guest house appeared, followed closely by a third and fourth. Property prices rocketed from around R300 for a vacant lot to R3000. A bakery, second café, speciality and souvenir shop, hardware shop and small cheese factory followed, and the Indian trading store became a supermarket. In 1995 more than 5000 bed nights were sold and the quantified investment in Wakkerstroom from 1990 to the end of 1995 was in excess of R6.5 million.

These changes occurred hand in hand with the founding of the Wakkerstroom Natural Heritage Association (WNHA) by Dr Warwick Tarboton and myself. The WNHA succeeded in gaining a ten-year lease of the wetland from the town council with effect from 1 July 1992. After thorough research, management guidelines were formulated.[38] While the dream of an inviolate wilderness area may appeal to many people it was, by virtue of the history and indivisibility of town and wetland, not an attainable or even necessarily a desirable goal. The goal had to be the multi-functional use of the system, bounded within conservation parameters. This large and beautiful wetland has a major role to play in raising wetland consciousness in general and as a management example in particular. Cattle still graze in the wetland and it is still burnt. The difference, however, is that the cattle numbers and areas in which they graze are strictly monitored and grazing is used as a tool to create a greater mosaic of habitats within the wetland. Fire is used in much the same way, with only a third of the wetland burnt in any year. The great difference is that the wetland now serves a large number of tourists as well. Vlei Street, running parallel and next to the wetland, was once the 'wrong side of the tracks', but it has been dramatically upgraded and is now the most sought-after address. Then, in 1997, the Mpumalanga Parks Board took over the management of the wetland together with a large section of Ossewakop.

Wakkerstroom entered a new era post-1990. The most dramatic change has been to the social profile, which has seen a reversal of the phenomenon of rural depopulation. The resultant positive effect on the human capital of the town bodes well for the future as it has supplied Wakkerstroom with the skill base it had lost and which is the single most necessary component of a thriving town.

The burning issues

Between 60 and 80 per cent of South Africa's grasslands have been irreversibly transformed and less than 2 per cent are formally conserved. The Wakkerstroom district lies in the centre of some one million hectares of relatively pristine grassland and as such has an obligation to conserve this heritage. This will be no easy task as there are many threats. The single major threat is afforestation[39] – the ploughing up of grassland for the establishment of large, monocultural, exotic tree plantations. This particular land-use conversion has a long history in South Africa, aspects of which are explored by Harald Witt in Chapter 7 of this book.

The Department of Water Affairs and Forestry classifies the entire area up to a line west of Volksrust as 'good for afforestation'. The northern sub-catchments of the Usutu system no longer support perennial rivers, whereas the southern sub-catchments do. The origins of the various rivers are so close together that these differences cannot be realistically ascribed to climatic differences. The major difference would appear to be the degree to which these catchments are planted with alien trees. The unplanted catchments of the Vaal, the Assegaai, the uThaka and the Slang are now the only rivers in the massive government water schemes that can guarantee a year-round water supply that is vital for the generation of 70 per cent of South Africa's power requirements. This includes virtually all the power requirements of the economically vital province of Gauteng. However, if these catchments are planted up – as it would appear that the Department of Forestry wishes to do – this guarantee may well not hold in the future. The effects of injudicious catchment management are all too obvious in other areas of Mpumalanga and the Northern Province, such as the northern Usutu, the Sabie – Sand and Letaba river catchments. In these cases, the catchments have been overdeveloped. Large-scale, indiscriminate afforestation of the upper catchments has been allowed in the past, with unfortunate results. Rivers that were once perennial now only flow during seasons with a higher than average rainfall. There is much evidence for the statement that 'trees are prodigious water users compared with natural grasslands'.[40] It is found that not only do trees use more water than grasses, but also the canopies of these trees intercept much of the rainwater.[41] In a relatively hot country such as South Africa much of this intercepted water evaporates long before it has the chance to reach the ground. Since at least half of the country's timber production is exported as wood chips, pulp and raw timber, South Africa's most precious long-term resource – water – is being used up in order to supply foreign countries with almost unprocessed timber.

The issue of access to land and the need to redress past injustices brings about a set of different pressures on the land. These are closely linked to the issue of the high rate of unemployment, quoted as a startling 40 to 60 per cent by various sources. The new political dispensation has committed itself to land reform. In the Wakkerstroom area this has deeper implications because of the 'labour tenant' system still practised by some of the farming fraternity. The Land Reform (Labour Tenants) Act 3 of 1966 grants labour tenants protection against arbitrary eviction – providing that they may be evicted only in prescribed circumstances, in terms of a court order issued by the Land Claims Court.

The Act also grants labour tenants the right to apply for ownership of that portion of the farm over which they have historically had use rights. It is the task of the Land Claims Court to decide whether such ownership rights should indeed be granted, or whether the granting of lesser rights or compensation would be more appropriate. Where ownership is granted to labour tenants, farm owners are entitled to fair compensation. It is the task of the Land Claims Court to determine the amount of such compensation. For those farm labourers who work on a straight contract basis the Extension of Security of Tenure Act was passed in November 1997 to protect rural occupiers of land (other than labour tenants) against arbitrary eviction. It provides that they may be evicted only in certain circumstances.

While many of the farmers are not against the principle, they have pointed out some practical difficulties. Land tenants often live far from the periphery of the farm. This means that a farmer has to accept granting title to a piece of land that would further necessitate right of way across the land. As most of the tenant homesteads are presently accessible only by foot or horseback, this could present a lot of problems. The farmers maintain that no cognisance has been taken of the onerous economic burden a change in the *status quo* could create. All tenant farmers own stock and many of them have a situation where the stock is dipped, dosed and generally cared for as part of the farmer's main herd. The reality of the situation is also that those farmers who have treated their tenants well will be the most severely 'penalised'. To illustrate this statement, if a farmer has allowed a tenant generous grazing for his cattle and not placed onerous limits on the numbers he may keep, the tenant could own up to eighty head of cattle. This could translate to a claim for 200 ha of the farmer's land when the Department of Agriculture's carrying capacity figures are used as a guideline. By contrast, those farmers who, mostly because of their harsh treatment, have ensured a steady turnover of tenants will not be subject to any claims as their tenants have not occupied the land long enough. The viability of small farms is highly questionable and examples across Africa suggest that this could lead to disaster. Farmers have reacted with feelings of being under threat and some of the tenants have responded by refusing to work for their landlord as they have been led to understand that they now own the land and do not have to work. In cases where the farmers have been able to prove a breach of contract, labour tenants have been evicted. These evicted tenants, together with their stock, have migrated to Wakkerstroom because of the commonage system. This is the only town that I know of where this system has survived, undoubtedly because of the economic decline of Wakkerstroom leading to a great dependency on an agro-economy by the town and surrounding smallholding owners.

The tenure on very large 'urban' plots (6882 m²) and 'rural smallholdings' of 5–25 ha, coupled to the right to own five cattle on the former and the right to hire adjacent municipal grazing land of up to 300 ha on the latter, makes of Wakkerstroom a farm with lots of houses on it. The growth in the urban population of eSizameleni has meant great growth in the cattle herd; estimates are as high as 400 per cent since 1991. The demand for land from these cattle owners is as obvious as it is fraught with problems both legal and moral. The townlands of Wakkerstroom are in excess of 10 000 ha in extent.

The utter lack of proactive land-use planning and integrated land-use management has created great problems. Neither the town nor the townlands have any zonation plan. Everybody – from farmers holding huge tracts of land to eSizameleni residents on their 300 m² – holds the view that their land is their domain on which they can pretty much do exactly as they please. The many laws that exist to the contrary do not challenge this assumption. The erosion, overgrazing, number of declared weeds, ploughing-in of wetlands and so on all bear testimony to this fact. Laws without buy-in by the rank and file and enforcement by the responsible agencies are just words on paper. Only the mining industry (since 1994) and Eskom know about Environmental Impact Assessments. At all times parties have to be extremely vigilant, and the balance of power that exists and the inaccessibility of the briefing documentation are fatal flaws in the system of Interested and Affected Parties Meetings.

In 1957 the coal reserves of the area were estimated at 2 358 million tons. Coal has been mined for many years in the vicinity of Heyshope Dam, but new extensions planned can dramatically increase the extent of the industry and cause environmental problems. The specific coal layers found in much of the area directly beneath and in the vicinity of Wakkerstroom are too thin or have too much dolerite intrusion to be mined economically. The early closure of the coal mine at Majuba Power Station was due to the latter fact. The history of coal mining in the area is unfortunately full of stories of unscrupulous operators. The abandoned coal dumps at what used to be the Wakkerstroom station bear testimony to such operations and the disastrous consequences, in this case the loss of a station.

'Relevant' environmental history

Research of any kind, like the development of technology, should be relevant. Many people argue that any and all research and technology is relevant, which is true if the time factor is removed. However, what is needed is relevancy in solving the most immediate problems. There are huge gaps in our understanding that need to be filled quickly. We need the biophysical data to ensure a sound decision-making support base. We need information on people's interface with the environment – both past and present – to enable us to understand the dynamics, but also for all people to understand that decisions imply consequences – whether positive or negative. Environmental responsibility is imperative as many people's livelihoods depend on South Africa's natural resource base.

I see the environmental history of the Wakkerstroom district in particular and the Grassland Biome in general as the foundation on which the compatible development strategies of both should be built. 'Economic growth, quality of life and environmental health are three interdependent elements which determine the prosperity and well-being of individuals and nations. Wise management of any two of these elements without care for the other is inadequate for sustained development.'[42] This quotation outlines what I believe to be the three main areas that need attention simultaneously to achieve sustainable conservation and development of an area. In the mainstream debate around sustainable development and utilisation, recognition has been given to the fact that this is only possible if a holistic approach is taken and if communities, or at least the majority within them, are committed to the concept. All of this needs, however, to be informed by our past history and our understanding of the dynamics that shaped it in order to ensure that we do not make the same mistakes again.

Chapter Twelve

The dynamics of ecological change in an era of political transformations: An environmental history of the Eastern Shores of Lake St Lucia

Georgina Thompson

In South Africa, the conundrum of 'parks versus people' remains largely unsolved and development versus conservation issues still present major problems to conservationists and policy-makers. This is nowhere more evident than in the Lake St Lucia region, which boasts a unique wetland of international importance and the largest inland body of water in southern Africa. The Eastern Shores of St Lucia exhibit in microcosm all the complex problems facing South African conservationists and policy-makers. It is for this reason, and in the belief that environmental history can and should make a contribution to current debate and policy relative to the issue of 'sustainability', that an exploratory environmental history of the area has been undertaken.

Due in large part to the country's history of colonial conquest and the subjugation of indigenous people which led ultimately to alienation from their land, conservation of the region is countered by land claims, poverty, a profound need for development in the region, and a proposal to mine within the region. How then does one reconcile the desire to maintain St Lucia as a conservation site when this option is set against the competing and desperate needs of the people of the area?

Resolving these issues will require innovation and strong political resolve, which are not often found in developing countries with large disadvantaged communities as exist around St Lucia. Solutions to the complex problems facing this region will require policy-makers not only to look into the future, but also to look back at the past. This is required to ensure that the problem is not viewed as simply an environmental conservation issue, but to broaden it to include the concept of sustainable development of St Lucia and the broader region.

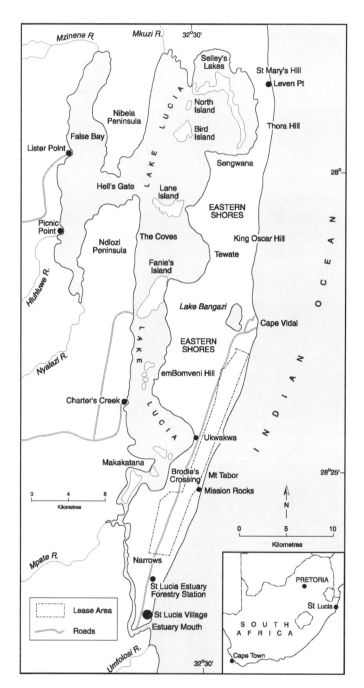

12.1 The St Lucia estuary

Source: adapted from Conlong, D. 1986. An ecological study of the grasslands on the Eastern Shores of Lake St Lucia. Masters thesis, University of Natal, Pietermaritzburg.

The biophysical environment

The Eastern Shores of Lake St Lucia form part of a much larger ecosystem which extends from the Mkuzi catchment and Mkuzi Game Reserve in the north, southwards to the Umfolozi Game Reserve and westwards to Vryheid (the catchment of the Umfolozi). The Lake St Lucia system itself is situated in north-eastern KwaZulu-Natal. It forms the largest natural body of water in South Africa, and constitutes more than 75 per cent of the total estuarine area of the whole coastline.[1]

The area is unique in that it includes estuarine, terrestrial and marine wildernesses with a rich biodiversity.[2] While the main focus of this chapter remains on the Eastern Shores area, some understanding of the working of the whole system and the history of the entire area is necessary in order to appreciate fully the ecological threats to the Eastern Shores region.

The Eastern Shores consist of a unique piece of land stretching from the St Lucia Estuary in the south to St Mary's Hill in the north, bordered on the east by the Indian Ocean and by Lake St Lucia on the west (Figure 12.1): an area roughly 260 square kilometres in extent.[3] Its landscapes range from gentle to majestic with fairly flat, rolling grasslands, giving way to an impressive cordon of sand dunes interspersed with wide depressions in which a diverse variety of wetlands occur. The continuous range of very high forested sand dunes, reputed to be amongst the highest vegetated dunes in the world, rises steeply from the shore and runs all the way along the sea shore. This varied topography is one of the factors that have led to a wide diversity of animal and plant species in the area.[4] The diversity of the Eastern Shores is further enhanced by the climatic, geological and hydrological conditions of the area. Lying where it does – in a transitional zone between the tropical and subtropical climatic regions – results in the Eastern Shores having species of flora and fauna belonging to both climatic zones, with a consequent unusually diverse number of plant and animal species occurring in the region, many of which represent the southerly limit of distribution.

The general geology, landform and soils have remained much the same since the known advent of human activity around AD 400. Land use of the area has, however, changed considerably in the last 50 years, resulting in drastic alteration of the vegetation, but with little effect on the geology and landform as yet. Topographically the Eastern Shores can be divided into four broad units. The first, and perhaps the most visually impressive, is the coastal dune cordon. The cordon has evolved over the last 25 000 years and morphologically is made up of a variety of dune forms, with bi-directional parabolic dunes predominating, but with other dune forms such as longitudinal or linear dunes, to form the fascinatingly complex dune field we see today. The dune cordon is between one

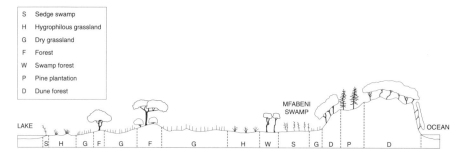

S	Sedge swamp
H	Hygrophilous grassland
G	Dry grassland
F	Forest
W	Swamp forest
P	Pine plantation
D	Dune forest

12.2   Transect from the coast to the shore of Lake St Lucia, showing the plant communities of the Eastern Shores area

Source: after Taylor, R. 1991. *The Greater St Lucia Wetland Park.* Natal Parks Board.

and two kilometres wide and rises to about 135 metres above sea level in the northern part of the region.[5] Immediately west of the dune cordon is a low-lying coastal plain, which never rises more than 15 metres above mean sea level. The coastal plain varies in width from about 500 metres to seven kilometres in places.[6] To the south-west is a depression running parallel to the coastline which features a fascinating mosaic of wetland types. The largest depression is the Mfabeni Depression (see Figure 12.1), which drains southwards to Lake St Lucia, but at times northwards towards Lake Bhangazi.[7] To the west of the Mfabeni Depression is an extensive coastal plain known as the Eastern Shores Plain, the elevations of which vary between fifteen and twenty metres above mean sea level, but in places, where fossil dune ridges occur, may rise to seventy metres. Drainage occurs westwards into Lake St Lucia and eastwards into the Mfabeni Depression.[8]

The vegetation of the Eastern Shores reflects the climatic, geological, hydrological and topographical conditions of the area, the sum of which renders this region unique in terms of plant diversity. Disturbances, such as those caused by shifting agriculture and fire, have also played a role, for example in the maintenance and, in some instances, creation of grasslands. It is thus the interaction of these factors (relating to both human and natural activity) which controls the formation of the structure of the different plant communities.[9] These conditions have led to a very varied land-based flora which are identifiable in a number of distinct types (Figure 12.2). Starting from the sea and then progressing inland towards the lake these are: pioneer dune vegetation, coastal thicket and forest, secondary dune forest, secondary grasslands, hygrophilous grassland, vegetated pans, swamp forest and mangrove forests.[10] The different types of vegetation are indicative of the complexity and uniqueness of the ecosystems of the Eastern Shores. They also reflect the fragility of their environment and the delicate balances between the prevalent sand formations and water balances, and the generally low-nutrient status of the soils in which the various plant communities have evolved and adapted.

These forests, grasslands and mosaic of wetlands of the Eastern Shores link together like a giant jigsaw puzzle to form a number of diverse habitats which are home for an equally diverse vertebrate fauna. The Eastern Shores are home to at least 450 vertebrate species of which 65 are mammals, 286 birds, 60 reptiles and 39 are amphibian species.[11] Other areas of the country of equivalent size have an equal or even greater number of species. What makes this area unique is the diversity of habitat, which has resulted in an unusual mix of species, located in uncommonly close proximity to one another.

Human ecosystems

The term 'ecosystem' and the concept of 'the ecosystem' are undergoing constant revision by scientists but even so are generally not thought to be directly associated with human beings. Studies of ecosystems have commonly been studies of natural ecosystems only. In reality, there are few, if any, ecosystems in the world today that have not been influenced by humans. What has often been overlooked is that humans are inhabitants of ecosystems as other animals are, and are influenced by the principles of ecology. Humans may influence the principles though not the laws of ecology. The implication is that when studying ecosystems one needs to look at human activity within the system. Furthermore, because human activity is rooted in social systems, we need to look at the social systems that govern and give meaning to those activities and interactions impacting on the ecosystem. It is necessary therefore to understand the dynamics of natural succession as well as the dynamics behind human change and the merging of the two. The merging of these dynamics has a direct bearing on diversity patterns and on future conservation and resource management. This is particularly important on the Eastern Shores, because natural scientists recognise that the dune system of the Eastern Shores 'has developed under the influence of man for over a 1000 years'.[12] What is especially important to this study is the changes in human interaction and interference with the environment and, perhaps even more significant, the shifting motives behind these changes, which in turn resulted in the introduction of a number of significant alterations to the flora and fauna, especially those species characteristic of the early stages of succession.

Current archaeological evidence shows that humans first inhabited the area about 1600 years ago,[13] although they had been living in the wider region for very much longer. This region has thus been exposed to communities ranging from hunter-gatherers, through mixed farmers, to today's capitalist, industrial societies. Research suggests that although the modes of resource use of the early inhabitants certainly had some impact on the environment, and that this impact increased with the development of pastoralism and agriculture until the advent of colonialism, the impact appears not to have been particularly damaging. The hunter-gatherers appear to have lived in relative harmony with nature, and even as early forms of agriculture began to develop (for instance the practice of slash-and-burn agriculture and the keeping of cattle) this sort of resource management seems to have been mutually supportive of both human and ecological development. Nonetheless, these early farmers did influence the composition of their environments; they changed the flora and so ultimately the fauna. Their system of shifting agriculture resulted in some replacement of dune forest by secondary grasslands, though the higher woodlands and forests would have remained intact throughout the Early Iron Age.[14]

The Early and Later Iron Age communities exploited marine resources to supplement their diet. Shell debris at many of the archaeological sites throughout the Iron Age indicates that marine resources were exploited for at least fifteen centuries. The fact that marine resources were not depleted suggests that some balance between uses and resources was reached. It has been suggested that this equilibrium was the result of the interaction of different components in the total economy over the annual cycle.[15] In the late summer and autumn the grasslands were at their lowest nutrient value, so the availability of secondary products of cattle would have been limited. At these times shellfish would have become more important as an alternative source of protein. This period coincided with the March equinox, which is characterised by low tides exposing the mussel zones and thus facilitating their collection. This heavy exploitation should not have had too much of a detrimental effect on the reproduction of the resource as it is known that in this region mussels spawn in winter and in spring.[16]

By the beginning of the twentieth century the use of slash-and-burn agriculture and the grazing of stock in this area had had a marked effect on the vegetation. It is argued that many of the grassland areas present at this time were once covered by natural forest. However, ecologists believe that this anthropogenically created grassland may in fact be viewed as an asset to the Eastern Shores area as it has increased the diversity of plant life and thus also of fauna habitats.[17]

More serious environmental alteration came with the arrival of white colonists and the technology of industrialisation. First came traders and hunters, who rapidly depleted many species of game,[18] leading to the disappearance of many of the larger species from the region. The removal of these species would have had its own impact on the environment. Thus with a change in human technological status and its inherently different attitudes towards nature came increasingly heavy impacts on the environment. It was not, however, until the growth of capitalist, industrial societies, which first appeared in the latter half of the nineteenth century in South

12.3 St Lucia wetland
Source: EnvironDev

Africa as a whole, and a little later in the St Lucia region, that widespread human-induced environmental alteration became increasingly common. In the wider St Lucia region industrial capitalist activity began with commercial agriculture after the arrival of white cattle farmers, who came shortly after the Lands Delimitation Commission of 1902–04 had made land available to white settlers. Next came sugar plantations, when the Mfolozi Flats were opened up to farmers in 1927. These activities, however, only had indirect effects on the Eastern Shores.

The St Lucia system has, then, since some time before the turn of the century, been adversely affected by the activities of humans. In the specific Eastern Shores region, however, the situation was a little different. Though there is an abundance of evidence of human activity in this region by the 1950s, there is relatively little evidence of any direct impacts of the generally environmentally ravaging, exploitative characteristics of industrial capitalism. Instead, from the time of the advent of human beings on the Eastern Shores until the 1950s, changes in the landscape and ecosystems, though largely the result of human interference, had been slow and evolutionary in nature.

Human-induced environmental change had, however, also resulted from human activity beyond the Eastern Shores themselves. It has been argued, for

12.4 Residents of the Eastern Shores
Source: EnvironDev

instance, that pre-Iron Age human activity in the river valleys of the catchment area created more marshlands and alluvial flats bordering the lake, which was thought to have been a much larger expanse of deeper and wider water.[19] This led to the establishment of rich hygrophilous grasslands and swamp areas into which Iron Age communities began to move. Once settled, their activities resulted in grasslands beginning to take the place of forest and scrub. Their use of fire, their cultivation of land, and their keeping of stock all served to hold back previous succession of vegetation and so cleared certain areas of forest vegetation. This type of vegetation alteration continued over the years and led to large areas of grasslands being created and maintained. Eventually settlements became permanent but interactions between the people and their environment remained essentially the same. These particular interactions with the environment were based on the establishment of subsistence-orientated agro-ecosystems, and it is generally accepted that while this type of agro-ecosystem induced major changes in nature, it managed to preserve and – in the case of the Eastern Shores in some areas – increase diversity and complexity. This achievement laid the foundation for future social stability.[20] From the 1950s onwards, however, human interactions with the environment on the Eastern Shores changed, and environmental alteration not only increased radically but did so at a much faster rate.

It was during the 1950s in the Eastern Shores region that a leap was made from subsistence agro-ecosystems to the monocultural agro-ecosystem typical of capitalist commercial agriculture. We see 'what had once been a biological community of plants and animals so complex that scientists could hardly comprehend it', being changed by traditional agriculturists into a still highly diversified system for the growing of foodstuffs and other materials, now become 'a rigidly contrived apparatus competing in widespread markets for economic success'.[21] We see an extreme example of environmental simplification – widespread production of a single species produced solely for gain – and we are made aware that the societies responsible for human interference on the Eastern Shores have strikingly different values, laws, aspirations and available technology governing their interaction with the environment. This sudden development – the product of a society very different from that of the indigenous communities who inhabited the area – was to have serious ramifications for both the original inhabitants of the region and for the environment.

Direct environmental impact came with state-controlled afforestation programmes. The plantations were established where grasslands had previously existed, and as a direct consequence the area of grasslands was seriously diminished. There were, however, other indirect environmental impacts. Afforestation necessitated the removal of the subsistence agriculturalists, whose ancestors created most of these grasslands in the first place. With the removal of this type of human interference, the remaining grasslands began to revert to indigenous forest. This succession took place along a number of different successional pathways, which depended largely on the type of previous interference as well as factors such as the hydrology, topography and soil type of a particular site.[22] Commercial forestry was then a major dynamic of change, but one that initiated other dynamics which in turn caused further change. Commercial forestry decreased the area of grassland on the Eastern Shores by a third. The consequent ripple effect meant that the habitat of herbivores was decreased, which in turn put pressure on the fauna and on the remaining grasslands. It is also believed that extensive afforestation significantly reduced seepage inflow into the lake, which in turn could have had an effect on salinity levels particularly during periods of drought. Terrestrial ecosystems could also have been modified by the lower ground-water levels resulting from increased transpiration losses caused by afforestation.[23]

The advent of state-controlled forestry in the area heralded heavy impacts not only on the environment but on the indigenous population as well because they were subjected to racially discriminatory policies and removed from the area. This in itself has led to environmental degradation in the surrounding areas because the people were forced to move into areas which were already inhabited and thus soon became over-exploited. In the light of the present government's new Land Reform Policy and the Restitution of Land Rights Act, passed in November 1994, this issue poses complex problems for both environmentalists and policy-makers. It poses a dilemma for the environmental historian too, for if one accepts that environmental history necessitates the study of the relationship between human beings and nature, South Africans have an enormous problem, as up until 1994 it has been the white minority which has controlled South Africa's biophysical world. This control has resulted in the attitudes and responses of the indigenous peoples to their environment being, firstly, largely unexplored and, secondly, warped by the inconsistencies and injustices of the apartheid system.[24] The implications of this are evident in the attitudes of the people who have invaded the Dukuduku Forest Reserve, situated at the entrance to Lake St Lucia, which they are now accused of exploiting. Their sceptical attitude towards conservation of the environment is worrying to environmentalists, but it is understandable. These people see no logic in environmental concerns after having been removed from a conservation area where the state subsequently replaced hundreds of thousands of acres of indigenous vegetation with pine and eucalyptus forests. Add to this the fact that white farmers in the surrounding regions have removed hundreds of thousands of hectares of indigenous vegetation to establish commercial monocultural agriculture, and the logic of environmental policy seems obscure indeed.

If we move to the broader catchment area the situation is just as complex, but it helps to highlight the need for extreme caution when policy-makers and environmentalists make decisions concerning development which involves exploiting the environment. Within the St Lucia catchment area there is an abundance of evidence to suggest that human resource management in this region has had adverse effects on the lake system. In the case of the Eastern Shores region, this impact is largely a consequence of the practices of commercial agriculture and the policies of the past apartheid government but there is the additional impact of mining and industry. These activities have much to do with the fact that in 1889 St Lucia Lake was more than twice the size it is today and its average depth was thought to be three metres; today the average depth is approximately half a metre.[25] These impacts have been partially caused by commercial agriculture and generally poor farming practices, which led to both a lowering of the water table and an increase in soil run-off. This has been exacerbated by the system of segregation which forced impoverished people into already overcrowded and environmentally denuded areas. In these areas soil erosion on a massive scale has occurred. The catchment area of St Lucia has suffered such severe ecological devastation that sections of the Black Mfolosi are little more than 'a storm-water drain'.[26] Add to this the negative effects of industrialisation and mining, and we cannot but be concerned for the environment generally, and for the St Lucia system in particular.

It would appear that there has been little recognition of the adverse effect of human activity on the environment of the St Lucia region. This impression is not entirely true. An awareness of environmental violation has in fact existed since the last decades of the nineteenth century when the wholesale slaughter of game led to the proclamation of St Lucia and four other reserves in 1895. These areas were reproclaimed in 1897 after Natal had annexed Zululand. Hunting was still permitted but the number of animals that could be shot was limited. Conservation ideals were simple and prompted not by any real concern for ecosystems or the environment, but by the fear of losing resources. It was, however, a start. During the twentieth century conservation ideals grew, but so did the pressures being placed on the environment. With industrial capitalism came the overwhelming belief that human beings should strive to control nature in order to exploit it and thus enhance human development. Industrial capitalism in the Lake St Lucia region came first in the form of commercial agriculture and, from this time on, attempts at conserving the environment and its natural resources were challenged by farmers, who managed to get the reserve deproclaimed in 1928. It was reproclaimed in 1938, but was smaller in extent.

The St Lucia system continued to suffer adverse environmental impact and remedies continued to be sought. In 1936 the swamps were drained and canalised to prevent the flooding of sugar farms, resulting in siltation of the lake and declining fish populations. In an effort to remedy this problem, the mouth of the Mfolosi River was diverted and dredging of the tidal basin was undertaken in 1952. These measures failed to prevent the mouth from closing and so failed to ensure the continued necessary interchange of fresh and salt water which was essential to ensure the continued functioning of the lake's ecosystem. From this time onwards, there were an increasing number of reports of deterioration of the viable functioning of the St Lucia system caused by human activity in both the immediate vicinity and in the catchment areas. Public concern grew when government announced its plans to build a dam on the Hluhluwe River in order to provide irrigation for sugar farmers. This led to a public outcry as a dam would affect the flow of fresh water into the lake, so aggravating its already deteriorating condition. In response to the outcry the government appointed a commission of inquiry, the Kriel Commission, which published its report in 1966.[27] Unfortunately, the commission's recommendations were largely ignored, but its work nevertheless constituted a turning point in the environmental history of St Lucia[28] because it was the first time an investigation into the entire ecosystem had been undertaken. Research was entrusted to experts, thus increasing the 'knowledge bank' of the area. Furthermore, the necessity of establishing a single, consolidated conservation area was highlighted. Mismanagement of the area continued, however, with increased acreage being put under pine forests, the construction of a missile testing base near Cape Vidal and the construction of the Hluhluwe Dam. Even attempts to remedy the malfunctioning of the lake system – such as the dredging of the narrows and the construction of link canals – proved to be detrimental.

It was, in fact, not until 1977 that an agreement was reached between the Department of Forestry and the then Natal Parks Board to manage the Eastern Shores jointly.[29] It was at this time that the Natal Parks Board was allowed to take over the management of Cape Vidal. The Department of Forestry had allowed limited numbers of campers access to Cape Vidal since about 1968 and it had become a very popular fishing camp.[30] The facilities were improved and the popularity of the Eastern Shores grew. Though the majority of visitors were there to fish, others came merely to enjoy the aesthetic beauty of the area. Wilderness trails along the lake were instituted in 1958, run at first by the resident game rangers, and later by the Natal Parks Board and the Wilderness Leadership School. These trails did not involve any exploitation of resources and were undertaken to learn something of the biodiversity and beauty of the area. In them we see the beginning of ecotourism and evidence of a different concept of conservation. Between 1958 and the present the number of wilderness trails has increased and self-guided walks were introduced. In 1986 conservation of the area received a boost when, despite all the human interference in the region, particularly the ongoing afforestation, the St Lucia system was declared a wetland of international importance at the Ramsar Convention. By 1992 the St Lucia Lake system appeared secure, and management of the Eastern Shores state forests was transferred to the Natal Parks Board.

The 1990s

The 1990s brought change, new hopes, new challenges and a new democracy to South Africa. The Eastern Shores of St Lucia illustrate all these factors, for in this region can be found all the examples of the mosaic that had come to constitute the South African 'system' with all its inherent cultural and political idio-syncrasies. Moreover, nowhere is it more evident than in the St Lucia region that development and economic growth are desperately needed to generate the means to rebuild the communities and redress the decades of neglect of the many needs of the majority of the population.

The 1990s began with a plan to mine sections of the dunes of the Eastern Shores. A mining company, Richards Bay Minerals, had been granted mining leases in 1972, at the height of the apartheid era. These leases were extended in 1976.

12.5 Dunes of the Eastern Shores

Source: EnvironDev

Despite the extension of these leases the St Lucia wetland area was declared a wetland of international importance in terms of the Ramsar Convention in 1986.[31] In 1989 Richards Bay Minerals, having completed a successful prospecting programme, applied for rights to mine the dunes in their lease areas for rutile, ilmenite and zircon. These minerals are common in South Africa but are not often found in the economically viable concentrations which occur in the coastal areas of northern KwaZulu-Natal, and more specifically on the dunes of the Eastern Shores. These deposits occur because of the erosion of inland rock formations which have been washed away over millions of years into the rivers and into the sea. Once in the Indian Ocean, the wave action deposited the minerals onto the beach along the Eastern Shores and the sands containing the minerals were blown into the dunes by the prevailing winds. These deposits posed a dilemma for the government. It was government policy at the time to increase the mining base of the country in order to help earn foreign exchange which was in short supply because of the sanctions applied against South Africa. Yet the area had also been recognised as a unique natural asset and part of a wetland of international importance.

In view of this dilemma, Richards Bay Minerals commissioned an environmental impact study of the lease areas. Completed in September 1989, the study covered most of the important issues relating to the mining option, but it was seen essentially as a mitigation report, as Richards Bay Minerals assumed that it had the legal right to mine.[32] The document was released at public meetings on 7 and 8 September 1989, and was also circulated to various interested and affected parties. The release of the document was met with considerable hostility and a public outcry against mining. These reactions were followed by an extensive national media campaign, which led to a cabinet decision in September 1989, requiring that a more comprehensive Environmental Impact Assessment (EIA) be carried out and that the findings be reported back to them before a decision on the implementation of a mining lease would be taken. In January 1990 the administrative structures for this decision were set in place and the EIA commenced.

The EIA team was instructed to investigate two land-use options for the area: the nature conservation and tourism option; and the mining option, which included conservation and tourism as far as they would be feasible in conjunction with mining. The EIA was also specifically required to address the question of irreparable damage.[33] While the EIA constitutes a thorough and competent scientific study, there were weaknesses in the processes that resulted in criticisms of the study and uncertainty about the future of St Lucia. This uncertainty remained in spite of the conclusions reached by the report that under strict conditions, including the rehabilitation of the affected areas, mining could proceed. This was overturned by a subsequent Review Panel. The panel concluded that no mining should be allowed in the Greater St Lucia Area. This decision was ratified by the South African Cabinet on 6 March 1996.[34] The major shortcoming was the limited terms of reference of the EIA, which failed to accommodate the complexity of issues involved in land-use options for the area. The design of the process excluded adjacent communities by producing an 'expert-led outcome instead of developing consensus over the issues'[35] in order to build a common vision. Thus, while the 'interested parties' were claiming victory for 'saving the dunes', the realities facing the 'affected parties' presented complex and serious problems needing to be resolved before a decision should be made on what land-use option or options should be implemented on the Eastern Shores.

In short, the processes of the EIA had not allowed for the complex and changing social and political dynamics of the issues involved. It is perhaps in this regard that the discipline of environmental history could have played an important role. The very nature of the methodology of the discipline serves to illuminate some of the intrinsic and intangible factors missed by other disciplines. For example, looking back at the history of the area would reveal the importance of the creation and maintenance of conservation areas being seen as more than merely a geographic area divorced from and independent of society,[36] and more than an area left exclusively to the controls of the laws of nature. Such areas are after all created by society and, as such, they form yet another type of human ecosystem. Conservation practices therefore tend to mirror socio-political structures and, in particular, the attitudes of those in power.[37] Environmental history illustrates that historically conservation involves allocation of resources, and this allocation must be seen to benefit society. To be successful, conservation must therefore be sensitive to the interests of society.

The terms of reference of the EIA did not allow for consideration of the complex and diverse land issues in the St Lucia region, which are inextricably linked to socio-economic as well as political problems. The most important factor to note is perhaps that mineral rights on the Eastern Shores cannot be separated from the land rights of the local communities. In order to understand this aspect it is necessary to look again at the history of the Eastern Shores region and at the political environment which characterised its development. We have noted that until the advent of colonialism the local communities' modes of resource use appear to have been sustainable. They altered their landscapes without jeopardising the underlying functioning and productivity of the ecosystem. This relationship with nature changed with the arrival of the first white settlers, and the delicate balance between sustainable resource use and unsustainable exploitation was soon shattered. The local communities and their environment were subjected to the influences of a market economy, firearms and industrialisation. They could only stand by as these new peoples first decimated much of the wildlife in the area and then later, with the expansion of commercial agriculture, watch as vast areas of indigenous vegetation were swallowed up by sugar and pine plantations.

Research has shown that the ancestors of the communities who were removed from the Eastern Shores had lived there since the reign of King Cetshwayo (1872–79)[38] and possibly since the reign of Shaka and before. These people practised shifting agriculture as described above, and continued to subsist in this way until they lost ownership of the land in 1897 in terms of the Zululand Annexation Act (37 of 1897). This position was consolidated in 1909 with the establishment of the Zululand reserves by means of the Deed of Grant No. 7638/1909, and all land that was not demarcated as reserve land became Crown land and, later, state land.[39]

The Eastern Shore communities were, however, allowed to remain where they were, though their rights were limited, and the state had the right to evict them provided that reasonable notice was given. Their access to the land was therefore severely limited. The situation was to deteriorate further with the passing of the

1913 Land Act, which prevented African ownership of land outside of the scheduled reserves. Dispossession of land rights was further entrenched by the 1936 Native Trust and Land Act. For the people of the Eastern Shores this legislation meant that they found themselves deprived of access to most of their pastures and farming land as well as fisheries and the marine resources upon which they had hitherto depended for their livelihood. Worse was to come. In 1956 Government Notice 1408 proclaimed the Cape Vidal and Eastern Shores Forest Reserves, in terms of the Forest Act of 1941. Many of the people living on the Eastern Shores would now be physically removed. Some were permitted to remain, but only if one member of the family was employed by the Department of Forestry. Those unable or unwilling to comply with this regulation were given three months' notice to vacate the land.

There was nothing that could be done other than comply with the regulations, or move. The people of the Eastern Shores had, since the arrival of the first white settlers, slowly but surely been rendered politically powerless. They had lost the legal basis to occupy the land in 1897 and had lived there only under the regulation and sufferance of the state. The exact number of people removed is not known. The 1951 census shows the population of this area to be 2075; other estimates vary from 3000 to 5000. Whatever the figure, the removals exacerbated an already untenable situation in the areas surrounding the St Lucia conservation area. The Eastern Shores communities were not given land of their own but were expected to 'khonza', which broadly translates as becoming vassals, to neighbouring chiefs. Nearby communities had themselves been territorially restrained and resettled in these areas, which were (and still are) for the most part without rudimentary infrastructure, and by the 1950s were already showing signs of overcrowding and land degradation.

This situation was the result of a number of complex factors, not least of which was the way in which South Africa obtained labour for industrialisation. Labour needs and regulation were facilitated by the evolution and entrenchment of discriminatory practices and the alienation of the indigenous population from the land. These practices had implications for all facets of South Africa's socio-economic make-up, but especially for the environment. Up until the arrival of the colonists, African agriculturists had practised subsistence agriculture and in the more marginal regions had developed a system of pastoralism which was environmentally sustainable. They had too, where markets existed, responded to these and in some regions a successful peasantry had evolved. With the creation of reserves and, later, 'homelands', which were confined to about thirteen per cent of South Africa's land mass, it became impossible for most African agriculturalists to maintain their previous relationships and interactions with their environment. The inadequacy of available land on which to subsist was aggravated by the fact that one of the most salient aspects of the apartheid system was its neglect of African agriculture. In fact, it has been argued that African agriculture was actively discriminated against while white agriculture was protected, subsidised and modernised. What had happened to African agriculturalists – and this is particularly relevant to those living in the St Lucia region – was that their method of resource use had been rendered unsustainable without the possibility of change to meet the needs and opportunities brought by industrialisation. It is these injustices that the South African government is trying to address through its new Land Reform and Redistribution Policy. It is in the light of past injustices and present policy that we must view solutions for the problems facing the future of the St Lucia conservation area and, more particularly, that of the Eastern Shores region.

Current land policy

The current government's land policy seeks to facilitate the redress of past political injustices and to use land as a tool for the empowerment of formerly disadvantaged people. The specific aims of the land reform programme are to redress the legacy of land dispossession, to ensure benefits to the poor, to contribute to reconciliation in South Africa,[40] and to ensure economic benefits to the nation. The framework within which these aims are to be achieved is embraced in land redistribution, land restitution and land tenure reform.

As far as land policy and St Lucia is concerned it is land restitution – the restoration of land or provision of compensation to those people who were dispossessed of their land by the discriminatory laws of apartheid – that is applicable. This policy is meant to work in conjunction with the Reconstruction and Development Programme (RDP), which should be accessed in order to facilitate necessary development in the area. This policy illustrates that there is now a quite different power structure. A highly emotive response inspired by the potential destruction of a unique wetland is logical in a world where the natural environment is under severe pressure. Now, though, any land-use strategy would need to be evaluated against a much broader set of criteria than the options set by the EIA. The sort of development necessary, besides seeking the normal tax revenues and foreign exchange, would have to bring appropriate levels of services and utilities to the area and fulfil the needs of the local communities and not just the institutional structures administering them. Development should also be undertaken in such a way that it helps to preserve the region's natural resources.[41] In the words of the joint statement made by the Ministers' Committee, the government sought '...an integrated development and land-use planning strategy for the Eastern Shores and the entire Greater St Lucia Region. This will enable various sectors (such as nature conservation, agriculture, ecotourism, forestry and existing mining) to work collectively toward the common goal of eradicating the region's poverty and thus promoting sustainable development.'[42]

It is in this context, then, that we need to view the future of the Eastern Shores of St Lucia and indeed the entire Greater St Lucia Wetland Park region. Today the former inhabitants of the Eastern Shores are scattered amongst various communities living in what is known as the Hlabisa district. Two claims to the Eastern Shores have been lodged with the KwaZulu-Natal regional office of the Commission on Restitution of Land Rights. The first of these was lodged on 27 September 1995 by Mr Phineas Mbuyazi on behalf of the Mbuyazi clan. The second was lodged soon afterwards, on 11 October 1995, by Inkosi Mkhwanazi on behalf of the Mpukonyoni Tribal Authority.[43] Both claims are for the same area and refer to the same history of removal, but the Mpukonyoni Tribal Authority disputes the authority of Mr Mbuyazi to represent the claim while the latter refutes the right of the Mpukonyoni to claim, as Inkosi Mkhwanazi and the Mpukonyoni never actually lived on the Eastern Shores. The custom of appointment of traditional leaders, however, gives Inkosi Mkwanazi authority over Mr Mbuyazi and his clan. To add to the complexity of the situation there have now been claims made by individuals who are tired of the political manoeuvring of the two leaders and merely want their land back or acceptable alternative land.[44] The legal complexities of this case are many and need clarification before a settlement can be made. The case has therefore been submitted to the Land Claims Court. It would appear that there is a strong case for restitution, and justice demands some fair accommodation for these people. Land restitution, however, does not dictate that people have an automatic right to a particular area. This leaves scope for some creative lateral thinking in offering alternative propositions.

The dynamics of change

Human disturbance of the Eastern Shores environment has come from a number of different sources, the most significant of which are silviculture, recreation, agriculture and, if one includes indirect interferences, industry and settlement. Between 1950 and 1996 the visual and aesthetic landscapes of the Eastern Shores underwent radical changes in places. The indigenous people were banished, and many hectares of pine forest replaced their small cultivated fields and the undulating grasslands on which the antelope they hunted and their cattle had grazed. On the beach near Cape Vidal, where they collected shellfish, there are now, over a weekend, anything up to 200 four-wheel-drive vehicles. On the dune overlooking Lake Bangazi, on an old kraal site, is a secluded luxury tourist camp.

What are the dynamics behind these changes and behind the way different human societies interrelate and interact with their environment? The societies responsible for human interferences on the Eastern Shores are radically different, being governed by vastly different goals, values, laws, aspirations and available technologies. The goals of a society will reflect its values and aspirations. The introduction of different goals will therefore provide a strong dynamic for change in relationships and interactions with the environment. It is clear from research undertaken that the goals, customs and beliefs of the community of subsistence agriculturists living on the Eastern Shores reflected the importance and respect – even reverence – given to the environment. It is this attitude that provides an important dynamic behind the type of impact this community had on its environment. Their method of resource use and thus their relationship with the environment was typically pre-industrial. They did not use industrial technology and did not harness the energy sources available to industrial societies. They had developed a method of resource use in response to their own particular goals and needs and to their environment. The limits on this system were those set by the environment and by the regulations of their traditional authority. These changed continually and so the dialectic between farming and the environment was never static. As a subsistence economy that was locally confined, its socio-political and environmental dynamics and characteristics were highly dependent on the region. The impacts this community made on their environment were conse-quently relatively slow and evolutionary in nature and, in general, not damaging to the environment.

The 1950s produced a radical change when the Eastern Shores came under the direct control of a very different society. It was now under the control of a state governed by industrial, capitalist ideals and with the added complication of a racist policy of segregation. The indigenous community had been removed from the area by the mid-1970s. For both political and economic reasons the state took control of the area and created an agro-ecosystem distinctive of industrial capitalism. We see on the Eastern Shores the establishment of the widespread production of a single exotic species solely for profit. Capitalism commodifies land and this has definite implications for the relationship that a capitalist society has with its natural environment.

It has been argued by Simmons and others that 'technology is the strongest cultural determinant of the impact a society can make on the environment'.[45] Indeed, it was not until the region had been subjected to a change in human technological status that dramatically different impacts on the environment occurred. The level of technology available to a society will impact on its ability to harness, store and use energy and also on its methods of resource use. In turn, the method of resource use will largely dictate the flow of matter, energy and information through the human ecosystem and thus ultimately the type of impact a society has on the environment. These are sound arguments, but the goals of a society have dynamics of their own even though those goals are only achievable if the level of technology enables them to be so. This is not to deny that each mode of production evolves its own corresponding ideology and institutions which will support that ideology. The argument is that it does not follow that a society gaining a certain level of technology will, for example, necessarily develop 'profit' as its motivating force. Thus when looking at the dynamics driving the increased environmental impacts of industrial capitalist societies, or any other society, one must look beyond the technology and energy sources to the social structures which uphold the method of resource use – in short, the set of ideas that justify and support the system.

Accepting the above argument has interesting implications when viewed in the light of the aims of South Africa's democratically elected government, which has introduced a transformed power structure with different aims and goals for the society which makes up its electorate. The overriding goal of this government is to redress the material backlog suffered by the majority of South Africans. From the new government's perspective any development strategy would need to be evaluated against a different and broader set of criteria than that of the past government. Any development would have to bring appropriate levels of services and utilities to the area and fulfil the needs of the local communities as well as the institutional structures administering them.

The Lake St Lucia region lies within the Hlabisa district, one of the poorest in KwaZulu-Natal. Growth and development are clearly needed. The question is: in light of the goals of the new government, what type of growth and development, and with what environmental impacts? The conventional view is that 'Post Apartheid South Africa will only be able to redress the inequalities of the past if it achieves growth'.[46] Sustainable development – 'development which meets the needs of the present, without compromising the ability of future generations to meet their own needs'[47] – is the new concept. This widely accepted definition of a global goal is broad and it is not clear whether it means the preservation of the existing resource and environmental component of the nation's total capital stock. This is a particular concern for the new South African government because, as in many less developed countries, the existing stocks have been significantly depleted already.[48] The concept of sustainable development, while admirable, is not very helpful without a more explicit definition and some sort of suggested strategy to achieve it.

Growth and development are generally seen to go hand in hand with growth in the free market and private sector. Economists who advocate sustainable development, however, are beginning to be more critical of what actually constitutes growth. Turck, for instance, points out 'that we do not want growth for growth's sake in the sense of a simple statistical indicator'.[49] He argues further that we also do not need 'an explosion of free market forces which will favour the powerful against the small business and informal sector'. He claims rather that what we need is growth in the private sector but it must be in a 'carefully nurtured form' that will lead to the disadvantaged being the main beneficiaries through a genuine increase in the resources they command and in their share of the national cake.[50] This view is in line with the new government's goals. They would like to promote growth that is not, for example, based on the production of luxury consumer goods but on providing for the needs of the impoverished people of South Africa.

Thus it would appear that development is being redefined to mean providing the impoverished with the means with which to survive sustainably. This redefinition of development creates the need for radical redistribution of access to resources as well as changes to the institutions and systems that had previously managed them. These changes will in turn change the relationship between the society and its environment and are indeed necessary if seen in the light of the claim that it is the combined destructive impacts of an impoverished majority struggling to stay alive and an affluent minority consuming resources to excess that are destroying the environment.[51] This set of circumstances is clearly observable in the environs of St Lucia, where industry, commercial agriculture and abject poverty have all taken their toll on an exceptionally unique environment. It is equally clear that the poor can no longer bear the blame nor the cost of these impacts. New solutions need to be found.

Conclusion

Given the explosive mix of imperatives in the St Lucia region, new solutions will not be found easily. Rationally there appear to be possibilities of a win-win solution for all, with perhaps a degree of sacrifice by mining interests. (There are alternative commercially viable deposits for them to mine.) The emotions whipped up by the past unjust political interference together with financial constraints could, however, bedevil the achievement of logical solutions. The question remains then: how are environmentalists and policy-makers going to reconcile the claims and needs of the communities in the light of the new land, economic and environmental policies?

During the course of this exploratory study, the approaches of environmental history have helped to identify crucial factors which need to be reconsidered in plotting the path to a resolution of the conundrum. These factors include the unique and irreplaceable biodiversity of international significance which the study area supports, and whose protection and conservation deserves attention not only from local communities, province or state but from the world; the land claims of removed people (be they legal, legitimate claims or merely demands for justice); the poverty and general lack of infrastructure in the local communities; the high unemployment figures; and the development potential that eco-tourism holds for the area, and how this potential can be used to uplift and sustainably develop the local communities.

To succeed, environmentalists and policy-makers must accept the goals of balancing the cost and benefits of conservation equally among the different sectors of the community, of widening environmental philosophy to include that of traditional societies such as those who existed on the Eastern Shores. This requires linking the struggle against social injustice and exploitation to the struggle for the environment;[52] and linking conservation to the process of rural development and the survival of agrarian societies.[53] By doing this they would fall in line with a new, evolving perception of development, driven by the goals of a new power structure which reflects the needs of a newly defined South African society. Consequently, the objectives of development and conservation will come to be regarded not as irreconcilable but as part of one and the same process. It would appear that, even given the complexities of the issues, with some creative planning the challenge of packaging these goals into a workable policy could be achievable. The problems facing the Eastern Shores and its environment are potentially resolvable, and its future conservation is possible.

Part III
Commentaries and Comparisons

Chapter Thirteen

South African environmental history in the African context

William Beinart

Environmental history written on South Africa has been strongest, firstly, on state regulation of natural resources and, secondly, on conflicts between the state and rural people over such policies. These emphases have been in part shaped by comparative material on, respectively, the anglophone settler world and colonial Africa. I will suggest that there are certainly some themes, explored briefly here, in African environmental studies that would repay closer examination by South Africanists – in particular, African knowledge of the natural world. And historians of both Africa and South Africa would profit from a more complex understanding of environmental change itself.

To take the first point: the United States of America and the British settler commonwealth have been a major comparative foil for historians of South Africa.[1] North America has been the key locus of the new environmental history that has evolved since the 1970s. Historiography has focused on expanding settler capitalist societies that drew deeply on the exploitation of natural resource frontiers, from bison and beavers to forests and pastures. Dispossession of indigenous people has been a co-equal concern. North American literature also searches out the antecedents of modern environmentalism. Some proponents of the natural world were influenced by aesthetic or preservationist priorities; most were concerned about the efficient use of natural resources and their long-term viability. By the early twentieth century, new settler states were engaged in systematic environmental regulation in the shape of national parks, forest protection, water conservation – as it was then called – and controls on land use.

Terence Ranger has suggested that South African environmental history may be too strongly influenced by this comparative settler dimension, which contributes to acceptance of that country's exceptionalism in Africa.[2] Yet there are echoes everywhere of the American experience in South African history and there is still a great deal to be discovered both about settler appropriation of natural resources, and about the interrelationship between settlers, African people and nature. To take one example: white settlement was deeply dependent on water and, as Guelke and Shell point out, nearly 50 per cent of new farm names by the mid-eighteenth century were water-related.[3] By the twentieth century, South Africa was an increasingly dammed society with a high proportion of its water channelled to irrigate farmlands. There is very limited historical writing on this key resource: the most innovative analysis of water politics is hidden in a local history of Graaff-Reinet by Kenneth Smith.[4] It would be valuable to test, with South African materials, Worster's ideas about the hierarchical, corporate, 'hydraulic' character of the American West. Perhaps, as some of Worster's American critics have suggested, individual settler enterprise was more significant than the state and corporations in enhancing usable water supplies.[5]

Beverley Ellis's discussion of nineteenth-century colonial Durban's impact on the environment in this volume also opens up new areas for investigation. It has not been replicated for other South African cities, despite exciting American comparative examples. Her approach could be extended to include the processing and distribution – locally and globally – of raw materials and agricultural commodities.[6] This would include not only sugar and wattle, but products of the hunt as well as the pastoral economy. Durban was intimately linked with the interior pastoral frontier: wool exports exceeded those of sugar in value through the late nineteenth and early twentieth centuries; the ox-drawn wagon traffic in and out of the port was huge.

Harald Witt's analysis of the history of industrial forestry in Natal, on the basis of exotic species, similarly breaks new ground and shows the potential for amalgamating agrarian and environmental history. Even in relatively well-explored areas, such as settler and imperial hunting, where there have been more extended discussions by Roger Wagner, John Mackenzie, Jane Carruthers and others, there remains a great deal of potential for further research.[7] Analysis of the sequential impact of settlement and firearms on particular species of wildlife in this, one of the regions richest in mammal species on a global scale, is still lacking.[8] Which species were favoured for consumption or trade? Which, aside from jackals, weathered the storm? Was animal behaviour itself significant in shaping this history? Can we write the history of wild animals – rather than simply what was done to them? Certainly the primacy of ivory in trade is acknowledged, but the market for this commodity has not been systematically analysed. Exploration of the skills and languages that evolved in hunting, including those of tracking and everyday zoology, as well as the equipment, technology and social forms that developed, remains preliminary.

Historians are now realising just how early it was that conservationist concerns were expressed in the Cape as settlers and officials came to terms with their new environment. Grove has canvassed the idea that environmentalism in the Cape had Scottish origins: he explores the interests and concerns of Robert Moffat, the missionary; Thomas Pringle, the settler, writer and political activist; and John Croumbie Brown, the missionary, botanist and writer.[9] Yet this thesis is by no means established and there are other strands of influence to be discovered both for the Cape and the country as a whole. Both English and Swedish travellers left a legacy of natural history, which was frequently referred to in later conservationist writing.[10] P.J. van der Merwe has demonstrated the awareness of desiccation as well as drought amongst frontier officials, who were keen to control trekboer transhumance, in the early nineteenth century.[11] We know very little about Afrikaner ideas about drought and the extent to which they were formalised into conservationist concerns.

The same point applies more generally to Afrikaner environmental knowledge. Although Jane Carruthers has her doubts about the significance of Afrikaners in the foundation of the Kruger National Park, nevertheless she shows that even in a state as rudimentary as the Transvaal, hunting regulation was a major preoccupation by the mid-nineteenth century.[12]

Nineteenth-century English settler farmers were certainly amongst the first to develop a systematic critique of the impact of livestock on the semi-arid environment of the Cape.[13] Patrick Harries points to more general missionary fascination with classifying the natural world.[14] It was certainly difficult for fledgeling colonial states to impose controls over natural resource usage in the nineteenth century. But there is an argument to be made that environmental and disease regulation – especially over the much underestimated commercial livestock economy – was a major and neglected feature in the formation of the Cape colonial state.[15] Van Sittert's chapter on prickly pear in this volume (Chapter 9) explores just one area of concern for the Cape government; it was replicated in such spheres as predator control, water provision, disease eradication, and other areas for which experts were employed.

Another theme that might draw fruitfully on the comparative model of settler states is the influence of scientists on environmental regulation. Initially, those employed in South Africa were externally trained – largely in Britain, India and the United States. By the early decades of the twentieth century, these South African-based scientific and conservation experts were beginning to have an important impact, not only in the country but in other parts of Africa – veterinary experts such as Hutcheon and Theiler; entomologists such as Lounsbury; botanists Bews and Philips; and water engineer Kanthack. Most of them were in thick contact with global, especially anglophone, scientific networks. South

Africa's role as a scientific and conservationist submetropole, especially in the first half of the twentieth century, before apartheid began to cut off international contacts, has probably been underestimated. In sum, even if the environmental history of South Africa has been unduly influenced by the comparative example of other anglophone settler societies, this vein of material has by no means been fully mined.

Conflict

As noted above, an equally central theme in writing about South Africa has been conflict between the state and African rural communities over natural resources. At the heart of the literature has been land-use planning during the apartheid period – especially 'Betterment' and rehabilitation. Here a broader Africanist literature has been particularly influential. The late colonial period in Africa, when British colonial states embarked on highly interventionist programmes of agricultural and natural resource management, reveals many parallels. There are certainly differences of opinion in South African literature over exactly what was intended by South African interventions and how similar they were to British colonial land-use planning. Fred Hendricks argues, for example, that South African rehabilitation policy – whatever its initial intention – had more to do with the control of settlement and population movements in pursuit of apartheid, than with environmental management.[16]

Historians and social scientists writing the history of South Africa's African societies in the reserve or homeland areas in the twentieth century find that they cannot escape this central theme. The significance of state intervention in stimulating rural protest and opposition has been densely covered – for example, in Peter Delius's book on Sekhukhuneland and Anne Mager's on the Ciskei.[17] Issues of natural resource management, and conflicting ideas about appropriate uses of nature, were often important in rural conflict. However, these studies place at their centre political and gender rather than environmental issues. My other chapter in this collection (Chapter 6) suggests how we might look behind immediate political conflicts and explore their deep environmental roots: in the case of Pondoland, locust control and forestry regulation.

This strategy of research would demand fuller understanding of environmental change and its impact on rural people rather than simply let us invoke environmental questions as an aid to discussing politics. Other contributors to this volume start to move more systematically into this realm of analysis. John Lambert discusses the weakening of homestead production not simply on the basis of economic decline and discrimination, which has been the major focus in the literature on African peasants, but environmental loss. Nancy Jacobs, drawing ironically on a North American rather than specifically African model, attempts to insert environmental issues into the history of the southern Tswana. There are valuable examples within African historical studies where sustained analysis of relationships between people and nature go beyond any material which is yet available on South Africa.

Robert Harms's study of the Nunu – a fishing community settled along the Zaïre River – from their first contacts with the Atlantic economy is a case in point.[18] A wide range of archaeological, linguistic and oral material has been brought to bear on pre-colonial African environmental history. Understandings of the gradual expansion of Bantu-speaking peoples through much of sub-Saharan Africa over three millennia are increasingly attuned to the environmental context.[19] New rural histories of Zimbabwe are particularly strong on the environmental dimensions of state intervention and responses in the colonial period.[20] There are strong signs that southern African – and even South African – studies are absorbing these new directions. In addition to Jacobs's work on the southern Tswana, research such as that by Emmanuel Kreike on Ovambo history will provide a new platform for analysing and teaching an environmentally informed history of Africans in southern Africa.[21] Kreike argues that most studies of African peasantries in southern Africa have concentrated too much upon the impact of the colonial state and neglected the details of African land use.[22]

There are other limits to approaches – thus far perhaps dominant in South African historiography – which focus largely upon the regulatory state and reactions by Africans to it. A growing Africanist literature has illustrated the depth of indigenous or local knowledge about the natural world. West African studies have been most fertile in this regard.[23] This is not entirely surprising, given the absence of settler colonialism, the vitality of African peasantries in the region, and their capacity to adapt and develop their agrarian systems in the colonial period and after. By contrast, early conquest and absorption of African societies in South Africa, as well as relative stasis in peasant production in the reserves, constrained examination of African local knowledge. Officials in the Native Affairs Department and various expert commissions emphasised the extent of degradation in African reserve areas of South Africa and the incapacity of Africans to manage their cattle and land. As Lambert notes in Chapter 4 of this volume, even sympathetic novelists such as Alan Paton have used soil erosion in the reserves as a literal and metaphorical sign of decline. Radical historians offered a different interpretation of rural decline, blaming external pressures and the migrant labour system rather than traditional African culture, but they used the same evidence of degradation.[24] This was not a model suited to an exploration of the strengths of local knowledge.

It may be difficult to research African ideas in pre-colonial and early colonial South Africa, yet not uniquely difficult in the context of African history. Some of the African kingdoms and chiefdoms of South Africa were conquered only in the late nineteenth century – at much the same time as the scramble for the rest of the continent. Moreover, historians of South Africa may even have some advantages in the density of early travel, mission and official records. Nancy Jacobs's chapter certainly suggests that there is a rich late-eighteenth- and early nineteenth-century literature.[25] Ecologists and archaeologists have also extracted a great deal of environmental information from early travel literature in an attempt to find a baseline for later environmental change.[26] European travellers were often particularly sensitive to the new environment they were encountering for the first time and a number brought with them a botanical and zoological training. They were of course limited by their 'imperial eyes' but at this time of enlightenment and romantic enthusiasm they could be sensitive and wide-ranging observers – and even reflect the perceptions of their African intermediaries.[27] Early literate African communities, and the press that served them, might also provide valuable source material. At least some of the new elite remained rooted in rural communities and took up their cause in respect of land.[28]

Nor should local knowledge be conceived simply as that which pertains to the distant past. African ideas were evolving and there is considerable scope for further interviewing and inventive use of ethnographic and other sources.[29] A number of major African chieftaincies such as the Thembu, Mpondo, Zulu, Swazi and Sotho held onto their core areas of settlement as well as their languages. There is continuity as well as change to be found here both in practices and in modes of understanding. South African social scientists, now drawing on the literature on African local knowledge, are rediscovering that African communities in some areas continue to make use of their landholdings in mixed farming systems. While they have absorbed many new ideas, techniques and crops, their land is still largely held in forms of customary tenure, and their land-use strategies would be recognisable to observers from the late nineteenth century. Furthermore, historians of South Africa may have been limited by their linguistic competence – and this leaves scope for a new generation of African scholars to make a particular contribution.

A related strand of literature on Africa has been to caution against diagnoses of crisis, which might invite external and inappropriate interventions. One interesting example concerns deforestation and fuelwood. A picture of massive and rapid deforestation has been widely presented, especially in more popular literature such as Lloyd Timberlake's *Africa in crisis,* subtitled *The causes, the cures of environmental bankruptcy.*[30] There have certainly been intense debates about effective solutions: agro-forestry or community forestry rather than established strategies of afforestation. But now scholars have gone further in their discussion of deforestation. There is a powerful counterthrust criticising 'narratives of deforestation' and arguing that rural Africans sometimes afforest their land, notably around settlements in treeless savannah zones.[31] A parallel discussion has attempted to qualify the idea of a universal fuelwood crisis. JoAnn McGregor argued on the basis of extensive oral interviews that even in densely settled communal reserves of Zimbabwe, women contrived to find wood locally. Local planting and management, new exotic species, recycling, the spread of indigenous acacia species, and even major planted forests were all important for local fuelwood supplies.[32]

The notion that Africans have deforested the areas they occupy remains a powerful one in South African literature, especially with respect to the former African homelands. It may be correct, and pockets of dense indigenous forest have certainly been reduced in some areas. But there is limited systematic study of vegetation in these areas of South Africa over the long term. In some districts, indigenous acacia species may have become more common during the second half of the twentieth century because of particular grazing and burning regimes.[33] Exotic species such as the black wattle are extensively grown around rural homesteads in KwaZulu-Natal and the Transkei for firewood and building purposes. South Africa as a whole is almost certainly more treed now than it has been for some centuries, because of widespread planting of exotic species in many different locales.[34]

An assumption that has abounded in literature on Africa, not least in crisis narratives, is that environmental scarcity is new, and that it intensifies conflicts. Jabulani Sithole makes a convincing case in Chapter 5 of this volume that long-term conflict within rural African communities in the Pinetown district, KwaZulu-Natal, should be analysed in the context of a shortage of natural resources. More generally, there is an almost unconscious reiteration in South African historical work that many conflicts – between white and black, on colonial frontiers, as well as within African societies – have been due to 'land shortage'. Archival material even on environmental issues has tended to accumulate around episodes of conflict, as is reflected in chapters in this collection. But we need to ask, in continental terms, firstly, whether there has in fact been greater scarcity in recent decades than there was in the past and, secondly, even if there is, whether scarcity has, overall, intensified conflict.[35]

Perceptions of environmental scarcity in Africa are clouded by memories of good times, and by the assumption that people in Africa should have land. Yet Africa as a whole now supports vastly more people than it did in the relatively recent past. Scarcity was almost certainly more of a brake on demographic increase prior to the twentieth century than it was in that century of massive population growth. Though millions of African people remain very poor, intensification of agriculture, urbanisation and more differentiated economies have arguably reduced overall scarcity – certainly in its life-threatening forms. Scarcity is often more intense in societies with non-commoditised, land-extensive forms of subsistence.

It is by no means clear, either, that the level of conflict over natural resources has increased. For example, the period in KwaZulu-Natal between the Bambatha rebellion in 1906 and the outbreak of violence between supporters of the United Democratic Front and Inkatha in the 1980s was probably more peaceful than the nineteenth century. Yet the twentieth century was also the period of the most rapid rural population increase. Nineteenth-century conflict in the Zululand area, it has been argued, was itself probably triggered in part by competition for natural resources.[36] The powers of the state to enforce peace were certainly far greater in this twentieth-century period than before or since.

In addition to understanding the multiple causes of the kind of factional conflict that Sithole illustrates, we need to ask harder questions as to what constitutes frequent violence in this context. Equally important, questions arise as to how negotiations are conducted over natural resource use and boundaries – how peace is made and sustained at a local level. It would be valuable for South Africanists to draw on anthropological literature about the regulation of disputes in African societies.[37] More broadly, has tension over environmental resources historically helped to precipitate negotiation and co-ordination, the extension of civil society, and indeed the formation of government and states, as much as violent conflict?

African knowledge and practice

Exploration of local knowledge in broader Africanist literature has included not only discovery, but also an advocacy of the salience of African practice. The literature reflects changing global arguments about the validity of different forms of knowledge and about rights to resources.[38] Scholars have developed a critique of Western science and of managerial development strategies controlled by insensitive outsiders or those with particular interests in intensifying commoditisation within Africa. The corollary has been an argument for community management of natural resources as an alternative development practice. This reassertion of an Africanist, pro-peasant or subaltern perspective is understandable. So many debates in African studies have hinged around the deleterious effects of external intrusion. In some sense this is ironic as Africans – to a greater extent than Native Americans, First Nations in Canada, Aborigines or Maoris in Australasia – have continued to shape their own environmental destinies.

Asserting the salience of African knowledge and countering crisis narratives have been central in new approaches to African environmental studies. Such advocacy has made an impact in South Africa, especially since 1994, when restitution of land and other resources has become more possible. But in drawing on comparative literature on Africa, South Africanists should be cautious. They need not be restricted to arguments that have their roots in a powerful moral anti-colonialism and a celebration of locality and community. While they should most certainly attempt to understand African local knowledge and resource use, they should also retain a critical perspective on local practices.

Not that historians of Africa are necessarily of one voice. Research has also opened the way for more diverse perspectives on the relationship between people and nature in Africa. Even people with limited technology could transform their environments, exterminate species, overwork their land and exacerbate drought. In North America, native peoples migrating down from Alaska probably played a significant role in the extinction of key species including wild equines.[39] It is an irony that their adoption of domesticated horses as well as firearms after European colonisation played a significant role in the demise of the bison.[40] Whatever the significance of African local knowledge, African states have by no means all been able to regulate and control environmental change. As Clark Gibson argues, the political economy of post-colonial African states such as Zambia has not always been favourable to sustainable management of natural resources – in his case, wildlife.[41] Local knowledge itself, imbricated as it is with many new influences, does not necessarily produce production regimes that are sympathetic to local resources. Much human knowledge about nature, whether in Africa or elsewhere, has evolved to facilitate exploitation. All human societies, from metropolitan industrial Britain to the Easter Islands, have had the capacity to destroy the natural resources on which they depend.

Nor should we assume that outside interventions aimed at regulating African use of natural resources were always rejected. Grace Carswell, writing on Kigezi, south-west Uganda, shows that colonial environmental regulation, notably terracing of sloping fields, was successfully introduced during the 1930s and 1940s.[42] Agricultural officials observed and worked with existing Bakiga practices and were prepared to adapt their techniques to local circumstances. Chiefly authority was relatively uncontested and the chiefs were won over to this project. Carswell's case raises the question of the balance of emphasis in existing historiography between resistance to and acquiescence in colonial planning. In debates over Betterment and rehabilitation in South Africa, there were also individuals – whether modernisers in Sekhukhuneland, or women seeking better state services in the Ciskei – who approved or acquiesced.[43] In respect of the Transkei, Andrew Charman has noted that the African elite, organised around the

Bunga or Council system, often approved the introduction of cattle dipping and veterinary controls, even when others organised to reject it. Like some white farmers, self-consciously progressive and modernising communities saw these strategies as helping to protect their livestock.[44] Historians need to move beyond an argument that sees colonialism as necessarily impoverishing environments or triggering environmental conflicts.

Drawing especially on East African examples and on ideas about local knowledge, radical range ecologists in South Africa are now arguing that contrary to widespread perceptions, rangelands in African areas with communal tenure are not generally degraded.[45] They are rejecting the old critiques that nightly kraaling of livestock destroyed the veld through endless tramping. They also question the expensive solution of fencing pasturelands in camps which are rotated through the year so that some can be rested. It may be that African rural communities cannot afford to fence and improve pasturelands, given the limited income that is available from livestock-farming and the withdrawal of subsidies from the agricultural sector. Yet South African environmental historians should also be cautious about applying these arguments historically. There is evidence of soil erosion in many of the former homeland areas; some of it at least is likely to have been caused by the intensification of peasant production and livestock holdings in the late nineteenth and early twentieth centuries under conditions of communal tenure.

Neither the comparative settler nor comparative African historiography has yet fully come to terms with an ecological history in which the dynamics of environmental change form a significant focus. This raises formidable problems for historical researchers in that it requires some grasp of scientific as much as historical sources, research techniques and debates. Historians should not, however, abandon the task before it is begun and there are increasing signs that some cross-disciplinary sharing of the enterprise of environmental history is possible. Environmental historians are in fact already littering their footnotes with references to ecological and scientific journals.[46] It is certainly easier to grasp older science than newer. Yet it is just as essential for historians to understand past scientific thinking because it shaped the approach of many of the historical actors on whom we focus. The history of science is a massively expanding area in itself, providing context and content for research into African environmental history.[47] A critical history of science does not have to be a condemnatory history of science.

Moreover, some scientists are writing history, and often choosing to do so in overarching, global and popular terms accessible to non-specialists. They both demonstrate the uncertainties in their disciplines and provide a means for historians to absorb and engage with debates. Texts such as Jared Diamond on

Guns, germs and steel or Tim Flannery's *The future eaters* are at their best in sketching the long evolution of interaction between plants, animals and people.[48] But they are not shy about entering into the documented historical age, and are prepared to risk highly determinist approaches most historians would eschew. If scientists can write about history in this way, perhaps historians should be no less rash in taking on scientific debates. Geography, as a discipline, has long provided an interface between these different time-scales and research strategies. As Edward Wilson argues in *Consilience* there is a strong case for prioritising such interdisciplinary approaches as a means of confronting global problems and their historical origins in the twenty-first century.[49] Here the comparative African literature will be of great value because there are rich and only partly tapped wells of accumulated scientific and medical research on Africa.

Historians tend to start with people and their influence upon the natural world. They are concerned with assigning human responsibility for change and, however indirectly, with the moral issues connected with such judgements. Scientists are more comfortable in attempting to assess the nature of environmental change itself, rather than perceptions of it, or human responsibility for it. As John McAllister suggests in Chapter 10 of this volume, the extent of human influence on natural environments – in this case, African rangelands – over the long term remains a central issue for analysis. There is a significant tradition in rangeland ecology which argues for a relatively small human impact.[50] McAllister certainly sees anthropogenic factors as important, but his concerns are less with the social causes and consequences of change, and more with the actual nature of change in grasslands consequent upon different fire regimes. In this case, and also in Elna Kotze's discussion of the interaction of fire and grasslands in Wakkerstroom (Chapter 11 of this volume), scientific research is seen as critical in management strategies which aim at approximating a natural environment. These new scientific histories of pasturelands are no longer based on the older notion of a climax vegetation, but stem from newer ideas of biodiversity. They may also stand at odds with the human-centred Africanist approach which prioritises human well-being and the right for humans to manage their resources. In defending community rights to manage and command resources in Africa, it is important that Africanists – and South Africanists in particular – do not neglect the fate of those natural resources themselves.

Global information flows are complex. Ideas about the environment and claims upon it by local communities might be generated from their own experience, but are also increasingly framed by international debates and pressure groups. Non-governmental organisations (NGOs) have spread 'social learning'.[51] Concepts such as community management of natural resources might describe what was done by local communities but they are now elaborate frameworks, developed by intellectuals and activists globally, absorbed and adapted by states, and invoked by local communities as part of their political strategy in a new internationally recognised language (although in some cases, such as Zimbabwe's Campfire programme, communities have not necessarily favoured the state's version of community management).

Conclusion

Environmental history can be, and is becoming, a significant element in a post-apartheid historiography. It lends itself towards a focus on the long term, and interactions between all humans and the environment. Racial discrimination in the region has certainly been a key factor in shaping access to natural resources. Segregation and apartheid policies were significant in shaping some manifestations of environmental degradation, notably the condition of land in the African reserves or homelands. But it would be myopic to attribute all forms of environmental degradation to this cause. South Africa's environmental history also has features in common with a number of other countries, including African countries, where settlers were unable to impose themselves: one such process has been massive demographic growth. Environmental history can help to push perspectives and debates beyond the central and anguished issue of race to explore how all human beings both shape the natural world and are constrained by it.

Perhaps environmental historians of South Africa need to think harder about how to structure university courses which might reflect both this interdisciplinary promise and post-apartheid innovations. The interdisciplinary environmental studies Master's programme at the University of Natal, Pietermaritzburg – the site of the conference on which much of this book is based – is a valuable model. Undergraduate teaching might be more difficult, but interdisciplinary approaches to environmental questions may also help to provide one lifeline for history as an undergraduate teaching discipline in South Africa.

Chapter   Fourteen

Commonalities and contrasts, pasts and presents: An Australian view

Stephen Dovers

I have had the good fortune to live at a time when a great debate took place on the nature of man and the future of society. I have had the impression that debate will not go on for much longer, that either the men who know the way forward will take over, and shut up all doubters and dissidents, or the barbarians will shut us all up in their own way.[1]

Today's preoccupations and the events and processes of the past can collide in contemporary political debates, sometimes with unfortunate results. Is collision inevitable or can there be a more informing and productive meeting? As this was being written, John Howard, Australia's prime minister, used the iconic occasion of Anzac Day – Australia's only real collective celebration – to lament the teaching of history in schools. Too many issues and not enough facts, he claimed. The facts he cited seemed to mostly concern Federation in 1901, Australia's roles in international wars and, especially, in the First World War, the brave, failed assault by the Australian and New Zealand Army Corps on the Gallipoli peninsula.[2]

The protestations of historians and those concerned with the unmentioned but strongly implicit 'issues' were as swift as they were predictable. After several decades of work by historians and teachers to spare us the deadening rote chanting of selective, celebratory lists of events, there is pressure to regress. Those lists of the 1950s and 1960s – I learned them at school and forgot much of them soon after – were easy, boring and unchallenging. They served up what went down smoothly, with the rough or spicy bits removed, much like the mainstream Australian cuisine of the same era. History that tries to follow and explain 'issues' is harder, it challenges and unsettles. But it is public history, tied to the public life of the nation's past and present, and with the potential to engage the future. Thus it must swerve –

too close for some – to the political. This is perhaps more obvious in today's South Africa than in Australia.

The tensions between fact and issue cannot be avoided. The extremes of the continuum are uninteresting; it is the mingling of the two that is interesting – politically and intellectually. It is also dynamic, as both fact and issue change constantly. There is scope for negotiating some of these tensions through opening the narratives of Australian environmental history up against those of other places, and this brief chapter wanders across a few connections between Australian and South African environmental history. Environmental history inevitably deals with current political and social issues as it seeks to unearth and reconcile different people's versions of 'facts', and thus it must be public history in the sense of engagement with public life.[3] It might also be public history in stricter senses of the term – supported by public (and other) agencies – a possibility that will be used to close this chapter.

Societies still settling

The Australian in South Africa – and I think vice versa – encounters comforting commonalities, only to be brought up short by the startling contrasts. This holds for the casual visitor or one who delves deeper. Similar landscapes and land uses, comparable climates (an unusual experience for Australians), familiar environmental problems, some historical patterns in rough sequence and accord. Both continue to reconcile the whole of nationhood with the identities and competitive purposes of constituent jurisdictions (the states and provinces) and both look equivocally to their imposed capitals and compromised structures of governance. South Africa's 'voluntary subsumptions of sovereignty in a greater whole... preceded by much hard bargaining' and 'a set of compromises' leading to Union in 1910 parallel Australia's move to Federation in 1901.[4] Both are said to be 'settler' societies.

Then come the jarring contrasts: wildly different regional context, incomparable cultural histories, different politics, different economies. Commonality and contrast occur across the ecological, biophysical, social and political domains of interest to the environmental historian, and can provide either a solid or a shaky base for joint inquiry. A search for commonality can cloud the inquiry just as a focus of contrasts can become an unhelpful list of negatives. As one sorts through the contrasts, some turn out to be real – differences in kind – such as the regional context: South Africa with its land borders to poor countries, Australia afloat in a mixed but economically very dynamic region. Others turn out to be differences in degree, but of great degree, such as the lack of power and resource access by minorities. Some of the similarities are true enough, and are supported by close intellectual relationships between the two countries, in the science of ecology for example. Some important historical themes can be compared, such as the series of pushes for closer land settlement and schemes for creating a white farmer landscape.[5] Two settler societies.[6]

If South Africa and Australia are to be labelled 'settler' societies, then it should be recognised that human settlement is a process and not an event. This is perhaps an obvious point, but it is not always evident in scientific, political or historical discussions. The two countries are still settler societies – 'settling' is still happening and that is a helpful heuristic for environmental history and much else besides. The realisation of the ongoing process of settlement is much stronger in South Africa, not surprisingly following the changes and upheavals of recent years. The opening vignette of this chapter – a prime ministerial plea for historical 'facts' – is indicative only. There are ongoing fights between those who view Australia's two centuries of white history through a selective, rose-coloured lens, and those who are derided as having a 'black armband' view of our past. Mostly, this centres on the past treatment of Aboriginal Australians and the present implications of that, but denial affects historical interpretations of the place of migrants, of women, of the environment. Even the word 'settlement' is tainted in Australia; jingoistic celebration of early white 'settlers' – occupiers and invaders, rather – denies recognition of at least 60 000 years of Australian human settlement.[7]

The notion of 'still settling' can help historians to connect their craft to the preoccupations of people now. It can also help modern environmental managers – be they in a government agency, a farming sector or a community group – to connect their task to a longer story of ongoing human creation of landscapes. It can weigh against a modern political hubris that is rational and managerial and both unable and unwilling to deal with uncertainty and complexity. The present challenge to manage resources and environments sustainably carries with it a clear instruction to think much further ahead. If sustainable development demands a further view forward, then the obvious corollary is a further view back. The core sustainability principle of intergenerational equity demands it, the fact of ongoing settlement demands it and, most importantly, the nature of ecological systems demands it. In ecology, the answer to long time-scales, pervasive uncertainty and complexity facing ecosystem managers is the notion of 'adaptive management', where management interventions are framed as hypotheses that can be tested and the results fed back into the process of management. This offers a marriage of the rigours of the scientific method and the contingent realities of politics and policy.[8] Taking the adaptive notion further and applying it to the political processes and institutional arrangements that frame our interactions with our environments can provide a broad approach to resource and environmental policy, one that embraces complexity and uncertainty and invites us to better connect past, present and future. We have a history of experimenting with Australian and South African environments – sometimes knowingly, sometimes not. We are still experimenting, and the past and present experiments might be brought together by the environmental historians who can tell the ongoing stories of settlement. The ecological ideas of uncertainty and complexity which inform the adaptive notion can inform history regarding natural systems, and historians can stretch the adaptive notion further back. Settlement as adaptation, adaptation as settlement.

What were once in both countries viewed as stories of pre-settlement are being tied more and more to the ongoing story. Settlement was, according to the 'facts' and recitation approach to Australian history, what white people started doing in 1788, obliterating the story of Aboriginal Australians and their thousands of years of prior settlement. From the 1960s on, cultural resurrection of indigenous peoples challenged this story. That task is ongoing. The landmark High Court *Mabo* judgment in 1992 overturned the crucial colonial legal assumption of *terra nullius* – land without law – and sped up that process.[9] With increasing indigenous ownership and/or management of land (one-seventh of the continent and rising), the environmental history of Aboriginal Australia is interesting and increasingly relevant. The tenure at the centre of the native title debate – pastoral leases – was used carefully and intently as a policy instrument for land management for a century and a half. But this history was lost in the rush to protect leases, minimise the possibility of sensible coexistence with native title, and even create a political move for the clean freehold that had been rejected as inappropriate by colonial administrations.[10]

Debate continues over the past impact of Aboriginal burning on Australian environments, and with fire regimes over large and sensitive areas being increasingly determined with reference to indigenous practice the answers are important.[11] Many argue the case one way or the other, absolutely. The more obvious answer is that the situation varied over space and time – to think otherwise would be to deny the heterogeneity of the Australian environment and the finely regionalised nature of indigenous societies. Finding out the more detailed story is a challenge requiring the input of indigenous communities, management agencies, historians, ecologists and more. Not dissimilar debates are carried on in South Africa (see John McAllister in Chapter 10 of this book).

The surprise (for many) and reshaping of historical and legal assumption delivered by the *Mabo* decision invite thought as to the source of possible future surprises that might spur or redirect or challenge the processes of settlement and our understanding of them. The common law is one source, given its evolutionary nature. The recent re-emergence of the legal doctrine of the public trust in Australia owes much to one environmental historian's research into century-old environmental disputes.[12] Are there others? The unfolding of biophysical events is a safe enough bet, as our understanding of the impact of El Niño deepens and events occur. How well do we know the broad parameters of climate variability, with relatively short records and scarce empirical research? That is an area of great potential collaboration between history and science. Who knows what the issues of tomorrow will be, other than that they are difficult to predict now, and that they will demand historical explanation? Many current concerns – climate change for instance – have only been on our research and policy agendas for a very short time. Therein lies a difficulty – as issues evolve and fresh ones emerge, will the sorts of historical material we need be available? McLoughlin explored the history of an activity with strong implications for modern environmental management, the dredging of the Sydney estuary, and raised important questions about the nature, assessment and disposal of key archival material.[13] My personal fascination with how environmental history might connect with present concerns produces many examples similar to these. Whether one accepts the usefulness of the connection or not, the topics remain valid ones for environmental historians.

The latest big series of experiments in settlement are now captured by the term 'sustainable development' – given the prefix 'ecologically' in Australian policy and law.[14] The issue of sustainability has attracted much intellectual and policy attention, with few uncontested developments of theory, method or policy prescription. Much of the attention has come from the fringes of disciplines and from new interdisciplinary alliances: environmental politics and policy, ecological economics, green social theory, and environmental history. Much work is constrained by the limits of disciplinary approaches that do not take sufficient account of the nature of sustainability problems: climate change, biodiversity, integrated land and water management, population–environment linkages and the like. The law, public policy and most economic analyses have this handicap, each reluctant to question the appropriateness of its theoretical assumptions and basic methodological approaches.

Sustainability problems are different in kind – and some would argue in degree – from other contemporary concerns, as they display problem attributes not so often encountered elsewhere, and especially not in combination.[15] Prime amongst these attributes are extended spatial and temporal scales, complexity and pervasive uncertainty, poorly defined policy and property rights and responsibilities, close involvement of communities in causes of and responses to environmental degradation, and the systemic roots of sustainability problems, deeply embedded in patterns of production, consumption, settlement and governance. It is to be expected that approaches that are shaped by past concerns and do not display these attributes so much will be found wanting. Sustainability as a contemporary concern, one that will be around for some time, is both a difficult and attractive target for historical explication. It will require the skills of the many disciplines which undertake 'environmental history': history, ecology, historical geography, law, geomorphology, anthropology, archaeology, and the rest. Could these fields ever be melded into an environmental history with theoretical and methodological coherence? Apart from the likely impossibility of that, I do not think it would even be a good thing as half the insights in a book such as this one would never emerge without disparate approaches.

If environmental history is to be maintained as an interdisciplinary arena rather than a subdiscipline, as Powell rightly says it should,[16] then some rules of interaction and etiquette are called for. Historians have much to tell scientists about competing narratives and the construction of histories, and scientists should listen and adopt some of the courtesies and safeguards of the historian's game. Vice versa, scientists should be open about the limits and narratives in their fields. Even subdisciplines of ecology do not present united fronts, let alone the whole discipline or other, relevant natural sciences – historians and others should not accept one scientific theory, assumption or method as representative of a broader epistemic consensus.

As a lapsed scientist, I will illustrate from that perspective. Strange uses and abuses of the term 'ecology' abound in environmental history and elsewhere. Too often it is used as an inadequate code for the environment, its processes and an array of disparate, antecedent areas of inquiry. Few seem to have looked closely at what the modern discipline of ecology has to say about the character and function of natural systems – and, just as important, what it does not or cannot say. That would seem a logical source of inspiration for non-ecologists who wish to think about the natural world, past, present or future. One needs to look fairly often, as ecology is a young discipline with frequent, important theoretical shifts and a constant building of the methodological and empirical base.[17] Sean Archer gives us a sample of the use of such a perspective in his Karoo chapter in this book (see Chapter 8), and interestingly a good deal of the ecological insight is shared between Australia and South Africa. The long-term, basic function of arid and semi-arid ecological systems is a rapidly evolving and far-from-settled area. Much insight has come from a small, dedicated group at the Centre for Arid Zone Research in Alice Springs: the 'prophets from the desert' of Australian ecology, whose account of ecological adaptations and implications of low-nutrient landscapes and climatic variability probably hold true enough for quite a few non-arid Australian environments as well.[18]

Environmental history holds much potential for attending sustainability problems and their troublesome attributes – temporal scales most apparently –

but contributing also to better coping with uncertainty, exploring the determinants of systemic causes, and examining the role of communities over time. One can view this as an invitation to relevance, or merely as serving to highlight previously under-examined themes and sources in history. Certainly, the potential for relevance to modern concerns should not become the prime imperative, or we risk constraining inquiry and sources. But relevance is worth considering nonetheless. This relevance may come in three forms.[19] The first is, as ever, the provision of a general historical context – an unexceptional claim of historical inquiry and unlikely to be contested. The second and most practical is the provision of human and ecological baselines, giving us more idea about the 'what was there before' question that plagues modern environmental manage-ment and is the stuff of environmental history. The third is more shaky, the unearthing of actual policy or institutional lessons. These are pragmatic categories of relevance that would attract the policy-maker or scientist. There is another contribution from a more historical explication of environmental issues: an enlivening of investigation and debate flowing from the entry of the humanities.

Returning to the pragmatic categories of relevance, both Australia and South Africa – for similar and dissimilar reasons – are refashioning land laws and uses, resource and environmental management regimes, and approaches to environmental protection. There are contrasts and commonalities in both initial conditions and driving imperatives. Like most countries, these renegotiations of settlement reflect the nature of emerging problems and challenges, global forces and political fashions, and the inertia or resilience of pre-existing institutions, customs and practices. Emerging strategies for land degradation, climate change, biodiversity conservation and the like are shaped by modern beliefs concerning the use of market mechanisms and the necessity of down-sizing the state.[20] This creates interesting tensions with another political trend of the time, the intellectual and practical push for more inclusive, discursive ways of doing politics and policy. These recent trends may succeed or fail to influence the preconditions of our current settlement. Natural systems, human institutions and social values often take great time to change (although when they do it may be sudden – threshold effects or revolution) and reflect historical determinants more often than those of the immediate present. Will some of the Westminster institutions of government in Australia such as statutory authorities and representative democracy survive unscathed from the movements toward, respectively, privatisation of government bodies and popular demands for more participatory democracy? Exposure of the historical determinants of existing settings – sometimes resilient, sometimes fragile – has a valuable place.

More glaring pressures operate. The declining social and economic fortunes of rural Australia influence modern policy immensely, and are a product of changing world markets and recent economic policy. They are also very much a product of long-past rural settlement schemes with their too-small property sizes, overlain on an impoverished landscape subject to two centuries of often degrading resource-use practices. Understanding of both sets of influences – the modern and past – is necessary to redress both economic and environmental decline. Yet such declines fade into insignificance beside the human development needs of modern South Africa. The Australian saying 'it's hard to be green when you're in the red' hardly translates. When human development and land management needs are so strongly flavoured by very recent, intense conflict and blatant dispossession, environmental history must also be very much political and social history. This shows clearly in the theme of conflict running through this book (see Chapter 2 by Nancy Jacobs, Chapter 5 by Jabulani Sithole, and Chapter 6 by William Beinart). While narratives of conflict and dispossession feature increasingly in Australian history, including environmental, the relevance to so many people and their very recent nature make this an overriding theme in South Africa. It does not touch so many people so directly in Australia, which is why the nay-sayers can be partially successful in seeking to discount such 'issues' of environment, minorities, race and dispossession. Ensuring that environmental history is also social, economic and political reflects rather well a basic instruction of sustainable development: to 'integrate' environmental, social and economic policy.

The various chapters in this book lead us to some commonalities and contrasts, past and present. The changing appreciation of natural systems and their use is shaped by scientific understanding and by evolving social values and aesthetic appreciation. The emergence of concern over previously disregarded grasslands discussed by John McAllister in Chapter 10 and Elna Kotze in Chapter 11 brings past and present together nicely, demonstrating the importance of what we know and what we do not yet know. Australia's grasslands have been similarly overlooked until recently, and their status, history and management raise similar issues.[21] Annoyingly for the environmental historian, few of those who wrote early accounts were very specific about plants other than the obvious trees. Language and units of description for describing natural systems change and reflect much. Acocks's veld classification, relied on and commented on by Archer, McAllister and Kotze in this book, is a case in point. For an Australian the depth of penetration of Acocks's classification of veld types into the literate non-specialist community is remarkable. Ecologists who gave Australia its various schemata of description are scarcely known. Attempts to change such classifications lead to spats among a few scientists; for the rest, it's just bush.

Unlike grasslands, the economic importance of forests and their better description by past sojourners have seen them much more deeply covered in Australian environmental history, indeed more so than any other ecosystem. The contribution of a small, dedicated and diverse group under the auspices of the Australian Forest History Society has been immense.[22] Yet there is the mixture of past and present here too. Australia's native forests have been subject to more and more intense debates than any other sectors over the past 30 years – countless protests, inquiries and temporary political decisions. In the latest, an astounding amount of resources, energy and detailed information have gone into the Regional Forest Agreement (RFA) process, producing a series of agreements between government, industry and conservationists that may or may not be just as contingent as previous 'settlements'. Interestingly, the conservation targets in the RFA process had as a baseline vegetation extent at 1750, a picture that will doubtless be questioned as time passes and knowledge grows. In part at least, historical work has naturally enough followed issues of current import, so perhaps the argument for relevance is not so necessary. But 'mainstream' history has not exactly led the way; rather, newcomers such as foresters and geographers have found their way into history. As William Beinart suggests in Chapter 13 of this book, if scientists can dare tread into documented history, historians should not hold back from incursions into science's arcane territories.

It is not just the case with history; other disciplines have always followed the dictated focuses of development and politics, with profound influence over the later evolution of those same disciplines and our understanding of their subject. In Australia, ecology and related sciences have been deeply shaped by research – especially longer-term research – that has followed major issues. Close attention to the Australian alps preceding and after the Snowy Mountains Scheme influenced ecology, just as current attention to the contested forests of Victoria's central tablelands will shape future understanding and research directions. Understanding of climate, ecology and geomorphology of northern Australia owes much to activities associated with the Ord Scheme and Lake Argyle in western Australia and the placement of the Ranger uranium mine in the Northern Territory. Battles over the Great Barrier Reef, and the remarkable state–Commonwealth resolution via the world's premier marine park, were both influenced by science and created a focus of reef and marine research in that vicinity. The influence of these political-scientific coincidences on later scientific understanding deserves closer attention by historians of science and environment. In Chapter 7 of this book, Harald Witt makes a valuable contribution to South Africa's forest history, in describing how local and global political and economic forces mesh somewhat patchily with the understanding of the natural sciences and the realities of natural systems. With so much attention being paid now to reforestation, catchment yields and to those unfortunate, imported Australians – the wattle and gum tree[23] – such explanations should be in great demand. Is there scope in such contests for a more orderly and strategic negotiation of history and present concern, allowing environmental history to both profit and contribute? Again, the environmental history will also be political, economic and social, in keeping with ongoing use of and debates about forests.

Of all modern policy achievements, Australia is best known for its Landcare movement, a community-based and government-sponsored response to rural land degradation. When 4500 local Landcare groups formed in one decade are stacked up with thousands of other 'watch' and 'care' groups (dunes, frogs, water, salt, fish), something remarkable is happening. Modern theorists of participatory approaches do not much engage with such reality – more's the pity. Whether it is the great turning point will not be apparent for some time, a judgement informed by the long history of 'policy *ad hocery* and amnesia' in Australia that has seen many encouraging starts falter and fade.[24] There is a latent conflict between the down-sizing of government, withdrawal of state programmes, and the 'empowerment' of communities. Empowerment or passing the buck? Landcare has attracted international attention and mimicry, in South Africa and elsewhere,[25] but care should be taken in transplanting Australian policy experiments to foreign soil. Landcare grew from particular conditions and historical precedents and it is not the 'new' thing that it appears, having its roots in a strong history of soil conservation and agronomic extension (now seriously diminished), and also in a history of community-based responses (for example, Pasture Protection Boards from 1912 in New South Wales, River Improvement Trusts from 1948).

The community dimension of environmental history is sometimes overlooked. Georgina Thompson's account of St Lucia in Chapter 12 identifies the sorts of very real conflicts between past and present, conservation and use. Communities engaged in resource management are a recipient of environmental history, but at least in Australia they are becoming environmental historians themselves as they seek to understand the evolution of their present land management issues. Planting trees furiously to arrest salinisation has prompted some to inquire as to the state of vegetation at European occupation. Communities may do history well or badly, but they will do it whether or not the relevant disciplines pitch in. Oral histories have a particular place here, and we have some way to go in reconciling the arts and crafts of documentary history, community-based oral history and science. Yet where this is done carefully – such as on the Lachlan River in Australia – the rewards can be significant for science, the community, historical understanding, and modern river management.[26]

All of these human–natural system interactions took place within institutional arrangements. The refashioning of institutions is a prime topic in sustainability debates right now. Yet appreciation of the nature of institutions and how they change is often absent. An argument has been put for an 'organisational approach' to environmental history, as a research principle and to avoid normative biases.[27]

I concur, but would prefer the broader term 'institutional', including the more immediate concrete manifestations of organisations and the more fluid institutions of political change. At root, most environmental history deals with changing institutions – law, custom, governance – but less often is it a central focus. The slowness of institutional change and the fortunes of our past institutional responses to environmental change are good history and a source of good lessons now. Some of Australia's best-known environmental institutions of today have long histories. The Murray Darling Basin (MDB) Commission and its supporting political agreement continue to struggle against a mammoth task, and this struggle began in 1915. That is a long haul, with many lessons and insights about environment and about the politics of a Federation garnered along the way. Powell characterised the MDB as one of our 'boldest throws of the institutional dice', but I would like to think that this need not be just a game of chance.[28] Other institutional responses, more recent but old enough to be beyond the memory of those wrapped in the present, are worthy of note too. Victoria's Land Conservation Council did good service combining politics, science and consultation for a quarter-century before its independence and consultative roles were severely compromised by a modern, rationalist government. The reasons for its establishment and why they still have relevance and currency have for most people faded already, but fortunately that story has now been superbly told.[29]

Such bodies are the closest we get to 'adaptive' and persistent institutions, and they are worthy of close examination both for what they do now and for how they got there. In an era of rapid and often unthinking institutional change, examples of adaptive persistence are valuable. South Africa's recent and current great pace of institutional change offers more of an opportunity for profiting from such insights of institutional pasts than does Australia, where basic institutional change is either resisted or forced suddenly through obeisance to imperatives other than the social or environmental.

Growing environmental history?

By now, my preoccupations about 'relevant' environmental history will be clear enough to have become wearying. Certainly, I would wish to see more such work, with historical explanations seasoning modern understanding and policy. Yet I cannot choose what should be left out of the current range of environmental history inquiries – they all are deeply interesting and necessary. Taking a cue from the 'growth answers everything' assumption underlying most post-war policy prescriptions in the Western world, the only answer seems to seek a growth in the size of the cake. How can environmental history grow as a field, allowing expansion, evolution and the maintenance of invigorating diversity?

On the face of it, environmental history is a growing field and continues to develop – in terms of the number of people engaged as well as theoretical, methodological and empirical advances. While some may be happy enough with the prospects for environmental history, these are hard times for new, innovative and interdisciplinary areas that do not offer a short-term economic pay-off. As unfortunate as it is, resources are the key. The humanities are shrinking in education and more generally – environmental history may not face a rosy or even stable future. But there is also an obsession with sustainability, and public interest and policy commitments should ensure that sustainability research and practice remain reasonably vibrant. So, relevance may be the lifeline for environmental history whether we like it or not. If that sounds grubbily pragmatic, then at least by considering it environmental historians can think strategically about how to use the possibilities on their own terms rather than take a reactive, mendicant role.

So far, much insight has come from detailed and finely located studies of districts and regions.[30] Exploration at a fine resolution of human–environment interactions is the bedrock of environmental history (this does not discount the value of broad sweeps). The theoretical testing and development provided in Nancy Jacobs's chapter in this book (Chapter 2) are made possible by the detail of research in Kuruman. We need more, but how? Except in rare cases of fortunate, remarkable or intensely committed individuals, I believe that in future these studies will be carried out increasingly as postgraduate research projects. Doctoral research is one of the few opportunities for the necessary time- and labour-intensive research to be carried out. If this is to happen, two challenges will need to be met, and these can serve to close this discussion. The first is the art and craft of postgraduate supervision in this new and complex field, which needs close attention. 'Supervision' of postgraduates is a touchy subject; individual academics may not respond positively to scrutiny, and too many disciplines still reek of the vertical, master–apprentice model. In interdisciplinary arenas, such individualistic approaches to supervision are less viable, and in my experience a collaborative journey of inquiry between student and multiple supervisors should be accepted as the norm.

Secondly, how to support such studies in constrained times? I would venture to propose a future where a good many studies would be undertaken in collaboration with resource and environmental managers – be they community groups or public agencies or industries – establishing the much-needed historical context to their pressing current concerns; a future where interdisciplinary environmental histories of places, sectors and communities will be at least partially funded or otherwise supported by such bodies. To return to an opening theme of this chapter, this would be *public* history in the normally understood sense. It would also be *applied* history, distilling lessons, and it could be *people's* history if it brings forth previously unheard voices.[31] Environmental histories attached to current issues will be undertaken anyway – management agencies and community groups are starting already – and it would be better if the appropriate skills are included and human resources developed. Commissioned histories have a mixed reputation, but we are used to the idea of them at least. Why not pursue commissioned environmental histories? At the core of Australia's literature on the environmental history of water lie the invaluable, agency-supported or commissioned histories by Joe Powell.[32] This could become a pattern of research 'investment' that would see environmental history prosper, and guarantee the future of the field. If those who might be wary of such a prospect have an alternative other than a noble struggle at the margins of hostile research and education funding debates, then we should hear it. Returning to the theme of public history, Davison's comments a decade ago regarding that field and the future of history in Australia are worth revisiting:

> after ten years in which national policy, including educational policy, has been largely determined by narrowly trained economists, in which public values have been denigrated and private interests made sacrosanct, and in which static and presentist modes of understanding have often displaced dynamic historical ones, the need for broadly educated, inventive, politically astute and socially responsible public historians is greater than ever before. The question is: where will such useful historians come from? And who will give them a job?[33]

We can make that twenty years now, although to heap singular blame on economists is inaccurate and simplistic. But the strictures for the humanities are tighter than ever. I have in this chapter given some clues for finding answers to the two hard, practical questions that end the quote above. Environment and sustainability may offer more fruitful engagement than any other topics – for historians and for other disciplines. There is the possibility for good, useful and widely supported public environmental history in Australia, and perhaps in South Africa too. Furthermore, these histories will have an audience. It will not be just 'historians' in a pure sense, though, but just as likely 'historicised' ecologists, geomorphologists, foresters, economists – and scientifically informed historians.

C h a p t e r   F i f t e e n

Environment and history in South America and South Africa

J.R. McNeill

South Africa is much smaller than Brazil and less than half the size of Argentina. If transplanted to South America, it would take up only six or seven per cent of the continent, about the same amount of space as Peru. South Africa's 44 million people are about one-fifth the number in Brazil, and roughly equal to the population of Argentina or Colombia, while South America as a whole has some seven times the population of South Africa. Viewing the two with the same lens can raise difficulties of scale, but scale does not always matter.

From some perspectives, the two areas have something in common. The main theatres of world historical development – of plant and animal domestication, of cities, of states, of metallurgy, of most influential technologies – lay far from South Africa or South America. Both were, before AD 1500, peninsular culs-de-sac into which only those things came that could pass through all the filters, geographical and cultural, that stood between these outposts and the rest of the world. They were, then, unusually isolated by world historical standards, and an unusually high proportion of their technology, culture, political tradition, as well as flora and fauna, had developed *in situ*. This comparative isolation was quite long in duration in both cases.

Until recently, the long isolation of both regions did not prevent sharply divergent histories. People first entered South America at least 13 000 years ago, but probably no more than 40 000 years ago. The first people, or hominids at any rate, in South Africa arrived more than three million years ago, and the direct ancestors of today's San and Khoikhoi have lived in South Africa for several thousand years. In both settings these populations were ordinarily sparse and mobile for millennia, although in South America there were, in time, some exceptions to this. In the Andean highlands of South America, agriculture evolved around 9000 years ago and irrigation was invented on the Peruvian coast around

240 | JOHN McNEILL

5000 years ago. In South Africa, agriculture came only around AD 500, with iron tools imported from the north. The stability (as well as ecological sustainability) of life in South Africa in the centuries before AD 500 was extraordinary by world standards. Indeed, the toolkit and foodstuffs employed at Gwisho (Zambia) around 1500 BC were easily recognised by San in the 1970s, implying more than 3000 years of stability in southern African subsistence strategies. Parts of South America may show the same stability (or stagnation if one prefers), such as Tierra del Fuego, but in much of the continent – especially the Andes – agriculture, irrigation, states and cities emerged independent of contacts with the wider world. This process culminated in the Inca Empire, which grew from modest origins beginning around AD 1440 to become one of the world's great empires, encompassing perhaps nine to sixteen million people and territory that ranged 4500 kilometres north to south, all linked together by 30 000 to 50 000 kilometres of state-controlled roads. This was a society and state on the scale of the Ottoman or Mughal empires; and nothing of the sort appeared in South African history.

When contacts with the wider world became routine, however, the long isolation told and the environmental histories of South America and South Africa converged. Both regions underwent quick transitions (still in train) to new systems of human ecology, with new diseases, plants and animals; with new pressures on forests and soils from new economic connections and new immigrant populations. This process – the creation of settler ecologies – will be the main focus of this chapter.

In 1498, on his third voyage to the Americas, Columbus spied the coast of Venezuela, but did not act on his sighting as he was aiming for China. In 1500, a Portuguese sea captain, Pedro Alvares Cabral, set out to follow Bartholomeu Dias around the Cape of Good Hope and into the Indian Ocean, aiming to open a Portuguese route to China and the spice islands. Winds drove him far west, however, and he accidentally landed on the Brazilian coast. Although he initially took it for an island, a follow-up expedition revealed that this was a continent. Soon a trade in dyewood developed along the Brazilian coast, the Portuguese established a political presence, and South America henceforth interacted continually with the rest of the world. This interaction was reinforced in the 1530s when Spanish adventurers intervened in a war of succession in the Inca Empire and seized the reins of power in that empire.

South Africa's entry into the web of intercontinental contacts came relatively soon after. Although Portuguese sailors rounded the Cape from 1488 onward, and seamen from the Indian Ocean may have done so too, systematic interaction with the rest of the world – the breakdown of isolation – came only in 1652 with the formal establishment of a Dutch presence at the Cape. After 1500 in South America, and after 1652 in South Africa, intercontinental connections provoked rapid ecological changes. Here I will address main themes from South America's environmental history – population catastrophe, introduced exotic species, mining and deforestation – and comment on their potential interest to South African history.

Demographic disaster

One of the several ways in which European mariners changed the world after 1450 was their transfer of animals, plants and diseases to new biogeographic provinces. This had always happened of course – with and without human agency. But never had it happened so rapidly as after 1450.[1] South America and South Africa had scarcely participated in intercontinental biological exchange before 1500, because they were far off the beaten tracks of sailing ships.[2] For South America, exotic microbes carried the most immediate consequences.

In 1500 South America was home to perhaps eighteen to thirty million people – estimates vary widely. Soon after Cabral's visit, however, that population began a long and sharp decline. Mesoamerica and North America experienced much the same catastrophe as, in later centuries, did Australasia and many Pacific islands when their populations first encountered the diseases that had become routine, endemic infections in most of northern Africa and Eurasia. Smallpox, typhus, influenza, measles, whooping cough, mumps and other diseases raged as epidemics in the Americas, killing adults as well as children, disrupting all facets of life and facilitating conquest by European powers. None of these diseases had existed in the Americas before, and Amerindian immune systems carried no inherited or conferred resistance to any of these killers. In many lowland areas, malaria, imported from Africa, added to the new disease burden. Indigenous populations fell by 80 to 90 per cent between 1500 and 1650. On many Caribbean islands and on several coasts, the depopulation approached or reached 100 per cent. In highlands in the southern Andes, the decline was less, perhaps 50 per cent. Whatever the local variations, the experience was catastrophic.[3]

Removing most of the people from ecosystems carried many consequences. South Americans in the broad forest expanses from Venezuela to southern Brazil had regularly burned off spontaneous vegetation as part of their shifting cultivation strategy. With the sharp depopulation after 1500, second-growth forests emerged widely. Where agriculture had involved terraces, as in the Peruvian Andes, the lack of labour meant that terraces could not be maintained, and instead soils washed down to the coastal plain and, eventually, out into the Pacific. The populations of hunted animals presumably rose, with the relaxation of hunting pressure. No doubt there were other ecological ramifications of the population disaster that befell South America (and the Americas generally).[4]

The establishment of the VOC (or Dutch East India Company) in 1652 at the Cape also exposed previously isolated populations to the routine infections of North Africa–Eurasia. The demographic consequences are at least as obscure as in South America, but devastating smallpox epidemics raged among Khoisan from at least 1713. Venereal diseases – a reliable cargo on sailing ships in those days – also affected South Africans, depressing fertility. What did this mean for the South African environment? Whatever role Khoisan had played in shaping South African ecology was presumably reduced. Did wildlife enjoy a respite from hunting pressure? Surely the incidence of fire declined, affecting vegetation patterns. How extensive such changes might have been depends on the extent of population decline in South Africa, and the role of the Dutch settlers' environmental impacts, which may in cases (for example, wildlife populations) have overridden all else.

Exotic introductions

Aside from diseases, maritime connections brought hundreds of exotic species to South America after 1500. Indeed, the process is still ongoing. Most introduced species failed to establish themselves – as a rule, about one in ten succeed. The most important invaders in South American history were large domesticated animals and food crops. South America had only about ten naturally occurring domesticable animals larger than 45 kilograms. Of these, only one – the llama – had been successfully domesticated before 1500. The llama and its cousin the alpaca were domesticated around 3500 BC, and were used as pack animals in the Andes. No other native animal of South America approached the llama in social and economic importance. South America had at least two smaller domesticated animals – the dog and the guinea pig – but it had none of the animals that proved historically important in North Africa and Eurasia: the pig, cow, goat, sheep and the horse.[5] After 1500, however, it acquired them all rather suddenly and, in the absence of predators and relevant animal diseases, these intruders usually flourished in their new surroundings. Feral herds developed soon and grew quickly. They often occupied terrain formerly farmed by Amerindians, which, in early stages of succession, afforded succulent new plant growth. But their favourite landscapes were the vast grasslands of the continent, the Venezuelan llanos, the Argentine pampas, and all the savannahs and pastureland in between.[6]

Wild or domesticated, the huge herds and flocks soon changed life in fundamental ways in South America. Migratory herds posed problems for farmers, whose crops were frequently trampled and eaten by livestock. This was an old problem elsewhere, but new to South America, and occasioned a new social struggle between herders and farmers.[7] The introduced livestock eventually created different ways of life for South Americans. Amerindians took to the horse to become *vaqueros* (cowboys), and horsemanship became an important index of manly virtue in parts of South America (as it had long been elsewhere in the world). Cattle-raising carried a certain cachet in Iberian culture and this outlook also transferred to South America, so that many settlers, *mestizos* (persons of mixed Amerindian and European ancestry) and Amerindians preferred cattle-raising to other occupations and pursued it wherever possible. Before 1900, that meant in the grasslands and parklands, where cattle helped to prevent the spread of bush and forest. After 1900 or so, it increasingly came to include former forest lands, as cattlemen found it worthwhile to undertake the tedious chore of clearing forest land to make room for pasture. In the Andes, shepherding became a way of life for hundreds of thousands, and probably made children more economically productive than they had formerly been. Cattle, sheep, goats and chickens provided cheap animal protein for Amerindians, who formerly had derived most of their proteins from beans. Sheep and goats also gave wool, which in South America had formerly come only from llamas, alpacas and vicuñas, which were hard to control. The new animals also made leather a common material for the first time.

With the new animals came new plants. Some were of no use or, worse, were weeds while others proved quite helpful for some people. Citrus fruits, bananas, grapes, apples and pears expanded the range of fruits available for South American consumption. Sugar cane created its own social and physical landscapes in coastal Brazil, Peru and elsewhere. The food grains of Eurasia – rice, rye, barley and wheat – all found niches in South America. Wheat proved especially well suited to parts of South America and eventually became a new staple food, although eaten only rarely by Amerindians. Spaniards and Portuguese liked wheat bread and encouraged wheat cultivation. Eating wheat bread became a sign of social status, an indication of Europeanness. In the fluid colonial societies of South America, where crafty and lucky people could get rich, Spaniards (and those of Spanish descent) in particular clung to social distinctions that marked them off from Amerindians, Africans and *mestizos*.[8]

Wheat did especially well in the pampas of Argentina and Uruguay, in the Mediterranean climate of central Chile, and in southern Brazil. It underpinned highly urbanised societies from the sixteenth century onwards: Peruvian cities ate Chilean wheat. Wheat also encouraged an agrarian order that bore strong resemblance to that of the grain lands of *ancien régime* Europe, with lord and peasant. The typical – but not universal – South American form, which survived into the twentieth century, was the *latifundio*, the big estate worked by a landless class of agricultural labourers but owned by one family that prized its distinctions from the toiling classes. This social form did not of course require wheat, but it spread to new landscapes because of wheat. It became the dominant crop on the Argentine pampas in the nineteenth century, and Argentine history thereafter was built on two imported species: wheat and cattle.

Coffee was a later introduction brought originally from Ethiopia in the eighteenth century. It prospered in the hills of Colombia and of southern Brazil. It became a small-holder crop in Antioquia (Colombia) but a *latifundio* crop in Brazil, showing that botany is not necessarily destiny. Coffee-growing took off in the mid- and late nineteenth century, when oceanic shipping costs fell rapidly and South American coffee could dominate markets in North America and Europe. Sizeable areas of Brazilian forest vanished in order to make room for coffee, a process still under way late in the twentieth century.[9]

In South Africa, exotic introductions also played a major role in shaping environmental history. In this volume, Harald Witt takes up this theme with regard to exotic timber trees (see Chapter 7), and Lance van Sittert with regard to prickly pear (see Chapter 9). But there is much more than this, most of which remains to be explored for its historical significance. The Cape, with its Mediterranean climate, was especially liable to invasion by species from the original Mediterranean world, which has proved itself a great exporter – mainly of plants, presumably because of their long adaptation to regimes of intensive human disturbance. Plants that did well there flourished in the Cape, in south-western Australia, in central Chile and in southern California, the other regions of the world with a Mediterranean climate.[10] Elements of Mediterranean agriculture, such as vines, also did well at the Cape.

Perhaps more significant than the imported crops in South African history was the curiously limited role of the horse. As in the Americas, the horse had not existed in South Africa before outsiders brought it with them. In the Americas – as elsewhere – the horse proved a political animal: a trained horse with rider became a decisive military instrument. Amerindians who took to the horse and became skilled riders adjusted their techniques with bow and arrow accordingly to become formidable forces in the geopolitics of the Americas. The most famous examples of this come from North America, where by the early eighteenth century the 'plains Indians' (as Americans call them) created a new way of life, based on efficient buffalo-hunting and vigorous raiding of their less formidable neighbours.[11] The Sioux managed to parlay this cultural synthesis into political power that lasted until the 1880s – the final gasp of horse-nomad power in world history. In South America, especially on the pampas flanking the Rio de la Plata, the gauchos developed a similar pattern of life, albeit hunting wild cattle instead of buffalo. The Guaycuru of the Chaco took to the horse, to cattle-hunting, and to mounted warfare, and fended off intruders well into the eighteenth century. As in North America, in the nineteenth century the repeating rifle replaced the spear or lance as the preferred complement to horses. But in South Africa the horse remained primarily a political instrument of settlers, and it helped to underwrite their power. Indeed, mastery of horses and of the techniques of mounted warfare allegedly helped to make the Anglo-Boer War a less unequal contest. But why did the horse not infiltrate indigenous African societies, revolutionising warfare and upsetting prior political arrangements? It did so on the West African savannahs, just north of the tsetse zone; why not to the south of it?

Alfred Crosby, in his book *Ecological Imperialism* (1986), which remains the most important work on the historical significance of introduced species, avoided extended discussion of South Africa. He found it 'too complicated'.[12] Complicated it surely is. South Africa may not fit well with Crosby's model of neo-Europes – lands where plants, animals, diseases and European settlers substantially replaced local species. South Africa was at most a very partial neo-Europe. But the successes and limits of ecological imperialism in South Africa, the importance of introduced species generally, the social and political reactions to the invaders – all this needs the attention from historians of South Africa that similar themes have attracted among historians of Australia and New Zealand.

Mining

Precious metals exercised a magnetic attraction upon Iberians, drawing them to the Americas. Nothing could make a man wealthier faster, and no doubt many dreamed of seizing gold from Amerindian potentates, as Francisco Pizarro did in Peru in 1533. The myth of golden cities (El Dorado) propelled many prospectors and explorers throughout South America in the sixteenth century. They found silver more often than gold. Silver mining became a major part of the South American economy from the 1540s with the rediscovery of abandoned Inca mines at Potosí, in today's Bolivia. For the next century, Potosí provided about half the silver of all Spanish America (which also included rich silver mines in Mexico), and helped to finance Habsburg political ventures in Europe. Potosí, and silver mining generally, had great social and economic significance for South America, and it had environmental significance too.

At first Spanish silver ore was smelted, using Amerindian techniques and grass or llama dung for fuel. But by 1572 the mercury amalgamation process prevailed at Potosí, whereby mercury was combined with crushed silver ore, latched on to the silver, was rinsed free of the ore, and then was evaporated away, leaving a honeycomb of pure silver. This technology required numerous watermills for power to crush the ore, and thus the streams around Potosí had to be reconfigured with dams and ponds. It required lots of mercury, which had to be mined, mainly at Huancavelica, in southern Peru (but also in Spain). It required fuel, to burn off the mercury. Timber for props had to come from afar, because Potosí stood above the tree line. Mining also generated huge amounts of air and water pollution, notably by highly toxic mercury, as well as enormous quantities of slag. Merely feeding the hundreds of thousands of people and mules who toiled there meant surrounding regions were turned over to stock-raising and food crops. By the 1590s, Potosí was one of the world's largest cities; the viceroyalty of Peru (that is, the colonial state) organised the draft of some 10 000 to 15 000 men annually from the Andean highlands to work the mines. Potosí remained the centre of Latin American silver mining for some 250 years, and remained active through the twentieth century. Its environmental impact, never carefully studied, was enormous.[13]

But Potosí accounts for only part of South America's mining history. In the 1690s in Minas Gerais (Brazil), great gold and diamond strikes attracted people from far and wide. Mining camps and towns grew up from nothing in landscapes formerly very sparsely populated. Brazilian gold mining was alluvial mining, with no deep shafts. Its environmental impact consisted of rerouting streams in the quest for gold, and the recasting of landscapes to provide supplies for thousands of miners. It peaked around 1720–50, moving the economic and political centre of gravity of Brazil to the south, where it remained thereafter.[14]

In the nineteenth and twentieth centuries the great copper veins of the Andes, especially in Chile, became a centre of South American mining. The usual range of environmental effects followed in the Andean copper mines, complicated by the impact of smelting. Copper ores were smelted close to the mines, because transporting ore was expensive. This required masses of fuel, which often came in the form of fuel wood or charcoal, that is from the local vegetation. Beyond this, copper smelting emitted toxic vapours, notably sulphur dioxide, which then rained down on surrounding lands. In the Peruvian case of the Cerro de Pasco smelter, pollution damaged crops for many kilometres all around, obliging farmers to cease farming and move away from the area. The Ilo smelter, opened in southern Peru in 1960, generated toxic rain as far as 200 kilometres downwind throughout the 1990s, provoking peasants to organise themselves and launch lawsuits against the smelter owners.[15]

Mining also shifted the centre of gravity of South Africa, from the Cape to the Witwatersrand, in the late nineteenth century. What were its environmental consequences? The volumes of earth moved? The slag, the slurry, the erosion? Did chemicals used in ore-processing pollute soils and waters? Where did the timber props come from? What were the consequences of drawing legions of young men away from their villages for years in the mines? Could the women remaining behind take up the slack in terms of environmental management, burning off encroaching bush, keeping fierce animals at bay? The direct and indirect effects of a development as large as South African mining must have been considerable, greater and more concentrated than in South America.

Forests and deforestation

Although it is the last 30 years of deforestation in Amazonia that attracts the most attention, forest clearance has a long history in South America. Amerindians burned off forests to make room for their fields and to drive game as well. Their demographic collapse after 1500 led to a resurgence of forest area. But by the nineteenth century, renewed clearances by farmers and ranchers reduced South American forest area to levels below those of 1500. Then, in the twentieth century, a more sustained assault on forests followed, shrinking South American forest area by about a quarter. The Atlantic coastal forest of Brazil covered perhaps one million square kilometres in 1500. It shrank little before 1820, but in the nineteenth century, however, its wood was used for mine props, railway ties, urban construction and fuel wood. Coffee planters firmly believed that their crop did best on recently cleared forest soils, so they burned off huge swathes of the coastal forest to make space for coffee. By 1900, some sixty per cent of the forest was gone and by the 1990s, only about eight per cent of the forest of 1500 remained. Similar pressures, if less well studied, reduced the forests of every country in South America after 1820.[16]

Between 1960 and 1997, the world's largest rainforest, that of Amazonia, shrank by about ten per cent. The main reason for this reduction was the conversion of forested land to farms and pastures; a secondary reason was the demand for timber. The government of Brazil sponsored colonisation schemes intended to secure Amazonia for Brazil and to reduce the social pressures generated by peasant landlessness, especially in the north-east. Without the government's initiatives, its road-building, its tax breaks, this rapid colonisation and deforestation would have happened only much more slowly. The Brazilian government chose to accelerate a process that was already under way, on smaller scales, in other countries sharing Amazonia – Bolivia, Peru, Ecuador, Colombia and Venezuela. Indeed the possibilities that settlers from these countries might encroach upon Brazilian national territory served as one of the chief motives, or at least public justifications, for Brazilian settlement policy in Amazonia. The rapid forest clearances in Amazonia do indeed constitute a major chapter in the forest history of the modern world, although only one of several in the nineteenth- and twentieth-century history of deforestation in South America.[17]

In South Africa forests were not as central to environmental history. Much less of the land supported forests. But here too there was a long campaign to convert forest to pasture or farmland, at least from the time of the introduction of iron tools (around AD 500). Several of the chapters in this book give brief glimpses of South African forest history, and those of Beverley Ellis (Chapter 3) and Harald Witt (Chapter 7) give more than that. Their concerns are, however, specific, while the general saga of South African forests still beckons, with the impacts of farmers, herders, miners and shipbuilders, of fire, animals and climatic change, of war, reforestation and the international timber economy yet to be explored.

Conclusion

Compared to the literature on Australia, India, the United States of America or East Africa, environmental history in both South America and South Africa appears as almost uncharted waters. This of course represents a great opportunity for enterprising scholars. One way to cope with high levels of uncertainty is to employ theory, which can result in useful questions that guide research (see Nancy Jacobs in Chapter 2 of this volume). Another way forward involves framing questions by looking at what happened elsewhere – in South America, in India, in Australia or elsewhere in Africa.

No doubt South African environmental history is unique in some respects, but in most it probably is not. This chapter, with its quick comparisons to themes prominent in South America, scarcely scratches the surface. The torrential urbanisation in the twentieth century – common to both South America and South Africa as well as to many other lands – cries out for attention as an environmental history. The Humboldt current and the Benguela current bring cold, oxygen-rich water to the western shores of South America and South Africa respectively, creating two of the world's richer fisheries. The saga of human involvement in these marine ecosystems is also a shared theme in environmental history. But different issues will require different frames of reference. South America's energy supply in the twentieth century came mainly from oil and hydropower. South Africa's energy regime, with plentiful coal but scant petroleum, bears comparison with Germany's or Japan's and so, perhaps, does its industrial pollution history.

Environmental historians of South Africa (on the evidence of this volume) are often aware of the historiography on the United States of America. That is a useful step, but they can hasten progress, particularly with regard to forming questions and hypotheses, by consulting other environmental histories as well. With respect to South America (indeed, all Latin America) the most convenient starting point is the on-line bibliography maintained by Lise Sedrez and colleagues.[18] It will not be long before environmental historians of other parts of the world will need to include South Africa in their frame of reference. This book will help them to do so.

Chapter Sixteen

'Degradation narratives' and 'population time bombs': Myths and realities about African environments

Gregory Maddox

In October of 1999, I travelled in the Eastern Cape Province. I stayed in East London and most days had to drive about 100 kilometres up the main coastal highway to the smaller town of Butterworth. The route ran through former white South Africa around East London with its large farms planted with tropical products. Then the road descended into the valley of the Kei River. Through the valley the snaking route of the road is called the 'Kei Cuttings' and it is the scene of frequent road accidents as trucks, cars and minibuses vie to negotiate the switchbacks. The day I arrived, an accident killed more than twenty people. The long bridge over the Kei River formerly served as a border post between South Africa and the nominally independent homeland of Transkei. The road then meandered back up out of the valley onto a plateau through an entirely different landscape. Instead of open fields, the roadside was filled with settlements, some laid out in regular patterns with a fenced few acres surrounding each collection of houses, others true shanty towns looking like urban slums transported to the countryside. In many of the open fields around the settlements, large gullies (*dongas*) marred the slopes of the gently rolling hills.

Such contrasts in landscapes are a common feature of South Africa and have an extended historiography to which this volume contributes.[1] The reservation of the majority of the land in the country for white farmers, to be worked by black labourers, and the attempt to restrict black residence in urban areas created rural slums. Despite money poured into homelands such as the Transkei during the last decades of apartheid, these areas have remained 'overcrowded', 'overstocked' and 'undeveloped', and significant environmental degradation has occurred.[2]

As commonplace (and commonsensical) as this historical explanation is, it is not the one I heard in South Africa. My travelling companions on these drives were administrators in a formerly black technical college. Though they were of

250 | GREGORY MADDOX

mixed background, all were distinctly urban. We talked often of the change in landscape across the Kei River. We discussed the fact that livestock wandered onto the road in the former Transkei, the omnipotence of exotic species such as wattle, eucalyptus and prickly pear, and the spread of photoelectric cells on top of mud huts. As I earnestly badgered them about land reform and tenants converting to freeholders, one turned to me and said, 'You know, black people don't really know how to farm.' Ironically, this was said as we passed a village where I saw two ploughs in action, in a context where most of the farm labour on white farms is performed by blacks, and with my questions arising from my reading of the literature of 'strangled peasantries'[3] and environmental degradation. I kept quiet in the face of such a radical disconnect – and at that moment we entered the Cuttings, where two minibuses on the first switchback were trying to get around an overloaded lorry before they hit us or were forced over the steep drop-off on the side.

This little discussion about a landscape in South Africa, set against the chapters in this volume and, in turn, this volume's relationship with the fields of African and environmental history, brings out a number of important points. It demonstrates how colonialism appropriated the landscape and alienated Africans from it. Such a naked vision in post-apartheid South Africa has its echoes throughout Africa – and the developing world generally – in everything from the gas flares of the Niger delta to the way that dollars for diamonds or oil provide impetus to wars in Angola, Sierra Leone or the Democratic Republic of the Congo. It is repeated in the expulsion of hungry herdsmen and spindle-thin cattle from national parks in East Africa so that tourists can see more wildebeest and the lions that prey on them.

My conversation with my colleagues contains another lesson about constructions of environments and causality that applies to the way scholars approach the issue of environmental change. I am now quite unfairly going to link the dialogue I had with my colleagues to some very powerful discourses about environmental change and human communities. This is in no way meant to imply that the scholars cited below think that 'black people don't know how to farm' or nurture an environment or do anything, in fact. I am going to attempt to demonstrate that a dominant narrative about environmental history perpetuates important myths about Africans and African environments. These myths form the background against which many of the chapters in this volume operate and against which many struggle. The basic narrative goes like this: until the twentieth century, technologically simple African societies lived at the mercy of their environments. Population densities remained low because African communities could not control diseases or generate large food surpluses. Population growth remained slow as crisis mortality from famine or epidemic worked as Malthus said it would, to keep population in check. Beginning in the 1870s, colonialism brought an end to warfare, much improved transportation and modern medicine: catalytic changes that allowed the population to spiral upwards. In the 1970s, technologically driven population growth put serious pressure on African environments and initiated a crisis. The Sahara expanded more rapidly, forest loss became excessive, and wildlife declined in numbers and range as more and more land – much of it marginally arable – was taken up for agriculture. Brian Fagan, for example, writes:

> Famine and disease stalked farmer and herder alike even when population densities were low. In the twentieth century, when colonial governments upset the delicate balance of climate and humanity on a continent that had never supported vast numbers of people or huge urban civilizations, these social disasters have come more frequently. Europe suffered through repeated subsistence crises during the Little Ice Age. Africa is enduring far more serious food shortage in the late twentieth century, caused by a combination of drought, population growth, and human activity.[4]

In this understanding, the African conflicts that have intermittently dominated headlines result from societies in crisis. The bold few have argued that the only hope for Africa's environments is that the rapid spread of HIV/AIDS will cause a demographic collapse.

Such a narrative can be compelling in some respects, but it is part of an ancient lineage. The vision of environmental degradation caused by African land-use practices and the growing population first appeared in the writings of British and French colonial officials. Despite labour migration to white-owned farms and mines, they blamed the perceived failures of African farmers either to produce more export crops or to feed themselves, on environmental degradation. Influenced by conservation arguments coming from the United States and elsewhere,[5] the colonial officials promoted extensive measures to rehabilitate African lands. In South Africa[6] – and other European-run colonies – settler-controlled or -influenced governments used this evidence to support continuing alienation of native land and subsidies for settler agriculture.[7]

Most strikingly, initiatives at forest and wildlife conservation intensified during this era. Colonial forestry officials justified conservation with a poignant refrain, the degradation narrative.[8] It was a loaded conceptualisation, as often conservation explicitly meant the transfer of the right to use resources away from African communities and toward extractive firms.[9] Likewise, the protection of wildlife and habitat responded both to concerns about perceived loss and to demands of lobbies in colonial and metropolitan governments for the reservation of resources.[10] In almost all cases, conservation meant the expulsion of Africans from territory to be conserved and the almost complete extinction of African use-rights to the resources. The transparent fashion in which conservation concerns covered appropriation of resources by colonial states and businesses was apparent to Africans. Consequently, by the 1950s in many parts of the continent, opposition to conservation policies became one of the most effective organising issues for anti-colonial nationalist movements.[11]

Independence for much of Africa by the mid-1960s brought some change. Post-colonial states temporarily abandoned attempts to promote conservation measures in farming communities. Simultaneously, however, they followed the pattern of colonial management and promoted the reservation of resources as a conservation measure. Conservation was merely a code since officials explicitly expected to maintain income to the state from resource use and tourism.[12] Farm-level efforts to enforce conservation reappeared by the 1970s, usually driven by foreign governments or non-governmental organisations. In some places, civil society collapsed in the new states leaving only brute force in its place and, in those places, conservation and rehabilitation efforts became impossible.[13] These collapses of civil society have increasingly been blamed on environmental crisis.

Despite the obvious differences, the environmental history of South Africa is closely connected to the general environmental history of Africa. In a provocative book Mahmood Mamdani has suggested that South Africa served as the model for colonialism throughout Africa.[14] Much the same is true of the environmental changes occurring in the region. South Africa's almost total alienation of Africans from the control of land and resources seems merely the most complete version of processes that occurred almost everywhere.[15] As in the rest of Africa, it remained African labour that made something of value out of those resources, despite the much higher level of capitalisation found in South African agriculture as well as mining and industry. Such a view of South Africa's experience as different in degree only can provide useful insights on some of the debates outlined in the chapters in this volume.

Degradation narratives have several important functions even today. They serve both within African societies and internationally to sanction the appropriation of resources by states from local communities. In South Africa – as the cases discussed by Jabulani Sithole (Chapter 5), William Beinart (Chapter 6) and Georgina Thompson (Chapter 12) show in this volume – such efforts occurred throughout the twentieth century, and they continue to be part of the struggle over redistribution of land and resources in the aftermath of the transition to majority rule. At the same time, they justify international organisations that take control of resources from African states. In a different context, governments of developed nations use these types of degradation narratives as a stick with which to beat their underdeveloped counterparts.

Furthermore, both African governments and people in local communities detect a certain hypocrisy in measures to promote environmental protection and conservation that come from Western governments, international organisations and non-governmental organisations. These very same bodies – the World Bank pre-eminent among them – simultaneously promote the development of more resources in the developing world by multinational corporations. As in the rest of Africa, in South Africa advocates of both environmental protection and exploitation have emerged. In a way that is undermining to the former, environmental protection is often regarded as anti-human and a continuation of colonial policies.[16] Environmental protection, as Western environmentalists understand it, often has very little purchase except as an adjunct to claims for greater local control over resources. While such claims can be the basis for sustainable resource use and environmental protection, they start from a different basis than those of most environmentalists. In South Africa, the environmentalists are often local inhabitants. This has facilitated the construction of alliances against unfettered resource destruction, but has often meant that such alliances remain extremely fragile. The tension between greater justice in the control of resources and environmental protection for the greater good can become too extreme to overcome.

Environmentalists often proceed from universal concerns about humanity's destruction of the environment. Such thought is not usually shy about claiming the theoretical authority to dictate acceptable human use of the environment in the name of preserving it or of promoting the sustainable use of it. Attempts to assert local (or national) control over resources usually reject universal claims, often accusing those making them of hypocrisy.

In the end, much of what we know about African environments is almost fatally compromised by the types of degradation narratives essential to colonial control and carried on to the present. Such narratives do not just come from either popular media or interested parties. Just as my colleagues in South Africa could ignore the evidence before their own eyes as they drove past thousands of Africans engaged in agriculture, so too can scholars believe the narrative instead of the evidence. Brian Fagan is a distinguished archaeologist who has done pioneering work at African sites as well as being the author of one of the most widely used introductory university-level texts in the field. In his recent book, quoted above, he repeats the classic degradation narrative for the Sudan.[17] In doing so he ignores the conclusions of scholars such as Roderick McIntosh, James Webb and George Brooks that climatic variability determined human land-use in the region.[18] Fagan ignores more recent scholarship that demonstrates what can only be called 'rehabilitation' as a result of a cycle of wetter years in the region since the 1980s.[19] Finally, he claims that cattle diseases – of which he repeatedly lists only rinderpest – kept herd sizes in check before the colonial era, and in a footnote he acknowledges that rinderpest only entered Africa in the 1890s, at roughly the same time as the colonial era began. His narrative required that something keep cattle populations low before the colonial era and he chose the most deadly and widespread of cattle diseases. Fagan seems to have let his narrative determine his evidence in this case rather than consider alternatives that might include an element of human agency in maintaining a rough-and-ready control over herd size.[20]

These debates have relevance both for longer-term and for more immediate analyses of South Africa's environments. The chapters in this volume move the debate forward as they display the tension inherent in struggles over landscapes in South Africa. I want to use this opportunity to highlight some recent works that provide possible models for rethinking the environmental history of South Africa. Such a presentation draws on a rapidly expanding body of scholarship based on both long-term and more recent evidence. A more nuanced perspective does not romanticise African societies' ability to nurture an environment, as has been the case in some works.[21] Nor does it mean that the dramatic expansion of the African population over the last several decades can be ignored. It does, however, mean that such changes must be put into historical and global contexts in ways that do not blame Africans for being unable to manage environments.

For as long as humans have walked the planet, African environments have been lived in and altered by humans.[22] Neither the rainforests of West Africa nor the Serengeti Plains have been primeval landscapes covered with 'natural' vegetation and inhabited only by natural fauna. Not only did humanity originate in Africa, but agriculture developed and spread in Africa at about the same time as it did in Europe. Iron-working developed in Africa at roughly the same time that it spread in the Mediterranean world.[23] In southern Africa, the spread of stock-raising, agriculture and iron-working generally occurred early in the first millennium of the current era.[24] Population generally grew as new ways of putting together labour, land, techniques of production, and crops and domestic animals emerged up to about AD 1600. Climate and climate variability played dominant roles in determining the course of change and in promoting the development of new techniques. In some cases, it appears to be possible that African societies' growth outstripped the ability of their environments to support them.[25] Long-distance trade across the Sahara and Indian Ocean promoted production of metals, the exploitation of timber, and agricultural production as well as bringing a variety of new crops to African societies. In South Africa, the beginnings of white settlement at the Cape simultaneously brought a displacement of the existing population in the area.[26]

By 1600, the fabled Columbian Exchange was in full swing. It brought new crops – especially cassava and maize – and new technologies to Africa, but its biggest impact was on the continent's population. The thirteen million or so Africans who became involuntary migrants to the new Atlantic system between 1450 and 1860 played a major role in domesticating the New World. The effect on African populations of this 'migration' and the violence used to produce it must be measured both temporally and spatially. The slave trade affected western Africa much more than it did southern or eastern Africa. Yet the net effect was to hold Africa's overall population growth in check and, according to Patrick Manning, to cause a reduction in population in much of western Africa.[27] In South Africa, outside the arid region of the Karoo, African populations did not feel this impact as greatly until the early nineteenth century. Thereafter, the interplay of expanding white settlement and African state formation resulted in a cycle of violence throughout the region that weakened the ability of African communities to survive in their environments.

The effects of this branch of the Columbian Exchange did not end with the Atlantic slave trade. The rapid development of commodity production in Africa for European, American and Asian markets during the nineteenth century redistributed the population dramatically and continued to promote involuntary servitude – which continued to act as a check on population growth – as a means of organising production. The final indignity of colonial conquest coupled with the spread of rinderpest, which decimated cattle herds throughout the continent in the 1890s, meant that sub-Saharan Africa's population in 1900, estimated at about 100 million, was, quite possibly, roughly comparable with what it had been in 1600.[28] This is not a collapse of the order of the one that occurred in the Americas between 1500 and 1600, but it is a striking case of demographic stagnation at a time when the populations of Europe, the Americas and regions in Asia grew dramatically.

Colonialism across Africa remade landscapes. A transportation revolution eventually made the movement of goods and people much more rapid. In South Africa the exploitation of diamond and gold deposits provided the engine for this remaking, and the eventual destruction of the autonomy of African societies followed. The remaking of agriculture in capitalist forms went hand in hand with the creation of a stable labour supply for the mines and eventually industry. Colonial states insisted that taxes be paid in money, forcing Africans to sell crops or to go to work for wages. These pressures reconfigured African communities by changing the demands on their members. After 1920, crisis mortality fell, but generalised poverty probably increased.[29]

Population on the African continent certainly began to increase by the Second World War, reaching about 600 million today. More reliable food supplies played a large role in reducing mortality, and modern medicine played a smaller one – until perhaps the 1960s in most places. Some scholars suggest that much of the growth came from an increase in fertility over the course of the twentieth century.[30] There was no singular African demographic regime before the twentieth century. Some areas had relatively low fertility and mortality rates, others higher ones.[31] But colonial political economies put new pressures on African communities and placed a premium on labour. Low returns for labour remain the norm in Africa even today, and hence the well-being of a household too frequently depends on how many people it contains.

Despite the differences in its history, South African environmental history can be connected to that of the rest of Africa. I would suggest that two of the themes emphasised in much of the literature could profitably be used in understanding South African environmental history. The first theme – perhaps best exemplified by the anthropologists James Fairhead and Melissa Leach in *Misreading the African landscape* – concentrates on understanding how African communities lived in their environments. Their work provides a detailed review of afforestation and deforestation in the forest–savannah borderlands of Guinea. European colonial officials and current state and international bureaucrats see forest remnants in derived savannahs; but these are actually forest colonies in 'natural' savannahs created by human settlement. Fairhead and Leach show that over the last 30 years, forest cover has expanded as population has increased, and they detail the methods used by communities to promote forest cover around settlements and the ways in which these methods, and the mix of trees, have changed.[32] In a more recent study drawing on materials from across West Africa, they show that while much forest has been cut, much has been regrown, and suggest that extractive industries – timber, rubber plantations, mining, usually for export markets in the developed world – should shoulder more of the blame than the expansion of African population for the transformation of forest.[33]

In the literature on South Africa, the work of Nancy Jacobs (see Chapter 2) has demonstrated a similar approach. Her work on the Kuruman region brings together close analysis of the ways that Tswana-speaking communities in the area utilised the resources at their disposal. Jacobs demonstrates the interaction between changes in both the physical and ideological landscapes as Christianity and irrigation, ploughs and labour migration spread. Her work carefully bridges the human–nature divide found all too frequently in environmental history.[34]

The second theme can be found in James McCann's *Green land, brown land, black land*. McCann's book draws on his long career as a promoter of the study of Africa and its environments.[35] He argues against allowing 'narratives' to dictate a representation of African environments. McCann illustrates how both late-nineteenth-century visitors to the Ethiopian highlands and American Vice-President Al Gore called treeless landscapes the result of recent deforestation when in fact these landscapes represented a more 'natural' state. The outsiders were confused again by the presence of trees around settlements. McCann also notes fairly sharp swings in the type of vegetative cover on the Serengeti Plain during the last 50 years despite the absence of appreciable human settlement.

McCann ends his book by noting that much of Africa's population growth during the last couple of decades has come in the form of rapid urbanisation. Some rural areas have actually lost population. Increasing urbanisation will surely change the nature of debates about Africa's environments. In this, as in so many other ways, South Africa again could provide the template for much of the rest of Africa. The effects of industrialisation and urbanisation, important themes for the chapters in this volume, have just begun to play a role in the analysis of African environments elsewhere.

Chapter Seventeen

The colonial eco-drama:
Resonant themes in the environmental history
of southern Africa and South Asia

Ravi Rajan

Although flamed by different fires, the burgeoning fields of environmental history in southern Africa and South Asia have at least one thing in common: a concern with examining the impacts of European colonialism.[1] This shared focus is therefore a good place to start any discussion of how the environmental histories of these two regions of the world compare.

The colonial eco-drama

In his playful discussion of the political ecological consequences of European imperialism, Timothy Weiskel invoked what, at first glance, seems a rather odd metaphor – of theatre – to describe the underlying historical phenomena.[2] Imperialism, Weiskel suggests,

> engenders a particular type of ecological drama involving several characteristic phases or acts. The play has been repeated many times, and as with all classical drama, the plot is now well understood. Indeed some might argue that there is a depressing repetitiveness to the successive enactments of the colonial eco-drama, as if man and nature knew how to write only one scenario and insisted upon staging the same play in theater after theater on an ever-expanding world-wide tour...[3]

Weiskel urges us to visualise the colonial eco-drama as though it were a five-act play.[4] The explosive opening act depicts the acute social and ecological disruption caused by European colonisers, their plant and animal species, and their biotic regimes, in the immediate aftermath of colonial intrusion. The second act involves the colonisers occupying previously under-occupied eco-niches and then expanding into and exploiting others. Act Three portrays the immediate impact of such expansions on local peoples: the disruption of colonised societies, their eco-niches and biotic regimes; and the many acts of resistance by colonised societies against their forced ecological dislocation. The fourth act is about the processes of re-configuration following the radical disruption caused by the colonial encounter, and depicts the colonising populations moving into 'neo-niches' such as the 'virgin lands' of the white settler agriculturists. Finally, the last act explores the 'mature predator–prey relationships within the colonial ecosystem' established during the earlier stages. These involve the creation of new kinds of relations, sometimes symbiotic and enduring, between indigenous and intrusive populations.

Central to Weiskel's colonial eco-drama are its narratives and slogans. Among the most important are those that extol the virtues of exploiting and 'improving' the environment. Such slogans recur throughout the play and serve to justify the course of events presented therein. In the third act, for example, they justify the displacement of indigenous peoples and their ecological regimes. Again, in the fourth act, they justify colonial expansions as movements into 'empty' territory and new frontiers. So potent are these narratives, argues Weiskel, that the powerful *dramatis personae*, the supporting actors, and often the spectators of the colonial eco-drama themselves, are to this day clamouring for repeat performances of Act Four, spurred on by ideologies of development and improvement.

Scripting the eco-drama: The terrain of environmental history in southern Africa and South Asia

Scholars engaged in writing environmental history in both South Africa and South Asia have, in significant ways, sought to write about specific aspects of the colonial eco-drama. Their broad agenda has consisted of investigating the role and place of nature in human society and politics and, in particular, the intersection between the spheres of the natural, the cultural, the economic and the political. To the extent that they are driven by such a broad-based intent, environmental historians in both these contexts are not vastly different from their counterparts in North America who, true to their continental predilection with advancing new frontiers, were the first to self-consciously stake out and define the field.[5] Although scholars in both South Asia and southern Africa never cease to describe their work as distinct from those of their American counterparts, it might be useful to read their work against the backdrop of a paradigmatic statement of the agenda of the discipline of environmental history.[6]

One place to start is Donald Worster's programmatic essay setting out the course for a new research field more than a decade ago, and the round table it spawned. In that essay, Worster had envisaged a discipline encompassing three main levels, each requiring distinctive methods of analysis.[7] The first level was meant to understand 'nature itself'; the second, to grapple with the 'socio-economic realm as it interacts with the environment'; and the third, with the 'perceptions, ethics, laws, myths and other structures of meaning' which are part of an 'individual's or group's dialogue with nature'.[8] Although the literature on South Asia and southern Africa does not sharply demarcate such 'levels', it is safe to say that these themes resonate therein.

Consider the so-called 'first level' of environmental history. As applied to colonised ecologies such as South Africa or South Asia, it is concerned with the role of nature and of natural processes in the unfolding of the colonial eco-drama. Of particular importance is the question of how specific plant and animal species and resource use practices of European colonialists aided imperial expansion.[9] Here, there is an interesting contrast to be drawn between South Asia and southern Africa. Whereas in the latter context there is a small but growing body of work that dwells on the theme of what Alfred Crosby referred to as 'ecological imperialism', there is as yet no evidence for such a process in the environmental history of South Asia during the colonial period.[10] However, the natural environment of South Asia had, prior to European colonialism, been altered to a tremendous degree by the introduction of non-native species. According to Stephen Pyne, only six and a half per cent of India's flowering plants are endemic.[11] If this is true, the thesis of ecological imperialism, while perhaps inapplicable to the European colonialists of the eighteenth century and onward, might well stand its ground for an earlier period.

Michael Dove's work on attitudes to nature in the Indian north-west and T.R. Trautmann's pioneering essay on the place of elephants in the Mauryan state again show a preference, both in contemporary as well as in classical times, for a mediated, as opposed to a wild, landscape.[12] There seems to be a *prima facie* resonance here with the attitudes to nature and resources among the Bantu-speaking people of sub-Saharan Africa generally, and of the Bemba in Zambia more specifically.[13] Such comparisons are, however, quite premature at this point because very little is really known, either in South Asia or southern Africa, about the precise interactions between the various historic communities and their natural environments in the past. Clearly, this is a fertile ground for further research, and opens up challenges for creative collaborations between environmental historians and archaeologists.

The resonance between the colonised ecologies of southern Africa and South Asia is greater at the second level of environmental history, which provides the content to script Acts Two, Three and Four of Weiskel's imaginary eco-drama. This is indeed where the bulk of the existing research has been directed. There has thus been a great deal of work on the relationship between human productive technology and the natural environment, and especially on the different ways in which human communities, including colonial and indigenous resource users, have attempted to transform nature – using technology – into regimes that produce resources for consumption.[14]

A related concern has been about how technologies have shaped and transformed human social systems and human–ecological relations.[15] Important here is the question of the relationship between modes of production, demographic change and transformations of the natural environment in the wake of European colonialism.[16] Also significant is the issue of how changes in modes of production affect human communities differentially, that is, who loses and who gains as modes of production change.[17] The literature in both South Asia and southern Africa therefore focuses a great deal on the processes of appropriation of agricultural land, water resources, forests, wildlife and minerals.[18] It also has two specific dimensions: the 'macro' aspect of the politics of imperial resource use and the 'micro' aspect of how colonial policies affected different indigenous communities differentially.[19] The latter point is particularly significant because the processes of European colonialism, both in South Asia and in southern Africa, involved specific resource alliances. As a consequence, not all of the indigenous communities were affected alike and there were many individuals and communities that prospered at the expense of others.[20]

The issue of resistance and contestations over the emergent colonial resource regimes has also been an important resonant theme in the literatures of South Asia and southern Africa. In South Asia such studies have origins in nationalist and, more recently, Marxist, feminist and 'subaltern' historiographies.[21] In southern Africa, this efflorescence of work was a result of considerable revisionist writing that focused on the role of race and class in shaping South African society.[22] It was also a response to a research agenda that stressed the importance of examining 'African agency, African initiative, and the salience and legitimacy of African resistance'.[23]

The so-called third level of environmental history, as applied to southern Africa and South Asia, is concerned with the narrative aspects of the colonial eco-drama.[24] Of particular importance here are the cognitive lenses through which the various human communities perceived their relations with nature.[25] There is therefore a considerable body of work, on both regions, that seeks to explore and document their respective perceptions of nature and their often conflicting cognitive maps which define what a resource is and what natural processes are. A related issue concerns the ideologies of environmental protection and transformation, and the systems of governance and the laws that maintain the social order of colonial communities, especially those that are about the allocation and regulation of natural resources, land and property rights. There is therefore considerable work, both in South Africa and South Asia, on the recurrent themes of colonial improvement and development, environmental law, the regulation of common property resources, and of 'coercive conservation'.[26]

Nature, science and colonial development

Underlying ideas such as colonial improvement and the policies they gave rise to were the colonial sciences, technologies, and economic models of regional and imperial development.[27] Indeed, scientific resource management was an important component of the British colonial state from the second half of the nineteenth century. Pure and applied scientific disciplines such as land surveying, soil science, water management, meteorology, botany, zoology, fisheries, entomology, geology, forestry, agriculture, the veterinary sciences and the medical sciences were increasingly deployed across the length and breadth of the British empire to tackle the complex problems associated with the determination of policy on natural resource use.[28] Even the science of ecology has imperial origins. Early ecology, for example, was largely influenced by the colonial studies of botanists, soil scientists and hydrologists such as A.F. Wilhelm Schimper, Johannes Mildbraed, Homer Le Roy Shantz, Curtis Fletcher Marbut, André Aubreville, T.F. Chipp, G.P. Milne, Fernand Moreau, Bernard Dearman Burtt and Clement Gillman.[29]

During the hundred years from 1850 to 1950, a vast network of scientific institutions ranging from centres of research and training to regional and international conferences was set up in various parts of the British empire.[30] As Figure 17.1 – adapted from a book on science in colonial Africa – illustrates, this framework encompassed a wide range of natural sciences interacting with social sciences such as demography and anthropology to produce a web of knowledge that would facilitate efficient exploitation of the natural resources of the colonial hinterland.[31] In the era after the First World War, this loose but elaborate chain of scientific institutions began to be systematically co-ordinated centrally. In the words of an ex-colonial official: 'Between the wars policy-making on a whole variety of issues from education to pest control increasingly radiated from a few centres of academic power and administrative influence, with the result that by the 1930s planning initiatives that previously would have been taken by the "man on the spot" had become the preserve of metropolitan experts...'[32]

After the Second World War, this elaborate imperial scientific framework and the environmental regimes it engendered were consciously nurtured to last well into the post-colonial era. An official statement in 1948 patronisingly defined the purpose of British colonial policy to be 'to guide the colonial territories to

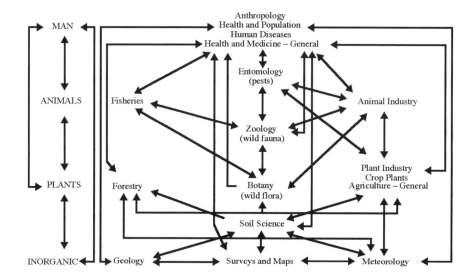

17.1 Networks of science in colonial Africa

responsible government within the Commonwealth'.[33] The dictates of formal colonialism were thus supplanted by the agendas of many colonial scientific officials, especially those influenced by the doctrines of Fabian Socialism, who set out to implement what they saw as a mandate to carry out 'the sacred trust of civilization' – to bring all native peoples who were under their suzerainty to a state of self-determination.[34] For imperial scientific officers working on natural resource management, this meant ensuring, often as an urgent priority, that they left an institutional and ideological legacy that would survive the demise of formal colonialism. An excellent illustration of such a spirit is the following poem, cited by one colonial forester as exemplifying the spirit of their sense of mission and the justification for their very presence in the empire:

> ...young men in your pride make haste
> The wrong to right, the bond to free
> And plant a garden in the waste...[35]

The existence of a vast scientific complex devoted to managing the empire of nature poses some important historiographical problems. At the outset, what exactly was and was not colonial about 'colonial' science? Equally important, what should historians make of the idea of redemptive mission as noted above? What indeed should be made of the fact that following the end of formal imperial rule, many of the 'colonial' scientists were invited back as 'experts'? Further, what would historians have to say to those environmental activists who have targeted regimes of scientific resource management promoted by governments and international developmental agencies,[36] arguing that the underlying resource-use priorities of these sciences are opposed to those of the general populace?[37] What, indeed, should the response of an environmental historian be to those social and cultural assumptions underlying these systems of scientific resource management which have become issues of public controversy?[38]

Much of the trend in the history of science, technology and medicine, in both southern Africa and South Asia, has been to *subsume* science within wider processes such as the political economy of imperialism. In doing so, scholars base their work on the assumption that science and scientific ideas were deeply embedded in imperial rule and not 'an independent lever externally brought to bear on contemporaneous political and economic events'.[39] Science and scientific institutions are thus seen as 'tools of empire',[40] and scientists in turn are seen as servants of the colonial state. This attitude is clearly manifest in the ideal-type 'state science' used by many scholars to explain the nature of the colonial sciences of resource management.[41] The principle implicit in the ideal-type 'state science' is that the efficacy of the imperial scientific institutions concerned with environmental management can be explained deductively with reference to the political and economic exigencies of imperialism.

Such an approach, however, only gets at part of the story. The reason is that most colonial scientific regimes of resource management first developed within specific social, economic and political milieux in Europe.[42] The deployment in colonial contexts of scientific frameworks developed in Europe therefore meant concomitant transfers of their initial agendas on natural resource use. They also involved the adoption, in a colonial setting, of their inherent modes of production and their implicit capacities to engineer specific forms of ecological and human change. Moreover, they often meant the carrying over to colonial contexts of their implicit values and ideologies about nature and resource use.[43] The vehicles of such transfers were the scientific communities involved in natural resource management. Trained in European institutions, they imbibed the traditions and perspectives of the European sciences. When they went to the empire, these scientists constituted 'epistemic communities' carrying with them agendas of resource use developed within a European context.[44]

In order to understand what these epistemic communities brought with them, it is important to appreciate the origins of the European resource management systems. Karl Polanyi provided a hint of what was involved in his classic, *The great transformation*, wherein he argued that in pre-modern societies, economic activities were embedded in the social relations that made up the community as a whole.[45] Borrowing a leaf from the nineteenth-century social reformer Robert

Owen, Polanyi argued that in modern societies, by contrast, the economy was 'disembedded' from its social base. In these societies nature and human labour were exploited to satisfy explicitly economic goals, under the assumption that economic growth would in turn yield societal benefit.[46]

Thus, in the case of forestry, traditional resource-use regimes made way for a system of management that combined the sciences of tree growth with the economics of cameralism. The emergent cameral science of forestry in Prussia and later in France and the rest of Europe sought to protect forests for the economy of the state, often against local peoples.[47] Such a science was, in this sense, clearly colonial, even within Europe. While it made sense for a modernising colonial state to import such resource management systems, it is therefore important to recognise that the colonialism that they produced stemmed primarily from the matrix of economics, knowledge and state embedded within them in Europe.[48] Moreover, with modernisation and the idea of development emerging as a progressive ideology in the first few decades of the twentieth century – both within the experts of the colonial state as well as in the various nationalist movements – the implicit violence engendered by the intrinsic colonialism of forestry was ignored. It is this shared commitment that explains the redemptive ideology and optimism alluded to earlier, and the reason for the retention of colonial experts by post-colonial regimes.

Conclusion: The revenge of history

The retention of these experts or, perhaps more importantly, their agendas, in both southern Africa and South Asia, provoked a number of social movements directed against the assumptions of 'colonial' expertise. This unease is reflected in recent historical scholarship in both contexts, which has emphasised the validity of local knowledge systems and regimes of common resource management.[49] In doing so, they have provoked fascinating new experiments in resource use and control, involving, among other things, joint or co-management between local users and agencies and experts of the state.

Seen from a historical vantage point, and especially through a Polanyian lens, what has been attempted – in cases such as Joint Forest Management in Bengal or Campfire in Zimbabwe, with a degree of success – has been the re-embedding of economies within societies and communities.[50] Such initiatives, needless to say, are ideologically at the opposite end of the spectrum from the more dominant policy frameworks of market triumphalism and neo-liberalism which, in both southern Africa and South Asia, threaten a new era of imperialism, albeit of the 'global' variety. What we are witnessing now, therefore, is a new double movement, one that will be as much about ideas and cognitive revolutions as old-fashioned revolt.[51] The colonial eco-drama thus isn't over yet, nor will topics for environmental historians in both South Asia and southern Africa be exhausted anywhere in the near future.

Notes

Chapter 1: Environmental history in southern Africa

1. Taylor, A. 1996. Unnatural inequalities: social and environmental history. *Environmental History*, 1(4): p.8.
2. See Chapter 15 of this book.
3. As summarised by Taylor in Unnatural inequalities, p.6.
4. Cronon, W. 1993. The uses of environmental history. *Environmental History Review*, 17(3): pp.4–5.
5. Worster's best known works include: *The ends of the earth: perspectives on modern environmental history*. New York, 1988; *Under western skies: nature and history in the American west*. Oxford, 1992; *The wealth of nature: environmental history and the ecological imagination*. New York, 1993.
6. Worster, D. 1996. Nature and the disorder of history. *Environmental History Review*, 18(2): p.2.
7. Griffiths, T. 1997. *Research School of Social Sciences: Annual Report*. Canberra: Australian National University, p.46.
8. Coates has written about environmental history in: Clio's new greenhouse. *History Today*, August 1996: pp.15–22.
9. Beinart, W. and Coates, P. 1995. *Environment and history: the taming of nature in the USA and South Africa*. London, p.1.
10. Quoted in Beinart and Coates, *Environment and history*, p.2.
11. Van der Merwe, P.J. *The migrant farmers in the history of the Cape Colony, 1657–1842*. Translated by Roger B. Beck (Athens, Ohio, 1995) and first published in 1938; *Die noordwaartse beweging van die boere voor die Groot Trek*. The Hague, 1937; *Trek: studies oor die mobiliteit van die pioniersbevolking aan die Kaap*. Cape Town, 1945.
12. Dicke, B.H. 1932. The tsetse-fly's influence on South African history. *South African Journal of Science*, 29: pp.792–96. See Steyn, P. 1999. A greener past? An assessment of South African environmental historiography. *New Contree*, 46: pp.7–27.
13. London, 1963.
14. See, for example, Powell, J.M. 1976. *Environmental management in Australia, 1788–1914*. Melbourne; Powell, J.M. 1988. *An historical geography of modern Australia: the restive fringe*. Cambridge.
15. An early example was Le Roy Vail's, Ecology and history: the experience of eastern Zambia. *Journal of Southern African Studies*, 1977, 3(2): pp.129–55.
16. Wagner, R. 1980. Zoutpansberg: the dynamics of a hunting frontier, 1848–1867. In: Marks, S. and Atmore, A., eds. *Economy and society in pre-industrial South Africa*. London.

17. Guy, J. 1980. Ecological facts in the rise of Shaka and the Zulu kingdom. In: Marks, S. and Atmore, A., eds. *Economy and society in pre-industrial South Africa*. London; Guy, J. 1983. *The destruction of the Zulu kingdom*. Pietermaritzburg.

18. Phimister, I. 1986. Discourse and the discipline of historical context: conservationism and ideas about development in Southern Rhodesia, 1930–1950. *Journal of Southern African Studies*, 12(2): pp.263–75.

19. Beinart, W. 1983. *The political economy of Pondoland, 1860–1930*. Johannesburg; Beinart, W. 1984. Soil erosion, conservationism and ideas about development: a southern African exploration, 1900–1960. *Journal of Southern African Studies*, 11(1): pp.52–83; Beinart, W., et al. 1986. *Putting a plough to the ground: accumulation and dispossession in rural South Africa, 1850–1930*. Johannesburg; Delius, P. 1983. *The land belongs to us*. Johannesburg; Keegan, T.J. 1986. *Rural transformations in industrializing South Africa: the southern highveld to 1914*. Johannesburg; Peires, J. 1981. *The house of Phalo*. Johannesburg; Shillington, K. 1985. *The colonisation of the southern Tswana*. Johannesburg.

20. Cambridge, 1987.

21. January 1989, 15(2).

22. Hackel, J.D. and Carruthers, E.J. 1993. Swaziland's twentieth century wildlife preservation efforts: the present as a continuation of the past. *Environmental History Review*, 17(3): pp.61–84; Khan, F. 1997. Soil wars: the role of the African National Soil Conservation Association in South Africa, 1953–1959. *Environmental History*, 2(4): pp.439–59; Van Sittert, L. 1993. 'More in the breach than in the observance': crayfish, conservation and capitalism c.1890–c.1939. *Environmental History Review*, 17(4): pp.21–46.

23. The most recent article in this connection has been by Phia Steyn and André Wessels. The emergence of new environmentalism in South Africa 1988–1992. *South African Historical Journal*, 2000, 42: pp.210–31.

24. *Past and Present*, August 1990, 128: pp.162–86.

25. *South African Historical Journal*, 1990, 23: pp.184–95.

26. Steyn, P. 1999. A greener past? An assessment of South African environmental historiography. *New Contree*, 46: pp.7–27.

27. December 2000, 26(4).

28. Griffiths, T., ed. 1996. *People and place: Australian heritage perspectives*. London, p.i.

29. Dovers, S. 1994. Sustainability and 'pragmatic' environmental history: a note from Australia. *Environmental History Review*, 18(3): pp.21–22.

30. Cape Town, 1991.

31. See also Van Sittert, L. 2000. 'The seed blows about in every breeze': noxious weed eradication in the Cape Colony, 1860–1899. *Journal of Southern African Studies*, 26: pp.655–74.

32. See also Witt, H.A. 1999. An economic, social and environmental study of afforestation: a case study of tree-growing in Natal, 1900–1960. Ph.D. thesis. University of Natal, Durban.

33. See Ellis, B. 1998. The impact of the white settlers on the natural environment of Natal, 1845–1870. MA thesis. University of Natal, Pietermaritzburg.

34. Griffiths, T., *Research School of Social Sciences Annual Report*, p.47.

35. Cambridge, 1995.

36. London.

37. See, for example, the work of Stuart A. Marks, including: *The imperial lion: human dimensions of wildlife management in central Africa*. Boulder, CO, 1984; his earlier *Large mammals and a brave people: subsistence hunters in Zambia*. Washington, 1976, and numerous articles. Also significant is the work of E.I. Steinhart: Hunters, poachers and gamekeepers: towards a social history of hunting in colonial Kenya. *Journal of African History*, 1989, 30: pp.247–64; as well as Steinhart, E.I. National parks and anti-poaching in Kenya, 1947–1957. *International Journal of African Historical Studies*, 1994, 27(1): pp.59–76.

38. 1989, 15(2).

39. 1995, 1(3).

40. Mackenzie, J.M. 1988. *The empire of nature: hunting, conservation and British imperialism.* Manchester; Mackenzie, J.M., ed. 1990. *Imperialism and the natural world.* Manchester.

41. Stephen Pyne, personal communication. Pyne's graduate student course HIS690 is such a comparative course.

42. Edinburgh, 1997.

43. Cambridge, 1999.

44. See, for example, Arnold, D. and Guha, R., eds. 1995. *Nature, culture, imperialism: essays in Indian environmental history.* Delhi; Gadgil, R. and Guha, R. 1992. *This fissured land: an ecological history of India.* Oxford.

45. See, for example, Gautier, D. 1994. Prudence and profligacy: the dialectic of ecology and humanity in the Underberg district in historical context. BA Honours dissertation. University of Natal, Pietermaritzburg; Nell, D. 1998. 'You cannot make the people scientific by Act of Parliament': farmers, the state and livestock enumeration in the north-western Cape, c.1850–1900. MA thesis. University of Cape Town, Cape Town; Payne, J. 1998. Re-creating home: British colonialism, culture and the Zuurveld environment in the nineteenth century. MA thesis. Rhodes University, Grahamstown.

46. Along the lines of Carolyn Merchant's *The death of nature: women, ecology and the scientific revolution.* New York, 1989; or Merchant, C. 1995. *Earthcare: women and the environment.* New York.

47. See, for example, Rosen, C.M. and Tarr, J.A. 1994. The importance of an urban perspective in environmental history. *Journal of Urban History,* 20(3): pp.299–310.

48. Jane Carruthers, 2001, *Wildlife and warfare: the life of James Stevenson-Hamilton.* Pietermaritzburg, deals with the life of one of South Africa's most significant early environmentalists.

49. For example, Hoffman, M.T. 1995. Environmental history and the desertification of the Karoo, South Africa. *Giornale Botanico Italiano,* 129(1): pp. 261–372.

50. J.M. Powell is the most prolific writer in this field. See, for example: Historical geography and environmental history: an Australian interface. *Journal of Historical Geography,* 1996, 22(3): pp.253–73.

51. For example, Barnard, D. 1999. *Environmental law for all.* Pretoria; Fuggle, R.F. and Rabie, M.A., eds. 1983. *Environmental concerns in South Africa: technical and legal perspectives.* Cape Town; Rabie, A. 1976. *South African environmental legislation.* Pretoria. There have been a number of useful articles in the *South African Journal of Environmental Law and Policy* which began in 1994.

Chapter 2: The colonial ecological revolution in South Africa

1. Merchant, C. 1989. *Ecological revolutions: nature, gender and science in New England.* Chapel Hill: University of North Carolina, pp.2–3.

2. McCann, J. 1995. *People of the plow: an agricultural history of Ethiopia.* Madison: University of Wisconsin, p.69.

3. Merchant, *Ecological revolutions,* p.11.

4. Ibid., pp.14–19.

5. Ibid., pp.19–26.

6. Ibid., p.2.

7. Ibid., pp.3–4.

8. Crosby, A. 1986. *Ecological imperialism: the biological expansion of Europe.* New York: Cambridge University Press. Crosby has virtually no discussion of the character of ecological imperialism in Africa.

9. Shillington, K. 1985. *The colonisation of the Southern Tswana, 1870–1900.* Johannesburg: Ravan, pp.12–16; Comaroff, J. and Comaroff, J.L. 1991. *Of revelation and revolution: Christianity,*

colonialism and consciousness in South Africa. Chicago: University of Chicago Press, 1: p.127. Regarding population statistics at the turn of the century, see note 70 below.

10. Acocks, J.H. 1988. 3rd edition. *Veld types of Southern Africa*. Memoirs of the Botanical Survey of South Africa 57: pp.44–47.

11. For a description of environmental conditions, see: Snyman, P.H.R. 1992. *Kuruman: vervloë pad na Afrika*. Pretoria: Raad vir Geesteswetenskaplike Navorsing, pp.5–12.

12. Rainfall statistics are from Snyman, *Kuruman*, pp.5–8 and 1: 500 000 maps Kimberley SE29/22 and Vryburg SE27/21. Pretoria: Government Printer, 1950.

13. Lichtenstein, W.H.C. 1973. *Foundations of the Cape and about the Bechuanas*. Edited and translated by Spohr, O.H. Cape Town: Balkema, p.66.

14. For evidence on the ethnicity of Kuruman foragers, see: Campbell, J. 1822. *Travels in South Africa undertaken at the request of the London Missionary Society; being a narrative of a second journey into the interior of that country*, 2 vols. London: London Missionary Society. Reprint, New York: Johnson Reprints, 1967, 1: p.289; Moffat, R. 1842. *Missionary labours and scenes in Southern Africa*. London: Snow, p.8.

15. Elphick, R. 1977. *Kraal and castle: Khoikhoi and the founding of white South Africa*. New Haven: Yale University Press, pp.30–42.

16. For an expansion of this argument, see Jacobs, N. Environment, production and social difference in the Kalahari Thornveld, c.1750–c.1820s. Forthcoming in *Journal of Southern African Studies*.

17. Comaroff, J. 1985. *Body of power, spirit of resistance: the culture and history of a South African people*. Chicago: University of Chicago Press, pp.54–60; Comaroff, J. and Comaroff, J.L., *Of revelation and revolution*, pp.126–60, 206–13.

18. Comaroff, J., *Body of power*, p.54.

19. On the chief and control over nature, see also: Landau, P. 1995. *In the realm of the word: language, gender, and Christianity in a Southern African kingdom*. Portsmouth, NH: Heinemann, pp.24–26; Schapera, I. 1971. *Rainmaking rites of Tswana tribes*. Leiden: Afrika-Studiecentrum, pp.17–42.

20. The present environmental approach to the history of the region rests upon earlier research into its economic and political history. This region saw significant political developments before significant contact with the Cape, such as the establishment of the Tlhaping as an important chiefdom and the immigration of the Korana and Griqua. See Legassick, M. 1969. The Griqua, the Sotho–Tswana and the missionaries, 1700–1840: the politics of a frontier zone, Ph.D. thesis, UCLA; Shillington, *The colonisation of the Southern Tswana*.

21. Merchant, *Ecological revolutions*, p.2.

22. Commonly cited examples of merrie Africanist environmental history are Kjekshus, H. 1977. *Ecology control and economic development in East African history*. Berkeley and London: University of California and Heinemann. Reprint, Athens and London: Ohio University and James Currey, 1996; Vail, L. 1977. Ecology and history: the example of eastern Zambia. *Journal of Southern African Studies*, 3: pp.129–55. For discussions of this tendency see Giblin, J. and Maddox, G. 1996. Introduction. In: Giblin, J. and Maddox, G., eds. *Custodians of the land: ecology and culture in the history of Tanzania*. Athens: Ohio University Press, pp.6–9; Koponen, J. 1988. *People and production in late precolonial Tanzania: history and structures*. Uppsala: Scandinavian Institute of African Studies, pp.21–23, 360–91.

23. Grove, R. 1989. Scottish missionaries, evangelical discourses and the origins of conservation thinking in Southern Africa. *Journal of Southern African Studies*, 15: pp.22–39.

24. Tyson, P.D. 1987. *Climatic change and variability in Southern Africa*. Cape Town: Oxford University Press, pp.59–61, 67–68.

25. Severe drought has received a strong emphasis in the turmoils of the 1820s. See Eldredge, E. 1992. Sources of conflict in Southern Africa, c.1800–1830: the Mfecane reconsidered. *Journal of African History*, 33: pp.1–35.

26. For a summary of game depletion in southern Africa, see MacKenzie, J.M. 1988. *Empire of nature: hunting, conservation, and British imperialism*. Manchester: Manchester University Press, pp.89–116.

27. Selous, F.C. 1872. Zimbabwe National Archives [hereafter ZNA] Selous Journal [hereafter SE] 1/4, 5 Feb. For more on game population, see: Anderson, A.A. 1888. *Twenty-five years in a waggon.* London: Chapman and Hall, p.87; Mackenzie, J. 1871. *Ten years north of the Orange River.* Edinburgh: Edmonston and Douglas. Reprint, London: Frank Cass and Company, 1971, p.70; Wookey, A. 1884. School of Oriental and African Studies, University of London, Council for World Mission Archive, London Missionary Society, Africa South, Incoming Letters [hereafter LMS] Box 42. Review of South Bechuanaland, Part 2, 11 June.

28. Bryden, H.A. 1893. *Gun and camera in Southern Africa.* London: Edward Stanford. Reprint, Prescott, Arizona: Wolfe, 1988, p.62; Gould, A.J. 1883. Kuruman to Morokweng. In: Sandilands, A., ed. 1977. *Botswana Notes and Records.* 9: pp.49–54. Querk, A. 1887. British Parliamentary Papers [hereafter BPP] c.4956. *Further correspondence respecting the affairs of Bechuanaland and adjacent territories.* Report on Patrol to Honing Vley, p.124.

29. Regarding missionary thinking about irrigation, see Comaroff, J. and Comaroff, J.L., *Of revelation and revolution,* pp.206–13.

30. Philip, J. 1831. LMS Box 12. Report on South African mission. The smaller Tlharo chiefdom remained downstream from the mission and in the Langeberg.

31. Moffat, *Missionary labours and scenes,* p.558.

32. Backhouse, J. 1844. *A narrative of a visit to the Mauritius and South Africa.* London: Hamilton, Adams and Co., p.455. Gordon Cumming, R.G. 1857. *A hunter's life in South Africa.* London: John Murray. Reprint Bulawayo: Books of Zimbabwe, 1980, p.225.

33. Jacobs, N. 1996. The flowing eye: water management in the Upper Kuruman Valley, South Africa. *Journal of African History,* 37: pp.237–60.

34. Ashton, W. 1865. LMS Box 33. From Dikgatlhong, 20 Dec; Selous, F.C. 1871. ZNA SE 1/4, 3 Nov; Backhouse, J. and Taylor, C. 1862. *The life and labours of George Washington Walker of Hobart Town, Tasmania.* London: A.W. Bennet, p.448.

35. Wookey, *Review of South Bechuanaland;* Mackenzie, J. 1887. *Austral Africa: ruling it or losing it.* London: Sampson Low, 1: p.30.

36. Shillington, K. 1982. The impact of the diamond discoveries on the Kimberley hinterland: class formation, colonialism and resistance among the Tlhaping of Griqualand West in the 1870s. In: Marks, S. and Rathbone, R., eds. *Industrialisation and social change in South Africa: African class formation, culture and consciousness 1870–1930.* London: Longman, pp.99–118. For the history of irrigated cultivation in a western Transvaal village, see Drummond, J.H. 1990. Rural land use and agricultural production in Dinokana village, Bophuthatswana. *GeoJournal,* 22: pp.338–40.

37. Wookey, *Review of South Bechuanaland.* For an overview of wood sales in the northern Cape, see Shillington, *Colonisation,* pp.102–06, 137–38.

38. Warren and Harell. 1883. BPP c. 3635. *Reports by Colonel Warren, R.E., C.M.G. and Captain Harell. Late 89th Regiment. On the Affairs of Bechuanaland, Dated April 3rd 1879 and April 27th 1880,* pp.12–13.

39. Moffat, *Missionary labours and scenes,* p.562.

40. See Comaroff, *Body of power;* Comaroff and Comaroff, *Of revelation and revolution;* Landau, *In the realm of the word.*

41. Mackenzie, J., *Ten years,* p.92.

42. Merchant, *Ecological revolutions,* p.109.

43. De Kiewiet, C.W. 1937. *The imperial factor in South Africa.* Cambridge: Cambridge University Press, pp.183–88; Shillington, *Colonisation,* pp.123–65.

44. Regarding North America, John Locke dismissed native rights on the grounds that a few nomadic hunters and gatherers had no rights to keep legions of European farmers out of a territory. Washburn, W. 1971. *Red man's land – white man's law.* New York: Charles Scribner's Sons, pp.38, 143, 253.

45. British Bechuanaland Land Commission. 1886. BPP c. 4889. *Report of the Commissioners Appointed to Determine Land Claims and to Effect a Land Settlement in British Bechuanaland,* p.4.

46. Shillington, *Colonisation,* pp.166–214.

47. Bryden, *Gun and camera*, pp 15–16.
48. Brown, J.T. 1895. LMS Box 53, 6 Jan. See also Bam, C.J. 1895. CTAR Bechuanaland Crown Colony [hereafter BCC] 117, Resident Magistrate Annual Report, 10 Apr. Ashton, W. 1895. LMS Box 52, at Barkly West, 12 Oct.
49. Crosby, *Ecological imperialism*, pp.195–216; McNeill, W.H. 1989. *Plagues and peoples.* Garden City, New York: Anchor, pp.176–207.
50. Ballard, C. 1986. The repercussions of rinderpest: cattle plague and peasant decline in colonial Natal. *International Journal of African Historical Studies*, 19: pp.421–50; Phoofolo, P. 1993. Epidemics and revolutions: the rinderpest epidemic in late nineteenth century Southern Africa. *Past and Present*, 88: pp.112–43; Van Onselen, C. 1972. Reactions to rinderpest in Southern Africa, 1896–97. *Journal of African History*, 3: pp.473–88.
51. Gould, A.J. 1896. LMS Box 53, 9 May; Price, R. 1896. LMS Box 53, 1 April, 12 April.
52. Bam, C.J. 1896. CTAR Kuruman Resident Magistrate Series [hereafter 1/KMN] 10/1, 6 Aug., 19 Aug., 18 Nov.
53. On Cape Colony game laws, see MacKenzie, J.M., *Empire of nature*, pp.202–04. For a missionary protest, see Brown, J.T. 1897. LMS Box 54, 27 Sep.
54. Brown, J. 1896. LMS Box 53. At Taung, 25 Oct. [Note: This is John Brown, not John Thomas Brown]; Shillington, *Colonisation*, pp.231–32.
55. These factors are reasons offered as causes for the rebellion among the Tlhaping. For accounts of the Langeberg war, see: Saker, H. and Aldridge, J. 1972. The origins of the Langeberg rebellion. *Journal of African History*, 12: pp.299–317; Shillington, *Colonisation*, pp.215–40; Snyman, *Kuruman*, pp.68–70.
56. Cape Colony Parliamentary Papers [hereafter CPP] G 42–'98, *Blue Book of Native Affairs*, p.66.
57. CPP G 72–'98, *Rinderpest statistics for the Colony of the Cape of Good Hope*.
58. Ministers to Governor. 1897. Public Records Office, London [hereafter PRO] Colonial Office Confidential Print Series [hereafter CO] 879/51 no. 547, 7 Feb.
59. McCarthy, J.P. 1898. CTAR NA 247, Monthly Report, Kuruman Inspector of Native Reserves, 2 Sept.
60. CPP G 42–'98, *Blue Book of Native Affairs*, p.66.
61. M. Seburu. 1898. PRO CO 879/51. Enclosure. 22 Feb.
62. The histories of imperialism in the region by Shillington and Agar-Hamilton exclude the history of the Anglo-Boer War. Snyman's work contains the only detailed account of the war in the area. See Snyman, *Colonisation*, pp.79–86.
63. Lyne, M.J. 1902. CTAR 1/KMN 10/4. Date illegible.
64. Brown, J.T. 1900. LMS Box 48, 23 Jan., 26 Feb. Snyman, pp.81–82.
65. Brown, J.T. 1901. LMS Box 59, 14 Feb., 14 Oct, 6 Nov.
66. CPP G 25–1902, *Blue Book of Native Affairs*, p.30.
67. CPP G 52–1901, *Blue Book of Native Affairs*, pp.20, 30.
68. Lyne, M.J. 1903. CTAR NA 605, Telegraph 2 May.
69. Merchant, *Ecological revolutions*, pp.92–96.
70. These are not entirely trustworthy figures, but they convey an understanding of demographic change. The prisoners indentured in the Western Cape account for almost 2000 of the decline and some would have returned by 1904. For population figures for 1896 and 1897, see Jan. Report for Native Affairs Blue Book. 1898. Cape Town Archives Repository 1/KMN 10/2.
71. Blenkins, W.G. 1899. CPP G 67–'99, *Reports by the Special Commissioner Appointed to inquire into the Agriculture Distress and Land Matters in the Division of Herbert, Hay, Barkly West, Vryburg and Kimberley*, p.8. Kuruman was included in the Vryburg Division.
72. M.J. Lyne. 1902. CTAR 1/KMN 10/4. Date illegible.
73. On government response to the 1903 food shortage, see correspondence between Lyne and the Native Affairs Department, in CTAR NA 605.
74. For 1904 see CPP G.19–1905, *Census of the Colony of the Cape of Good Hope*, 1904.

75. See, for example, Walker, C. 1990. Gender and the development of the migrant labour system, c.1850–1930. In: Walker, C., ed. *Women and gender in Southern Africa to 1945*. London: James Currey, pp.168–96.

76. Merchant, *Ecological revolutions*, p.111.

77. For Merchant's discussion of consciousness, see *Ecological revolutions*, pp.44–50 (northern foragers), pp.70–74 (southern cultivators).

78. There are few explorations of attitudes toward nature among whites in southern Africa. On missionaries, see Grove, R. and Ranger T. 1987. Taking hold of the land: holy places and pilgrimages in twentieth-century Zimbabwe. *Past and Present*, 117: pp.158–94. For general comparisons of the environmental history of settler societies see Griffiths T. and Robin, L., eds. 1997. *Ecology and empire: environmental history of settler societies*. Pietermaritzburg: University of Natal Press.

79. Regarding northern foragers, Merchant does discuss conversion to Christianity, see *Ecological revolutions*, pp.58–61, but she sees it as a reaction to rather than part of the process of change. There is no similar discussion about changing consciousness among southern cultivators.

80. See Merchant, *Ecological revolutions*, p.6, Figure 1–1 for a specific list of significant items deserving consideration at each level.

Chapter 3: White settler impact on the environment of Durban

All archival references are to be found in the Natal Archives Depot, (NAD) Pietermaritzburg, and the Durban Archives Repository (DAR).

1. Maggs, T. 1980. The Iron Age sequence south of the Vaal and Pongola rivers: some historical implications. *Journal of African History*, 21: pp.1–15.

2. Bjorvig, A.C. 1994. Durban 1824–1910: the formation of a settler elite and its role in the development of a colonial city. Ph.D. thesis, University of Natal, Durban: p.18.

3. Colenso, J.W. 1855. *Ten weeks in Natal*. Durban: p.9.

4. Henderson, W.P.M. 1904. *Fifty years of municipal history*. Durban: p.6.

5. Bjorvig, Durban 1824–1910, pp.47–49.

6. Davies, R.J. 1963. The growth of the Durban metropolitan area. *South African Geographical Journal*, 45: p.19.

7. Bjorvig, Durban 1824–1910, p.174.

8. Robinson, J., ed. 1872. *Notes on Natal: an old colonist's book for new settlers*. Durban. Reprint, Pretoria, 1967: p.xii.

9. Bjorvig, Durban 1824–1910, pp.235, 236.

10. Ibid., pp.240, 241.

11. Swanson, M. 1984. 'The fate of the natives': black Durban and African ideology. *Natalia*, 14: p.59.

12. The only figure that could be found is the one cited for 1871, taken from Robinson, *Notes on Natal*, p.xii.

13. Russell, G. 1899. *The history of old Durban and reminiscences of an emigrant of 1850*. Durban. Reprint, Durban, 1971: p.324.

14. Henderson, *Fifty years*, p.49.

15. For discussion on Milne's role, see Heydenrych, L. 1985. Port Natal harbour, c.1850–1897. In: Guest, B. and Sellers, J.M., eds. *Enterprise and exploitation in a Victorian colony*. Pietermaritzburg, 1985: pp.19–20.

16. GH 1210, p.503, no. 60, Col. H. Cooper to Sec. of State, 19 October 1855.

17. Heydenrych, Port Natal harbour, p.23.

18. GH 1217, no. 130, R. Keate to E. Grenville, 21 December 1869.

19. Russell, *Old Durban*, p.91.

20. Henderson, *Fifty years*, p.49.

21. Child, D., ed. 1979. *A merchant family in early Natal: diaries and letters of Joseph and Marianne Churchill, 1850–1880*. Cape Town: p.10.

22. Sanderson, J. 1868. Rough notes on the botany of Natal. In: Chapman, J. *Travels in the interior of South Africa*. Vol. 2. London: p.446.
23. *Natal Mercury*, 28 January 1858.
24. Durban Local History Museum, water colour by James West, View of Durban Bayhead from Bluff, 1856; Russell, *Old Durban*, p.72.
25. Sanderson, Rough notes on the botany of Natal, pp.451, 452.
26. *Natal Mercury*, 9 July 1867.
27. *Government Gazette*, 1869. Government Notice No. 141: p.487.
28. *Natal Mercury*, 23 May 1855.
29. DAR *Minutes of the Durban Town Council*, Vol. 1, 24 April 1863: p.472.
30. Russell, *Old Durban*, p.287.
31. *Natal Mercury*, 10 June 1859.
32. *Government Gazette*, 1849, Gazette No. 30, Government Notice No. 56 of 1849.
33. Proclamation of 24 September 1853.
34. SGO 111/1/9: p.8, R. Boyne to Surveyor-General, 14 January 1854.
35. DAR *Minutes of Durban Town Council*, Vol. 1, 24 April 1863: p.472.
36. Sanderson, Rough notes on the botany of Natal, pp.446–54.
37. Holliday, J.H. 1890. *Dottings on Natal as published in 1865, and sundry tit-bits of colonial experience*. Pietermaritzburg: p.5.
38. DAR Office of the Durban Town Clerk, File 51, R. Jameson to the Mayor, 15 November 1869. Note: The grass is now [2002] called *Bromus wildenowii*, used for winter green pastures.
39. *Natal Commercial Advertiser*, 8 July 1854.
40. *Natal Mercury*, 7 May 1857; Leslie, D. 1875. *Among the Zulus and Amatongas*. Glasgow: p.219.
41. SGO 111/1/3, T. Okes to W. Stanger, 24 July 1846; Drayson, A.W. 1858. *Sporting scenes among Kaffirs of South Africa*. London: p.77.
42. Russell, *Old Durban*, p.96.
43. Leslie, *Among the Zulus and Amatongas*, p.6.
44. Mackenzie, J.M. 1987. Chivalry, Social Darwinism and ritualized killing: the hunting ethos in Central Africa up to 1914. In: Anderson, D. and Grove, R., eds. *Conservation in Africa: people, policies and practice*. Cambridge: pp.41–61.
45. *Natal Herald*, 9 September 1869.
46. Ibid., 28 October 1869.
47. Russell, *Old Durban*, p.96.
48. *Durban Observer*, 19 September 1851; Colenso, *Ten weeks in Natal*, p.29; *Natal Mercury*, 6 July 1867.
49. *Natal Mercury*, 7 July 1856; Russell, *Old Durban*, pp.72, 96.
50. *Natal Times*, 30 January 1852; *Natal Mercury*, 14 March 1856, 19 September 1867; *Natal Herald*, 11 April 1870.
51. Holden, W.C. 1855. *History of the Colony of Natal, South Africa*. London: p.17.
52. Russell, *Old Durban*, pp.96, 97.
53. Slater, H. 1980. The changing pattern of economic relationships in rural Natal, 1838–1914. In: Marks, S. and Atmore, A., eds. *Economy and society in pre-industrialized South Africa*. London: p.156.
54. *Natal Blue Book*, 1865, p.Y9.
55. *Natal Mercury*, 29 November 1866; *Natal Herald*, 13 December 1866.
56. *Natal Herald*, 13 December 1866.
57. *Government Gazette*, p.440. Law No. 13, 1867.
58. *Natal Blue Book*, 1868, p.Y11.
59. Russell, *Old Durban*, p.92.
60. *Natal Mercury*, 29 May 1866, 16 February 1867.
61. *Natal Mercury*, 16 February 1865; *Natal Blue Book*, 1856, p.315.
62. *Natal Mercury*, 3 May 1866.

Chapter 4: 'The titihoya does not cry here any more'

1. Paton, A. 1948. *Cry, the beloved country: a story of comfort in desolation*. Harmondsworth: Penguin, p.7. Three members of the plover family are known by the Zulu name, *iTitihoye*; Paton is possibly referring to the blacksmith plover, a common resident in Natal's well-watered regions.
2. Evans, M.S. 1916. *Black and white in south-east Africa: a study in sociology*. 2nd ed. London: Longmans, Green, p.131.
3. The information on the pre-colonial homestead economy is taken from Lambert, J. 1995. *Betrayed trust: Africans and the state in colonial Natal*. Pietermaritzburg: University of Natal Press, pp.39–40.
4. For environmental conditions in Natal, see *Archaeology and natural resources of Natal*. 1951. Natal Regional Survey. Vol.1. Cape Town: Oxford University Press, passim; Lambert, J. 1986. Africans in Natal, 1880–1889: continuity, change and crisis in a rural society. D.Litt. et Phil., University of South Africa, Pretoria, Chapter 1; Phillips, J. 1973. *The agricultural and related development of the Tugela basin and its influent surrounds: a study in subtropical Africa*. Natal Town and Regional Planning Report 19, Pietermaritzburg: Natal Town and Regional Planning Commission, passim.
5. Natal, *Proceedings of the Commission Appointed to inquire into the Past and Present State of the Kafirs in the District of Natal... 1852*. Pietermaritzburg. III, Peppercorne, p.66; see also Welsh, D. 1971. *The roots of segregation: native policy in colonial Natal, 1845–1910*. Cape Town: Oxford University Press, p.178
6. Natal, *Proceedings of the Commission... 1852*. VI, Mesham, p.11; Tyler, J. 1891. *Forty years among the Zulu*. Boston: Congregational Sunday School and Publishing Company, pp.38, 73–82.
7. See Hedges, D.W. 1978. Trade and politics in southern Mozambique and Zululand in the eighteenth and early nineteenth century. Ph.D. thesis, University of London, London.
8. Bryant, A.T. 1907. *A description of native foodstuffs and their preparation*. Pietermaritzburg: Times Printing and Publishing Company. This provides an excellent description of African diet; see also Shooter, J. 1857. *The Kafirs of Natal and the Zulu country*. London: E. Stanford, p.28.
9. Lambert, *Betrayed trust*, pp.25–27.
10. Ibid., p.25.
11. Ballard, C. 1989. Traders, trekkers and colonists. In Duminy, A. and Guest, B., eds. *Natal and Zululand from earliest times to 1910: a new history*. Pietermaritzburg: University of Natal Press and Shuter & Shooter, p.119.
12. Methley, J.E. 1850. *The new colony at Port Natal with information for emigrants*. London: Houlston and Stoneman, p.24.
13. Welsh, *Roots of segregation*, pp.12–13, 177.
14. Natal, *Proceedings of the Commission... 1852*. VI, Mesham, p.11; Tyler, *Forty years*, pp.38, 73–82.
15. Natal Parliamentary Papers (NPP). Natal Archives. 107, no.5, Report of Commission... to Enquire into the Existing Relations between Masters and Native Servants, 31 July 1871.
16. Secretary for Native Affairs (SNA). Natal Archives. 1/6/6, 257/76, Magistrate, Umsinga to SNA, 23 March 1876; Smith, R.H. *Labour resources of Natal*. Natal Regional Survey, Report no.1. Cape Town: Oxford University Press, p.47.
17. See *Natal Mercury*, 23 November 1875; SNA, 1/6/6, 253/76, Magistrate, Upper Umkomanzi to SNA, 28 June 1876.
18. *Natal Blue Books* (NBB), 1867, p.X7; 1882, p.X6. These would be very rough estimates; official agricultural statistics in colonial Natal have to be treated with great circumspection.
19. Natal, *Proceedings of the Commission... 1852*. III, Peppercorne, p.66; VI, Shepstone, p.85; *NBB*, 1876, pp.J8–9; 1882, p.GG63.
20. Natal, *Report on the Condition of the Native Population, 1879*, pp.7, 12, 24, 26, 45. As this chapter focuses on homestead society, the experience of the black Christian elite, the *amakholwa*, is not looked at.

21. Natal, *Evidence taken before the Natal Native Commission, 1881*. Pietermaritzburg. Maweli, p.203, Kukelela, p.232, Madude, p.240, Umsutu, p.367.

22. *Legislative Council (LC) Hansard*, VII, 19 August 1884, Robinson and Hulett, p.485; Natal Land and Colonisation Company (NL&C). Natal Archives, 183, no.142, Haynes to General Manager, Durban, 13 January 1887. By the 1880s many of the sales were to Indian purchasers while absentee landowners now preferred Indian rent tenants who could afford to pay higher rents.

23. *NBB*, 1884–1889; *NBB Departmental Reports*, 1890/1, p.H107.

24. *NBB*, 1883, p.GG54; *NBB Departmental Reports*, 1884, pp.B16–17; Upper Umkomanzi Magistracy. Natal Archives. 3/2/2, 109/92, Magistrate to SNA, 26 March 1892.

25. *NBB*, 1881, p.GG8; SNA, 1/1/94, 945/86, SNA to Colonial Secretary, 13 January 1887.

26. Natal, *Correspondence Relative to the Eviction of Native Occupants from Crown Lands, 1883*. Pietermaritzburg. Acting SNA's report, 18 August 1882, p.13.

27. Natal, *Report of the Natal Native Commission, 1881–2*. Pietermaritzburg. p.50; Natal, *Report...Native Population*, 1894/5, p.12.

28. This was evident even in the early 1880s, see Natal, *Evidence...Natal Native Commission, 1881*. Mahoba, p.376, Ncapie, p.384.

29. *NBB*, 1892/3, p.X21. Incorrectly added as 17 772.

30. Allan, W. 1965. *The African husbandman*. Westport: Greenwood Press, pp.30f.

31. Natal, *Report on the Natal Forests, 1889*. Pietermaritzburg, pp.6, 12, 20, 48, 50.

32. See NL&C, 208, no.85, Weller to General Manager, Durban, 26 August 1893; *Natal Witness*, 29 July 1891.

33. Natal, *Report on the Natal Forests, 1889*, pp.13, 15.

34. Palmer, R. and Parsons, N., eds. 1977. *The roots of rural poverty in Central and Southern Africa*. London: James Currey, p.7.

35. Jenkinson, T.B. 1882. *Amazulu: the Zulus, their past history, manners, customs and language*. London: W.M. Allen, p.10.

36. *NBB*, 1869, p.X12; 1882, p.xii; *Natal Statistical Yearbook (NSYB)*, 1896, p.P15.

37. Bransby, D.I. 1977. The ecology of livestock production in Natal and Zululand. Workshop on production and reproduction in the Zulu kingdom, University of Natal, Pietermaritzburg, p.3.

38. *NSYB*, 1896, p.P15

39. *NBB*, 1894, pp.78, 83; 1895, p.46.

40. *Natal Mercury*, 19 April 1893.

41. Natal, *Report...Native Population*, 1894, p.83.

42. SNA, 1/1/124, 472/90, Magistrate, Weenen to SNA, 13 April 1890.

43. SNA, 1/1/163, 1209/92, SNA to Governor, 2 December 1892.

44. *NBB*, 1888–1893; *NBB Departmental Reports*, 1888–1893; SNA, 1/1/137, 94/91, Fayle diary, 11 January 1891; see also Booth, A. 1985. Homestead, state and migrant labour in colonial Swaziland. *African Economic History*, 14: pp.107–45.

45. *NBB*, 1882, p.GG13; Natal, *Report on the Natal Forests, 1889*, p.15; *Natal Mercury*, 2 February 1891, 2 October 1892; Act 3, 1884, *To prevent the indiscriminate destruction of certain valuable wild animals*; Act 28, 1890 and Act 16, 1891, *To make provision for the better preservation of game*.

46. Hobsbawm, E.J. 1978. Review of peasants, politics and revolution . . . by J.S. Migdal. *Journal of Peasant Studies*, 5(2): p.254.

47. See NPP, 146, no.111, 1886, Report of SNA, 16 July 1884; SNA, 1/1/169, 441/93, Fayle diary, 8 April 1893.

48. See Lambert, J., *Betrayed trust*, Chapter 8.

49. Natal, *Report...Native Population*, 1897, pp.104–05.

50. By 1905 African-owned cattle numbered 276 997, far short of the 494 382 of 1896 (Natal, Department of Native Affairs, *Annual Report*, 1905, pp.129f); population numbers had increased to 607 229 in 1904 compared to 455 983 in 1891 (Natal, *Census of 1891: report with tables and appendices*, Pietermaritzburg; Natal, *Census of the Colony of Natal, 17th April 1904...*,

Pietermaritzburg). All figures exclude Zululand and the northern districts of Vryheid and Utrecht annexed after the South African War.

51. *NSYB*, 1902–04.
52. See *South African Native Affairs Commission, 1903–1905*, Cape Town. Vol.3, Mahashi, p.896.
53. Natal, *Report...Native Population*, 1901, p.B35; 1902, pp.A6, 27; 1903, pp.A11, 21, 25; *SANAC*, 3, R.C. Samuelson, p.505.
54. Natal, Department of Native Affairs, *Annual Report*, 1905, p.10.
55. Ibid., p.48.
56. Stuart Papers. Killie Campbell Library. File 2, What then is to be done?, p.3.

Chapter 5: 'I can see my *umuzi* where I now am...'

1. There are several terms that I use in this chapter which I should like to explain. I use the term *izimpi zemibango* for the fights which broke out in the Umlazi location during the 1930s. When translated literally from Zulu, it means 'fights or wars originating from disputes'. I prefer this term because it is open-ended, and it enables the possibility of a variety of disputes. The term also enables us to explore the possibility of a variety of actors, issues and interests. There is not the simple closure involved in the term 'faction fights'. I use the terms *Umlazi location* and *Pinetown district* to describe the territory which is nowadays (2001) known as the *Umbumbulu* reserve and district. The Umbumbulu magistracy was established in February 1938. Prior to this the district magistracy seat was in Pinetown, and the Umbumbulu reserve areas were referred to as Umlazi location. The terms *Mkhize* and *abaMbo* are used interchangeably in this chapter. *Mkhize* is used for the numerous chieftaincies which emerged when the Mkhize reached southern Natal during the 1830s. The *abaMbo* is the *isithakazelo* (form of polite address) for the Mkhize. I do not use the terms *inkosi/ubukhosi* because of the ideological baggage which these terms have assumed in the provincial politics of KwaZulu-Natal. I prefer the words *chief* and *chiefship*.
2. Chief Native Commissioner (CNC) 92A, 26 February 1920, Secretary for Native Affairs (SNA) to CNC.
3. See Beinart, W. 1992. Political and collective violence in southern African historiography. *Journal of Southern African Studies (JSAS)*, 18: pp.455–86.
4. Rider-Haggard, H. 1985 (first published in 1885). *King Solomon's mines*. Cape Town: A.D. Donker; Buchan, J. 1987 (first published in 1910). *Prester John*. London: Penguin; Gwayi, J.J. 1974. *Shumpu*. Pretoria: J.L. van Schaik Ltd.
5. The Minister of Native Affairs (MNA) declared that the Mkhize were 'a warlike lot and liked a little blood-letting occasionally'. *Hansard*, 1936: p.441.
6. See Meli, F. 1985. *South Africa belongs to us: a history of the ANC*. London: James Currey, pp.213–15; African National Congress. 1997. *Second Submission to the Truth and Reconciliation Commission*. Johannesburg: ANC's Department of Information and Publicity, pp.3–5; Beinart, Political and collective violence, pp.458–60.
7. Clegg, J. 1981. *Ukubuyisa Isidumbu: 'Bringing back the body'*. *Working Papers in Southern African Studies*. Johannesburg: Witwatersrand University Press, pp.164–99; Lambert, J. 1995. *Betrayed trust: Africans and the state in colonial Natal*. Pietermaritzburg: University of Natal Press, Chapter 5.
8. Beinart, Political and collective violence, p.473.
9. Crummey, D., ed. 1986. *Banditry, rebellion and social protest in Africa*. London: James Currey, pp.1–3.
10. Byerley, M.A. 1989. Mass violence in Durban's settlements in the 1980s. MA thesis, University of Natal, Durban.
11. Homer-Dixon, T.F., et al. 1993. Environmental change and violent conflict. *Scientific American*, February: pp.38–45.

12. Brookes, E.H. and Hurwitz, N. 1957. *The native reserves of Natal*. Cape Town: Oxford University Press (OUP), Chapter 1; Welsh, D. 1971. *The roots of segregation 1845–1910*. Cape Town: OUP, pp.7–15.
13. Alsop, M.H. 1952. *Population of Natal*. Cape Town: OUP, pp.104, 115.
14. CNC 89A, 25 October 1935, CNC to Secretary for Native Affairs (SNA).
15. Brookes and Hurwitz, *The native reserves of Natal*, p.63.
16. Alsop, *Population*; Fair, T.J.D. 1955. *The distribution of the population of Natal*. Cape Town: OUP, pp.86–87; Kelly, C. 1989. Durban's industrialisation and life and labour of black workers, 1920–1950. MA thesis, University of Natal, Durban, p.21.
17. My research has not enabled me to verify details about the soil texture, grass types and trees found in the Umlazi reserve areas. The description given here has been drawn from Reader, D.H. 1966. *Zulu tribe in transition*. Manchester: Manchester University Press; Pentz, J.A. 1945. *'n Agro-ekologiese opname van Natal*. Pretoria: Departement van Landbou en Bosbou; Acocks, J.P.H. 1988. *Veld types of South Africa*. Pretoria: Botanical Research Institute, Department of Agriculture and Water Supply, South Africa.
18. Reader, *Zulu tribe*, p.29; Pentz, *'n Agro-ekologiese opname*, pp.1–10.
19. Pentz, *'n Agro-ekologiese opname*, pp.1–10.
20. Reader, *Zulu tribe*, p.30; Acocks, *Veld types*, p.17; Fair, *The distribution of population*, p.87.
21. Reader, *Zulu tribe*, Chapter 3.
22. Schellnack, I.S. 1990. East Coast fever in Natal from the early 1900s to 1957. Honours thesis. University of Natal, Pietermaritzburg, pp.17–40.
23. Ibid., p.88.
24. Hurwitz, N. 1957. *Agriculture in Natal, 1860–1950*. Cape Town: OUP, pp.87–90.
25. CNC 18A, 1918, Report of locust plagues in the Pinetown district; CEN 954, 21 October 1933, Reports of locust swarms.
26. CNC 92A, 12 September 1921, Native Commissioner (NC) for Pinetown to CNC.
27. CNC 92A, 14 March 1922, NC for Pinetown to CNC.
28. CNC 92A, 12 October 1921, G.L. Kirby to NC for Pinetown.
29. CNC 92A, August 1925, Bell to CNC; also 24 July 1928, Lewis to CNC; and 28 October 1929, Pearce to CNC.
30. CNC 92A, 25 September 1930, SNA to CNC; and 1 October 1930, CNC to SNA.
31. CNC 92A, 10 October 1924, A.L. Barret to Kirby.
32. CNC 92A, 3 December 1924, Kirby to CNC.
33. *Hansard*, 4 June 1936, p.423.
34. SNA 1/1/192, 22 September 1894, SNA for Natal to colonial SNA.
35. SNA 1/6/27, 30 July and 15 August 1906, Court martial of Tilongo and Sikhukhukhu.
36. SNA 1/1/356, 9 November 1906, 'The amalgamation of the abaMbo chiefdoms'; CNC 89A, 17 October 1934, CNC to SNA; *Natal Mercury*, 10 September 1934; and Lugg, H.C.1970. *A Natal family looks back*. Durban: Adams and Griggs, p.94.
37. CNC 1, 9 January 1911, B. Evans (farmer) to SNA; CNC 3, 30 January 1911, L.G. Wingfield-Stratford (farmer) to SNA; CNC 5, 18 February 1911, CNC to SNA.
38. *Hansard*, 4 June 1936, p.423.
39. See Nuttall, T.A. 1991. Class, race and nation: African politics in Durban, 1929–1949. D.Phil. thesis, Oxford University, Oxford, pp.126–27, 246.
40. *Government Gazette No.1883*, 19 June 1930; Government Notice No.1119; CNC 89A, 17 October 1934, CNC to SNA. CNC 89A, 23 November 1934, NC for Pinetown to Attorney General (AG); 1/CPD 3/2/2/6, 24 September 1934, Minutes of meeting; *Hansard*, 4 June 1936, p.424.
41. URU (Executive Documents), 1126, 9 April 1930, Amalgamation of the Mkhize chiefdoms under acting chiefs Bhinananda and Mgadlela, the retirement of these chiefs, and the appointment of Nkasa as chief over the amalgamated sections of the 'Mbo Tribe'; CNC 89A, 6 October 1934, Thrash to CNC.

42. 1/RMD 3/3/1/1, 6 March 1931, Const. Hagel to NC for RMD; 1/RMD 3/3/1/1, 12 June 1931, CNC to NC for Pinetown; *Government Gazette No.1991*, 4 December 1931; Government Notice No.1893; CNC 89A, 17 October 1934, CNC to SNA. CNC 89A, 23 November 1934, NC for PTN to AG; *Hansard*, 4 June 1936, pp.428–30; Reader, *Zulu tribe*, pp.25–26.

43. *Natal Mercury*, 30 March 1931; CNC 91A, 17 June 1935, SNA to meeting; Edgar, R.R. and kaMsumza, L., eds. 1996. *Freedom in our life time: the collected writings of Anton Muziwakhe Lembede*. Johannesburg: Ravan, p.3; and Bradford, H. 1988. *A taste of freedom: the ICU in rural South Africa, 1924–30*. Johannesburg: Ravan, Chapter 2.

44. CNC 95A, 21 November 1933, F.S. Heaton to Lugg.

45. CNC 89A, 23 November 1934, NC for Pinetown; *Hansard*, 4 June 1936, p.428.

46. 1/CPD 3/2/2/6, 21–26 April 1933, NC for Camperdown to CNC; 1/CPD 3/2/2/6, 19 July 1933, CNC to NC for Pinetown; CNC 89A, 23 November 1934, NC for Pinetown to AG; *Hansard*, 4 June 1936, p.429; Reader, *Zulu tribe*, p.27.

47. 1/CPD 3/2/2/6, 12 April 1934, CNC to NCs for Pinetown, Umzinto and Camperdown; CNC 89A, 17 October 1934, CNC to SNA.

48. *Natal Mercury*, 4 August 1934; *Hansard*, 4 June 1936, p.433.

49. 1/RMD 3/3/1/1, 16 October 1934, Minutes of meeting.

50. CNC 89A, 9 October 1935, SAP, Isipingo to District Commissioner, Durban; CNC 89A, 8 November and 5 December 1935, NC for Pinetown to CNC.

51. CNC 77A, 8 July 1936, DC to Deputy Commissioner of Police (DCP).

52. CNC 77A, 1 November 1934, O.J. Askew and Company to NC for Pinetown.

53. CNC 89A, 2 December 1935, Shange's testimony to Inquiry.

54. CNC 91A, 17 June 1935, Minutes of meeting.

55. 1/RMD 3/3/1/1, 9 August 1935, Meeting at the Mid-Illovo.

Chapter 6: Environmental origins of the Pondoland revolt

1. Mbeki, G.. 1964. *South Africa: the peasants' revolt*. Penguin: Harmondsworth; Lodge, T. 1985. *Black politics in South Africa since 1945*. Longman: London.

2. Delius, P. 1996. *A lion amongst the cattle: reconstruction and resistance in the Northern Transvaal*. James Currey: Oxford.

3. Beinart, W. 1992. Transkeian smallholders and agrarian reform. *Journal of Contemporary African Studies*, 11(2).

4. For background, see Beinart, W. 1984. Soil erosion, conservationism and ideas about development: a southern African exploration, 1900–1960. *Journal of Southern African Studies*, 11(1); Hendricks, F.T. 1990. The pillars of apartheid: land tenure, rural planning and the chieftaincy. *Studia Sociologica Uppsaliensia*, 32; and Hendricks, F.T. 1989. Loose planning and rapid resettlement: the politics of conservation and control in Transkei, South Africa, 1950–1970. *Journal of Southern African Studies*, 15(2).

5. Beinart, W. 1982. *The political economy of Pondoland 1860–1930*. Cambridge: Cambridge University Press, p.107.

6. Transkeian Archives, Umtata, Chief Magistrate's papers (UTA CMT), Box 57, File 3/1/1/6, I, Resident Magistrate (RM) Bizana to Chief Magistrate of the Transkeian Territories, Umtata (CMT), 26.6.1926.

7. *Farming in South Africa*, vol. X (December 1935), Department of Agriculture and Forestry, Annual Report: Year ended 31 August 1935, pp.502–04, 526. This was an unusually large amount which was not again rivalled. The departmental budget did not include agricultural export subsidies, which were by then eight million pounds.

8. Beinart, *The political economy*, pp.173–74.

9. Cape Archives, papers of the Resident Magistrate of Bizana (CA 1/BIZ) 6/52, N1/1/5(6) King Langasiki to RM Bizana, 31.12.1934.

10. CA 1/BIZ 6/52, N1/1/5 (6), King Langasiki to RM Bizana, 6.2.1935.
11. UTA CMT 57, 3/1/1/6, Minutes of meeting held at Mpetsheni, in Headman King Langasiki's location, no.6. Bizana District on the 13th day of February, 1935.
12. CA 1/BIZ 6/52, S. Hilarius, locust officer, Report on meeting with location 16, 7.7.1935.
13. CA 1/BIZ 6/25, 4/26/3, McDonald Mlomo to RM Bizana, 29.7.1935 and following correspondence.
14. CA 1/BIZ 6/52, S. Hilarius, locust officer, Report on meeting with location 16, 7.7.1935.
15. Beinart, W. and Bundy, C. 1987. *Hidden struggles in rural South Africa: politics and popular movements in the Transkei and Eastern Cape, 1890–1930.* London: James Currey.
16. McKinnon, A. 1996. Land, labour and cattle: the political economy of Zululand, c.1930–1950. Ph.D. thesis, University of London, London.
17. UTA CMT 57, 3/1/1/6, Bantu Affairs Commissioner Bizana to CMT, 19.4.1960.
18. UTA CMT 57, 3/1/1/6, Statement by Headman Meje, 25.8.1960.
19. Feely, J.M. 1987. *The early farmers of Transkei, Southern Africa before AD 1870.* Oxford: B.A.R. series.
20. Cape Archives, papers of the RM of Lusikisiki (CA 1/LSK) 12, 71/10/1.
21. Beinart, *The political economy.*
22. Cape Archives, papers of the Chief Magistrate (CA CMT) 3/1327, 24/9/2, RM Lusikisiki to CMT, 7.9.1934, enclosing list: Squatters in Lusikisiki Forests.
23. CA 1/BIZ 6/26, 10/1/2, Government Notice 1862 of 1939. This was the same year as the promulgation of the Betterment proclamation.
24. Proclamation 224 of 1932, revising proclamations of 1912 and 1913.
25. These were defined in various proclamations, consolidated in Proclamation 193 of 1935.
26. CA CMT 3/1326, 24/9/1, Reservation of Trust Forests, Lusikisiki vol. I, RM Lusikisiki to CMT, 22.11.1937.
27. CA CMT 3/1326 24/9/1, RM Lusikisiki to CMT, 12.12.1945 and enclosures.
28. CA CMT 3/1326 24/9/1, E.A. Goodwin, District Forest Officer Kokstad to Conservator of Forests Umtata, 12.1.1946.
29. CA CMT 3/1326, 24/9/1, L. Watt, Director of Forestry, Pretoria to Secretary of Native Affairs Pretoria, 8.2.1946.
30. CA CMT 3/1327, 24/9/4, RM Lusikisiki to CMT, 6.1.1950.
31. CA CMT 3/1326, 24/9/1, RM Lusikisiki to CMT, 17.5.1947
32. CA 1/BIZ 6/25 4/5/2, RM Bizana to CMT, 12.8.1943
33. CA 1/BIZ 6/25, 4/5/2, Conservator of Forests Umtata to CMT, 27.4.1945
34. CA CMT 3/1327, 24/9/4, RM Lusikisiki to CMT, 29.12.1949.
35. Ibid.
36. CA CMT 3/1327, 24/9/4 vol. 1, Lusikisiki Encroachments, statement by Native constable G.N. Mtantato, 13.12.1949.
37. CA 1/BIZ 6/26, 10/1/2, District Forest Officer Bizana to RM Bizana, 15.3.1949.
38. CA CMT 3/1327, 24/9/4, Minutes of a meeting held at the Lusikisiki Magistrate's office on 15 May 1950.
39. CA CMT 3/1327, 24/9/4, Interview granted by Chief Magistrate to taxpayers of the Lusikisiki district, 7.2.1950.
40. CA CMT 3/1327 24/9/4, Minutes of a meeting held at the Lusikisiki Magistrate's office on 15 May 1950.
41. CA 1/BIZ 6/25, 4/5/5; CA CMT 3/1642, 67/6, RM Lusikisiki to CMT, 5.6.1951.
42. CA CMT 3/1327 24/9/2, W.R. Long, District Forest Officer Kokstad to Conservator of Forests Umtata, 20.9.1951.
43. CA CMT 3/1327, 24/9/2, E. Goodwin, Conservator of Forests, Umtata to Chief Native Commissioner Umtata, 30.7.1952.
44. CA CMT 3/1642, C7/6, Acting RM Lusikisiki to CMT, 16.4.1952.

45. CA CMT 3/1642, C7/6, 'Notes of meeting held at Sea View turn-out, near Gem Vale Store, Lower Ntafufu Location in connection with land enquiry, on 11th June, 1952'.

46. For a similar dispute in the 1920s see: Amafelandawonye (the Die-hards): popular protest and women's movements in Herschel District in the 1920s, in Beinart and Bundy, *Hidden struggles in rural South Africa.*

47. CA CMT 3/1642, C.7/6, Notes of meeting held at Sea View. Chains were used to make rough measurement of plots.

48. CA CMT 3/1642, C.7/6, Notes of meeting held at Sea View.

49. CA CMT 3/1642, C7/6, Extract from *The Torch*, 15.7.1952.

50. CA CMT 3/1327, 24/9/2, vol. 2, Bantu Affairs Commissioner Lusikisiki to Chief Bantu Affairs Commissioner Umtata, 28.10.1959.

51. Ibid.

52. CA CMT 3/1327, 24/9/2, vol. 2, Chief Regional Forest Officer Transkei to Acting Chief Magistrate Umtata, 28.11.1959.

53. For example, Munslow, B. 1988. *The fuelwood trap: a study of the SADCC region.* London: Earthscan.

54. Mortimore, M. 1989. *Adapting to drought: farmers, famines and desertification in West Africa.* Cambridge: Cambridge University Press; Fairhead, J. and Leach, M. 1996. *Misreading the African landscape: society and ecology in a forest-savannah mosaic.* Cambridge: Cambridge University Press; Tiffen, M., Mortimore, M. and Gichuki, F. 1994. *More people, less erosion: environmental recovery in Kenya.* Chichester: John Wiley.

55. Kepe, T. 1996. *Environmental entitlements in Mkambati: livelihoods, social institutions and environmental change on the Wild Coast of the Eastern Cape.* Research Report 1. Programme for Land and Agrarian Studies, University of the Western Cape.

Chapter 7: The emergence of privately grown industrial tree plantations

1. This chapter discusses primarily introduced tree species other than wattle, which were and are planted in plantations for the production of wood, timber, pulp and related products: mainly pines (conifers) and eucalypts.

2. Commercial hardwoods such as *Eucalyptus* were harvested on a rotational basis of approximately 8 to 12 years (sometimes less). Softwoods rotated on a 25-year cycle on private plantations and between 30 and 40 years (or more) on state plantations. Initially it was thought, however, that softwoods would need up to 60 years to grow before being harvested.

3. Sherry, S.P. 1971. *The black wattle.* Pietermaritzburg: University of Natal Press, p.108.

4. An extract from 'Natal sketches' in *London Society*, xiv (1868) referring to a 1862 trip to Pietermaritzburg in Hattersley, A.F. 1940. *The Natalians: further annals of Natal.* Pietermaritzburg: Shuter and Shooter, p.48. This was confirmed in a diary entry by J.S. Dobie in the same year when he noted that the streets were lined with syringas interspersed with 'tall blue-gums'. Hattersley, A.F., ed. 1945. *John Shedden Dobie: South African journal 1862–6.* Cape Town: Van Riebeeck Society, p.15.

5. Hattersley, *John Shedden Dobie*, pp.20, 21, 27, 28, 147.

6. McCracken, D.P. 1992. The economic function of imperial botanic gardens in Natal. Paper presented at the Seventh Biennial Conference of the Economic History Society of Southern Africa, Pietermaritzburg, July 1992, p.11.

7. Ibid.

8. Colony of Natal, *Natal Government Gazette*, 26 October 1886. Copies of dispatches from Sir H. Bulwer to Sir F. Stanley MP, 2 April 1886, p.1036.

9. Ibid.

10. Ibid.

11. Hutchins, D.E. 1905. Forestry in South Africa. In: Flint, W. and Gilchrist, J.D.F., eds. *Science in South Africa*. Cape Town: Maskew Miller, p.403.
12. *Natal Mercury*, 23 August 1889.
13. An individual who features prominently in the growing of alien timber trees in South Africa and Natal is T.R. Sim. Sim was initially employed as curator of the King William's Town botanical garden before joining the Cape Forestry Department in 1894, starting off as the forester at Fort Cunnyngham. In June 1895, he was promoted to superintendent of plantations for the Eastern Conservancy, followed by another promotion in September 1898, when he was appointed as the district forest officer at King William's Town, a position he held for four years. Following the decision of the Natal government to establish a department of forestry in 1902, Sim was recommended to the post, a position he retained until 1907. During this period, Sim was responsible for the establishment of some of the first state tree plantations in the colony. Upon his dismissal Sim established a nursery business in Pietermaritzburg. Using the nursery as a base, Sim was highly instrumental in the encouragement of private wattle-growing, before shifting his allegiance to the more profitable *Eucalyptus* species. As Sim was based in Natal for more than three decades, his personal contribution to tree-growing in the region is difficult to assess, yet can certainly not be dismissed.
14. Sim, T.R. n.d. 1889 and afterwards in South Africa. Unpublished autobiography. Stellenbosch Forestry Library, pp.104–05.
15. Sim was probably referring to *E. citriodora*.
16. Sim, T.R. n.d. Then and since. Book 3. Unpublished autobiography. Stellenbosch Forestry Library, p.145.
17. Hutchins, Forestry in South Africa, p.404.
18. Not all these tree-planting experiments took place under the auspices of the state, however, and private individuals continued to experiment on their own. The first stand of *E. fastigata* in South Africa, for example, was established on the farm Sneezewood in the Umzimkulu district in 1904–05. (Poynton, R.J. 1957. *Notes on exotic forest trees in South Africa*. Bulletin No. 38. Pretoria: Government Printer, p.30.)
19. The first recorded fertiliser experiments with eucalypts occurred in Zululand when a series of experiments was conducted with *E. grandis* in 1952. In the 1960s this was followed by the NTE experiments in the Seven Oaks and Richmond areas. The first fertiliser experiments with pines were carried out in the southern Cape in 1935. Experiments in Natal began in 1964, conducted by the Wattle Research Institute (Schönau, A.P.G. 1983. Fertilisation in South African forestry. *South African Forestry Journal*, 125: pp.5, 9, 12). Fertiliser experiments with wattle had begun much earlier.
20. These included eucalypts such as *E. microcorys, globulus, sideroxylon, eugenoides, maidenii, pilularis, maculata* and *paniculata*.
21. Although fungoid and bacterial diseases have not contributed to the large-scale demise of eucalypt species in Natal and Zululand, Mycosphaerella leaf disease did influence the propagation of some species, and led to the abandonment of *E. globulus* and *E. maidenii* as trees grown for commercial purposes (Lundquist, J.E. 1987. A history of five forest diseases in South Africa. *South African Forestry Journal*, 140: p.56).
22. Sim claims that the snout-beetle was first noticed in 1916 and was imported into the country among apple stocks (Sim, T.R. 1927. *Treeplanting in South Africa*. Pietermaritzburg: Natal Witness, pp.403–04). Bigalke believes that the insect was introduced two years earlier (Bigalke, R. 1937. The naturalisation of animals with special reference to South Africa. *South African Journal of Science*, 33: p.58).
23. Tooke, F.G.C. 1943. Progress of forest entomology. *Journal of the South African Forestry Association*, 10: p.5.
24. These included *Pinus roxburghii, P. taeda, P. pinaster, P. radiata, P. palustris*, and others.
25. Fungal disease, for example, was primarily responsible for causing *P. radiata* to be abandoned in the summer rainfall areas.

26. Poynton, *Notes on exotic forest trees*, p.75.

27. CAD, FOR, 355 (A. 1514). Forest Department Communication. Correspondence between Conservator of Forests and Department of Agriculture Press Service, 7 April 1930.

28. Diplodia dieback, considered to be the most important tree disease in South Africa, was first reported in Natal in 1911 although it may have been present before this date (Lundquist, Five forest diseases, p.52).

29. King, N.L. 1934. *Some notes on tree-planting with special reference to Natal*. Bulletin No. 29. Pretoria: Department of Forestry, p.16.

30. Poynton, *Notes on exotic forest trees*, p.65.

31. Lister, M.H. 1957. Joseph Storr Lister, the first Chief Conservator of the South African Department of Forestry. *Journal of the South African Forestry Association*, 29: p.18. The competition was primarily aimed at the lessees of Crown Lands on the Cape Flats and Downs. The Cape government offered prizes of £100, £50 and £25 for tree plantations in each of the five selected areas in the Cape. Not less than 100 000 trees were to be planted. In other words, not less than 1000 trees per acre. There were also age limitations. In 1901 there had been forty-three entries although only nine were judged, with Sim and Heywood the judges (Sim, Then and since. Book 2: p.92). Keet claims that the competition was first introduced by the British administration in the Cape in 1849 (Keet, J.D.M. 1983. *Historical review of the development of forestry in South Africa*. Pretoria: Directorate of Forestry, p.148). Shaughnessy states that the competition started in 1877 yet by 1883 there were no more entries (Shaughnessy, G.L. 1980. Historical ecology of alien woody plants in the vicinity of Cape Town. Ph.D. thesis, University of Cape Town, Cape Town: p.169).

32. Schoepflin had suggested, in 1891, that the state should be responsible for long-term tree-planting projects while the private sector should concentrate on short-term tree crops suitable for the production of poles and firewood.

33. Henkel, J.S. 1916. Tree-planting competitions in Natal. *South African Journal of Science*, 13: p.306.

34. At least one farmer established a sizeable plantation. This was a farmer called Niemack, from Ingeli near Harding.

35. The minimum entry was a ten-acre plantation that would then be judged in 1910. The first prize was to be £50 in every electoral division with the exception of the Alfred, Alexandra. Eshowe and Melmoth districts where only a £25 prize was offered (*The Natal Agricultural Journal*, 15[1]: p.92).

36. *The Natal Agricultural Journal*, 15(1): p.92.

37. A sum of £180 was subsequently collected from members for the competition.

38. Additional support came from the Trade and Industries Commission in 1912, which also encouraged the use of prizes for tree-planting.

39. Henkel, Tree-planting competitions, p.306.

40. This section was never well represented as the area was dominated by sugar.

41. Sim, Then and since. Book 3: pp.246–47. Figures in parentheses are taken from official reports: Department of Forestry. *Annual Reports*, U.G.7, 1921, p.23; U.G.8/1922, p.270; UG9/1924, p.326; U.G.21/1926, p.411; U.G.6/1927, p.351, U.G.42/1927, p.27; U.G.4/1929, p.27; U.G.54/1929, p.28; and U.G49/1930, p.33. As will be noted there are several inconsistencies in the figures produced by Sim and those recorded by state officials. These discrepancies may have arisen by confusing the number of contestants who initially entered a competition with the number that were finally judged.

42. Report of the Conservator of Forests, Natal Conservancy. 1917. Department of Water Affairs and Forestry Collections, p.1.

43. Sim, Then and since. Book 3: p.247. Sim also argued that not all farmers entered the competition solely for the prize money, but many did so for the value of the trees themselves (p.245). By 1927 there had been 2920 acres planted at a 'cost' of £2520 (Sim, T.R. 1927. *Treeplanting in South Africa*. Pietermaritzburg: Natal Witness, p.55).

44. Sim, Then and since. Book 3: p.246–47. These 4000 acres proved to be invaluable during and after the Second World War as a propaganda tool. Although profit levels from timber which was harvested during the war were inflated, astute farmers rapidly took note of the potential profits which could be realised from commercial tree-growing, a factor which contributed much to the expansion of tree-growing in Natal in the post-war period.
45. Report of the Conservator of Forests, Natal Conservancy. 1917. Department of Water Affairs and Forestry Collections, p.1.
46. Department of Forestry. *Annual Report*. U.G. 11/1932, p.24.
47. Department of Forestry. *Annual Report*. U.G. 35/1933, p.48.
48. *Cape Times*, 26 August 1935.
49. Sim, Then and since. Book 3: p.249.
50. CAD, FOR 192, A 331, N 2 216/71. Correspondence between Conservator of Forests (Natal) and Chief Conservator of Forests, 16 September 1915.
51. *The Natal Farmer*, 8 April 1927.
52. *The Farmer*, 19 September 1941. Originally there had been 65 plots entered in both competitions.
53. Sim, *Treeplanting*, p.41.
54. Hurwitz, N. 1957. *Agriculture in Natal, 1860–1950*. Cape Town: Oxford University Press, p.22.
55. Colony of Natal. Natal Agricultural Department. *Annual Report*, 1902–1903, p.28. See also Sim, 1889 and afterwards. Book 2: p.109.
56. Stayner, F.J. 1908. Coniferae. *The Natal Agricultural Journal*, 11(6): p.726. (Taken from a lecture delivered to the Dundee Farmers' Association, 18 June 1908.)
57. *The Natal Agricultural Journal*, 1908, 11: p.9.
58. Union of South Africa. 1924. *House of Assembly Debates*. Vol. 1: p.885 (Gibson, L.D.).
59. Department of Forestry. *Annual Report*. U.G. 15/1925, p.347.
60. *The Natal Farmer*, 14 September 1927, p.19; *Natal Witness*, 3 September 1927. Several months later it was reiterated that accessible stands of virgin softwoods would last only another 25 years (*Natal Farmer*, 23 March 1928, p.29). See also *Natal Witness*, 19 May 1928.
61. In 1927 the *East London Dispatch* carried an article which again referred to the world scarcity of timber. According to the article, timber in the Americas was being ruthlessly exploited with consumption in the United States eight times that of annual growth. Supplies would only last another 37 years (*East London Dispatch*, 26 September 1927).
62. Sim, *Treeplanting*, p.39.
63. Sim, 1889 and afterwards, p.103. In 1928 Major G.P. Ahern published a book, with a foreword by G. Pinchot, entitled *Deforested America*. In this book, Ahern claimed that in 1919 the annual drain on forest resources in America had been estimated at four times the annual growth.
64. Sim, Then and since. Book 2: pp.402–03.
65. *Natal Advertiser*, 31 August 1935.
66. Editorial. 1965. Notes and comments. *South African Forestry Journal*, 54: p.3.
67. Ironically, in 1977 it was reported that there was a 'low ebb in the timber industry', and the 'great shortage of timber predicted a few years ago has become an unreal picture in the eyes of more farmers who are unable to market even their present production'. Furthermore, the report added, the agricultural land in the Natal Midlands was highly productive and 'simply cannot be surrendered to timber' (Wilhelmij, H.A. 1977. *Report on forestry landuse and forestry advisory services in the northern part of the Natal Midlands*. Pretoria: Department of Forestry, p.1). Such fluctuations in market demand have continued to characterise the timber industry.
68. See, for example, *The Natal Farmer*, 21 January 1927, p.37
69. *The Natal Farmer*, 16 May 1924, p.31.
70. Ibid.
71. Colony of Natal, 1902 Natal Agricultural Department. *Annual Report*, p.28.
72. Sim listed Sir G. Sutton, Sir G. Leuchars, Sir T.K. Murray, Sir T. Heslop, Hon. F. Angus, Hon. W. L'Estrange, Senator M. Campbell, Hon. W.A. Deane, Colonel Fawcus, Major Newmarch, T.M.

Mackenzie, G.C. Mackenzie, A. Mackenzie, Hunt Holley, W.A. Angus, E.W. Evans, C. Hitchins, B.B. Evans, T. Adison, J. Leuchars, W.A. Hutchinson, Von Bulow, Pope Ellis, Hill, Crowe, Crooks, I.A. Dales, P. Otto, K. Fraser and many others.

73. *The Natal Farmer*, 16 May 1924, p.31.

74. *The Natal Farmer*, 23 May 1924, p.21.

75. *The Natal Farmer*, 16 May 1924, p.31.

76. *The Natal Farmer*, 10 June 1927.

77. Department of Forestry. *Annual Report*. U.G. 11/1932, p.23.

78. Other companies included the UVS Company Ltd., while individuals such as E.A.M. Erlandson from the Boomerang estate soon followed suit. Another prominent North Coast grower was J.H. Badenhorst, who established the Salpine Company. Ironically, Badenhorst the tree-grower became a tree-destroyer when, after selling the Salpine Company in 1943, he was responsible for the large-scale clearing of trees in northern Zululand to make way for pineapple plantations.

79. *Cape Times*, 26 August 1935.

80. *Natal Witness*, 28 August 1935.

81. Van der Zel, D. 1989. *Strategic forestry development plan for South Africa*. Pretoria: Department of Forestry, p.34.

82. De Villiers, P.C. 1951. Die ekonomiese ontwikkeling van die bosbou onderneming in Suid-Afrika. Ph.D. thesis, Stellenbosch University, Stellenbosch, p.28.

83. *The Natal Farmer*, 21 January 1927, p.37.

84. *The Sun and Agricultural Journal of South Africa*, April 1928, p.349.

85. Nicholson, H.B. 1961. The development of the market for Saligna gum in South Africa. *Journal of the South African Forestry Association*, 37: p.12; and Stephens, R.P. 1940. Mining timber in South Africa with special reference to wattle silviculture. *Journal of the South African Forestry Association*, 4: p.62.

86. By 1960 wattle made up about twelve per cent of the total.

87. Kotze, J.J. 1937. Forestry in relation to the mining industry. *South African Journal of Science*, 33: p.359.

88. The international reputation of eucalypts as 'thirsty trees' was well known in lay circles where the tree had been extensively used to drain swamps. Coupled with the endless acres of wattle, these emerging eucalypt plantations soon became the subject of intense speculation with regard to their impact on groundwater supplies in Natal. Non-tree-growing farmers argued that the effects of periodic droughts were being exacerbated by the absorbent nature of the commercial tree plantations that were increasingly beginning to dominate the Natal landscape.

89. Grut, M. 1965. *Forestry and the forest industry in South Africa*. Cape Town: A.A. Balkema, p.87. In the late 1980s this figure had dropped slightly to twenty per cent, which was still a substantial amount. To give an indication of the volume of timber involved, the *Strategic forestry development plan for South Africa* mentions the case of a leading timber company (probably operating in the former Eastern Transvaal) which, in the 1980s, cut down 35 000 trees and dispatched 120 trucks of timber to the mines on a daily basis (Van der Zel, *Forestry development plan*, pp.34–35). The recent crisis in the gold-mining industry has, however, almost certainly affected this insatiable appetite for timber although the development of an export market will have compensated for this decrease in demand.

90. *The Farmer's Weekly*, 21 May 1930.

91. Department of Agriculture. 1937. *Farming in South Africa*. Pretoria: Department of Agriculture, p.479.

92. De Villiers, Die ekonomiese ontwikkeling, p.73.

93. Editorial. 1948. Editorial notes and comments. *Journal of the South African Forestry Association*, 16: p.2.

94. Ibid.

95. The contemporary tree-growing giant, Mondi Paper, later purchased NTE. This paved the way

for the penetration of Anglo American timber interests in KwaZulu-Natal. Anglo American had already acquired the extensive tree plantations of South African Forest Industries (SAFI) in the former Eastern Transvaal (Mpumalanga). In 1966 Anglo American unveiled plans to build a pulp mill in the Mondi valley near Creighton in the Natal Midlands. To facilitate this development a new company, Mondi Paper, was registered. As Anglo American's interests in the growing and processing of timber expanded, it was finally decided to incorporate all related investments under Mondi Paper Company. It would appear that the original name 'Mondi' comes from the plant Modia. A railway siding in southern Natal was subsequently called Mondi. Incidentally, due to the perceived negative impact on local water supplies, the particular pulp mill was never established.

96.   Hocking, A. 1987. *Paper chain: the story of SAPPI*. Bethulie: Hollard, p.22. The South African Pulp and Paper Industries Limited company had been formally registered in December 1936.

97.   Johns, M. 1993. Are all trees green? *Africa Environment and Wildlife*, 1(3): p.79.

98.   By the mid-1960s, the SAPPI mill sourced approximately 50 per cent of its softwood fibre from private growers, 45 per cent from state plantations, and only 5 per cent from its own plantations (*Financial Mail*, 26 August 1966, p.26). In addition to the SAPPI mill there was a smaller paper mill at Felixton, which produced fluting paper, although the raw material used was primarily bagasse.

99.   Lack, C.E. 1957. Forestry development in Natal. *Journal of the South African Forestry Association*, 29: p.20. The wood requirements for the SAICCOR plant came from its subsidiary, the Saligna Forestry Company, although standing plantations were also purchased. SAICCOR also entered into long-term contracts with Zululand tree-growers for their harvested tree crops. Initially not a single ton of standard quality pulp was sold in South Africa, while between 1955 and 1962, 462 258 tons were exported. This was produced from 1 500 000 million tons of air-dried timber. The factory rapidly emerged as one of the top earners of foreign exchange in the manufacturing sector (Cantacuzene, M. 1962. The manufacture of rayon pulp in South Africa. *South African Forestry Journal*, 42: p.16).

100.   Lack, Forestry development in Natal, p.20.

101.   Together with smaller plants in Springs and Cape Town, the company was the dominant producer of paper boards (folding boxboard) and felt base papers (*Financial Mail*, 26 August 1966, p.54).

102.   Lack, Forestry development in Natal, p.20.

103.   Mechanisation in the tree-growing sector has been aimed primarily at exploitation where labour costs are high, rather than on the growing side of tree-farming. Mechanised debarkers, for example, have greatly enhanced the capacity of tree-farmers to harvest trees.

104.   Lack, Forestry development in Natal, p.22.

105.   Although farmers in certain areas, such as the Natal Midlands, have historically alternated or switched between wattle, commercial tree species and sugar-cane, this switching has recently resulted in growing acrimony, as vested interests become threatened or market values are distorted by powerful players in the respective industries.

106.   Lack, Forestry development in Natal, p.21.

107.   Lückhoff, H.A. 1955. The establishment and regeneration of *Eucalyptus saligna* plantations in the coastal belt of Zululand. *Journal of the South African Forestry Association*, 25: p.2. This was primarily due to the state and private individuals such as Rattray.

108.   See Union of South Africa. 1950. *House of Assembly Debates*. Vol. 72: pp.1391–93; pp.3567–70; p.3607; and pp.6530–32 for part of the parliamentary debate on the subject.

109.   Union of South Africa. 1952. *House of Assembly Debates*. Vol. 79: p.6234 (D.E. Mitchell). Apparently rice was grown in areas where in the past *Eucalyptus* trees had been planted for the sole purpose of drying up the soil. The planting of eucalypts was resumed in the early 1950s.

110.   Union of South Africa. 1952. *House of Assembly Debates*. Vol. 79: p.6325.

111. Editorial. 1960. Notes and comments. *Journal of the South African Forestry Association*, 34: p.3.

112. *The Farmer,* 10 October 1941, p.11. The problem of over-production would eventually be solved through the development of an export market.

113. Editorial. 1959. Notes and comments. *Journal of the South African Forestry Association*, 33: p.2.

114. Ackerman, D.P. 1974. Meeting South Africa's future demand for wood. *South African Forestry Journal*, 88: p.9.

115. Keet, *Historical review*, pp.161–62.

116. *Financial Mail*, 26 August 1966, p.15.

117. Grut, *Forestry and the forest industry*, pp.91–93.

118. Although research into the appropriate silvicultural and conservational principles for *Eucalyptus* species in South Africa was only initiated in the 1950s at Kwambonambi and Mtubatuba (Lückhoff, Establishment and regeneration, p.2).

Chapter 8: Technology and ecology in the Karoo

1. Vanclay, F. 1992. The social context of farmers' adoption of environmentally sound farming practices. In: Lawrence, G., Vanclay, F. and Furze, B., eds. *Agriculture, environment and society.* Melbourne: Macmillan, p.104.

2. This paper was presented to the African Environments conference, Oxford, July 1999. For advice and guidance to the literature I am indebted to Timm Hoffman, Paul McCabe, Sue Milton and Piet Roux, as well as two anonymous referees. A shorter version of the paper appeared in the *Journal of Southern African Studies*, 2000, 26(4).

3. Rutherford, M. 1997. Categorization of biomes. In: Cowling, R., Richardson, D. and Pierce, S., eds. *Vegetation of Southern Africa.* Cambridge: Cambridge University Press.

4. Calow, P., ed. 1998. *The encyclopaedia of ecology and environmental management.* Oxford: Blackwell Science, pp.639, 728.

5. Pimm, S. 1984. The complexity and stability of ecosystems. *Nature*, 26 January 1984, 307: p.322.

6. Walker, B. 1988. Autoecology, synecology, climate and livestock as agents of rangeland dynamics. *Australian Rangeland Journal*, 10: p.69:
   'When I was an undergraduate, in a Department of Rangelands Science in South Africa, there was little opposition to the one basic paradigm that underlaid most principles of range management, and that paradigm was of course Clementsian succession and the so-called climax. Variations of this theory were presented at various times but the basic tenets were propounded in all rangelands texts and they are still there today…The attraction of the equilibrium view and its logical consequence – Clementsian succession – is its seductive simplicity.'

7. Westoby, M., et al. 1989. Opportunistic management for rangelands not at equilibrium. *Journal of Range Management*, 42: p.266.

8. South Africa. 1923. *Final Report of the Drought Investigation Commission.* Cape Town: Cape Times Limited/Government Printers, p.11.

9. South Africa. 1951. *Report of the Desert Encroachment Committee*, UG 59/1951. Pretoria: Government Printers, p.25.

10. Talbot, W. 1961. Land utilization in the arid regions of Southern Africa, Part I: South Africa. In: Stamp, L.D., ed. *A history of land use in arid regions.* Paris: UNESCO, p.329.

11. Acocks, J. 1979. The flora that matched the fauna. *Bothalia*, 12: p.685.

12. DeAngelis, D., and Waterhouse, J. 1987. Equilibrium and non-equilibrium concepts in ecological models. *Ecological Monographs*, 57(1): p.16:
    'A key transition in ecological thinking, made largely during the 1970s, was the gradual de-emphasis of the classical mathematical models of ecology that assume the existence of equilibrium points. Both internal biotic feedback interactions and stochasticity were seen as

prevalent and capable of disrupting ecological systems. The long-term survival of species and of ecological organization were then perceived as facts that needed explanation.'

13. When the first borehole, as distinct from a well sunk by human effort and explosives, was drilled on private property in the Karoo remains to be established. But the date is not likely to differ by much between different arid regions of the world containing the same commercial farming system. The first success is recorded in South Australia in 1881, 'and from there the number of boreholes drilled grew exponentially [across Australia]'. Landsberg, J., James, C., Morton, S., Hobbs, T., Stol, J., Drew, A. and Tongway, H., eds. 1997. *The effects of artificial sources of water on rangeland biodiversity.* Canberra: Environment Australia and CSIRO, p.121.

14. Perrings, C. and Walker, B. 1995. Biodiversity loss and the economics of discontinuous change in semiarid rangelands. In: Perrings, C., Maler, K., Folke, C., Holling, C. and Jansson, B., eds. *Biodiversity loss: economic and ecological issues.* Cambridge: Cambridge University Press, p.194.

15. Fleischner, T. 1994. Ecological costs of livestock grazing in western North America. *Conservation Biology,* 8: p.634.

16. Holling, C.S., Schindler, D., Walker, B. and Roughgarden, J. Biodiversity in the functioning of ecosystems: an ecological synthesis. In: Perrings, et al., *Biodiversity loss*, p.48.

17. Holling, et al., Biodiversity in the functioning of ecosystems, p.49.

18. Holling, C. and Meffe, G. 1996. Command and control and the pathology of natural resource management. *Conservation Biology,* 10: p.335.

19. Westoby, et al., Opportunistic management, p.268.

20. Holling, et al., Biodiversity in the functioning of ecosystems, pp.51–52; Calow, *The encyclopaedia of ecology*, p.640.

21. Ellis, J. and Swift, D. 1988. Stability of African pastoral ecosystems: alternative paradigms and implications for development. *Journal of Range Management,* 41: pp.450–59; Behnke, R., Scoones, I. and Kerven, C., eds. 1993. *Range ecology at disequilibrium.* London: Overseas Development Institute.

22. Behnke, et al., *Range ecology*, p.9.

23. Ellis and Swift, Stability of African pastoral ecosystems, p.458.

24. Tainton, N., Morris, C. and Hardy, M. 1996. Complexity and stability in grazing systems. In: Hodgson, J. and Illius, A., eds. *The ecology and management of grazing systems.* Wallingford: CAB International, pp.275–99.

25. An interesting simulation of changes in Karoo plant communities over lengthy time periods, allowing for realistic rainfall variations, broadly shows the following. (1) The time-scales required for simulated changes in the state of the ecosystem are long compared with human lifespans. (2) Simulated resting of an overgrazed area containing the five dominant plant species selected for modelling shows that little improvement is likely during a time span of 60 years. (3) The simulation model 'supports the proverbial view that the next two generations will bear the high opportunity [cost] of rangeland overexploitation, but presents a moderately optimistic view that, in the long-term, recovery is possible'. Wiegand, T. and Milton, S. 1996. Vegetation change in semiarid communities: simulating probabilities and time scales. *Vegetatio,* 125: p.180.

26. Rubidge, R. 1979. *The merino on Wellwood: four generations.* Graaff-Reinet: Richard Rubidge, p.15; *Wellwood Farm diaries* (unpublished, Graaff-Reinet, 1877 and 1905).

27. Noble, J. 1875. *Descriptive handbook of the Cape Colony.* Cape Town: Juta, pp.146, 259–60.

28. Cape of Good Hope. 1876. *Blue Book 1875.* Cape Town: Saul Solomon, p.JJ 37.

29. Walton, J. 1998. *Windpumps in South Africa.* Cape Town: Human and Rousseau, p.9.

30. 'American-made mills began appearing in South Africa in the 1880s, and even in that decade American manufacturers proudly published engravings showing their mills pumping water at exotic South African ostrich ranches.' Lindsay Baker, T. 1985. *A field guide to American windmills.* Norman: University of Oklahoma Press, p.104.

31. Rolls, E. 1984. *A million wild acres.* Melbourne: Penguin Books Australia, p.166.

32. Cape of Good Hope. 1889. *Report of the Select Committee on Fencing or Enclosing Lands,* A10–89. Cape Town: W.A. Richards & Sons; Bryden, H. 1889. *Kloof and Karroo.* London: Longmans.

33. South Africa. 1919. *Agricultural Census 1918*, UG53–1919. Cape Town: Cape Times, p.9.

34. British South Africa and South Africa. 1906–1910, 1910–1950. *Annual Statements of the Trade and Shipping of the South African Customs Union*. Cape Town: Whitehead, Morris & Co.

35. Cape of Good Hope. 1905. *Results of the Census 1904*. Cape Town: Cape Times Ltd, p.clxxxvi.

36. South Africa. 1960. *Union Statistics for Fifty Years*. Pretoria: Bureau of Census and Statistics, pp.1–22.

37. Wailes, R. 1956. A note on windmills. In: Singer, C., ed. *A history of technology*, Volume II. Oxford: Clarendon Press, p.623.; Braudel, F. 1974. *Capitalism and material life*. London: Fontana Books, p.263:
   'The great event in the West – as opposed to China where mills turned horizontally for centuries – was the transformation of the windmill into a wheel fitted vertically, as had happened to water-mills. Engineers say that the modification was a stroke of genius and that power was greatly increased. It was this new style of mill, a creation in itself, that spread in Christendom.'

38. White, L. 1969. The expansion of technology. In: *Fontana economic history of Europe*, Volume 1. London: Fontana Books, p.39 (emphasis added).

39. Webb, W. 1931. *The Great Plains*. Boston: Ginn and Co.

40. Hills, R. 1994. *Power from wind: a history of windmill technology*. Cambridge: Cambridge University Press, p.239.

41. Webb, *The Great Plains*, p.338.

42. McGraw-Hill. 1992. *Encyclopedia of science and technology*: vol. 19. 7th edition. New York: McGraw-Hill, p.470.

43. Hills, *Power from wind*, p.251; '[In] America they became recognised as "the Cadillacs of the windmills because of their outstanding design and quality of workmanship."' Baker, T.L. *A field guide*, quoted in Walton, *Windpumps in South Africa*, p.24.

44. Noble, *Descriptive handbook*, p.261; Cape of Good Hope, *Blue Book 1875*, p.JJ 24.

45. Jaffe, A. and Stavins, R. 1994. The energy paradox and the diffusion of conservation technology. *Resource and Energy Economics*, 16: p.95. Farms just north of the Sneeuberg proper were fenced as late as the mid-twenties. 'During 1927 Rietpoort's 15,000 morgen was completely fenced and divided into ten camps. It was the first farm in the Murraysburg district to be jackal-proofed.' Kingwill, A. 1953. *A Karoo farmer looks back*. Pretoria: Futura Press, p.105.

46. Cape of Good Hope, Department of Agriculture. 1903. *Agricultural Journal*. 23: pp.691–92.

47. South Africa. 1910–1950. *Annual Statements of the Trade and Shipping*.

48. Archer, S. 1990. Poverty and production in a rural microcosm: Hanover, Cape. *Africa*, 60: pp.471–96.

49. Landsberg, et al., *The effects of artificial sources of water*, pp.124–25.

50. South Africa. 1954. *Annual Report of the Secretary for Agriculture for the Year 1953*. Pretoria: Government Printers, p.73.

51. Rolls, *A million wild acres*, p.166.

52. Deacon, H. 1992. Human settlement. In: Cowling, R., ed. *The ecology of Fynbos*. Cape Town: Oxford University Press, pp.263–66.

53. Noble, *Descriptive handbook*, pp.258ff.; Bryden, *Kloof and Karroo*, p.238; Cape of Good Hope, *Report of the Select Committee on Fencing*.

54. Cape of Good Hope, *Report of the Select Committee on Fencing*, pp.15–16, 22–23; South Africa, *Final Report of the Drought Investigation Commission*; Beinart, W. 1998. The night of the jackal: sheep, pastures and predators in the Cape. *Past and Present*, 158: pp.172–206; Cape of Good Hope, Department of Agriculture. 1896. *Agricultural Journal*, 9: p.491:
   'At a late meeting of the Graaff-Reinet Farmers' Association Mr S. Hobson read the following paper on the subject of [deterioration of the veld]…1st The Kraaling System – Every farmer knows full well to his cost that this system is slowly but surely injuring his stock and run; morgen of veld are being trodden into sluits, and the soil around the roots of the various shrubs carried away by the water, when it does fall, to lower levels, to smother other parts with silt;

and nearly half of the animal droppings, which should be laid down again on the veld, are piled up to form a useless waste at the out-stations. We as farmers cannot allow this wear and tear to go on much longer, without finding out that our candle has been burning at both ends…I do not blame farmers wholly, the blame rests a good deal on the Government of this country.'

55. Rubidge, *The merino on Wellwood*, p.31. The comment in parentheses was added for publication in 1979.

56. Cape of Good Hope, *Agricultural Journal*, 1896, p.591.

57. South Africa, *Final Report of the Drought Investigation Commission*, pp.10, 15.

58. Cary, J. and Barr, N. 1992. The semantics of 'forest' cover: how green was Australia? In: Lawrence et al., *Agriculture, environment and society*, pp.60–76; Dovers, S. 1994. Still discovering Monaro: perceptions of landscape. In: Dovers, S., ed. *Australian environmental history*. Melbourne: Oxford University Press, pp.119–40.

59. Cape of Good Hope, *Blue Book 1875*, pp.JJ 24–25, 28. The testimony of casual observers of the Karoo environment in the past must be interpreted with circumspection. But the following two passages dating from 1775 are particularly striking on the 'overstocking' theme. Swellengrebel is writing about the Camdeboo, which included the Sneeuberg in the eighteenth century. Sparrman's area here described is less easy to pin down, although he mentions the 'Carrow-veld' and the 'Zuure-velden' in the immediately preceding pages of his journal, which probably means the country south and east of the Sneeuberg:
'There are about 30 farms in the Camdebo of which some 25 are inhabited. Unless people begin to conserve the grazing for cattle intelligently, it is to be feared that the luxuriousness, that has been declining noticeably since this region began to be occupied 7 or 8 years ago, will not last and this veld, similar to that lying closer to the Capital [Cape Town], will grow totally wild. It has already gone so far that one Jac. Botha evacuated to the Great Fish River as he had no grazing for his animals here, and one A. van den Berg talks about wanting to move elsewhere, as he could not continue on his farm.' (Swellengrebel Familie-argief: Reisverhaal van Swellengrebel [1776], translated from the Dutch quoted in Van der Merwe, P. 1945. *Trek*. Cape Town: Nasionale Pers, p.73.)

'In direct contradiction to the custom and example of the original inhabitants the Hottentots, the colonists turn their cattle out constantly into the same fields, and that too in a much greater quantity than used to graze there in the time of the Hottentots; as they keep not only a number sufficient for their own use, but likewise enough to supply the more plentiful tables of the numerous inhabitants of Cape Town, as well as for the victualling of the ships in their passage to and from the East-Indies with fresh, and even with salted provisions. In consequence of the fields being thus continually grazed off, and the great increase of the cattle feeding on them, the grasses and herbs which these animals most covet are prevented continually more and more from thriving and taking root; while, on the contrary, the rhinocerus-bush, which the cattle always pass by and leave untouched, is suffered to take root free and unmolested, and encroach on the place of others…' (Sparrman, A. 1786. A voyage to the Cape of Good Hope…from the year 1772 to 1776. Translated from the Swedish original in two volumes. London: G.G.J. & J. Robinson, vol. I, pp.251–52.)

60. Hoffman, M., Cousins, B., Meyer, T., Petersen, A. and Hendricks, H. 1999. Historical and contemporary land use and the desertification of the Karoo landscape. In: Dean, W. and Milton, S., eds. *The Karoo: ecological patterns and processes*. Cambridge: Cambridge University Press, p.270; Hoffman, M. 1995. Environmental history and the desertification of the Karoo, South Africa. *Giornale Botanico Italiano*, 129: pp.261–73; Hoffman, M., Bond, W. and Stock, W. 1995. Desertification of the eastern Karoo, South Africa: conflicting paleontological, historical, and soil isotopic evidence. *Environmental Monitoring and Assessment*, 37: pp.1–19; Dean, W., Hoffman, M., Meadows, M. and Milton, S. 1995. Desertification in the semi-arid Karoo, South Africa: review and assessment. *Journal of Arid Environments*, 30: pp.247–64; Bond, W., Stock, W. and Hoffman, M. 1994. Has the Karoo spread? A test for desertification using carbon isotopes from soils. *South African Journal of Science*, 90: pp.391–97.

61. Tainton, N. and Hardy, M. 1999. Introduction to the concepts of development of vegetation. In: Tainton, N., ed. *Veld management in South Africa*. Pietermaritzburg: University of Natal Press, p.20.

62. Fleischner, T. Ecological costs of livestock grazing, p.635, quoting Hastings, J. 1959. Vegetation change and arroyo cutting in southeastern Arizona. *Journal of the Arizona Academy of Science*, 1: pp.60–67.

63. Brooks, H. 1986. The typology of surprises in technology, institutions, and development. In: Clark, W. and Munn, R., eds. *Sustainable development of the biosphere*. Cambridge: Cambridge University Press, p.331.

64. Wilson, A. and MacLeod, N. 1991. Overgrazing: present or absent? *Journal of Range Management*, 44: p.475.

65. Landsberg, et al., *The effects of artificial sources of water*, p.129.

66. Archer, S. 1996. Assessing and interpreting grass-woody plant dynamics. In: Hodgson, J. and Illius, A., eds. *The ecology and management of grazing systems*. Wallingford: CAB International, p.102.

67. Archer, Assessing and interpreting grass-woody plant dynamics, p.104, emphasis added.

68. Tainton, et al., Complexity and stability in grazing systems, p.288.

69. Hoffman, et al., Historical and contemporary land use, pp.270–73.

70. Ash, A., McIvor, J., Corfield, J. and Winter, W. 1995. How land conditions alter plant-animal relationships in Australia's tropical rangelands. *Agriculture, Ecosystems and Environment*, 56: p.89.

71. Nix, H. 1994. The Brigalow. In: Dovers, *Australian environmental history*, p.220.

72. Talbot, Land utilization in the arid regions of Southern Africa, p.330.

73. South Africa, *Annual Report of the Secretary for Agriculture for the Year 1953*, p.7.

74. *Wellwood Farm diaries*, Graaff-Reinet.

75. Landsberg, et al., *The effects of artificial sources of water*, p.123.

76. Dean, R. and MacDonald, I. 1994. Historical changes in stocking rates of domestic livestock as a measure of semi-arid and arid rangeland degradation in the Cape Province, South Africa. *Journal of Arid Environments*, 26: pp.281–98.

77. Vanclay, The social context of farmers' adoption of environmentally sound farming practices; Dovers, Still discovering Monaro; Fry, K. 1994. Kiola: a history of the environmental impact of European occupation, 1830–1980. In: Dovers, *Australian environmental history*.

78. Stafford Smith, D. and Morton, S. 1990. A framework for the ecology of arid Australia. *Journal of Arid Environments*, 18: pp.255–78.

79. Aguilera-Klink, F. 1994. Some notes on the misuse of classic writings in economics on the subject of common property. *Ecological Economics*, 9: p.222; Hardin, G. 1994. The tragedy of the unmanaged commons. *Trends in Ecology and Evolution*, 9(5): p.199.

80. Walker, B. 1999. Maximising net benefits through biodiversity as a primary land use. *Environment and Development Economics*, 4: p.206.

81. Brussard, P., Murphy, D. and Tracy, C. 1994. Cattle and conservation biology – another view. *Conservation Biology*, 8: p.920; on the same theme, a 1936 document expressing New Deal conservation ideas about the Great Plains in the United States set out the accepted presumptions of the time:
'All of the attitudes identified were those found at the heart of the expansionary, free-enterprise culture. First on the…list was the domination-of-nature ethic, which, it was objected, reduced the land to nothing more than raw material for man to take advantage of and to exploit for his own ends. That natural resources were inexhaustible was a corollary view, a self-deception preventing environmental adaptation and restraint. Other destructive values of the plainsmen were more social than ecological: that what is good for the individual is good for everybody, that an owner may do with his property what he likes, that markets will grow indefinitely…The remedy, it would seem, therefore, would have to involve a pronounced shift away from that economic order…That conclusion, however, was not at all the one arrived at in the report [entitled *The Future of the Great Plains*].' (Worster, D. 1979. *Dust bowl: the Southern Plains in the 1930s*. Cambridge: Cambridge University Press, p.195.)

82. Haas, C. and Fraser, J. 1995. Letters. *Conservation Biology*, 9: p.234.
83. Illius, A. and Hodgson, J. 1996. Progress in understanding the ecology and management of grazing systems. In: Hodgson, J. and Illius, A., eds. *The ecology and management of grazing systems*. Wallingford: CAB International, pp.429–57; Illius, A. and O'Connor, T. 1999. On the relevance of non-equilibrium concepts to arid and semi-arid grazing systems. *Ecological Applications*, 9: pp.798–813.
84. Walker, Maximising net benefits through biodiversity; see also Barnes, J., et al., Comments; and Stafford Smith, M. Management of rangelands: paradigms at their limits. In: Hodgson and Illius, *The ecology and management of grazing systems*.
85. The *real* price of wool in cents per kilogram was 522 in 1960, 337 in 1970, 397 in 1980, 435 in 1990, and 199 in 1999. Data supplied by Cape Wools SA, February 2000.
86. Lee, K. 1995. Deliberately seeking sustainability in the Columbia River Basin. In: Gunderson, L., Holling, C. and Light, S., eds. *Barriers and bridges to the renewal of ecosystems and institutions*. New York: Columbia University Press, p.233.

Chapter 9: 'Our irrepressible fellow colonist'

This is an edited version of a paper appearing in the *Journal of Historical Geography* in 2002.
1. See, for example, Di Castri, F. 1989. History of biological invasions with special emphasis on the Old World. In: Drake, J.A., et al., eds. *Scope 37 biological invasions: a global perspective*. Chichester: Wiley.
2. See, for example, Wolf, E.R. 1982. *Europe and the people without history*. Berkeley: University of California Press.
3. Crosby, A. 1986. *Ecological imperialism: the biological expansion of Europe 900–1900*. Cambridge: University of Cambridge Press.
4. See, for example, Bazzaz, F.A. 1984. Life history of colonising plants: some demographic, genetic and physiological features. In: Moody, H.A. and Drake, J.A., eds. *Ecology of biological invasions of North America and Hawaii*. New York: Springer-Verlag; Kruger, F.J., et al. 1986. Processes of invasion by alien plants. In: MacDonald, I.A.W., et al., eds. *The ecology and management of biological invasions in Southern Africa*. Cape Town: Oxford University Press; Noble, I.R. 1989. Attributes of invaders and the invading process: terrestrial and vascular plants. In: Drake, J.A., et al., eds. *Scope 37 biological invasions*; Roy, J. 1990. In search of the characteristics of plant invaders. In: Di Castri, F., et al., eds. *Biological invasions in Europe and the Mediterranean Basin*. Dordrecht: Kluwer.
5. See Di Castri, F. 1990. On invading species and invaded ecosystems: the interplay of historical chance and biological necessity. In: Di Castri, F., et al., eds. *Biological invasions in Europe and the Mediterranean Basin*, for colonial biological invaders in Europe.
6. See, for example, Cronon, W. 1983. *Changes in the land*. New York: Hill and Wang; and Silver, T. 1990. *New faces in the countryside*. Cambridge: Cambridge University Press, for eastern North America; Hecht, S. and Cockburn, A. 1990. *The fate of the forest*. London: Penguin, for South America; and Pyne, S. 1991. *Burning bush*. New York: Holt, for Australia.
7. See Deacon, J. 1986. Human settlement in South Africa and archaeological evidence for alien plants and animals. In: MacDonald, I.A.W., et al., eds. *The ecology and management of biological invasions in Southern Africa*; Cowling, R., ed. 1992. *The ecology of fynbos: nutrients, fire and diversity*. Cape Town: Oxford University Press.
8. Uekoetter, F. 1998. Confronting the pitfalls of current environmental history: an argument for an organisational approach. *Environment and History*, 4: p.32.
9. For the classic statement of this argument and an extensive bibliography see Janzen, D.H. 1986. Chihuahuan desert nopaleras: defaunated big mammal vegetation. *Annual Review of Ecology and Systematics*, 17: pp.595–636. Janzen, however, rejects the theory that flora outstripped

megafauna in the evolutionary arms race thus causing their extinction, as suggested by Guthrie, R.D. 1984. Mosaics, allelochemics and nutrients: an ecological theory of late Pleistocene megafaunal extinctions. In: Martin, P.S. and Klein, R.G., eds. *Quaternary extinctions: a prehistoric revolution*. Tucson: University of Arizona Press.

10. Nobel, P.S. 1988. *Environmental biology of agaves and cacti*. Cambridge: Cambridge University Press, pp.2–15.

11. Cape of Good Hope, *Report of the Select Committee on the Eradication of the Prickly Pear and Poisonous Melkbosch, 1890* [C3–90], Evidence of G.M. Palmer, p.14; Cape of Good Hope, *Report of the Select Committee on the Prickly Pear, 1891* [A9–91], Evidence of E.R. Hobson, pp.1 and 6 and A.C. MacDonald, pp.20–21. For an alternative source of origin based on the Dutch name for the plant, 'turksche vijgen' ('turkish fig'), see Wells, M.J., et al. 1986. The history of introduction of invasive alien plants to Southern Africa. In: MacDonald, I.A.W., et al., eds. *The ecology and management of biological invasions in Southern Africa*, p.29, who quote an unpublished manuscript by C.A. Smith suggesting opuntia may have been imported with 'turkish corn' (*Zea mays*) from Morocco in 1656.

12. A9–91, Evidence of A.C. MacDonald, pp.20–21.

13. Thunberg, C. 1823. *Florae Capensis*. Stuttgart: Cottae; Sparrman, A. 1977. *A voyage to the Cape of Good Hope…1772–1776*, Volume II. Cape Town: Van Riebeeck Society, p.260.

14. Wellington, J.H. 1928. Some physical factors affecting the economic development of the Eastern Cape Province and adjoining areas. *South African Geographical Journal*, 11: pp.29 and 33. See also Rennie, J.V.L. 1945. The Eastern Province as geographical region. *South African Geographical Journal*, 27: pp.1–27; Cole, M.M. 1961. *South Africa*. London: Methuen and Co., pp.561–68.

15. See MacLennan, B. 1986. *A proper degree of terror*. Johannesburg: Ravan Press; Peires, J.B. 1989. *The dead will arise*. Johannesburg: Ravan Press; Crais, C. 1992. *The making of the colonial order*. Johannesburg: Witwatersrand University Press; Mostert, N. 1992. *Frontiers*. New York: Knopf, for recent accounts of European conquest and settlement of the Eastern Cape.

16. Compiled from Cape of Good Hope, *Statistical Registers* and Department of Agriculture *Annual Reports*, 1884–1910; the selected rainfall stations are Aberdeen, Cradock, Fort Beaufort, Graaff-Reinet, Grahamstown, Humansdorp, Port Elizabeth, Somerset East, Uitenhage and Willowmore.

17. Nobel, *Environmental biology*.

18. A9–91, Evidence of A.C. MacDonald, pp.20–21; Baines, T. 1961. *Journal of residence in Africa 1842–1853*, Volume I. Cape Town: Van Riebeeck Society, p.106; Cape of Good Hope, *Report of the Select Committee on Xanthium Spinosum, 1860* [A15–60].

19. Bryden, H.A. 1889. *Kloof and Karroo*. London: Longmans Green, p.88.

20. Compiled from CA, AGR 74, 244 and PAS 3/155, N77; Bergh, J.S. and Visagie, J.C. 1985. *The Eastern Cape frontier zone 1660–1980*. Durban: Stoneham Butterworths, p.65.

21. See, for example, Schaffner, J.H. 1938. Spreading of Opuntia in overgrazed pastures in Kansas. *Ecology*, 19(2): pp.348–50; Cook, C.W. 1942. Insects and weather as they influence growth of cactus on the central Great Plains. *Ecology*, 23(2): pp.209–14; Anthony, M. 1954. Ecology of the Opuntiae in the Big Bend region of Texas. *Ecology*, 35(3): pp.334–47; Benson, L. and Walkington, D.L. 1965. The Southern California prickly pears: invasion, adulteration and trial-by-fire. *Annals of the Monterey Botanical Garden*, 52: pp.262–73; Pearson, L.C. 1965. Primary production in grazed and ungrazed desert communities of eastern Idaho. *Ecology*, 46(3): pp.278–85; Harris, D.R. 1966. Recent plant invasions in the arid and semi-arid Southwest of the United States. *Annals of the American Association of Geographers*, 56: pp.408–22; Baskin, J.M. and Baskin, C.C. 1977. Seed and seedling ecology of *Opuntia compressa* in Tennessee cedar glades. *Journal of the Tennessee Academy of Science*, 52: pp.118–22; Berry, J. 1977. The effects of grazing pressure on Opuntia populations. *Proceedings of the South Dakota Academy of Science*, 56: pp.271–72; Cohn, J.P. 1982. Of prairies and prickly pears. *Nature Conservation News*, 32(6): pp.17–21.

22. Cape of Good Hope, *Report of the Select Committee on Eradication of Prickly Pear, 1898* [A29–98], Evidence of R.P. Botha, p.23; Cape Archives [CA], AGR 503, F6, E.A. Nobbs, 'Report Prickly Pear', October 1906, p.1.

23. C3–90, vii and Evidence of G.M. Palmer, p.7; A9–91, Evidence of E.R. Hobson, p.4.

24. C3–90, Evidence of J.H. Smith, p.18 and J.O. Norton, p.25; A9–91, Evidence of A.C. MacDonald, pp.28 and 30; A29–98, Evidence of R.P. Botha, p.32 and C.G. Lee, p.37.

25. C3–90, Evidence of J.H. Smith, p.22.

26. A9–91, Evidence of E.R. Hobson, p.7, P.J. du Toit, p.16 and A.C. MacDonald, p.25; CA, AGR 503, F6, E.A. Nobbs, 'Report prickly pear', October 1906, p.1.

27. CA, AGR 503, F6, E.A. Nobbs, 'Report prickly pear', October 1906, p.1, and MacOwan, P. 1897. The prickly pear and the kaal-blad. In: *Agricultural Miscellanea.* Cape Town: Department of Agriculture, p.1.

28. Cape of Good Hope, *Report of the Select Committee on Prickly Pear, 1906* [A8–06], Evidence of D. Hutcheon, pp.7–8 and J.J. Vosloo, p.54; and C3–90, Evidence of J.O. Norton, pp.22 and 26.

29. A8–06, Evidence of J.J. Vosloo, pp.58–59; see also Osmond, C.B. and Monro, J. 1981. Prickly pear. In: Carr, D.J and Carr, S.G.M., eds. *Man and plants in Australia.* New York: Academic Press, pp.200–01 for similar attempts to control opuntia's spread in Australia by exterminating frugarious emu, magpies and crows.

30. A8–06, Evidence of E.A. Nobbs, p.29.

31. A9–91, Evidence of B.J. Keyter, p.14 and P.J. du Toit, p.18.

32. A9–91, Evidence of A.C. MacDonald, pp.26–27.

33. MacOwan, The prickly pear, p.3 and Bryden, Kloof and Karroo, p.88.

34. A29–98, Evidence of C.G. Lee, p.41; A8–06, Evidence of R. Marloth, p.18 and E.A. Nobbs, p.26.

35. C3–90, Evidence of P.H. du Plessis, p.26; A9–91 Evidence of B.J. Keyter, p.14 and P.J. du Toit, p.18.

36. A9–91, Evidence of A.C. MacDonald, p.25; C3–90, Evidence of J.H. Smith, p.18; A8–06, Evidence of J.J. Vosloo, p.59.

37. A29–98, Evidence of C.G. Lee, pp.41–42; and CA, PAS 3/155, N77, Civil Commissioner Fort Beaufort to the Department of Agriculture, 23 July 1906 forwarding Report of Sub-Inspector T. Delaney, Cape Mounted Police.

38. Cape of Good Hope, *Legislative Council Debates*, 1893, p.97; A8–06, Evidence of D. Hutcheon, pp.11–12.

39. Jackal proof fencing: its advantages and economies. 1904. *Agricultural Journal of the Cape of Good Hope (AJCGH)*, 25(5): p.561.

40. Miscellaneous. 1891. *AJCGH*, 4(10): p.122.

41. How to destroy prickly pears with arsenite of soda. 1896. *AJCGH*, 9(12): p.298; and Cape of Good Hope, *House of Assembly Debates*, 1893, p.215.

42. A8–06, Evidence of D. Hutcheon, p.6.

43. The labour question. *AJCGH*, 4(18): pp.203–04. See also Middleton, K. 1999. Who killed 'Malagasy cactus'? Science, environment and colonialism in southern Madagascar (1924–1930). *Journal of Southern African Studies*, 25: pp.215–248 for another instance of opuntia as a source of underclass subsistence in preference to wage labour.

44. A29–98, Evidence of R.P. Botha, p.31; CA, PAS 3/155, N77, Resident Magistrate Jansenville to the Department of Agriculture, 10 August 1906.

45. C3–90, Evidence of G.M. Palmer, p.7; and A9–91, Evidence of A.C. MacDonald, p.28.

46. C3–90, Evidence of G.M. Palmer, pp.7 and 11.

47. A9–91, Evidence of A.C. MacDonald, p.28.

48. A8–06, Evidence of J.J. Vosloo, p.56.

49. See A8–06, Evidence of G.H. Maasdorp, p.41 and J.J. Vosloo, p.58 for contradictory evidence that 'kaalblad' opuntia does not affect and even enhances the value of farms.

50. C3–90, Evidence of G.M. Palmer, p.8, J.H. Smith, p.18 and J.O. Norton, p.23; A9–91, Evidence of E.R. Hobson, p.5, P.J. du Toit, p.17 and A.C. MacDonald, p.27.

51. A8–06, Evidence of J.J. Vosloo, p.55

52. A29–98, Evidence of C.G. Lee, pp.37 and 39.

53. A29–98, p.iv.

54. A8–06, p.iv; see C3–90, pp.viii–ix, Evidence of R.P. Botha, p.3, G.M. Palmer, pp.8ff. and J.H. Smith, pp.16–17; A9–91, p.iv, Evidence of E.R. Hobson, pp.3–5, A.C. MacDonald, pp.33–35, Appendix A, pp.i–ii; Meetings of farmers' associations and agricultural shows. 1892. *AJCGH*, 4(18): p.213 for detailed discussion of the recommended form and administration of this legislation.

55. C3–90, Evidence of R.P. Botha, p.5, G.M. Palmer, p.10 and J.H. Smith, p.16; A8–06, Evidence of R.F. Hurndall, p.35.

56. Cape of Good Hope, *Legislative Council Debates*, 1893, p.97.

57. See Cape of Good Hope, Xanthium Spinosum Act (No. 27, 1864); Cape of Good Hope, *Report of the Select Committee on Xanthium Spinosum Act, 1880* [A5–80], and Cape of Good Hope, Divisional Councils Act (DCA) (40, 1889), VI, 1, for the problematic precedents informing the agitation for a Prickly Pear Act.

58. Cape of Good Hope, *Legislative Council Debates*, 1890, p.63; C3–90, Evidence of G.M. Palmer, pp.12–13; and Van Zyl, D.J. 1984. *Phylloxera vastatrix* in die Kaapkolonie, 1886–1900: voorkoms, verspreiding en ekonomiese gevolge. *South African Historical Journal*, 16: pp.26–48.

59. MacOwan, The prickly pear, pp.1–2; Cape of Good Hope, *Report of the Department of Agriculture, 1891–92 [G 19–92]*, 18.

60. See MacOwan, The prickly pear; Phillips, E.P. 1940. Opuntias in South Africa II. Some species of *Opuntia* cultivated or naturalised in South Africa. *Farming in South Africa*, 15: pp.125–28; Annecke, D.P. and Moran, V.C. 1978. Critical reviews of biological pest control in South Africa. 2. The prickly pear, *Opuntia ficus-indica* (L.) Miller. *Journal of the Entomological Society of South Africa*, 41(2): pp.163–66 for the varied scientific classifications of opuntia in South Africa over the past century.

61. A9–91, Evidence of A.C. MacDonald, pp.21–22 and 40; CA, AGR 503, F6; Nobbs, 'Report prickly pear', October 1906, p.3.

62. This was not the only folk botanical classification of opuntia. See A8–06, Evidence of R. Marloth, pp.17–18 for the differentiation of 'mannetjies' ('little men') and wyfies ('little wives'). Marloth confessed that he had 'not been able to arrive at a clear understanding of what is meant by these two terms' as 'one description of the difference was contradicted by another description' and held 'The other terms are much better, "kaalblad" and "doornblad."'

63. Compare with, for example, Smith, C.A. 1966. *Common names of South African plants*. Pretoria: Government Printer, pp.151–53 who suggests that the newly arrived and 'useless' burrweed *Xanthium spinosum* only acquired a vernacular name, 'boetebossie' ('little fine bush'), in the wake of Act 27 of 1864.

64. A9–91, Evidence of P.J. du Toit, p.15.

65. C3–90, Evidence of E.R. Hobson, p.7; A9–91, Evidence of A.C. MacDonald, pp.22–23; CA, AGR 455, 3431, H. Fehr to W.W. Thompson, 15 August 1903; CA, AGR 242, 5, Assistant Magistrate Montagu to the Under Secretary for Agriculture, 20 January 1904.

66. A9–91, Evidence of P.J. du Toit, p.19 and A.C. MacDonald, p.29; CA, AGR 503, F6, A.E. Nobbs, 'Experiments upon the destruction of the prickly pear, 1907: final report', 6 September 1907, pp.6–8 (unnumbered).

67. See A9–91, Evidence of B.J. Keyter MLA Oudtshoorn, P.J. du Toit MLA Richmond and A.S. le Roex MLA Victoria West for opuntia cultivation throughout the Karoo.

68. A9–91, Evidence of A.C. MacDonald, pp.28–29.

69. Ibid., pp.29–30.

70. See, for example, Cape of Good Hope, *House of Assembly Debates*, 1892, p.234; and 1893, p.215.

71. See A9–91, Evidence of A.C. MacDonald, pp.23–24, 35–36 and 38–39; Does kaalblad change into doornblad? 1891. *AJCGH*, 4(7): pp.82–83; Does a kaalblad change into a doornblad? 1891.

AJCGH, 4(9): pp.106–07; A8–06, Evidence of D. Hutcheon, p.8 and R. Marloth, pp.15–18 and 22–24 for the main public exchanges in this debate.

72. Does kaalblad change into doornblad? 1891. *AJCGH*, 4(7): p.83; Cape of Good Hope, *House of Assembly Debates*, 1891, p.297.

73. A9–91, Evidence of A.C. MacDonald, p.33; Cape of Good Hope, *House of Assembly Debates*, 1892, p.234.

74. The relevant legislation is Cape of Good Hope DCA (40, 1889), VI, 1; DCA Amendment Act (No. 18, 1898); Extirpation of . . . Weeds in Native Locations Act (No. 22, 1905); DCA Amendment Act (No. 17, 1907). See A8–06, Evidence of E.A. Nobbs, pp.24–26; CA, AGR 503, F6, E.A. Nobbs, 'Report prickly pear', October 1906, pp.5–6 for an envious description of the comparable Australian legislation described as 'curiously similar' to the Cape Colony's scab laws.

75. Cape of Good Hope, *House of Assembly Debates*, 1891, p.297; A8–06, Evidence of E.A. Nobbs, p.26.

76. See C3–90, Evidence of G.M. Palmer, p.12; A9–91, Evidence of E.R. Hobson, p.4 and A.C. MacDonald, pp.31–32; A29–98, Evidence of M.J. du Plessis, pp.2 and 7, R.P. Botha, pp.22 and 34, and C.G. Lee, p.35 for descriptions of manual eradication.

77. A29–98, Evidence of R.P. Botha, pp.34–35.

78. C3–90, Evidence of G.M. Palmer, p.12; A29–98, Evidence of M.J. du Plessis, p.8 and H.J. Raubenheimer, p.18.

79. A29–98, Evidence of Mr Lee and M.J. du Plessis, p.7.

80. A9–91, Evidence of E.R. Hobson, pp.7–8 and A.C. MacDonald, pp.31–32.

81. C3–90, Evidence of J.O. Norton, p.23.

82. A9–91, Evidence of A.C. MacDonald, pp.31–32.

83. See Cape of Good Hope, *House of Assembly Debates*, 1905, p.122 for convict labour; MacOwan, The prickly pear, p.5; A8–06, Evidence of J.J. Vosloo, p.57 for toxins.

84. Cape of Good Hope, *House of Assembly Debates*, 1906, p.80; Koen and Gouws's prickly pear destroyer. 1910. *AJCGH*, 36(6): p.631.

85. CA; AGR 74, 244 (10), Alfred Blackie to A.C. MacDonald, 19 February 1894.

86. See G19–92, 21–23; Cape of Good Hope, *Reports of the Agricultural Assistants, 1893* [G61–94], pp.6–10; Arsenite of soda as an exterminator for prickly pear. 1893. *AJCGH*, 6(15): p.276.

87. A8–06, Evidence of E.A. Nobbs, p.13.

88. G61–94, 6–10; Arsenite of soda as an exterminator for prickly pear. 1893. *AJCGH*, 6(15): pp.276–77; and CA, AGR 74, 244 (10), B. de Smidt van der Riet to the Under Secretary for Agriculture, 8 August 1894. Murchison's contained 66 per cent and Smith's 75 per cent white arsenic according to the analysts.

89. Wallace, R. 1896. *Farming industries of Cape Colony*. London: P.S. King.

90. A29–98, Appendix, W. Hammond Tooke, 'Prickly pear memorandum', pp.i–v.

91. Scrub exterminator. 1893. *AJCGH*, 6(13): p.249.

92. How to destroy prickly pears with arsenite of soda. 1896. *AJCGH*, 9(12): p.298.

93. A29–98, pp.iv–v; A8–06, Evidence of D. Hutcheon, pp.10–11, E.A. Nobbs, pp.27–29 and J.J. Vosloo, pp.53 and 55–56; CA, AGR 503, F6, E.A. Nobbs 'Report prickly pear', October 1906, p.5. Vosloo reported cases of farmers travelling 6–7 hours by wagon to obtain supplies, only to be told by the magistrate none was expected until the end of the month and others applying 4–5 times without success.

94. See Cape of Good Hope *Government Gazette*, No.8110, 14 March 1899, Government Notice No. 219 reprinted under heading 'Scrub exterminator for (eradication of) prickly pear'. 1899. *AJCGH*, 16(3–4 and 7–9).

95. Compiled from information contained in A8–06, Appendix A, p.i; Cape of Good Hope *Government Gazette*, No. 8932, 1 February 1907, p.340, Government Notice 119; Cape of Good Hope *Government Gazette*, No. 9078, 26 June 1908, p.1831, Government Notice 711; 1910. *AJCGH*, 36(2): p.144; 1910. *AJCGH*, 36(6): p.628; 1910. *AJCGH*, 37(6): pp.656–57; Cape of Good Hope *Estimates of Expenditure*, 1905–1910.

96. Extirpation of the prickly pear. 1900. *AJCGH*, 16(10): pp.621–24.

97. See Successful destruction of the prickly pear. 1893. *AJCGH*, 6(16): p.311; Scrub exterminator and arsenite of soda. 1893. *AJCGH*, 6(17): pp.330–31; CA, AGR 74, 244 (10), John G. Nash to the Under Secretary for Agriculture, 29 October 1895; A8–06, Evidence of R.F. Hurndall, p.32, and P.J. Pienaar, p.65; Nobbs, E.A. 1907. Experiments upon the destruction of prickly pear, 1907: final report. *AJCGH*, 31(6): p.682.

98. A8–06, Evidence of D. Hutcheon, p.4, R.F. Hurndall, p.31 and G.H. Maasdorp, p.38.

99. For rare examples see CA, 74, 244 (10), John G. Nash to the Under Secretary for Agriculture, 29 October 1895; Scrub exterminator for prickly pear. 1900. *AJCGH*, 17(1): p.50; Poisoning of ostriches. 1906. *AJCGH*, 28(5): pp.730–31.

100. Hobson, W.G. 1896. How to destroy prickly pears with arsenite of soda. *AJCGH*, 9(12): p.298.

101. Nobbs, E.A. 1907. Experiments upon the destruction of prickly pear, 1907: final report. *AJCGH*, 31(6): p.681.

102. Nobbs, E.A. 1908. Experiments upon the destruction of jointed cactus, 1907: final report. *AJCGH*, 32(3): p.343; Hobson, W.G. 1896. How to destroy prickly pears with arsenite of soda. *AJCGH*, 9(12): p.298.

103. Cape of Good Hope, *Reports of the Agricultural Assistants, 1899* [G20–1900], pp.6–7 reprinted as Extirpation of the prickly pear. 1899. *AJCGH*, 15(8): pp.548–50, and 1900. *AJCGH*, 16(10): pp.621–24.

104. Cape of Good Hope, Department of Agriculture, *Report of the Acting Director of Agriculture, 1905* [G47–1906], p.23. The state justified removing the 100 per cent subsidy to eliminate wastage and because it was only intended as a temporary measure until the poison's efficacy against opuntia had been proved.

105. Reitz, D. 1929. *A journal of the Boer War*. London: Faber and Faber, p.253.

106. See, for example, CA, AGR 74, 244, W.H. Trebble to Prof. Fisher, 25 and 29 November 1891; CA, AGR 239, 2597, M.A.M. Oosthuyzen to D. Versfeld, 5 January 1892; A8–06, Evidence of R.F. Hurndall, p.36, P.J. Pienaar, pp.59–70 and J.F. Cairns, pp.70–75; CA; AGR 503, F6, J.L. Neuper to the Under Colonial Secretary, 11 July 1908, and Alex Innes to the Secretary for Agriculture, 9 September 1908; Another prickly pear exterminator. 1910. *AJCGH*, 36(4): p.488. Also CA, AGR 503, F6, H.A. Taylor to Dr Smartt, 26 October 1907 and 26 February 1908 and R. McPhail to the Premier of the Cape Colony, 27 November 1907 for Australian hucksters attempting to peddle scrub exterminator patents and secrets to the Cape government.

107. Compare CA, AGR 507, G5, E.A. Nobbs to the Acting Director of Agriculture, 21 December 1905 and D. Hutcheon to the Under Colonial Secretary, 11 January 1906 for different opinions within the Department of Agriculture on P.J. Pienaar's scrub exterminator. Also A8–06, Evidence of G.H. Maasdorp, p.40 who warned against bonuses to inventors 'because there are so many who claim to have found the correct stuff'.

108. CA, 503, F6, E.A. Nobbs, 'Report prickly pear', October 1906, p.6; Nobbs, E.A. 1907. Experiments upon the destruction of prickly pear, 1907: final report. *AJCGH*, 31(6): p.678.

109. Nobbs, E.A. 1907. Experiments upon the destruction of prickly pear, 1907: final report. *AJCGH*, 31(6): p.680.

110. Jansen's prickly pear exterminator. 1909. *AJCGH*, 35(4): pp.372–73; The destruction of prickly pear by the use of Jansen's extirpator. 1910. *AJCGH*, 36(3): p.354.

111. CA, AGR 503, F6, A.E. Nobbs 'Experiments upon the destruction of the prickly pear, 1907: final report', 6 September 1907, pp.6–8 (unnumbered).

112. CA, AGR 455, 3431, H. Fehr to W.W. Thompson, 15 August 1903.

113. Vines on prickly pear. 1891. *AJCGH*, 4(6): p.73; CA, AGR 168, 852(3), Christian Wharmby to Cecil J. Rhodes, 24 August 1892; CA, AGR 453, 3377, S. Barrett Cawood to Sir Gordon Sprigg, 24 April 1901; Brandy from prickly pears. 1903. *AJCGH*, 22(4): p.474; Planting prickly pears to prevent sluiting. 1905. *AJCGH*, 26(4): p.603; CA, PAS 3/146 and 3/147, N12, N14 and N15.

114. CA, AGR 503, F6, E.A. Nobbs, 'Report prickly pear', October 1906, p.7.

115. Prickly pear for stock. 1895. *AJCGH*, 8(17): p.447.

116. The much abused prickly pear. 1899. *AJCGH*, 14(12): p.817.
117. Kaalblad prickly pears. 1905. *AJCGH*, 27(1): p.2.
118. See MacOwan, P. 1897. A plea for pricklies. *AJCGH*, 11(4): p.161 for the similar role played by species of the indigenous succulent *Euphorbia*.
119. Ibid., pp.158–59.
120. Ibid., p.159.
121. CA, AGR 357, 866, A. MacDonald to the Under Secretary for Agriculture, 20 September 1897; Analysis of prickly pear. 1898. *AJCGH*, 13(13): pp.848–50; Prickly pear ensilage. 1899. *AJCGH*, 14(9): pp.550–51; A8–06, Evidence of D. Hutcheon, pp.5–6.
122. See, for example, Prickly pear for pigs. 1897. *AJCGH*, 10(3): pp.143–44; CA, AGR 357, 866, A. Fittig to the Secretary for Agriculture, 3 August 1897; Prickly pear as a fodder. 1897. *AJCGH*, 11(13): pp.739–40; *Reports of the Agricultural Assistants, 1897* [G34–98], pp.22–23; A29–98, Evidence of G. Wilhelm, pp.14–17; CA, AGR 357, 866, A.A. Fouché to the Secretary for Agriculture, 4 July 1898; Prickly pear for stock. 1899. *AJCGH*, 15(3): p.170; Prickly pear ensilage. 1900. *AJCGH*, 16(1): p.52; Prickly pears as forage. 1902. *AJCGH*, 20(11): pp.643–44; Singed prickly pear as forage. 1904. *AJCGH*, 25(2): pp.124–25; Singeing prickly pear for fodder. 1904. *AJCGH*, 25(4): pp.473–74; CA, AGR 619, T102, H. Stevenson to the Director of Agriculture, 27 August and 17 September 1906.
123. See A8–06, Evidence of D. Hutcheon, pp.11–12; CA, AGR 503, F6, E.A. Nobbs, 'Report prickly pear', October 1906, pp.6–7 for the final word on the matter.
124. See, for example, Pettey, F.W. 1948. *Science Bulletin 271: The biological control of prickly pears in South Africa*. Pretoria: Department of Agriculture and Forestry; and Annecke, D.P., et al. 1969. Improved biological control of the prickly pear, *Opuntia megacantha* Salm-Dyck, in South Africa through the use of an insecticide. *Phytophylactica*, 1: pp.9–13.
125. See for example Turpin, H.W. and Gill, G.A. 1928. *Bulletin No. 36: Insurance against drought. Drought resistant fodders: with special reference to cactus*. Pretoria: Department of Agriculture; Brutsch, M.O. and Zimmerman, H.G. 1993. The prickly pear (*Opuntia ficus-indica* [Cactaceae]) in South Africa: utilization of the naturalized weed, and of the cultivated plants. *Economic Botany*, 47(2): pp.154–62 and S. Gray, 'Prinsloo's turksvy treats' in *Mail & Guardian*, 30 April–7 May 1998, p.6.
126. See Mackenzie, J.M. 1997. Empire and the ecological apocalypse: the historiography of the imperial environment. In: Griffiths, T. and Robin, L., eds. *Ecology and empire: environmental history of settler societies*. Pietermaritzburg: University of Natal Press.
127. Worster, D. 1996. Two cultures revisited: environmental history and the environmental sciences. *Environment and History*, 2(1): pp.5, 13 and 9.
128. Ibid., pp.9–13.
129. Ibid., p.10; and Grundmann, R. 1991. The ecological challenge to Marxism. *New Left Review*, 187: pp.111–14.
130. Crosby, *Ecological imperialism*, p.150.
131. See MacDonald, I.A.W. 1989. Man's role in changing the face of southern Africa. In: Huntley, B.J., ed. *Biotic diversity in Southern Africa: concepts and conservation*. Cape Town: Oxford University Press, pp.51–78; Hoffman, M.T., et al. 1995. Desertification of the eastern Karoo, South Africa: conflicting paleoecological, historical, and soil isotopic evidence. In: Mouat, D.A. and Hutchinson, C.F., eds. *Desertification in developing countries*. Dordrecht: Kluwer Academic, pp.159–77; and Kruger, et al., Processes of invasion, p.150.
132. See, for example, Beinart, W. and Coates, P. 1995. *Environment and history*. London: Routledge, pp.2–3; and Worster, Two cultures revisited, pp.4–5.
133. Worster, Two cultures revisited, pp.4 and 13.
134. Grundmann, The ecological challenge, p.112.
135. Ibid., p.114.
136. Ibid., p.106.

Chapter 10: Fire and the South African Grassland Biome

1. Roux, E. 1969. *Grass: a story of Frankenwald.* Oxford: Oxford University Press.
2. Rutherford, M.C. and Westfall, R.H. 1986. Biomes of southern Africa – an objective categorisation. *Memoirs of the Botanical Survey of South Africa* No. 54. Pretoria: Botanical Research Institute, Department of Agriculture and Water Supply.
3. Van der Zel, D.W. 1989. *Strategic forestry development plan for South Africa.* Mimeographed publication, Pretoria: Directorate of National Forestry Planning, Department of Environment Affairs. Note: for the purposes of this chapter, 'South Africa' includes the Republic and the kingdoms of Lesotho and Swaziland.
4. Acocks, J.P.H. 1975. Veld types of South Africa. *Memoirs of the Botanical Survey of South Africa* No. 40. Pretoria: Botanical Research Institute, Department of Agricultural Technical Services; Manry, D.E. 1982. Habitat use by foraging Bald Ibises *Geronticus calvus* in western Natal. *South African Journal of Wildlife Research*, 12: pp.85–93; Tainton, N.M. and Mentis, M.T. 1984. Fire in grassland. In: Booysen, P. de V. and Tainton, N.M., eds. *Ecological effects of fire in South African ecosystems.* Ecological Studies series no. 48. Berlin: Springer-Verlag.
5. Rutherford and Westfall, Biomes of southern Africa; Matthews, W.S., Van Wyk, A.E. and Bredenkamp, G.J. 1993. Endemic flora of the north-eastern Transvaal escarpment, South Africa. *Biological Conservation*, 63: pp.83–94; Low, A.B. and Rebelo, A.G., eds. 1996. *Vegetation of South Africa, Lesotho and Swaziland.* Pretoria: Department of Environment Affairs and Tourism.
6. Komarek, E.V. 1962. The use of fire: an historical background. *Proceedings of the Tall Timbers Fire Ecology Conference*, 1: pp.7–10; Lemon, P.C. 1968. Fire and wildlife grazing on an African plateau. *Proceedings of the Tall Timbers Fire Ecology Conference*, 8: pp.71–82.
7. Komarek, E.V. 1971. Lightning and fire ecology in Africa. *Proceedings of the Tall Timbers Fire Ecology Conference*, 11: pp.473–511; Manry, D.E. and Knight, R.S. 1986. Lightning density and burning frequency in South African vegetation. *Vegetatio*, 67: pp.67–76.
8. West, O. 1971. Fire, man and wildlife as interacting factors limiting the development of climax vegetation in Rhodesia. *Proceedings of the Tall Timbers Fire Ecology Conference*, 11: pp.121–45.
9. Komarek, Lightning and fire ecology.
10. Hall, M. 1984. Man's historical and traditional use of fire in southern Africa. In: Booysen, P. de V. and Tainton N.M., eds. *Ecological effects of fire in South African ecosystems.* Ecological Studies series no. 48. Berlin: Springer-Verlag.
11. Inskeep, R.R. 1978. *The peopling of South Africa.* Cape Town: David Philip.
12. Hall, Man's historical and traditional use of fire.
13. Ibid.
14. Ibid.
15. Edwards, D. 1984. Fire regimes in the biomes of South Africa. In: Booysen, P. de V. and Tainton N.M., eds. *Ecological effects of fire in South African ecosystems.* Ecological Studies series no. 48. Berlin: Springer-Verlag.
16. Bayer, A.W. 1955. The ecology of grasslands. In: Meredith, D., ed. *The grasses and pastures of South Africa.* Union of South Africa: Central News Agency; Gordon-Gray, K.D. and Wright, F.B. 1969. *Cyrtanthus breviflorus* and *Cyrtanthus lutens* (Amaryllidaceae). Observations with particular reference to Natal populations. *Journal of South African Botany*, 35(1): pp.35–62; Manry, D.E. 1983. Ecology of the Bald Ibis *Geronticus calvus* and fire in the South African grassland biome. M.Sc. thesis, University of Cape Town, Cape Town; Manry and Knight, Lightning density and burning frequency.
17. Komarek, Lightning and fire ecology.
18. Roux, *Grass: a story of Frankenwald*; Edwards, Fire regimes.
19. Ibid.
20. Trollope, W.S.W. 1984. Fire in savannah. In: Booysen, P. de V. and Tainton, N.M., eds. *Ecological effects of fire in South African ecosystems.* Ecological Studies series no. 48. Berlin: Springer-Verlag.

21. Komarek, Lightning and fire ecology.
22. Scott, J.D. 1981. Fire as a natural ecological factor. In: Tainton, N.M., ed. *Veld and pasture management in South Africa*. Pietermaritzburg: Shuter & Shooter and University of Natal Press.
23. Manry and Knight, Lightning density and burning frequency.
24. Edwards, Fire regimes; Mentis, M.T., Meiklejohn, M.J. and Scotcher, J.S.B. 1974. Veld burning in Giant's Castle Game Reserve, Natal Drakensberg. *Proceedings of the Grassland Society of Southern Africa*, 9: 26–31.
25. Edwards, Fire regimes.
26. Acocks, Veld types.
27. Davidson, R.L. 1964. An experimental study of succession in the Transvaal highveld. In: Davis, D.H.S., ed. *Ecological studies in Southern Africa*. The Hague: W. Junk.
28. Huntley, B.J. 1984. Characteristics of South African biomes. In: Booysen, P. de V. and Tainton, N.M., eds. *Ecological effects of fire in South African ecosystems*. Ecological Studies series no. 48. Berlin: Springer-Verlag.
29. Tainton. N.M. 1981. The ecology of the main grazing lands of South Africa. In: Tainton, N.M., ed. *Veld and pasture management in South Africa*. Pietermaritzburg: Shuter & Shooter and University of Natal Press.
30. Mentis, M.T. and Huntley, B.J. 1982. A description of the Grassland Biome Project. *South African National Scientific Programmes Report* No. 62. Pretoria: CSIR.
31. Trollope, W.S.W. 1971. Fire as a method of eradicating macchia vegetation in the Amatole Mountains of South Africa – experimental and field scale results. *Proceedings of the Tall Timbers Fire Ecology Conference*, 11: pp.99–120; Trollope, W.S.W. 1973. Fire as a method of eradicating macchia (fynbos) vegetation in the Amatole Mountains of the Eastern Cape. *Proceedings of the Grassland Society of Southern Africa*, 8: pp.35–41.
32. Tainton and Mentis, Fire in grassland.
33. Trollope, Fire as a method of eradicating macchia vegetation.
34. Galpin, E.E. 1926. Botanical survey of the Springbok Flats. *Memoirs of the Botanical Survey of South Africa* No. 12. Cape Town: Advisory Committee for the Botanical Survey of South Africa and Cape Times Ltd.
35. Acocks, Veld types.
36. Mentis, Meiklejohn and Scotcher, Veld burning; Scotcher, J.S.B. and Clarke, J.C. 1981. Effects of certain burning treatments on veld condition in Giant's Castle Game Reserve. *Proceedings of the Grassland Society of Southern Africa*, 16: pp.121–27.
37. Everson, C.S., George, W.J. and Schulze, R.E. 1989. Fire regime effects on canopy cover and sediment yield in the montane grasslands of Natal. *South African Journal of Science*, 85: pp.113–16.
38. Mentis, M.T. 1984. Monitoring in South African grasslands. *South African National Scientific Programmes Report* No. 91. Pretoria: CSIR.
39. Cooke, H.B.S. 1964. The Pleistocene environment in Southern Africa. In: Davis, D.H.S., ed. *Ecological studies in Southern Africa*. The Hague: W. Junk.
40. Acocks, Veld types.
41. Killick, D.J.B. 1978. The Afro-Alpine region. In: Werger, M.J.A., ed. *Biogeography and ecology of Southern Africa*. Vol. 1. The Hague: W. Junk.
42. Mentis and Huntley, The Grassland Biome Project.
43. Van Oudtshoorn, F.P. 1991. *Gids tot grasse van Suid-Afrika*. Pretoria: Briza Publikasies; Cooke, The Pleistocene environment.
44. Acocks, Veld types; Mentis and Huntley, The Grassland Biome Project.
45. MacDonald, I.A.W. 1989. Man's role in changing the face of southern Africa. In: Huntley, B.J., ed. *Biotic diversity in Southern Africa: concepts and conservation*. Cape Town: Oxford University Press; Acocks, Veld types.
46. Tainton, The ecology of the main grazing lands.
47. Rutherford and Westfall, Biomes of Southern Africa.

48. Acocks, Veld types.
49. Sunquist, F. 1986. Peering into the secrets of grasslands. *International Wildlife*, 16(2): 52–58; Moll, E.J. 1987. The Grassland Biome – a heritage lost? *Veld and Flora*, 72(4): 128–29.
50. Low and Rebelo, *Vegetation of South Africa, Lesotho and Swaziland*.
51. Harrison J.A., Allan, D.G., Underhill, L.G., Herremans, M., Tree, A.J., Parker, V. and Brown, C.J., eds. 1997. *The atlas of Southern African birds*. 2 vols. Johannesburg: BirdLife South Africa; Stattersfield, A.J., Crosby, M.J., Long, A.J. and Wege, D.C. 1998. *Endemic bird areas of the world: priorities for biodiversity conservation*. Cambridge: BirdLife International.
52. Komarek, Lightning and fire ecology.
53. Edwards, Fire regimes.
54. Manry and Knight, Lightning density and burning frequency.
55. Komarek, Lightning and fire ecology.
56. Mentis, Meiklejohn and Scotcher, Veld burning.
57. Everson, C.S. and Tainton N.M. 1984. The effect of thirty years of burning on the Highland Sourveld of Natal. *Journal of the Grassland Society of Southern Africa*, 1(3): pp.15–20.
58. Acocks, Veld types; Tainton, The ecology of the main grazing lands; Huntley, South African biomes.
59. Killick, The Afro-Alpine region; Mentis and Huntley, The Grassland Biome Project; Tainton and Mentis, Fire in grassland.
60. Mentis and Huntley, The Grassland Biome Project.
61. Acocks, Veld types; Huntley, South African biomes; Tainton, The ecology of the main grazing lands; Tainton and Mentis, Fire in grassland.
62. Davidson, An experimental study.
63. Mentis, Meiklejohn and Scotcher, Veld burning; Scotcher and Clarke, Effects of certain burning treatments.
64. Everson, George and Schulze, Fire regime effects.
65. Manry and Knight, Lightning density and burning frequency.
66. Mentis, Meiklejohn and Scotcher, Veld burning.
67. Killick, D.J.B. 1963. An account of the plant ecology of the Cathedral Peak areas of the Drakensberg. *Memoirs of the Botanical Survey of South Africa* No. 34. Pretoria: Botanical Research Institute, Department of Agricultural Technical Services.
68. Smith, F.R. and Tainton, N.M. 1985. Effects of a season of burn on shrub survival, regeneration and structure in the Natal Drakensberg. *Journal of the Grassland Society of Southern Africa*, 2(2): pp.4–10.
69. Scotcher and Clarke, Effects of certain burning treatments.
70. Tainton, N.M. 1981. Veld burning. In: Tainton, N.M., ed. *Veld and pasture management in South Africa*. Pietermaritzburg: Shuter & Shooter and University of Natal Press; Tainton and Mentis, Fire in grassland; Everson, C.S., Everson, T.M. and Tainton, N.M. 1985. The dynamics of *Themeda triandra* tillers in relation to burning in the Natal Drakensberg. *Journal of the Grassland Society of Southern Africa*, 2(4): pp.18–25.
71. Mentis and Huntley, The Grassland Biome Project.
72. Schulze, R.E. and McGee, O.S. 1978. Climatic indices and classifications in relation to the biogeography of Southern Africa. In: Werger, M.J.A., ed. *Biogeography and ecology of Southern Africa*. Vol. 1. The Hague: W. Junk.
73. Manry and Knight, Lightning density and burning frequency.
74. Komarek, Lightning and fire ecology.
75. Trollope, W.S.W. and Tainton, T.M. 1986. Effect of fire intensity on the grass and bush components of the Eastern Cape Thornveld. *Journal of the Grassland Society of Southern Africa*, 3(2): pp.37–42.
76. Trollope, W.S.W. 1987. Effect of a season of burning on grass recovery in the False Thornveld of the Eastern Cape. *Journal of the Grassland Society of Southern Africa*, 4(2): pp.74–77.

77. Manry and Knight, Lightning density and burning frequency.
78. Kruger, F.J. and Bigalke, R.C. 1984. Fire in fynbos. In: Booysen, P. de V. and Tainton, N.M., eds. *Ecological effects of fire in South African ecosystems*. Ecological Studies series no. 48. Berlin: Springer-Verlag.
79. Manry and Knight, Lighting density and burning frequency.
80. Mentis and Huntley, The Grassland Biome Project; Trollope, Fire as a method of eradicating macchia vegetation.
81. Trollope, Fire as a method of eradicating macchia (fynbos).
82. Everson, George and Schulze, Fire regime effects.
83. Edwards, P.J. 1969. Veld burning in the Giant's Castle Game Reserve. *Lammergeyer*, 10: pp.64–67.
84. Killick, The plant ecology of the Cathedral Peak areas.
85. Rutherford and Westfall, Biomes of Southern Africa.
86. Rutherford, M.C. 1980. Annual plant production-precipitation relations in arid and semi-arid regions. *South African Journal of Science*, 76: pp.53–56.
87. Manry and Knight, Lightning frequency and burning density.
88. Tainton, N.M., Groves, R.H. and Nash, R. 1977. Time of mowing and burning veld: short term effects on production and tiller development. *Proceedings of the Grassland Society of Southern Africa*, 12: pp.59–64; Everson, Everson and Tainton, The dynamics of *Themeda triandra* tillers.
89. Komarek, Lightning and fire ecology.

Chapter 11: Wakkerstroom: Grasslands, fire and war

1. Moll, E J. 1987. The Grassland Biome – a heritage lost? *Veld and Flora*, 72(4): pp.128–29.
2. Sunquist F. 1986. Peering into the secrets of grasslands. *International Wildlife*, 16(2): pp.52–58.
3. Tarboton, W.R. and Tarboton, M. n.d. *Wakkerstroom: a bird and nature guide*. Wakkerstroom: Wakkerstroom Natural Heritage Association.
4. Huntley B.J. 1984. Characteristics of South African biomes. In: Booysen, P. de V. and N.M. Tainton, eds. *Ecological effects of fire in South African ecosystems*. Ecological Studies 48. Berlin: Springer-Verlag.
5. Tarboton and Tarboton, *Wakkerstroom*; Du Toit, A. 1954. *The geology of South Africa*. 3rd ed. Edinburgh: Oliver and Boyd.
6. Van Oudtshoorn, F.P. 1991. *Gids tot grasse van Suid-Afrika*. Pretoria: Briza Publications.
7. Acocks, J.P.H. 1975. Veld types of South Africa. *Memoirs of the Botanical Survey of South Africa*, 40: pp.1–128. Pretoria: Botanical Research Institute, Department of Agricultural Technical Services.
8. Van Wyk, A.E. and S.J. Malan. 1988. *Field guide to the wild flowers of the Witwatersrand and Pretoria region*. Cape Town: Struik.
9. Tarboton, W.R. 1991. The Eastern Transvaal highveld and its birdlife. *WBC News*, 155: pp.2–5; Van Wyk and Malan, *Field guide*.
10. Van Oudtshoorn, *Gids tot grasse*.
11. Van Wyk and Malan, *Field guide*.
12. Huntley, B.J. 1984. Characteristics of South African biomes. In: Booysen, P. de V. and Tainton, N.M., eds. *Ecological effects of fire in South African ecosystems*. Ecological Studies 48. Berlin: Springer-Verlag.
13. McAllister, J.I. 1997. *Some grasslands facts*. Unpublished information leaflet.
14. Komarek, E.V. 1971. Lightning and fire ecology in Africa. *Proceedings of the Tall Timbers Fire Ecology Conference*, 11: pp.473–511.
15. Frost, P.G.H. 1984. The response and survival of organisms in fire-prone environments. In: Booysen, P. de V. and Tainton, N.M., eds. *Ecological effects of fire in South African ecosystems*.

Ecological Studies 48. Berlin: Springer-Verlag; Manry, D.E. 1985. Reproductive performance of the Bald Ibis *Geronticus calvus* in relation to rainfall and grass-burning. *Ibis*, 127: pp.159–73.

16. Manry, D.E. and R.S. Knight. 1986. Lightning density and burning frequency in South African vegetation. *Vegetatio*, 67: pp.67–76.

17. Roux, E. 1969. *Grass: a story of Frankenwald*. Oxford: Oxford University Press; Edwards, D. 1984. Fire regimes in the biomes of South Africa. In: Booysen, P. de V. and Tainton, N.M., eds. *Ecological effects of fire in South African ecosystems*. Ecological Studies 48. Berlin: Springer-Verlag.

18. Trollope, W.S.W. 1984. Fire behaviour. In: Booysen, P. de V. and Tainton, N.M., eds. *Ecological effects of fire in South Africa*. Ecological Studies 48. Berlin: Springer-Verlag; Komarek, Lightning and fire ecology.

19. McAllister, J.I. 1992. *Fire and the Grassland Biome in South Africa*. Term paper. Saasveld School of Forestry.

20. Skotnes, P. 1994. Personal communication, Wakkerstroom.

21. Hall, M. 1984. Man's historical and traditional use of fire in southern Africa. In: Booysen, P. de V. and Tainton, N.M., eds. *Ecological effects of fire in South Africa*. Ecological Studies 48. Berlin: Springer-Verlag.

22. McAllister, *Fire and the Grassland Biome*.

23. Ibid.

24. Edgecombe, R. 1986. The Mfecane or Difaqane. In: Cameron, T., ed. *A new illustrated history of South Africa*. Cape Town: Human and Rousseau.

25. Ibid.

26. Benyon, J. 1968. The British colonies. In: Cameron, T., ed. *A new illustrated history of South Africa*. Cape Town: Human and Rousseau, pp.168, 174, 175.

27. Shabalala, M.R. 1998. Personal communication with student researchers, Newcastle.

28. Oral history sources (interviewers' names given in parentheses): Mrs Jessie Mazibuko, born in 1912, still residing in eSizameleni and a relative of the scouts who fought on the side of the Boers in the Anglo-Boer War (Mandla Sithole); Gogo Mbatha Mndebele and Mr A.G. Dladla (Sipho Dladla); Mr and Mrs S. Thusi and Ms N. Masangu (Themba Thusi); Elders Ngobese, Mthembu and Nkambule, all from KwaNgema (Pinky Buthelezi); B.P. Mposula and I.S. Nkosi (Norman S. Mncube); Elders Ngobese, Mthembu and Nkambule (Mandla Sithole); Nonozi Nhlabathi (Johannes Nsibande); N.H. Mlambo who served as the guide and introduction to Malunguza Reuben Shabalala, descendant of the first Shabalala, who now resides in Newcastle (interviewed by all of the above seven students).

29. Uys, I.S. 1974. *Die Uys geskiedenis*. Kaapstad: Kaap & Transvaal Drukkers Bpk., p.87.

30. Begg, G.W. 1988. *Wetlands of Natal. Part 2: An overview of their extent, role and present status*. Report 71. Pietermaritzburg: Natal Town and Regional Planning Commission.

31. Oral history sources as per note 28.

32. Anon. 1992. *Luneburg: the historical background of Luneburg since its constitution in 1879 to 1992*. Private publication, pp.7–12.

33. Tarboton and Tarboton, Wakkerstroom.

34. Reitz, D. 1929. *Commando – a Boer journal of the Boer War*. London: Faber and Faber, pp.20–24.

35. Acocks, Veld types.

36. Anon. 1959. *Wakkerstroom eeufees 1859–1959 centenary*. Kroonstad: O.V.S. Afrikaanse Pers Bpk, p.14.

37. Smit, C.A. 1992. Personal communication, Wakkerstroom.

38. Kotze, D.C. n.d. *A management plan for Wakkerstroom Vlei: provisional guidelines*. Pietermaritzburg: Department of Grassland Science, University of Natal.

39. Kotze, E. and J.I. McAllister. 1996. *Wakkerstroom – Inter Flumina ad Montes*. Paper delivered at Environmental History Workshop, University of Natal, Pietermaritzburg, July 1996.

40. Duthie, A. 1992. Wood for the trees. *Bushcall*, June: pp.6–7.

41. Teklehaimanot, Z. and Jarvis, P.G. 1991. Direct measurement of intercepted water from forest canopies. *Journal of Applied Ecology*, 28: pp.603–18.

42. Huntley, B.J., Siegfried, R. and Sunter, C. 1989. *South African environments into the 21st century.* Cape Town: Human and Rousseau, Tafelberg.

Chapter 12: The dynamics of ecological change in an era of political transformations

1. Noble, R.G. and Hemens, J. 1996. *Inland water ecosystems in South Africa: a review of research needs.* Pretoria: CSIR, p.64.
2. *Environmental Impact Assessment* (hereafter cited as *EIA*), *Eastern Shores of Lake St Lucia, Kingsa/Tojan Lease Area. Review Panel Report.* 1993. Pretoria: CSIR, p.64.
3. *Report of the Commission of Inquiry into the Alleged Threat to Animal and Plant Life in St Lucia Lake. 1964–1969.* 1996. Pretoria, p.366.
4. *EIA Review Panel Report*, p.64.
5. Davies, L., et al. 1992. Landform, geomorphology and geology. In: *EIA Eastern Shores of Lake St Lucia, Kingsa/Tojan Lease Area. Specialist Reports. Vol. 1 Part 1.* Grahamstown: Coastal and Environmental Services, pp.17–31.
6. Ibid.
7. Ibid.
8. Ibid.
9. Lubke, R.A., Avis, A.M. and Phillipson, P.B. 1992. Vegetation and floristics. In: *EIA Eastern Shores of Lake St Lucia, Kingsa/Tojan Lease Area. Specialist Reports. Vol. 1 Part 1*, p.210.
10. Ibid., p.190.
11. Berruti, A. and Taylor, P.J. 1992. Terrestrial vertebrates. In: *EIA Eastern Shores of Lake St Lucia, Kingsa/Tojan Lease Area. Specialist Reports. Vol. 1 Part 1*, p.308.
12. Macdevette, D.R. and Gordon, I.G. 1991. Current vegetation patterns on the Zululand coastal dunes. In: Everard, D.A. and Von Maltitz, G.P., eds. Dune forest dynamics in relation to land use practices. *Environmental Forum Report*, 1991: p.67.
13. Maggs, T., Whitelaw, G. and Moon, M. 1992. Archaeology. In: *EIA Eastern Shores of Lake St Lucia, Kingsa/Tojan Lease Area. Specialist Reports. Vol. 1 Part 1*, p.408.
14. See Hall, M. 1981. *Settlement patterns in the Iron Age of Zululand: an ecological interpretation.* Oxford: Oxford University Press, pp.153–55.
15. Ibid.
16. Ibid.
17. Avis, A.M. Ecological implications of past and present land use. In: *EIA Eastern Shores of Lake St Lucia, Kingsa/Tojan Lease Area. Specialist Reports. Vol. 1 Part 1*, p.454.
18. Frost, S. 1990. Lake St Lucia: public opinion, environmental issues and the position of government, 1964–1966 & 1989–1990: a case study in changing attitudes to conservation. Honours Thesis, University of Natal, Pietermaritzburg, p.17.
19. Conlong, D.E. and Van Wyk, R.E. 1991. Current understanding of grasslands of the dune systems of the Natal north coast. In: Everard, D.A. and Von Maltitz, G.P., eds. Dune forest dynamics in relation to land use practices. *Environmental Forum Report*, 1991: p.82.
20. Worster, D., ed. 1988. *The ends of the Earth: culture, environment, history.* Cambridge: Cambridge University Press.
21. Worster, D. 1990. Transformations of the Earth: toward an agroecological perspective in history. *Journal of American History*, March: pp.1101.
22. See Avis, Ecological implications of past and present land use, p.450.
23. See Kelbe, B.E. and Rawlins, B.K. Hydrology. In: *EIA Eastern Shores of Lake St Lucia, Kingsa/Tojan Lease Area. Specialist Reports. Vol. 1 Part 1*, pp.80–83.

24. *EIA Eastern Shores of Lake St Lucia, Kingsa/Tojan Lease Area. Report. Vol. 4 Part 2*, p.311.
25. Kriel Commission Evidence. W.D. Wearne: Notes on the ecological history of the St Lucia Lake and environs: for the St Lucia Lake Commission of Inquiry, see pp.11–15.
26. Richard Bay Minerals, Video, 1993.
27. *Report of the Commission of Inquiry into the Alleged Threat to Animal and Plant Life in St Lucia Lake. 1964–1966.* 1996. Pretoria.
28. Frost, *Lake St Lucia*, pp.21–22.
29. Note: The Natal Parks Board and the erstwhile KwaZulu Department of Nature Conservation were amalgamated to form the KwaZulu-Natal Conservation Service in 1998, and amended again in 2001 to Ezemvelo KwaZulu-Natal Wildlife.
30. Bruton, M.N. and Cooper, K.H. 1980. The development of recreation at Sodwana and Cape Vidal. In: Bruton, M.N. and Cooper, K.H., eds. *Studies on the ecology of Maputaland.* Grahamstown: Rhodes University, p.595.
31. *EIA Summary Report*, p.1.
32. See Minerals Act (50 of 1991).
33. *EIA Summary Report*.
34. The Government of South Africa. Joint Statement by Ministers' Committee. March 1996.
35. Baskin, J. and Stavrou, A. 1995. *Synthesis report on the issues related to various land use options in the Greater St Lucia Area.* Data Research Africa Development Researchers and Policy Analysts, p.5.
36. Carruthers, J. 1995. *The Kruger National Park: a social and political history.* Pietermaritzburg: University of Natal Press, p.1.
37. Ibid., pp.2–6.
38. Guy, J. 1995. Political power and land distribution in the St Lucia area from the nineteenth century. *Memorandum to Regional Land Claims Commissioner, KwaZulu-Natal.*
39. Ibid.
40. See Department of Land Affairs. 1996. *Green Paper on South African land policy.* Pretoria: The Department of Land Affairs.
41. See Baskin and Stavrou, *Synthesis report.*
42. The Government of South Africa. Joint Statement by the Ministers' Committee, March 1996 at 14h15. Mining Disallowed on Eastern Shores of St Lucia.
43. Commission on Restitution of Land Rights. 1995. *Preliminary report: land claims in the Eastern Shores of Lake St Lucia.*
44. Private interviews, Richards Bay, November 1996.
45. Worster, *Transformations of the Earth*, p.1101.
46. Turck, B. 1993. South Africa's skyscraper economy: growth or development? In: Hallowes, D., ed. *Hidden faces, environment, development, justice: South Africa and the global context.* Pietermaritzburg: Earthlife Africa, p.240.
47. World Commission on Environment and Development. 1987. *Our common future.* Oxford: Oxford University Press.
48. Lumby, A. 1993. Environmental economics: terra incognita in the formulation of environmental policy. In: Hallowes, D., ed. *Hidden faces, environment, development, justice: South Africa and the global context.* Pietermaritzburg: Earthlife Africa, p.252.
49. Turck, *South Africa's skyscraper economy*, p.241.
50. Ibid.
51. Ledger, J. 1991. Biodiversity: the basis of life. South Africa's endangered species. In: Cock, J. and Koch, E., eds. *Going green: people, politics and the environment in South Africa.* Cape Town: Oxford University Press, p.326.
52. Cock and Koch, *Going green*, p.1
53. Anderson, D. and Grove, R., eds. 1987. *Conservation in Africa: people, policies and practice.* Cambridge: Cambridge University Press, p.1.

Chapter 13: South African environmental history in the African context

1. Dunlap, T.R. 1999. *Nature and the English diaspora: environment and history in the United States, Canada, Australia, and New Zealand*. Cambridge, has a recent overview of the anglophone settler areas which excludes South Africa.
2. Ranger, T. 1996. Review of William Beinart and Peter Coates. 1995. *Environment and history: the taming of nature in the USA and South Africa*. London. In *Journal of Southern African Studies* (hereafter *JSAS*), 22(1).
3. Guelke, L. and Shell, R. 1992. Landscapes of conquest: frontier water alienation and Khoikhoi strategies of survival. *JSAS*, 18(4).
4. Smith, K.W. 1976. *From frontier to midlands: a history of the Graaff-Reinet district, 1786–1910*. Grahamstown.
5. Worster, D. 1985. *Rivers of empire: water, aridity and the growth of the American West*. New York; Pisani, D.J. 1992. *To reclaim a divided West: water, law, and public policy 1848–1902*. Albuquerque; compare Powell, J.M. 1989. *Watering the Garden State: land, water and community in Victoria 1834–1988*. Sydney, and Enterprise and dependency: water management in Australia. In: Griffiths, T. and Robin, L., eds. 1997. *Ecology and empire: environmental history of settler societies*. Edinburgh.
6. Cronon, W. 1991. *Nature's metropolis: Chicago and the Great West*. New York.
7. Wagner, R. 1980. Zoutpansberg: some notes on the dynamics of a hunting frontier, 1848–1867. In: Marks, S. and Atmore, A., eds. *Economy and society in pre-industrial South Africa*. London; Mackenzie, J.M. 1988. *The empire of nature*. Manchester; Carruthers, J. 1988. Game protection in the Transvaal. Unpublished Ph.D. thesis, University of Cape Town, Cape Town; Carruthers, J. 1995. *The Kruger National Park: a social and political history*. Pietermaritzburg, omits much of the material in her thesis on the history of hunting in the nineteenth century.
8. An excellent resource on which to start such an analysis would be Skead, C.J. 1980, 1987. *Historical mammal incidence in the Cape Province*. 2 vols. Cape Town.
9. Grove, R. 1989. Scottish missionaries, evangelical discourses and the origins of conservation thinking in South Africa. *JSAS*, 15(2); and Scotland in South Africa: John Croumbie Brown and the roots of settler environmentalism. In: Griffiths, T. and Robin, L., eds. *Ecology and empire: environmental history of settler societies*. Edinburgh.
10. Beinart, W. 1998. Men, science, travel and nature in the eighteenth and nineteenth century Cape. *JSAS*, 24(4).
11. Van der Merwe, P.J. 1938. *Die noortwaartse beweging van die Boere voor die Groot Trek (1770–1842)*. Den Haag, especially Chapter VI.
12. Carruthers, Game protection.
13. This is demonstrated in my book in progress on the environmental history of livestock farming in the Cape, provisionally entitled *Debating degradation*.
14. Harries, P. 2000. Field sciences in scientific fields: entomology, botany and the early ethnographic monograph in the works of H.-A. Junod. In: Dubow, S., ed. *Science and society in southern Africa*. Manchester.
15. Beinart, W. Forthcoming. Animals' stories: settlers, livestock and environmental regulation in the Cape. In: Wynn, G. ed. *Nature, culture and colonialism*. Vancouver.
16. Hendricks, F. 1989. Loose planning and rapid resettlement: the politics of conservation and control in Transkei, South Africa, 1950–1970. *JSAS*, 15(2).
17. Delius, P. 1996. *A lion amongst the cattle: reconstruction and resistance in the Northern Transvaal*. Oxford; Mager, A.K. 1999. *Gender in the making of a South African bantustan*. Oxford.
18. Harms, R. 1987. *Games against nature: an eco-cultural history of the Nunu of Equatorial Africa*. Cambridge; see McCann, J. 1999. *Green land, brown land, black land: an environmental history of Africa, 1800–1990*. Oxford, for other examples and Akyeampong, E. 2001. *Between the sea and the lagoon: an ecosocial history of the Anlo of southeastern Ghana, c.1850 to recent times*. Oxford.

19. Schoenbrun, D. 1998. *A green place, a good place: agrarian change, gender and social identity in the Great Lakes Region to the 15th century*. Oxford.
20. Ranger, T. 1999. *Voices from the rocks: nature, culture and history in the Matopos Hills of Zimbabwe*. Oxford; Alexander, J., McGregor, J. and Ranger, T. 2000. *Violence and memory: one hundred years in the 'Dark Forests' of Matabeleland*. Oxford.
21. Kreike, E. 1996. Recreating Eden: agro-ecological change and environmental diversity in southern Angola and northern Namibia, 1890–1960. Ph.D. thesis, Yale University, New Haven.
22. For a systematic view of land use in an environmental framework see, Mandala, E. 1990. *Work and control in a peasant economy: a history of the lower Tchiri Valley in Malawi, 1859–1960*. Madison.
23. Perhaps the most influential text was Richards, P. 1985. *Indigenous agricultural revolution: ecology and food production in West Africa*. London; Fairhead, J. and Leach, M. 1996. *Misreading the African landscape: society and ecology in a forest-savanna mosaic*. Cambridge; for a recent collection see Reij, C., Scoones, I. and Toulmin, C., eds. 1996. *Sustaining the soil: indigenous soil and water conservation in Africa*. London.
24. Bundy, C. 1979. *The rise and fall of the South African peasantry*. London.
25. See also Newton-King, S. 1999. *Masters and servants on the Cape eastern frontier*. Cambridge, which, while it focuses on other issues, suggests similarly that a more systematic environmental history of this area at the time is possible.
26. Hall, T.D. 1934. South African pastures: retrospective and prospective. *South African Journal of Science*, 31; Hoffman, T.M. and Cowling, R. 1990. Vegetation change in the semi-arid eastern Karoo over the last 200 years – fact or fiction. *South African Journal of Science*, 86; Garth Sampson, C. 1995. Acquisition of European livestock by the Seacow River bushmen between AD 1770–1890. *South African Field Archaeology*, 4.
27. Pratt, M.L. 1992. *Imperial eyes: travel writing and transculturation*. London.
28. Khan, F. 1994. Rewriting South Africa's conservation history: the role of the Native Farmers Association. *JSAS*, 20(4).
29. Showers, K. and Mahlahlela, G. 1992. Oral evidence in historical environmental impact assessment: soil conservation in Lesotho in the 1930s and 1940s. *JSAS*, 18(2).
30. Timberlake, L. 1985. *Africa in crisis: the causes, the cures of environmental bankruptcy*. London; Harrison, P. 1987. *The greening of Africa*. London; King, P. 1986. *An African winter*. Harmondsworth, UK; Munslow, B., et al. 1988. *The fuelwood trap: a study of the SADCC region*. London.
31. Fairhead and Leach, *Misreading the African landscape*; McCann, *Green land, brown land*; Fairhead, J. and Leach, M. 1998. *Reframing deforestation: global analysis and local realities, studies in West Africa*. London.
32. McGregor, J. 1991. Ecology, policy and ideology: an historical study of woodland use and change in Zimbabwe's communal areas. Ph.D. thesis, Loughborough University of Technology; and Conservation, control and ecological change: the politics and ecology of colonial conservation in Shurugwi, Zimbabwe. *Environment and History*, 1995.
33. Barnes, R., Filer, D.L. and Milton, S.J. 1996. *Acacia Karoo, monograph and annotated bibliography*. Oxford.
34. When I made this suggestion at the Pietermaritzburg conference in 1995, responses were mixed. Kwazulu-Natalians in the audience confirmed that despite great clearances for sugar and other agricultural crops, the overall landscape in the province had probably become more densely treed. Others stressed that the pine and wattle plantations, such as those discussed in Witt's chapter, were more industrial than natural and hardly qualified as part of the concept 'treescape'.
35. Gleditsch, N. 1997. *Conflict and the environment*. Dordrecht, and Armed conflict and the environment – a critique of the literature. *Journal of Peace Research*, 1998, 35(3).
36. Guy, J. 1980. Ecological factors in the rise of the Zulu Kingdom. In: Marks, S. and Atmore, A., eds. *Economy and society in pre-industrial South Africa*. London.
37. Comaroff, J.L. and Roberts, S. 1981. *Rules and processes: the cultural logic of dispute in an African context*. Chicago.

38. For an outline and critique see, Beinart, W. 2000. African history and environmental history. *African Affairs*, 99(395).

39. Diamond, J. 1998. *Guns, germs and steel: a short history of everybody for the last 13,000 years*. London, for a popular account.

40. For a restatement of this argument see Isenberg, A.C. 2000. *The destruction of the bison*. Cambridge.

41. Gibson, C.C. 1999. *Politicians and poachers: the political economy of wildlife policy in Africa*. Cambridge; Barbier, E.B., et. al. 1990. *Elephants, economics and ivory*. London.

42. Carswell, G. 1997. African farmers in colonial Kigezi, Uganda, 1930–1962: opportunity, constraint and sustainability. D.Phil. thesis, School of Oriental and African Studies, University of London.

43. Delius, *Lion amongst the cattle*; Mager, *Gender*.

44. Charman, A. Progressive elites in Bunga politics: African farmers in the Transkeian Territories, 1904–1946, Ph.D. thesis, University of Cambridge, Cambridge.

45. Homewood, K. and Rodgers, W.A. 1987. Pastoralism, conservation and the overgrazing controversy. In: Anderson, D. and Grove, R., eds. *Conservation in Africa*. Cambridge; Behnke, R., Scoones, I. and Kerven, C., eds. 1993. *Range ecology at disequilibrium*. London.

46. McNeill, J. 2000. *Something new under the sun: an environmental history of the twentieth century*. London.

47. Tilley, H. 2001. Africa as a living laboratory. D.Phil. thesis, University of Oxford, Oxford; for South Africa see, Dubow, *Science and society*.

48. Diamond, *Guns, germs and steel*; Flannery, T.F. 1994. *The future eaters*. Sydney.

49. Wilson, E.O. 1998. *Consilience: the unity of knowledge*. London.

50. Malin, J.C. 1947. *The grassland of North America: prolegomena to its history*. Lawrence, Kansas; for South Africa see, Hoffman and Cowling, Vegetation change.

51. Princen, T. and Finger, M., eds. 1994. *Environmental NGOs in world politics: linking the local with the global*. London.

Chapter 14: Commonalities and contrasts, pasts and presents

I thank Libby Robin for thoughtful comments that improved this chapter. However, any further, unattended areas requiring improvement remain my responsibility.

1. Clark, C.M.H. 1978. *A history of Australia*, Volume IV: *the Earth abideth forever*. Melbourne: Melbourne University Press, p.viii.

2. Ironically, at Gallipoli on 25 April 2000, there were – as always – hordes of mostly young Australians, following the marvellous tradition of including that homage in the world backpacker tour. The Anzac 'fact' is probably the most known of any event in Australia's recent history, suggesting that Mr Howard's fear was misplaced.

3. For a discussion of public history's various manifestations and faces see Davison, G. 1991. Paradigms of public history. *Australian Historical Studies*, 24(96): pp.4–15.

4. Ross, R. 1999. *A concise history of South Africa*. Cambridge: Cambridge University Press, pp.79–80.

5. Williams, M. 1975. More and smaller is better: Australian rural settlement 1788–1914. In: Powell, J.M. and Williams, M., eds. *Australian space, Australian time: geographical perspectives*. Melbourne: Oxford University Press.

6. On this theme, see Griffiths, T. and Robin, L., eds. 1997. *Ecology and empire: environmental history of settler societies*. Melbourne: Melbourne University Press.

7. Dovers, S. 2000. Still settling Australia: environment, history and policy. In: Dovers, S., ed. *Environmental history and policy: still settling Australia*. Melbourne: Oxford University Press.

8. Lee, K.N. 1993. *Compass and gyroscope: integrating science and politics for the environment*. Washington DC: Island Press; Gunderson, L.H., Holling, C.S. and Light, S.S., eds. 1995. *Barriers*

and bridges to the renewal of ecosystems and institutions. New York: Columbia University Press; Dovers, S. and Mobbs, C. 1997. An alluring prospect? Ecology, and the requirements of adaptive management. In: Klomp, N. and Lunt, I., eds. *Frontiers in ecology: building the links*. London: Elsevier.

9. Mabo vs. Queensland. *Australian Law Reports*, 107: p.1.

10. Holmes, J. 2000. Pastoral lease tenures as policy instruments, 1847–1997. In: Dovers, S., ed. *Environmental history and policy: still settling Australia*. Melbourne: Oxford University Press.

11. See Bowman, D.M.J.S. 1997. Tansley review 101. The impact of Aboriginal burning on the Australian biota. *New Phytologist*, 140: pp.385–410.

12. Bonyhady, T. 2000. An Australian public trust. In: Dovers, S., ed. *Environmental history and policy: still settling Australia*. Melbourne: Oxford University Press.

13. McLoughlin, L. 1999. Environmental history, environmental management and the public record: will the records be there when you need them? *Australian Journal of Environmental Management*, 6: pp.207–18.

14. For reviews see, Hamilton, C. and Throsby, D., eds. 1998. *The ecologically sustainable development process: evaluating a policy experiment*. Canberra: Academy of the Social Sciences; Fitzgerald, P., McLennan, A. and Munslow, B., eds. 1997. *Managing sustainable development in South Africa*. 2nd ed. Cape Town: Oxford University Press.

15. Dovers, S. 1997. Sustainability: demands on policy. *Journal of Public Policy*, 16: pp.303–18.

16. Powell, J.M. 1996. Historical geography and environmental history: an Australian interface. *Journal of Historical Geography*, 22: pp.253–73.

17. Peters, R. 1991. *A critique for ecology*. Cambridge: Cambridge University Press; Dovers, S., Norton, T. and Handmer, J. 1996. Uncertainty, ecology, sustainability and policy. *Biodiversity and Conservation*, 5: pp.1143–67.

18. See, for example, Stafford Smith, D.M. and Morton, S.R. 1990. A framework for the ecology of arid Australia. *Journal of Arid Environments*, 18: pp.255–78.

19. This is discussed more in Dovers, S. 2000. On the contribution of environmental history to current policy and debate. *Environment and History*, 6: pp.131-50. (This is an article drawn from a paper presented at the 1996 meeting at the University of Natal that was the genesis of this book.)

20. Dovers, S. and Gullett, G. 1999. Policy choice for sustainability: marketisation, law and institutions. In: Bosselman, K. and Richardson, B., eds. *Environmental justice and market mechanisms*. London: Kluwer Law International.

21. Kirkpatrick, J., McDougall, K. and Hyde, M. 1995. *Australia's most threatened ecosystems: the southeastern lowland grasslands*. Sydney: Surrey Beatty.

22. Dargavel, J. 1995. *Fashioning Australia's forests*. Melbourne: Oxford University Press; Dargavel, J. and Libbis, B., eds. 2000. *Australia's ever-changing forests IV*. Canberra: Centre for Resource and Environmental Studies, Australian National University.

23. An Australian apology for these two can be given at this point but, after all, South Africa reciprocated with Bitou Bush (Boneseed) (*Chrysanthemoides monilifera*) and Cape Weed (*Arctotheca calendula*).

24. Dovers, S. 1995. Information, policy and sustainability. *Australian Journal of Environmental Management*, 2: pp.142–56.

25. Nabben, T. and Nduli, N. 2000. International landcare partnership between Australia and South Africa. *Proceedings, International Landcare 2000 Conference*. Melbourne: Department of Natural Resources and Environment.

26. Roberts, J. and Sainty, G. 2000. Oral history, ecological knowledge and river management. In: Dovers, S., ed. *Environmental history and policy: still settling Australia*. Melbourne: Oxford University Press.

27. Uekoetter, F. 1998. Confronting the pitfalls of current environmental history: an argument for an organisational approach. *Environment and History*, 4: pp.31–52.

28. Powell, J.M. 1993. *MDB: the emergence of bioregionalism in the Murray-Darling Basin*. Canberra: Murray Darling Basin Commission.

29. Robin, L. 1998. *Defending the Little Desert: the rise of ecological consciousness in Australia.* Melbourne: Melbourne University Press.
30. For example, in Australia, the Pilliga, Brigalow and Little Desert, see Rolls, E. 1981. *A million wild acres: 200 years of man and an Australian forest.* Melbourne: Thomas Nelson; Nix, H. 1994. The Brigalow. In: Dovers, S., ed. *Australian environmental history: essays and cases.* Melbourne: Oxford University Press; Robin, *Defending the Little Desert.*
31. Davison, Paradigms of public history.
32. Powell, J.M. 1989. *Watering the Garden State: water, land and community in Victoria 1834–1988.* Sydney: Allen and Unwin; 1991. *Plains of promise, rivers of destiny: water management and the development of Queensland 1824–1990.* Brisbane: Boolarong Press; 1998. *Watering the western third: water, land and community in Western Australia, 1826–1996.* Perth: Water and Rivers Commission.
33. Davison, Paradigms of public history, p.15.

Chapter 15: Environment and history in South America and South Africa

Thanks to Erick Langer, Lise Sedrez and John Tutino for their help with this chapter.
1. See Burney, D. 1996. Historical perspectives on human-assisted biological invasions. *Evolutionary Anthropology,* 4: pp.216–21.
2. There were exceptions. South America acquired maize from Mesoamerica several thousand years ago, and exported sweet potato (by means unknown) to Polynesia by about AD 1000. See Hather, J. and Kirch, P.V. 1991. Prehistoric sweet potato (*Ipomea batatas*) from Mangaia Island, Central Polynesia. *Antiquity,* 65: pp.887–89.
3. A recent survey is Cook, N.D. 1998. *Born to die.* New York: Cambridge University Press.
4. See the *Annals of the Association of American Geographers,* 82(3), 1992, a special issue entitled 'The Americas before and after 1492', edited by Karl Butzer.
5. Details on the distribution of domesticable species are in Diamond, J. 1997. *Guns, germs and steel.* New York: Norton, Chapter 9.
6. Brailovsky, A.E. and Foguelman, D. 1991. *Memoria verde: historia ecológica de la Argentina.* Buenos Aires: Editorial Sudamerica.
7. Melville, E. 1994. *A plague of sheep: the environmental consequences of the conquest of Mexico.* New York: Cambridge University Press.
8. Super, J. 1988. *Food, conquest and colonisation in sixteenth century Spanish America.* Albuquerque: University of New Mexico Press.
9. Foweraker, J. 1981. *The struggle for land.* Cambridge: Cambridge University Press; McNeill, J.R. 1988. Deforestation in the araucaria zone of southeastern Brazil, 1900–1983. In: Richards, J.F. and Tucker, R.P., eds. *World deforestation in the twentieth century.* Durham: Duke University Press, pp.15–32.
10. Di Castri, F. and Mooney, H. 1973. *Mediterranean ecosystems: origins and structure.* Berlin: Springer-Verlag.
11. Isenberg, A. 2000. *The destruction of the bison.* New York: Cambridge University Press.
12. Alfred Crosby, personal communication.
13. Dore, E. 2000. Environment and society: long-term trends in Latin American mining. *Environment and History,* 6: pp.1–29; Bakewell, P., ed. 1997. *Mines of silver and gold in the Americas.* Aldershot: Variorum.
14. Furtado, J. 1999. Chuva de estrelas na terra: o paraíso e a busca dos diamantes nas Minas setecentiastas. In: Vieira, A., ed. *História e meio-ambiente: o impacto da expansão Europeia.* Funchal: Centro de Estudios da História do Atlântico, pp.445–58.
15. On Ilo see McNeill, J.R. 2000. *Something new under the sun: an environmental history of the twentieth-century world.* New York: Norton, pp.85–86; on Cerro de Pasco see, Mallon, F. 1983.

The defense of community in Peru's central highlands. Princeton: Princeton University Press, pp.169, 223–30, 350–51.

16. Monteiro, S. and Kaz, L. 1992. *Floresta atlântica.* Rio de Janeiro: Edições Alumbramento; Dean, W. 1995. *With broadaxe and firebrand.* Berkeley: University of California Press; Houghton, R.A., Lefkowitz, D.S. and Skole, D.L. 1991. Changes in the landscape of Latin America between 1850 and 1985. I: Progressive loss of forests. *Forest Ecology and Management,* 38: pp.143–72.
17. Faminow, M. 1998. *Cattle, deforestation and development in the Amazon.* Wallingford UK: CAB International; Rudel, T.K. and Horowitz, B. 1993. *Tropical deforestation: small farmers and land clearing in the Ecuadorian Amazon.* New York: Columbia University Press; Barbosa, L. 2000. *The Brazilian Amazon rainforest: global ecopolitics, development, and democracy.* Lanham MD: University Press of America; Pandolfo, C. 1994. *Amazônia brasileira.* Belém: Editora Cejup.
18. www.stanford.edu/group/LAEH/index.html

Chapter 16: 'Degradation narratives' and 'population time bombs'

Versions of this paper have been presented at the World History 2000: Teaching World History and Geography conference in Austin, Texas, 10 February 2000, and the Houston Area African Studies Seminar at Rice University, 28 April 2000. I would like to thank the participants and Hal Rothman for comments on drafts of the paper.

1. Beinart, W. 1982. *The political economy of Pondoland, 1860–1930.* New York: Cambridge University Press; 1984. Soil erosion, conservationism and ideas about development: a Southern African exploration, 1900–1966. *Journal of Southern African studies,* 11(1): pp.52–85; 1989. Introduction: the politics of colonial conservation. *Journal of Southern African Studies,* 15(2): pp.143–62; 1996. Soil erosion, animals and pasture over the longer term: environmental destruction in southern Africa. In: Leach, M. and Mearns, R., eds. *The lie of the land: challenging received wisdom on the African environment.* Portsmouth, NH: Heinemann, pp.54–72; Beinart, W. and Bundy, C., eds. 1987. *Hidden struggles in rural South Africa: politics and popular movements in the Transkei and Eastern Cape, 1890–1930.* London: James Currey; Beinart, W., Delius, P. and Trapido, S., eds. 1986. *Putting a plough to the ground: accumulation and dispossession in rural South Africa, 1850–1930.* Johannesburg: Ravan Press.
2. See McCann, J. 1999. *Green land, brown land, black land: an environmental history of Africa, 1800–1990.* Portsmouth: Heinemann, pp.141–76.
3. Bundy, C. 1979. *The rise and fall of the South African peasantry.* Berkeley: University of California Press.
4. Fagan, B. 1999. *Floods, famines and emperors: El Niño and the fate of civilizations.* New York: Basic Books, p.204.
5. Anderson, D.M. 1984. Depression, dust bowl, demography, and drought: the colonial state and soil conservation in East Africa during the 1930s. *African Affairs,* 83: pp.321–43.
6. Phillips, S.T. 1999. Lessons from the dust bowl: dryland agriculture and soil erosion in the United States and South Africa 1900–1950. *Environmental History,* 4(2): pp.245–66.
7. Beinart, W. and Coates, P. 1995. *Environment and history: the taming of nature in the USA and South Africa.* London: Routledge.
8. Fairhead, J. and Leach, M. 1996. *Misreading the African landscape: society and ecology in a forest-savanna mosaic.* Cambridge: Cambridge University Press.
9. Neumann, R.P. 1997. Forest rights, privileges and prohibitions: contextualising state forestry policy in Tanganyika. *Environment and History,* 3: pp.45–68.
10. Neumann, R.P. 1998. *Imposing wilderness: struggles over livelihood and nature preservation in Africa.* Berkeley: University of California Press.
11. Throup, D.W. 1987. *Economic and social origins of Mau Mau 1945–1953.* Athens, Ohio: Ohio University Press.

12. Fairhead and Leach. *Misreading*, pp.262–63.
13. Richards, P. 1996. *Fighting for the rain forest: war, youth and resources in Sierra Leone*. Portsmouth: Heinemann.
14. Mamdani, M. 1996. *Citizen and subject: contemporary Africa and the legacy of late colonialism*. Princeton: Princeton University Press.
15. See, for example, Chapter 2 by Nancy Jacobs and Chapter 4 by John Lambert in this volume.
16. Giles-Vernick, T. 1999. 'We wander like birds': migration, indigeneity, and the fabrication of frontiers in the Sangha basin of Equatorial Africa. *Environmental History*, 4(2): 168-97.
17. Fagan, *Floods*, pp. 215–22.
18. Brooks, G.E. 1993. *Landlords and strangers: ecology, society, and trade in western Africa, 1000–1630*. Boulder: Westview Press; McIntosh, R.J. 1993. The pulse model: genesis and accommodation of specialization in the Middle Niger. *Journal of African History*, 34(2): pp.181–220; and Webb, J.L.A., Jr. 1995. *Desert frontier: ecological and economic change along the western Sahel, 1600–1850*. Madison: University of Wisconsin Press.
19. Fairhead, J. and Leach, M. 1998. *Reframing deforestation: global analyses and local realities: studies in West Africa*. London: Routledge.
20. Fagan, *Floods*, p.215.
21. Kjekshus, H. 1977. *Ecology control and economic development in East African history: the case of Tanganyika, 1850–1950*. London: Heinemann.
22. In this volume see Chapter 10 by John McAllister and Chapter 11 by Elna Kotze, for example.
23. Ehret, C. 1998. *An African classical age: eastern and southern Africa in world history, 1000 BC to AD 400*. Charlottesville: University Press of Virginia.
24. Maggs, T. 1996. The Early Iron Age in the extreme south: some patterns and problems. In: Sutton, J.E.G., ed. *The growth of farming communities in Africa from the Equator southwards*. Nairobi: British Institute in Eastern Africa, pp.168–70; Prins, F.E. 1996. Climate vegetation and early agriculturist communities in Transkei and KwaZulu-Natal. In: Sutton, J.E.G., ed. *The growth of farming communities in Africa from the Equator southwards*. Nairobi: British Institute in Eastern Africa, pp.179–86; Van Schalkwyk, L. 1996. Settlement shifts and socio-economic transformations in early agriculturist communities in the lower Thukela basin. In: Sutton, J.E.G., ed. *The growth of farming communities in Africa from the Equator southwards*. Nairobi: British Institute in Eastern Africa, pp.187–98.
25. Schmidt, P.R. 1997. Archaeological views on a history of landscape change in East Africa. *Journal of African History*, 38: pp.393–421.
26. Elphick, R. 1977. *Kraal and castle: Khoikhoi and the founding of white South Africa*. New Haven: Yale University Press.
27. Manning, P. 1990. *Slavery and African life: Occidental, Oriental and African slave trades*. Cambridge: Cambridge University Press.
28. See Iliffe, J. 1995. *Africans: the history of a continent*. Cambridge: Cambridge University Press, where he tries to balance both general environmental and political economy causes for the stagnation.
29. Iliffe, J. 1987. *The African poor: a history*. Cambridge: Cambridge University Press.
30. Cordell, D.D. and Gregory, J.W., eds. 1987. *African population and capitalism: historical perspectives*. Boulder: Westview Press.
31. Koponen, J. 1988. *People and production in late precolonial Tanzania: history and structures*. Uppsala: Scandinavian Institute of African Studies.
32. Chapter 7 by Harald Witt in this volume provides an interesting contrast to the views of Fairhead and Leach. Witt documents 'afforestation' of a type, using exotic species in commercial enterprises, and views it critically while Fairhead and Leach seem more positive about human-induced afforestation, even though it involves both domesticated and exotic species.
33. Fairhead and Leach. 1998. *Reframing deforestation*.
34. See, The flowing eye: water management in the upper Kuruman Valley, South Africa, c.1800–1962. *Journal of African History*, 1996, 37: pp.237–60; and The great Bophuthatswana

donkey massacre: the politics of class and grass, American Society of Environmental History Annual Meetings, Tucson, 15 to 18 April 1999.

35. McCann, J.C. 1987. *From poverty to famine in northeast Ethiopia: a rural history 1900–1935.* Philadelphia: University of Pennsylvania Press; 1995. *People of the plow: an agricultural history of Ethiopia, 1800–1990.* Madison: University of Wisconsin Press; and 1997. The plow and the forest: narratives of deforestation in Ethiopia, 1840–1992. *Environmental History,* 2: pp.138–59.

Chapter 17: The colonial eco-drama

1. For an excellent account of the development of South Asian environmental history see, Grove, R., Damodaran, V. and Sangwan, S., eds. 1998. *Nature and the Orient: the environmental history of South and Southeast Asia.* New Delhi: Oxford University Press. For an account of the development of South African environmental history see, Beinart, W. 1999. *African history, environmental history and race relations.* Oxford: Oxford University Press; and Steyn, P. 2000. The greening of our past? An assessment of South African environmental historiography, Unpublished paper presented to the American Society for Environmental History Annual Meetings in Tucson in March 2000.

2. For a definition of 'political ecology', see Greenberg, J.B and Park, T.K. 1994. Political ecology. *Journal of Political Ecology.* (http://dizzy.library.arizona.edu/ej/jpe/)

3. Weiskel, T.C. 1987. Agents of empire: steps toward an ecology of imperialism. *Environmental Review,* Winter: p.275.

4. Ibid., pp.276–79.

5. For an excellent account of the emergence of environmental history as a research field in the United States, see Worster, D., ed. 1988. *The ends of the Earth.* New York: Cambridge University Press.

6. See, for example, Grove, et al., *Nature and the Orient*; and Beinart, W. and Coates, P. 1995. *Environment and history: the taming of nature in the USA and South Africa.* New York: Routledge.

7. Worster, D. Doing environmental history. In: Worster, D., ed. 1988. *The ends of the Earth.* New York: Cambridge University Press, pp.289–308.

8. Worster, *The ends of the Earth*, p.293.

9. Worster, D. 1990. Transformations of the Earth. In: A round table: environmental history. *Journal of American History*, 76(4): p.1090; see also, Crosby, A. 1986. *Ecological imperialism: the biological expansion of Europe.* New York: Cambridge University Press; and Worster, D. 1985. *Rivers of empire: water, aridity, and the growth of the American West.* New York: Cambridge University Press.

10. Rangarajan, M. 1996. Environmental histories of South Asia: a review essay. *Environment and History*, 2: p.134.

11. Pyne, S.J. 1995. *World fire: the culture of fire on Earth.* New York: Holt, p.150.

12. Dove, M. 1992. The dialectical history of 'jungle' in Pakistan: an examination of the relationship between nature and culture. *Journal of Anthropological Research*, 48: pp.90–115; Trautmann, T.R. 1982. Elephants and the Mauryas. In: Mukherjee, S.N., ed. *India, history and thought: essays in honor of A.L. Basham.* Calcutta: Subarnarekha, pp.254–73.

13. Beinart, *African history*, p.14.

14. Worster, Transformations of the Earth, p.1090. This is a central issue in imperial environmental history. See, for example, Beinart, W. 1989. Introduction: the politics of colonial conservation. *Journal of Southern African Studies*, 15: pp.143–62, especially the section on popular protest and technical mishap in Herschel. See also, Guha, R. 1989. *The unquiet woods: ecological change and peasant resistance in the Himalaya.* Delhi: Oxford University Press; Guha, R. 1983. Forestry in British and post-British India: a historical analysis. *Economic and Political Weekly*, 29 October and 5–12 November; and Guha, R. and Gadgil, M. 1992. *This fissured land: an ecological history of India.* Berkeley: University of California Press.

15. The question of how technology shapes human systems and human-ecological themes is again one of the major themes of colonial environmental history at the present. See, for example, Guha, *The unquiet woods*; Peluso, N.L. 1992. *Rich forests, poor people: resource control and resistance in Java.* Berkeley: University of California Press; Beinart, Introduction: the politics of colonial conservation, especially the section entitled 'Soil erosion and rehabilitation schemes' and various other articles in the 1989 special issue of the *Journal of Southern African Studies* entitled *The politics of conservation in southern Africa*, 15(2); and Kjekshus, H. 1977. *Ecology control and economic development in East African history.* London: Heinemann.

16. Merchant, C. 1990. Gender and environmental history. In: A round table: environmental history. *Journal of American History*, 76(4): p.1120; Merchant, C. 1987. The theoretical structure of ecological revolutions. *Environmental Review*, 11: pp.265–74. See also Guha and Gadgil, *This fissured land.*

17. Worster, Transformations of the Earth, p.1090. The idea of *mode of production* incorporates the various senses of the ideal type developed by Karl Marx. The question of who loses and who gains is again an important issue in imperial environmental history. See, for example, Beinart, Introduction: the politics of colonial conservation, especially the section entitled 'Whose nature?'

18. For South Asia see, Grove, et al., eds. *Nature and the Orient*; Arnold, D. and Guha, R., eds. 1995. *Nature, culture, imperialism: essays on the environmental history of South Asia.* Delhi: Oxford University Press; and Rangarajan, Environmental histories of South Asia. For southern Africa see, Beinart, *African history, environmental history and race relations*; Beinart, W. 1989. Introduction: the politics of colonial conservation. *Journal of Southern African Studies*, 15(2); Steyn, P. The greening of our past; and Carruthers, J. 1990. Towards an environmental history of Southern Africa – some perspectives. *South African Historical Journal*, December, 23: pp.184–95.

19. An excellent illustration of work at the macro level is Guha, R. 1983. Forestry in British and post-British India: a historical analysis. *Economic and Political Weekly*, 29 October and 5–12 November. A good example of work at the micro level is Tucker, R.P. 1988. The depletion of India's forests under British imperialism: planters, foresters and peasants in Assam and Kerala. In: Worster, ed., 1988. *The ends of the Earth.* New York: Cambridge University Press.

20. See, for example, Richard Tucker's excellent discussion of forest contractors: Tucker, R.P. 1988. The British Empire and India's forest resources: the timberlands of Assam and Kumaon, 1914–1950. In: Richards, J.F. and Tucker, R.P., eds. *World deforestation in the twentieth century.* Durham: Duke University Press; and Tucker, R.P. 1983. The British colonial system and the forests of the Western Himalayas, 1815–1914. In: Tucker, R.P. and Richards, J.F., eds. *Global deforestation and the nineteenth century world economy.* Durham: Duke University Press. See also William Beinart's discussion of interactions, Beinart, *African history*, pp. 11–13.

21. See, for example, the various volumes of *Subaltern studies: writings on South Asian history and society.* Delhi: Oxford University Press.

22. See Saunders, C. 1988. Historians and apartheid. In: Lonsdale, J., ed. *South Africa in question.* Cambridge: African Studies Centre, University of Cambridge and Portsmouth NH: Heinemann; Saunders, C. 1988. *The making of the South African past: major historians on race and class.* Totowa NJ: Barnes and Noble Books; and Smith, K. 1988. *The changing past: trends in South African historical writing.* Johannesburg: Southern Book Publishers.

23. See Beinart, *African history*, p.3; and Ranger, T.O. 1969. *The recovery of African initiative in Tanzanian history.* Dar es Salaam: University College.

24. For an erudite explanation of this historiographical genre see, Cronon, W. 1993. The uses of environmental history. *Environmental History Review*, Fall: pp.1–22.

25. Worster, Transformations of the Earth, p.1091; and Merchant, Gender and environmental history, p.1120.

26. See, for example, Hill, Christopher V. 1997. *River of sorrow: environment and social control in riparian North India, 1770–1994.* Ann Arbor, MI: Association for Asian Studies; Adas, M. 1983. Colonization, commercial agriculture, and the destruction of the deltaic rainforests of

British Burma in the late nineteenth century. In: Tucker, R.P. and Richards, J.F., eds. *Global deforestation and the nineteenth-century world economy*. Durham NC: Duke University Press, pp.95–110; Beinart, W. 1984. Soil erosion, conservationism and ideas about development: a Southern African exploration, 1900–1960. *Journal of Southern African Studies*, 11(1): pp.52–83; Guelke, L. and Shell, R. 1992. Landscape of conquest: frontier water alienation and Khoikhoi strategies of survival 1652–1780. *Journal of Southern African Studies*, 18(4): pp.803–24.

27. See, for example, Cowen, M.P. and Shenton, R.W. 1996. *Doctrines of development*. London and New York: Routledge.

28. See, for example, Jefferies, C. 1964. *A review of colonial research 1940–1960*. London: H.M. Stationers Office; Worthington, E.B. 1938. *Science in Africa*. Oxford: Oxford University Press; Worthington, E.B. 1945. *Middle Eastern science*. London: H.M. Stationers Office; Lord Hailey. 1956. *An African survey*. London: Oxford University Press; and the Inter-Faculty Committee for African Studies, University of Oxford. 1975. *Symposium on Africa in the colonial period I – the conservation and development of natural resources* (hereafter, *IFCAS Symp*). Oxford: Unpublished manuscript.

29. Keay, R.W.J. 1975. *IFCAS Symp*, p.83.

30. See the articles on Land Surveying, Water Resources, Geology, Forestry, Agriculture and Animal Resources in *IFCAS Symp*.

31. Worthington, *Science in Africa*, p.2.

32. McCracken, J. 1982. Experts and expertise in colonial Malawi. *African Affairs*, 81: p.102.

33. Cmd. 7433, as quoted in Jefferies, *A review of colonial research*, p.43.

34. Sangster, R.G. 1975. *IFCAS Symp*, p.71.

35. Sangster, *IFCAS Symp*, p.71. The poem is attributed to John Buchan.

36. For a general idea of the extent of the critique see, Hayter, T. 1989. *Exploited Earth: British aid and the environment*. London: Rainforest Information Centre; and Hayter, T. 1990. *The World Bank Tropical Action Plan for Papua New Guinea: a critique*. Lismore: Rainforest Information Centre; Colchester, M. and Lohmann, L. 1990. *The Tropical Forestry Action Plan: what progress?* Dorset: The Ecologist; and Agrawal, A., et al. 1982, 1984–85. *Citizens reports on the state of the environment in India*. Delhi: Centre for Science and Environment.

37. See, for example, Guha, *The unquiet woods*; Peluso, N.L. 1992. *Rich forests, poor people: resource control and resistance in Java*. Berkeley: University of California Press.

38. See, for example, Nandy, A., ed. 1988. *Science, hegemony and violence*. Delhi: Oxford University Press; Marglin, F.A. and Marglin, S.A., eds. 1990. *Dominating knowledge: development, culture and resistance*. Oxford: Clarendon Press and New York: Oxford University Press; and the journal *The Ecologist*.

39. Mackenzie, J.M. 1990. Introduction to *Imperialism and the natural world*. Manchester: Manchester University Press.

40. See Headrick, D.R. 1981. *Tools of empire: technology and European imperialism in the nineteenth century*. Oxford: Oxford University Press.

41. See, for example, Guha, *The unquiet woods*.

42. This is true for both agriculture and forestry.

43. The dynamics and politics of such transfers have been an important theme of discussion in the growing critique of science and technics referred to at the beginning of this chapter. See, for example, Nandy, *Science, hegemony and violence*; and Marglin and Marglin, *Dominating knowledge*.

44. The idea of scientists as epistemic communities occurs widely in the sociology of science and has only recently begun to be deployed in discussions of the international politics of the environment. See Hurrell, A. and Kingsbury, B. 1992. The international politics of the environment: an introduction. In Hurrell, A. and Kingsbury, B., eds. *The international politics of the environment*. New York: Oxford University Press.

45. Polanyi, K. 1957. *The great transformation*. Boston: Beacon Press.

46. See, for example, Bowler, R.C. 1996. Bildung, bureaucracy and political economy: Karl Heinrich Rau and the development of German economies. Ph.D. thesis, UCLA, Los Angeles.

47. See, for example, Whited, T.L. 2000. *Forests and peasant politics in modern France.* New Haven: Yale University Press; and Sahlins, P. 1994. *Forest rites: the War of the Demoiselles in nineteenth-century France.* Cambridge, Mass: Harvard University Press.

48. This argument is developed in depth in my forthcoming book, *Modernizing nature: tropical forestry and the contested legacy of colonial ecodevelopment, 1800–2000.* Oxford: Oxford University Press.

49. See, for example, Amirthalingam, M. 1998. *Sacred groves of Tamilnadu: a survey.* Chennai: C.P.R. Environmental Education Centre; Kalam, M.A. 1996. *Sacred groves in Kodagu District of Karnataka (South India): a socio-historical study.* Pondichéry: Institut Français de Pondichéry, p.53.

50. See, for example, Nhira, C. and Matose, F. 1995. *Lessons for the resource sharing project in Zimbabwe from the Indian Joint Forest Management and Campfire programme experiences.* Mount Pleasant, Harare: Centre for Applied Social Sciences, University of Zimbabwe.

51. The term 'double movement' was coined by Karl Polanyi to describe the tension between the pulls of a self-regulating market, on the one hand, and the various social movements that historically sought to protect societies and cultures from its impact on the other hand.

Index